汉英对照

诗　经

Book of Poetry

许渊冲　英译

刘文娟　崔晶晶　中文注释

中国出版集团
中国对外翻译出版公司

图书在版编目（CIP）数据

诗经：汉英对照/ 许渊冲译. —北京：中国对外翻译出版公司，2009.9

（中华传统文化精粹·中译经典文库）
ISBN 978-7-5001-2020-9

Ⅰ. 诗… Ⅱ. 许… Ⅲ. ①汉语—英语—对照读物 ②古体诗—中国—春秋时代 Ⅳ. H319.4:I

中国版本图书馆 CIP 数据核字（2009）第 062455 号

出版发行 / 中国对外翻译出版公司
地　　址 / 北京市西城区车公庄大街甲 4 号物华大厦六层
电　　话 / (010) 68359376　68359303　68359101　68357937
邮　　编 / 100044
传　　真 / (010) 68357870
电子邮箱 / book@ctpc.com.cn
网　　址 / http://www.ctpc.com.cn

总 经 理 / 林国夫
出版策划 / 张高里
策划编辑 / 李育超
责任编辑 / 徐小美

排　　版 / 北京巴蜀阳光图文设计有限公司
印　　刷 / 保定市中画美凯印刷有限公司
经　　销 / 新华书店

规　　格 / 880×1230 毫米　1/32
印　　张 / 15.125
字　　数 / 250千字
版　　次 / 2009 年 9 月第一版
印　　次 / 2009 年 9 月第一次

ISBN 978-7-5001-2020-9　　　　　　定价：36.00 元

版权所有　侵权必究
中国对外翻译出版公司

前　言

　　欧美国家很少有人知道：世界上最早的诗集是中国的《诗经》。《诗经》包括三百零五篇诗歌，大约产生于两千五百年前。最早的一篇据陈子展《诗经直解》，是《商颂》中的《长发》，约作于公元前1713年。最晚的一篇，一说是《秦风》中的《无衣》，公元前505年申包胥哭秦庭时，秦哀公为代赋《无衣》之诗；一说是《陈风》中的《株林》，是刺陈灵公"淫乎夏姬"之诗，据《诗经直解》，约作于公元前599年。两说都是公元前6世纪。

　　《诗经》按照音乐类型分为《国风》、《小雅》、《大雅》和《颂》四个部分。《国风》一百六十篇包括周王室的乐官在十五个诸侯国的封地采集到的民歌民谣。《小雅》七十四篇多是西周贵族宴会用的乐章，《大雅》三十一篇多用于朝廷庆典。《颂》四十篇是用于宗庙祭祀的赞歌，又分为《周颂》三十一篇，《鲁颂》四篇，《商颂》五篇。《商颂》最早，约作于公元前17世纪至12世纪，相传是西周后期宋国大夫正考甫从周太师处得到的；一说是正考甫所作，商王室的后人宋襄公祭祀祖先所用，但是证据不足。

　　西周早期的诗篇约作于公元前11世纪至9世纪，包括全部《周颂》，一部分《大雅》和一小部分《国风》。大部分诗篇都是"赋"（叙事诗）或史诗，最出色的是《大雅》中的《生民》、《公刘》、《緜》、《皇矣》和《大明》,这些史诗描写了周王朝是如何建立,商王朝是如何灭亡的。西周后期的诗篇约作于公元前9至8世纪,包括大部分《大雅》,几乎全部《小雅》,还有一小部分《国风》。有些雅歌赞颂了中兴的周宣王(公元前9世纪末至8世纪初在位)南征北战的赫赫武功,如《大雅·常武》描写了宣王东征徐国的胜利;《小雅·六月》记载了尹吉甫北伐玁狁的史实;《小雅·采芑》叙述了方叔南征荆楚的武功。这些意气风发、斗志昂扬、威震四方的赞歌颂词的作者,有的是朝廷的史官,有的却是统率三军的大将,如《六月》的作者是"张仲孝友",而《大雅》中的《崧高》和《烝民》却是"文武吉甫"赠别申伯和仲山甫时所作。这些诗篇虽然极尽了赞颂之能事,但是比起《小雅》中描述士兵亲身经历的《采薇》来,却又显得稍逊一筹;《采薇》中的"昔我往矣,杨柳依依;今我来思,雨雪霏霏"传诵千古,被誉为"《诗》三百中最佳之句"。

  《诗经》中最好的作品还是《国风》,包括东周时期采集到的民歌民谣,大部分作于公元前8至6世纪。民歌大都纯朴自然,反映了古代人民各方面的生活,劳动斗争,思想感情,喜怒哀乐。如《豳风·七月》描写了农民一年的劳动生活,他们耕地,织布,打猎,为主人酿酒,修建房屋,自己却不得温饱。《魏风·伐檀》讽刺了不劳而获、贪得无厌的贵族;《周南·芣苢》是农村妇女采集车前子的劳动之歌。《召南·野有死麕》描写了猎人如何爱上了一个美丽的少女。《周南·关雎》叙述一对青年男女如何在春天钟情,在夏天求爱,在秋天订亲,在冬天结合的过程。《唐风·鸨羽》表达了农民在外服役的辛苦;《邶风·日月》写出了弃妇的不幸。《击鼓》抒发了士兵思家之情,而《燕燕》和《绿衣》却描写了生离死别的痛苦。

  孔子说过:"诗可以兴,可以观,可以群,可以怨。"用今天的话来说，就是诗可以启发，可以反映，可以交流，可以讥讽。在我看来，《国风》主要反映了劳动人民的生活，启发他们去做好事，讽刺了统治者的丑恶行为。如《周南》、《召南》反映了古代人民的家庭生活；《卫风》、《邶风》讽刺了贵族腐化堕落的习俗；《郑风》、《陈风》反映了民间的爱情生活；《豳风》启发了人民对周公的拥戴。

《小雅》主要用于贵族之间交流，反映了贵族的生活，也指责了他们的错误。如《鹿鸣之什》中有六篇用于王家宴会；《南有嘉鱼之什》中有两篇用于诸侯宴会，两篇描写王家狩猎；《鸿雁之什》中第一篇发泄了对乱世的不满，《祈父》却是士兵对大臣的怨言；《节南山之什》都是对周幽王宠爱褒姒的批评；《谷风之什》中有被压迫贵族的呼声；《甫田之什》中有收获时贵族祭神求福的乐歌，其中《宾之初筵》写贵族酗酒的醉态，栩栩如生，是不可多得的佳作；《鱼藻之什》则多是对周厉王暴虐无道的批评。不过《小雅》有些诗篇可以收入《国风》或《大雅》中，如《采薇》、《出车》记载西伯、南仲西征的事，可以算是《大雅》。

《大雅》记载史实，反映统治者的生活。如《文王之什》中有六篇记文王事，两篇记武王事，《緜》记古公亶父自豳迁岐，《皇矣》记太王、王季及文王伐密伐崇的事，都是史诗；《生民之什》中第一篇叙述周民族始祖后稷的神话，《假乐》、《泂酌》、《卷阿》是成王的诗，《民劳》、《板》是刺厉王的诗；《荡之什》中有三篇讽刺厉王，《云汉》等三篇赞美宣王，《崧高》赞美申伯，《烝民》赞美仲山甫，《韩奕》赞美韩侯，《瞻卬》、《召旻》讽刺幽王。所以《大雅》可以算是西周王室的兴衰史。

《颂》主要用来赞美王室祖先的丰功伟绩，启发后人对祖先的崇拜，达到齐家治国的目的。《周颂·清庙之什》中歌颂文王、武王、成王的各有三篇，《思文》一篇歌颂后稷。《臣工之什》第一篇是农事诗，第十篇《武》是宗庙舞歌，其他八篇都是祭祀诗。《闵予小子之什》据说是周公摄政时所作，前七篇都与成王有关；《访落》是成王登基的赞歌，《敬之》写成王君臣关系，《小毖》写成王自我批评，《载芟》是农事诗，《良耜》、《丝衣》是祭祀诗，《酌》等四篇和《武》一样是宗庙舞歌。《鲁颂》只有四篇，都是赞美鲁僖公的，僖公其实是个平庸之辈，但是作为周公的后裔，享受了王室祭典的特权，受到过孔子的批评。《商颂》是《诗经》中最古的诗篇。《长发》是商王朝的开国史；《那》等三篇歌颂汤武开国之君，《殷武》赞美武丁中兴之举。从内容看，说《商颂》是宋人祭祖乐章，似乎不能令人信服。大致说来，《颂》可以兴，《大雅》可以观，《小雅》可以群，《国风》可以怨。

《诗经》中常用的三种修辞手法是"赋"、"比"、"兴"，"赋"是直叙其事，"比"包括明喻、暗喻，"兴"是"先言他物以引起所咏之辞也"。《魏风·硕鼠》就是以动物比人的一个好例子。在这首诗中，硕鼠的形象和全诗主题有关；有时，"先言他物"和"所咏之辞"并无直接关系，只有作者感情上的联系，也就是说，同为作者爱憎的对象，如《鄘风·墙有茨》，"茨"与"中冓之言"并无关系，只是同为作者所憎。有时，"先言他物"不过是为了押韵顺口的缘故，如《召南·草虫》。

《诗经》的另一个特点是重调叠咏很多，可以增强诗歌的情韵，加深读者的印象。有时一行只变换一两个字，韵也变了，诗情也发展了；有时整行重复，有时整段重复；如《周南·芣苢》和《召南·摽有梅》。中国古诗的句式大致可以分为四言体、五言体、七言体和杂言体。四言诗出现最早，在《诗经》中也最多，可以说是已臻成熟了。四言体每行只有两个音步，比起五、七言体来，节奏更加干脆利落。《诗经》中的绝大部分诗歌都押韵，韵式多种多样：有的每行押韵，有的隔行押韵，有的整段一韵到底，有的行内有韵，有的还用双声加强音乐效果。

《诗经》中的词汇丰富，尤其是叠字、双声、韵语等的运用，变化多端，使得诗歌描写生动，声调悦耳。此外，还有叠句、合唱等等，也是民间歌谣常用的手法。

《诗经》的"风、雅、颂、赋、比、兴"叫做六艺，受到后世高度评价，对历代诗人产生了重要的影响。试比较下列引文，可见一斑。

1. 《周颂·桓》：保有厥士，于以四方。

   刘邦《大风歌》：安得猛士兮守四方？

2. 《唐风·蟋蟀》：今我不乐，日月其除！

   《古诗十九首》：为乐当及时，何能待来兹？

3. 《邶风·燕燕》：瞻望弗及，泣涕如雨。

   苏武《别妻》：握手一长叹，泪为生别滋。

4. 《卫风·氓》：三岁为妇，靡室劳矣。

   夙兴夜寐，靡有朝矣。

   《孔雀东南飞》：鸡鸣入机织，夜夜不得息。

   三日断五匹，大人故嫌迟。

5. 《陈风·衡门》：衡门之下，可以栖迟。

   泌之洋洋，可以乐饥。

   陶潜《归园田居》：户庭无尘杂，虚室有余闲。

   久在樊笼里，复得返自然。

6. 《陈风·月出》：月出皎兮！佼人僚兮！

   李白《越女词》：镜湖水如月，耶溪女如雪。

7. 《鲁颂·閟宫》：泰山岩岩，鲁邦所詹。

   杜甫《望岳》：岱宗夫如何？齐鲁青未了。

8. 《齐风·东方之日》：东方之日兮。

彼姝者子，在我室兮。
在我室兮，履我即兮。

李商隐《无题》：金蟾啮锁烧香入；
玉虎牵丝汲井回。

9. 《魏风·硕鼠》：硕鼠硕鼠，无食我黍！
三岁贯女，莫我肯顾。

曹邺《官仓鼠》：官仓老鼠大如斗，
见人开仓亦不走。
健儿无粮百姓饥，
谁遣朝朝入君口？

10. 《陈风·东门之杨》：东门之杨，其叶牂牂牁。
昏以为期，明星煌煌。

欧阳修《生查子》：去年元夜时，花市灯如昼。
月上柳梢头，人约黄昏后。

从以上十例可以看出《诗经》对历代诗人影响多大。《诗经》在国内虽然非常重要，但在国外并不广为人知，直到18世纪威廉·琼斯爵士才把部分诗篇译成英文散体和韵体，据说对英国19世纪诗人拜伦，雪莱、丁尼生等产生了巨大影响（见《外国语》总15期8页）。到了19世纪60年代，英国理雅各才把全部《诗经》译成散体英文，在香港出版；到1871年，他又在伦敦出版了《诗经》三百零五篇的韵体译本，并于1967年在纽约重印。他的译本注释丰富，是学者的译文，但不如原文简朴。1891年伦敦又出版了艾伦和詹宁斯的《诗经》英译本：艾本押韵，译文随意改动原文，有增有删，与其说是翻译，不如说是改写。吕叔湘编《中诗英译比录》选了几篇艾译；詹本则没有见到，不好妄评。

到了20世纪，1906年伦敦出版了克拉默宾的韵体译本，他译的《玉笛集》(中国诗选) 十年之内重印十次，可算畅销；从

《中诗英译比录》中选的《氓》看来，他的译文不像艾译那样自由，而且格律也不如艾严谨。1913年在波士顿出版了海伦·华德尔的韵体译本，从她译的《氓》看来，删节太多，而且重新组织。她的译本销路较好，二十年内重印六次。和她相反，路易丝·哈芒德走了另外一个极端，她试图把一个中文字译成一个英文音节，毫不增减，而且保持原诗韵律。她的《邶风·式微》译得很成功，但不知道她译了多少篇《诗》。

《诗经》的早期译者都用韵体。庞德是在理雅各之后，第一个把《诗经》译成自由体的诗人。他的译本于1915年在剑桥出版，1954年在哈佛大学出版社重印。他认为译诗是个创造性的问题，他的译文经常被当成创作而选入近代英美诗选，影响很大，但译文错误很多，不能算是佳译。另外一个把《诗经》译成自由诗的是韦理，他的译本于1937年在伦敦出版。他在《译自中文》的序中说：中国的旧诗句句都有一定的字数，必须用韵，很像英国的传统诗，而不像欧美今天的自由诗。但他译诗却不用韵，因为他认为用韵不可能不因声损义；他用一个重读音节来代表一个汉字，并将这种格律比之为英诗的无韵体。庞德和韦理都不知道：译诗如不传达原诗的音美，就不能保存原诗的意美。《诗经》总的说来是用韵的，译诗如不用韵，绝不可能产生和原诗相似的效果。恰恰相反，用韵的音美有时反而有助于传达原诗的意美。这就是说，用韵固然可能因声损义，不用韵则一定因声损义，用韵损义的程度反比不用韵小。试比较韦理《周南·关雎》和本书的译文，韦译"关关雎鸠"，无论意美、音美，都远不如本书。

诗无达诂，就以《关雎》而论，"雎鸠"到底是什么鸟？"君子"到底是什么人？"荇菜"到底是什么菜？众说纷纭。而"左右流之"，有人说"流"是"求"或"采"，韦理就是这样译的，但读来觉得牵强。我认为译诗要博采众家之长，而对《关雎》解释得最好的，是《诗经鉴赏集》王气中的文章。他说"关关"两句表示时令，夏历二月春分季节，鸟兽开始交配。"荇菜"开春发芽，入夏才浮出水面；"左右流之"，是说明荇菜在水面或左或右浮动的样子。"左右采之"，是说荇菜到了夏秋之间长大可采，比兴新郎新娘双方的恋爱已经达到成熟阶段；"琴瑟友之"说明还举行过订婚的仪式。"左右芼之"说明他们的结婚季节，是在秋冬农事生活闲隙，荇菜成熟的时候，人们要把它熟食了。总之，《关雎》歌唱新婚夫妇在一年内由相识、求爱、热恋、订盟以至结婚的全过程。这样一讲，才会明白孔子为什么把《关雎》列为《诗经》之首，因为这篇诗概括了我国礼乐治国的哲学。由此可见。外国译者对中国传统文化没有深刻的了解，是不大可能译好《诗经》的。一些诗有不同的解释，难分高下。如《周南·卷耳》，余冠英说"这是女子怀念征夫的诗。她在采卷耳的时候想起了远行的丈夫，幻想他在上山了，过冈了，马病了，人疲了，又幻想他在饮酒自宽"。钱锺书认为这不是幻想，而是实事："作诗之人不必即诗中所咏之人，妇与夫皆诗中人，诗人代言其情事，故各曰'我'。……夫为一篇之主而妇为宾也。男女两人处两地而情事一时，批尾家谓之'双管齐下'，章回小说谓之'话分两头'。"从真的观点看来，钱说更高；但从美的观点来看，则又以余说为上，因为"不言己之怀人，而愈见怀人情笃"。因此，我在河南译本中采用余说，而在湖南译本中则采用钱说；这样更可以看出《诗经》内涵的丰富。又如《召南·小星》，传统的解释是指小妾，以致"小星"成了妾的代称；今天一般认为是写小臣出差；我也是在河南本中用前说，在湖南本中用后说。但如《唐风·无衣》，一般认为是览衣感旧，睹物思人；《诗经楚辞鉴赏辞典》却认为是伤逝，情真意切，不胜依依，我就两本都按伤逝译了。总而言之，我的英译希望尽可能传达《诗经》的意美、音美和形美，并且与以往的各种语体译文也不尽相同。

《诗经》是我国古代的教科书，对建立及维护我国几千年的传统文化起了非常重大的作用。概括起来，儒家治国之道就是"礼乐"二字。"礼"模仿自然外在的秩序，"乐"模仿自然内在的和谐；"礼"可以养性，"乐"可以怡情；"礼"是"义"的外化，"乐"是"仁"的外化。做人要重"仁义"，治国要重"礼乐"，这就是中国文化几千年不衰的原因。世界各国，希腊罗马有古无今，英美法德俄有今无古，印度埃及都曾遭受亡国之痛，只有中国屹立世界东方，几千年如一日，对世界文明作出了独一无二的贡献。因此，把中国文化的瑰宝《诗经》译成具有意美、音美和形美的韵文，对东西文化的交流，对21世纪世界文化的建立，一定会有不可低估的意义。

许渊冲

1993年4月18日

北京大学畅春园舞山楼

Preface

Few people in Europe and America know that the earliest anthology of verse in the World is the *Book of Poetry* compiled in China 2500 years ago. This book consists of 305 poems dating from 1713 B.C. ("The Rise of Shang") to 505 B.C. ("Comradeship"). It is divided according to the type of music into four main sections: 160 *Songs* sung by the people in 15 city states and collected by royal musicians; 74 *Odes* and 31 *Epics* sung by the no nobles at court or at banquets, and 40 *Hymns* used during sacrifice to the gods and ancestors. The section of *Hymns* is subdivided into "Hymns of Zhou", "Hymns of Lu" and "Hymns of Shang", the last of which is said to be the oldest, dating from between the 17th and the 12th century B.C.

Songs of the early Western Zhou dynasty composed from the 11th to the 9th century B.C. include all the "Hymns of Zhou", a small part of the *Epics* and a few lyrical *Songs*. The majority of these songs are narrative or historical poems, the most outstanding being "Hou Ji, the Lord of Corn", "Duke Liu", "The Migration in 1325 B.C.", "the Rise of Zhou" and "Three Kings of Zhou" in the *Epic*, all of which describe the founding of the Zhou House. Songs of the later Western Zhou period during the 9th and 8th centuries B.C. include most of the *Epics* and practically all the *Odes* as well as a few folk *Songs*. Some *Epics* and *Odes* extol the military prowess of King Xuan who reigned at the end of the 9th and the beginning of the 8th century and led expeditions against the frontier tribes. "Expedition against Xu" describes his attack on the Xu tribes in the east, in which we find the embryo of Sun Wu's military strategy; "General Ji Fu" narrates King Xuan's north ern expedition against the Huns and "General Fang" his southern campaign against the Chu tribes. These spirited, vigorous yet dignified *Odes* were composed by officials or historians, for example, "General Ji Fu" by Zhang Zhong, "Count of Shen" and "Premier Shan Fu" by General Ji Fu. Although competent enough, they cannot compare with soldiers' song like "A Homesick Warrior", of which the last stanza was considered as the most beautiful verse in the *Book of Poetry*.

The best verse comes from the *Book of Songs* collected in the Eastern Zhou dynasty from the 8th to the 6th century B.C. Most of the folk songs, written in a simple and natural style, reflect the life and struggle, labor and love, joys and sorrows of the people in ancient times. For instance, "Life of Peasants" gives a fairly comprehensive picture of the work of the peasants; "The Woodcutter's Song" satirizes against those idle and greedy lords, "Plantain Gathering" sings of the labor of women who gathered plantain seed; "A Deer Killer and a Jadelike Maiden" describes a hunter's love, "Cooing and Wooing" narrates the life and love of a young man and a fair maiden from spring to winter and their joy at wedding; "The Peasants' Complaint" expresses the sorrows of peasants, "Complaint of a Soldier" that of a homesick soldier, "A Farewell Song" and "My Green Robe" describe grief at parting and over death.

As Confucius said, "Poetry may serve to inspire, to reflect, to communicate and to admonish," we may say that the *Book of Songs* serves chiefly to reflect the life of the labouring people, to inspire them to do good and to admonish the rulers against doing wrong. For instance, the first and second sections reflect the domestic life of the ancient Chinese people, the third to fifth sections serve to admonish the lords of their faults, the seventh and twelfth sections are mostly love songs, the thirteenth and fourteenth sections reflect the general decay of the State and the last section inspires the people to admire their Duke.

The *Book of Odes* serves chiefly to communicate, to admonish and to reflect the life of the nobles. For instance, the first decade contains six *Odes* used at the royal banquet, the second decade includes two *Odes* used in district entertainment and two describing the royal hunting, the third decade contains an official's complaint against the disorder of the time ("The Toilers") and a soldier's against the minister of war ("To the Minister of War"), the fourth decade is composed of complaints against King You and his favorite Lady Shi of Bao (from "To Grand Master Yin" to "A Eunuch's Song"), the fifth decade consists of *Odes* of the oppressed nobles and "Revelry" is a very good picture of the dissipation of the time, the sixth decade is remarkable for "Harvest" and "Farm Work", and the last decade is chiefly censure on King Li's misgovernment, "A Homesick Warrior", "A Soldier's Wife", etc. might be classified as *Epics* for they describe the life of soldiers and generals.

The *Book of Epics* records historic deeds and reflects the life of the rulers. For instance, in the first decade there are six epic odes about King Wen, two about King Wu and two about their ancestors King Tai and King Ji ("The Migration in 1325 B.G.", "The Rise of Zhou"). In the second decade "Hou Ji, the Lord of Corn" tells us the story of Hou Ji, Lord of Grain or Corn, founder of the Zhou House, there are three epic odes about King Cheng, and another three are censures on King Li. The first three epic odes in the third decade are admonitions against King Ping, King Li and King Xuan respectively, the next three epic odes record the deeds of "Count of Shen", "Premier Shan Fu" and "The Marquis of Han" and the last two are censures on King You.

The *Book of Hymns* serves chiefly to glorify the ancestors of the rulers and inspire their descendents to worship them as gods. The book is subdivided into three sections: "Hymns of Zhou", "Hymns of Lu" and "Hymns of Shang". In the first decade of the "Hymns of Zhou" there are three odes singing the praises of King Wen, three of King Wu, four of King Cheng and one of Hou Ji, Lord of Grain or Corn. The second decade begins with an ode on husbandry and ends with a hymn to Kingi Wu sung to the music regulating the dance in the temple. Other *Hymns* are sacrificial odes. The third decade is said to be composed by the Duke of Zhou himself as regent. The first seven Hymns are all concerned with King Cheng, his ascension, his consultation with his ministers, his self-criticism, his cultivation of the ground and his thanks-giving sacrifiee. The last four are said to belong to the same series as "Hymn to King Wu Great and Bright", sung to accompany the dance in honor of King Wu.

The "Hymns of Lu" contain only four odes celebrating Duke Xi of Lu, who was in fact a mediocre ruler, but as the deseendent of the Duke of Zhou, he wes privileged to employ royal ceremonies and sacrifices, which was condemned by Confucius.

The "Hymns of Shang" contain five oldest *Hymns* in the Book. Some critics said the "Hymns of Shang" were written in the eighth century B.C. by Shang descendents in the State of Song, but there is no authentic proof for it.

Two devices are commonly employed in the *Book of Poetry*, the frequent use of simile and metaphor, and the practice of "evocation" or "association," that is, starting a song by evoking images quite apart from the central subject. "Large Rat" is a good example of a song in which an animal is compared to certain type of man. Sometimes the images first mentioned are related to the general theme like this, but again there may be no close connection between them, for instance, the grasshopper in "The Rat" is not closely related to the wife's longing for her husband. Certain images have emotional associations, others are chosen solely for the sake of rhyme.

Another striking feature of the *Songs is* the repetition of whole phrases and stanzas, done perhaps simply for effect. Occasionally a few words of the first stanza are altered to show the development of some action, or to introduce a new rhyme or produce a more melodious effect. The form of repetition varies: sometimes certain stanzas are repeated, sometimes a few lines only, sometimes whole lines and phrases as in "Plantain Gathering" and "An Old Maid".

The metres of traditional Chinese poetry may be roughly divided into tetrasyllabic, pentasyllabic and heptasyllabic lines as well as lines of irregular length. The tetrasyllabic lines were the earliest and most songs

诗经 Book of Poetry

in the *Book of Poetry* are in this form, which had already reached maturity. Those four-character lines have only two feet each; hence the rhythm is brisk compared with the five- and seven-character lines which won popularity later. The great majority of the songs in this book are rhymed, but the rhyme schemes show a rich variety. Rhymes may be at the end of every line or every other line, certain stanzas retain the same rhyme throughout, elsewhere rhymes come in the middle of a line, and sometimes they are reinforced by alliterations.

The vocabulary of the *Book of Poetry* is a rich one; so notably is the use of epithets, double-adjectives, rhyming words and alliterations, which are employed in a variety of ways to heighten the descriptive effect or musical quality of the songs. In addition there are choruses and refrains too, another characteristic feature of folk-poetry.

This anthology was highly appraised by later generations and came to exercise a great influence on Chinese poets through the ages. For instance, we may compare the follow verse from (A) the *Book of Poetry* with (B) later poems.

1. A. How mighty did King Wu appear

    With his warriors and cavaliers

    Guarding his four frontiers! —"Hymn to King Wu"

    B. Where are my warriors brave to guard my four frontiers!

    —"Song of the Big Wind" by Liu Bang (256–195 B.C.), the first emperor of Han dynasty

2. A. The present not enjoyed at all,

    We'll miss the passing days,— "The Cricket"

    B. Enjoy the present time with laughter!

    Why worry about the hereafter?—*19 Old Poems*

3. A. You go home with a sigh.

    When your car disappears,

    I stantd there long in tears. —"A Farewell Song"

  B. Holding your band I sigh again;

    Letting it go, my teardrops rain. — "Su Wu to His Wife"

4. A. Three years I was his wife

    And led a toilsome life.

    Each day I early rose

    And late I sought repose. — "A Faithless Man"

  B. At daybreak, I begin to weave;

    At night the loom I dare not leave.

    I've finished five rolls in three days,

    Yet I am blamed for my delay. —"Peacocks Southeast Fly"

5. A. Beneath my door of single beam

    I can sit and rest at my leisure;

    Beside the gently flowing stream

    I drink to stay hunger with pleasure. —"Contentment"

  B. Into my courtyard no one should intrude,

    Nor rob my private rooms of peace and leisure.

    After long years of abject servitude,

    Again in nature I find homely pleasure.

    — "Return to Nature" by Tao Qian (365−427 A.D.)

6. A. The bright moon gleams;

    My dear love beams.

    Her face so fair,

    Can I not care? — "The Moon" 143

  B. The waves of Mirror Lake look like moonbeams;

The maiden's dress like snow on waterside.

The rippling dress vies with the rippling stream,

We know not which by which is beautified.

——"Song of the Southern Lass" by Li Bai (701—762)

7. A. Lofty is Mountain Tai

   Looked up to from Lu State.

   Mounts Gui and Meng stand nigh

   And eastward undulate. ——"Hymn to Marquis of Lu"

   B. O Peak of Peaks, how high it stands!

   One boundless green overspreads two States.

   A marvel done by Nature's hands,

   Over light and shade it dominates.

   ——"Gazing at Mount Tai" by Du Fu (712—770)

8. A. The eastern sun is red;

   The maiden like a bloom

   Follows me to my room.

   The maiden in my room

   Follows me to the bed. —— "Nocturnal Tryst"

   B. When doors were locked and incense burned, I came at night;

   I went at dawn when windlass pulled up water cool.

   ——"Nocturnal Tryst" by Li Shangyin (812—858)

9. A. Large rat, large rat,

   Eat no more millet we grow!

   Three years you have grown fat.

   No care for us you show. ——"Large Rat"

   B. The rats in the public granary so fatted grow,

When they see man came in, they do not run away.

The soldiers not provided, the people hungry go.

Who allow them to eat so much from day to day?

—"The Rats in Public Granary" by Cao Ye (816−875)

10. A. On poplars by east gate

The leaves are rustling light.

At dusk we have a date;

The evening star shines bright. —"A Date"

B. Last festival of Vernal Moon,

The blooming lanterns bright as noon,

The moon above a willow tree

Shone on my lover close to me.

—"Mountain Hawthorn" by Ouyang Xiu (1007−1072)

From the examples cited above, we can see what great influence the *Book of Poetry* has exercised on Chinese poets through the ages. Influential as it was, it was not translated into English until the 18th century by Sir William Jones (1746−1794) who rendered a fragment of the book into two versions, one verbal and the other metrical. In the 1860s James Legge (1814−1897) had his verbal version of *The Shi King or the Book of Ancient Poetry* published in Hong Kong, and his metrical version published in London in 1871 and reprinted in New York in 1967. His is a scholarly rendition which reads unlike the simple and plain original. In 1891 appeared *The Shih Ching* or *Classic of Poetry* translated by C.F.R. Allen, and *The Shi King, the Old "Poetry Classic" of the Chinese* translated by William Jennings, both published in London. Allen assumes the liberty to vary from the words and sense of the original, and his metrical version is more like adaptation than translation.

When the 20th century opened, in 1906 appeared in London the *Book of Odes, Shih-king* translated by L.Cranmer-Byng, whose metrical version is not so free in sense nor so regular in form as Allen's. In 1913 appeared at Boston *Lyrics from the Chinese* translated by Helen Waddell, who omits a great deal in her version though she adds little or nothing, and who makes an organization of her own. Her book found a large sale and reached its sixth printing in 1934. On the other hand, Louis S. Hammond pushed the close translation to the extreme. She tried to use one syllable in English to represent one word in Chinese and at the same time preserve the original rhyme scheme in her translation. For example, the first stanza of her version of "Toilers" reads as follows:

Oh woe! Oh woe!

Why not go?

Because of you

We are drenched with dew.

Almost all the earlier translators tried to render the *Book of Poetry* into English rhyme. Ezra Pound (1885–1972) was the first after Legge to render Chinese poetry into free verse in *The Classic Anthology as Defined by Confucius* published in 1915 at Cambridge and reprinted in 1954 by Harvard University Press. In spite of its extravagant errors, his book possessed abundant color, freshness and poignancy, but it is rather his recreation than his translation. Another remarkable free verse translator was Arthur Waley (1889–1966), whose version of *The Book of Songs* was published in London in 1937. In his book he said, "the essentials of English poetry are rhyme, stress and alliteration, whereas those of Chinese poetry are rhyme, length of line and tone." But he did not use rhyme in his translation, for "if one uses rhyme, it is impossible not to sacrifice sense to sound." As to stress, he made one stressed syllable represent one word in Chinese. But neither Pound nor Waley knew that beauty in sense could not be preserved at sacrifice in sound. The *Book of Poetry*, as a whole, was written in rhyme, so no English version could reproduce an effect similar to the original if no rhyme were used. On the contrary, rhymes or beauty in sound would help to bring out the beauty in sense. For instance, we may read Waley's version of "Cooing and Wooing".

"Fair, fair," cry the ospreys
On the island in the river.
Lovely is this noble lady,
Fit bride for our lord.

In patches grows the water mallow;
To left and right one must seek it.
Shy was this noble lady;
Day and night he sought her.

Sought her and could not get her;
Day and night he grieved.
Long thoughts, oh, long unhappy thoughts,
Now on his back, now tossing on to his side.

In patches grows the water mallow;
To left and right one must gather it.
Shy is this noble lady;
With great zithern and little we hearten her.

In patches grows the water mallow;
To left and right one must choose it.
Shy is this noble lady;
With gongs and drums we will gladden her.

If you compare Waley's version with mine in this book, you will find that Waley has sacrificed both sense and sound for "fair, fair" is neither faithful to the original in sense nor so beautiful in sound as "cooing" which rhymes with "wooing." In other words, by using rhymes both the beauty in sense and that in sound are preserved. This is an example to show that beauty in sound may help to bring out beauty in sense. Waley did not know that a water bird would cry and a turtledove would coo in spring to find a mate and the water plant would emerge on water in summer, so he said in line 6 "one must seek it," which is not related neither to the hero nor to the heroine of this song. According to my interpretation, "seek" should be read "flow" and its subject should be "water" instead of "one," so the first two lines of the first two stanzas show the time of wooing. In the last two stanzas the water plant was gathered in autumn and the lute and zither were played on the occasion of the engagement and bells would ring and drums would beat on the occasion of the wedding in winter. But we can find no trace of engagement and wedding in Waley's version, so we may say that he has not preserved the beauty of the original, neither in sense nor in sound. What is true of Waley's version is equally true of other free verse translations. Therefore, we may come to the conclusion that without a deep understanding of Chinese culture, no translator would be competent to translate the *Book of Poetry*.

The poetry in the Book is susceptible of various interpretations, so a poem may have different English versions, and that is the reason why this anthology is different from my previous edition entitled *The First Branch Blooming on Earth* published in Henan.

The *Book of Poetry* formed an important part of the education of Chinese intellectuals for thousands of years and became one of the classical canons of Confucianism. In this book the ancients learned the way how to regulate a family and how to govern a State, which may be summed up in two words: "rite" and "music." "Rite" imitates the order of the universe; "music" imitates the harmony of Nature. All things burst forth in spring, grow in summer, mature in autumn and rest in winter, so man should woo in spring, love in summer, be engaged in autumn and wedded in winter in accordance with rite and with the accompaniment of music as shown in *Song* 1. Thus we see rite is instituted to secure the mean in man's desires and music to secure the mean in man's sentiments. Music is benevolence and rite is justice externalized. If a State is governed with rite and music, the people will be just and benevolent and the world will be peaceful and happy. Rite and music are the essence of Confucianism or tranditional Chinese culture. In comparison with them, government and law are but secondary. The main function of government and law is but to provide the conditions that make rite and music possible. Educated in

Confucianism, China has been standing among the great powers for thousands of years, outshining Egypt and India, Greece and Rome which have only a glorious past, and America and England, France, Germany and Russia which have only a glorious present. From this we can see what an important role the *Book of Poetry*, gem of Chinese culture, will play if translated into an English version as beautiful as the original in sense, in sound and in form.

X. Y. Z.

Peking University
April 18, 1993

目 录
CONTENTS

前言 Introduction ·· (1)

国风 BOOK OF SONGS

周南 Songs Collected South of the Capital, Modern Shaanxi and Henan ·· (2)

 关雎 Cooing and Wooing ·························· (2)
 葛覃 Home-Going of the Bride ···················· (3)
 卷耳 Mutual Longing ······························ (4)
 樛木 Married Happiness ·························· (5)
 螽斯 Blessed with Children ························ (6)
 桃夭 The Newly-Wed ······························ (6)
 兔罝 The Rabbit Catcher ·························· (7)
 芣苢 Plantain Gathering ·························· (8)
 汉广 A Woodcutter's Love ························ (9)
 汝坟 A Wife Waiting ································ (10)
 麟之趾 The Good Unicorn ······················ (11)

召南 Songs Collected South of Zhao, Modern Henan ······ (12)

 鹊巢 The Magpie's Nest ·························· (12)
 采蘩 The Sacrifice ································ (12)
 草虫 The Grasshoppers ·························· (13)
 采蘋 Sacrifice before Wedding ···················· (14)
 甘棠 The Duke of Zhao ·························· (15)
 行露 I Accuse ···································· (16)
 羔羊 Officials in Lamb Furs ······················ (17)

CONTENTS

殷其雷 Why Not Return? ……………………… (17)
摽有梅 An Old Maid ……………………………… (18)
小星 The Starlets ………………………………… (19)
江有汜 A Merchant's Wife ……………………… (20)
野有死麕 A Deer Killer and a Jadelike Maiden …… (21)
何彼秾矣 The Princess' Wedding ………………… (21)
驺虞 A Hunter ……………………………………… (22)
邶风 Songs Collected in Bei, Modern Hebei ……… (23)
柏舟 Depression …………………………………… (23)
绿衣 My Green Robe ……………………………… (24)
燕燕 A Farewell Song ……………………………… (25)
日月 Sun and Moon ……………………………… (27)
终风 The Violent Wind ……………………………… (28)
击鼓 Complaint of a Soldier ……………………… (29)
凯风 Our Mother …………………………………… (30)
雄雉 My Man in Service ……………………………… (31)
匏有苦叶 Waiting for Her Fiance ……………… (32)
谷风 A Rejected Wife ……………………………… (33)
式微 Toilers ………………………………………… (35)
旄丘 Refugees ……………………………………… (36)
简兮 A Dancer …………………………………… (37)
泉水 Fair Spring …………………………………… (38)
北门 A Petty Official ……………………………… (39)

2

目 录

CONTENTS

　　北风 The Hard Pressed ·············· (40)

　　静女 A Shepherdess ················ (41)

　　新台 The New Tower ··············· (42)

　　二子乘舟 Two Sons in a Boat ········ (43)

鄘风 Songs Collected in Yong, Modern Shandong ········ (44)

　　柏舟 A Cypress Boat ··············· (44)

　　墙有茨 Scandals ··················· (45)

　　君子偕老 Duchess Xuan Jiang of Wei ········ (46)

　　桑中 Trysts ······················ (47)

　　鹑之奔奔 Misfortune ··············· (48)

　　定之方中 Duke Wen of Wei ········· (49)

　　蝃蝀 Elopement ··················· (50)

　　相鼠 The Rat ···················· (51)

　　干旄 Betrothal Gifts ··············· (52)

　　载驰 Patriotic Baroness Mu of Xu ········ (53)

卫风 Songs Collected in Wei, Modern Henan ········ (55)

　　淇奥 Duke Wu of Wei ············· (55)

　　考槃 A Happy Hermit ············· (56)

　　硕人 The Duke's Bride ············ (57)

　　氓 A Faithless Man ················ (59)

　　竹竿 A Lovesick Fisherman ········· (62)

　　芄兰 A Widow in Love ············ (63)

　　河广 The River Wide ·············· (63)

3

CONTENTS

伯兮 My Lord ················· (64)
有狐 A Lonely Huskand ················· (65)
木瓜 Gifts ················· (66)
王风 Songs Collected around the Capital, Modern Henan (67)
黍离 The Ruined Capital ················· (67)
君子于役 My Man Is Away ················· (68)
君子阳阳 What Joy ················· (69)
扬之水 In Garrison ················· (70)
中谷有蓷 Grief of a Deserted Wife ················· (71)
兔爰 Past and Present ················· (72)
葛藟 A Refugee ················· (73)
采葛 One Day When I See Her Not ················· (74)
大车 To Her Captive Lord ················· (75)
丘中有麻 To Her Lover ················· (76)
郑风 Songs Collected in Zheng, Modern Henan ················· (77)
缁衣 A Good Wife ················· (77)
将仲子 Cadet My Dear ················· (78)
叔于田 The Young Cadet ················· (79)
大叔于田 Hunting ················· (80)
清人 Qing Warriors ················· (82)
羔裘 Officer in Lamb's Fur ················· (83)
遵大路 Leave Me Not ················· (84)
女曰鸡鸣 A Hunter's Domestic Life ················· (84)

目 录
CONTENTS

有女同车 Lady Jiang ……………………… (85)

山有扶苏 A Joke ………………………… (86)

萚兮 Sing Together ……………………… (87)

狡童 A Handsome Guy …………………… (87)

褰裳 Lift up Your Robe …………………… (88)

丰 Lost Opportunity ……………………… (88)

东门之墠 A Lover's Monologue ………… (89)

风雨 Wind and Rain ……………………… (90)

子衿 To a Scholar ………………………… (91)

扬之水 Believe Me ………………………… (92)

出其东门 My Lover in White …………… (92)

野有蔓草 The Creeping Grass …………… (93)

溱洧 Riverside Rendezvous ……………… (94)

齐风 Songs Collected in Qi, Modern Shandong ………… (96)

鸡鸣 A Courtier and His Wife …………… (96)

还 Two Hunters …………………………… (97)

著 The Bridegroom ……………………… (98)

东方之日 Nocturnal Tryst ……………… (99)

东方未明 A Tryst before Dawn ………… (99)

南山 Incest ………………………………… (100)

甫田 Missing Her Son …………………… (102)

卢令 Hunter and Hounds ………………… (103)

敝笱 Duchess Wen Jiang of Qi ………… (103)

目 录

CONTENTS

 载驱 Duke of Qi and Duchess of Lu ·················· (104)

 猗嗟 The Archer Duke ···························· (105)

魏风 Songs Collected in Wei, Modern Shanxi ············ (107)

 葛屦 A Well-Drest Lady and Her Maid ··············· (107)

 汾沮洳 A Scholar Unknown ························ (108)

 园有桃 A Scholar Misunderstood ··················· (109)

 陟岵 A Homesick Soldier ························· (110)

 十亩之间 Gathering Mulberry ····················· (111)

 伐檀 The Woodcutter's Song ······················ (112)

 硕鼠 Large Rat ································· (114)

唐风 Songs Collected in Tang, Modern Shanxi ·········· (116)

 蟋蟀 The Cricket ······························· (116)

 山有枢 Why Not Enjoy? ························· (117)

 扬之水 Our Prince ······························ (118)

 椒聊 The Pepper Plant ··························· (119)

 绸缪 A Wedding Song ·························· (120)

 杕杜 A Wanderer ······························· (121)

 羔裘 An Unkind Lord in Lamb's Fur ··············· (122)

 鸨羽 The Peasants' Complaint ···················· (123)

 无衣 To His Deceased Wife ······················ (125)

 有杕之杜 The Russet Pear Tree ··················· (125)

 葛生 An Elegy ·································· (126)

 采苓 Rumor ···································· (127)

目 录
CONTENTS

- 秦风 Songs Collected in Qin, Modern Shaanxi ………… (129)
  - 车邻 Lord Zhong of Qin ………… (129)
  - 驷驖 Winter Hunting ………… (130)
  - 小戎 A Lord on Expedition ………… (131)
  - 蒹葭 Where Is She? ………… (133)
  - 终南 Duke Xiang of Qin ………… (134)
  - 黄鸟 Burial of Three Worthies ………… (135)
  - 晨风 The Forgotten ………… (136)
  - 无衣 Comradeship ………… (137)
  - 渭阳 Farewell to Duke Wen of Jin ………… (138)
  - 权舆 Not As Before ………… (139)
- 陈风 Songs Collected in Chen, Modern Henan ………… (140)
  - 宛丘 A Religious Dancer ………… (140)
  - 东门之枌 Secular Dancers ………… (141)
  - 衡门 Contentment ………… (141)
  - 东门之池 To a Weaving Maiden ………… (142)
  - 东门之杨 A Date ………… (143)
  - 墓门 The Evil-Doing Usurper ………… (144)
  - 防有鹊巢 Riverside Magpies ………… (145)
  - 月出 The Moon ………… (145)
  - 株林 The Duke's Mistress ………… (146)
  - 泽陂 A Bewitching Lady ………… (147)
- 桧风 Songs Collected in Gui, Modern Henan ………… (149)

CONTENTS

    羔裘 The Last Lord of Gui …………………………… (149)

    素冠 The Mourning Wife …………………………… (150)

    隰有苌楚 The Unconscious Tree ………………… (151)

    匪风 Nostalgia ……………………………………… (151)

曹风 Songs Collected in Cao, Modern Shandong ……… (153)

    蜉蝣 The Ephemera ………………………………… (153)

    候人 Poor Attendants ……………………………… (154)

    鸤鸠 An Ideal Ruler ………………………………… (155)

    下泉 The Capital …………………………………… (156)

豳风 Songs Collected in Bin, Modern Shaanxi ………… (158)

    七月 Life of Peasants ……………………………… (158)

    鸱鸮 A Mother Bird ………………………………… (164)

    东山 Coming Back from the Eastern Hills ………… (165)

    破斧 With Broken Axe ……………………………… (167)

    伐柯 An Axe-Handle ……………………………… (168)

    九罭 The Duke's Return …………………………… (169)

    狼跋 Like an Old Wolf ……………………………… (170)

小雅 BOOK OF ODES

鹿鸣之什 First Decade of Odes ……………………… (172)

    鹿鸣 To Guests ……………………………………… (172)

    四牡 Loyalty and Filial Piety ……………………… (173)

    皇皇者华 The Envoy ……………………………… (175)

    常棣 Brotherhood …………………………………… (176)

目 录
CONTENTS

伐木 Friendship and Kinship ·················· (178)

天保 The Royalty ·················· (180)

采薇 A Homesick Warrior ·················· (182)

出车 General Nan Zhong and His Wife ·················· (184)

杕杜 A Soldier's Wife ·················· (187)

鱼丽 Fish and Wine ·················· (189)

南有嘉鱼之什 Second Decade of Odes ·················· (191)

南有嘉鱼 Southern Fish Fine ·················· (191)

南山有台 Longevity ·················· (192)

蓼萧 Southernwood ·················· (193)

湛露 The Heavy Dew ·················· (195)

彤弓 The Red Bow ·················· (196)

菁菁者莪 Our Lord Visiting the School ·················· (197)

六月 General Ji Fu ·················· (198)

采芑 General Fang ·················· (200)

车攻 Great Hunting ·················· (203)

吉日 Royal Hunting ·················· (205)

鸿雁之什 Third Decade of Odes ·················· (207)

鸿雁 The Toilers ·················· (207)

庭燎 Early Audience ·················· (208)

沔水 Water Flows ·················· (209)

鹤鸣 The Crane Cries ·················· (210)

祈父 To the Minister of War ·················· (211)

目录

CONTENTS

白驹 The White Pony ……………………………… (212)

黄鸟 Yellow Birds ………………………………… (213)

我行其野 A Rejected Husband …………………… (215)

斯干 Installation …………………………………… (216)

无羊 The Herdsmen's Song ……………………… (219)

节南山之什 Fourth Decade of Odes …………… (221)

节南山 To Grand Master Yin …………………… (221)

正月 Lamentation ………………………………… (224)

十月之交 President Huang Fu …………………… (229)

雨无正 Untimely Rain …………………………… (232)

小旻 Counselors ………………………………… (235)

小宛 Reflections ………………………………… (237)

小弁 The Banished Prince ……………………… (239)

巧言 Disorder and Slander ……………………… (243)

何人斯 Friend or Foe? …………………………… (245)

巷伯 A Eunuch's Complaint …………………… (248)

谷风之什 Fifth Decade of Odes ………………… (250)

谷风 Weal and Woe ……………………………… (250)

蓼莪 The Parents' Death ………………………… (251)

大东 East and West ……………………………… (253)

四月 Banishment to the South …………………… (256)

北山 Injustice …………………………………… (258)

无将大车 Don't Trouble ………………………… (259)

目 录
CONTENTS

小明 A Nostalgic Official ······ (260)

鼓钟 Bells and Drums ······ (263)

楚茨 Winter Sacrifice ······ (264)

信南山 Spring Sacrifice at the Foot of the Southern Mountain ······ (267)

甫田之什 Sixth Decade of Odes ······ (270)

甫田 Harvest ······ (270)

大田 Farm Work ······ (272)

瞻彼洛矣 Grand Review ······ (274)

裳裳者华 A Noble Lord ······ (275)

桑扈 The Royal Toast ······ (276)

鸳鸯 The Love-Birds ······ (277)

頍弁 The Royal Banquet ······ (278)

车舝 On the Way to the Bride's House ······ (280)

青蝇 Blue Flies ······ (281)

宾之初筵 Revelry ······ (282)

鱼藻之什 Seventh Decade of Odes ······ (286)

鱼藻 The Fish among the Weed ······ (286)

采菽 Royal Favours ······ (287)

角弓 Admonition ······ (289)

菀柳 The Unjust Lord ······ (291)

都人士 Men of the Old Capital ······ (292)

采绿 My Lord Not Back ······ (293)

目 录
CONTENTS

  黍苗 On Homeward Way after Construction ⋯⋯⋯⋯ (294)

  隰桑 The Mulberry Tree ⋯⋯⋯⋯⋯⋯⋯⋯⋯⋯ (296)

  白华 The Degraded Queen ⋯⋯⋯⋯⋯⋯⋯⋯⋯ (297)

  绵蛮 Hard Journey ⋯⋯⋯⋯⋯⋯⋯⋯⋯⋯⋯⋯ (299)

  瓠叶 Frugal Hospitality ⋯⋯⋯⋯⋯⋯⋯⋯⋯⋯ (300)

  渐渐之石 Eastern Expedition ⋯⋯⋯⋯⋯⋯⋯⋯ (301)

  苕之华 Famine ⋯⋯⋯⋯⋯⋯⋯⋯⋯⋯⋯⋯⋯⋯ (302)

  何草不黄 Nowhere but Yellow Grass ⋯⋯⋯⋯⋯ (303)

大雅 BOOK OF EPICS

文王之什 First Decade of Epics ⋯⋯⋯⋯⋯⋯⋯⋯⋯ (306)

  文王 Heaven's Decree ⋯⋯⋯⋯⋯⋯⋯⋯⋯⋯⋯ (306)

  大明 Three Kings of Zhou ⋯⋯⋯⋯⋯⋯⋯⋯⋯ (309)

  绵 The Migration in 1325 B.C. ⋯⋯⋯⋯⋯⋯⋯ (312)

  棫朴 King Wen and Talents ⋯⋯⋯⋯⋯⋯⋯⋯ (315)

  旱麓 Sacrifice and Blessing ⋯⋯⋯⋯⋯⋯⋯⋯⋯ (316)

  思齐 King Wen's Reign ⋯⋯⋯⋯⋯⋯⋯⋯⋯⋯ (317)

  皇矣 The Rise of Zhou ⋯⋯⋯⋯⋯⋯⋯⋯⋯⋯ (319)

  灵台 The Wondrous Park ⋯⋯⋯⋯⋯⋯⋯⋯⋯ (323)

  下武 King Wu ⋯⋯⋯⋯⋯⋯⋯⋯⋯⋯⋯⋯⋯⋯ (325)

  文王有声 Kings Wen and Wu ⋯⋯⋯⋯⋯⋯⋯⋯ (326)

生民之什 Second Decade of Epics ⋯⋯⋯⋯⋯⋯⋯⋯ (329)

  生民 Hou Ji, the Lord of corn ⋯⋯⋯⋯⋯⋯⋯⋯ (329)

  行苇 Banquet ⋯⋯⋯⋯⋯⋯⋯⋯⋯⋯⋯⋯⋯⋯ (333)

目 录
CONTENTS

既醉 Sacrificial Ode ·················· (334)

凫鹥 The Ancestor's Spirit ·················· (336)

假乐 King Cheng ·················· (338)

公刘 Duke Liu ·················· (339)

泂酌 Take Water from Far Away ·················· (342)

卷阿 King Cheng's Progress ·················· (342)

民劳 The People Are Hard Pressed ·················· (346)

板 Censure ·················· (348)

荡之什 Third Decade of Epics ·················· (352)

荡 Warnings ·················· (352)

抑 Admonition by Duke Wu of Wei ·················· (355)

桑柔 Misery and Disorder ·················· (360)

云汉 Great Drought ·················· (366)

崧高 Count of Shen ·················· (370)

烝民 Premier Shan Fu ·················· (373)

韩奕 The Marquis of Han ·················· (377)

江汉 Duke Mu of Zhao ·················· (380)

常武 Expedition against Xu ·················· (383)

瞻卬 Complaint against King You ·················· (385)

召旻 King You's Times ·················· (388)

颂 BOOK OF HYMNS

周颂 Hymns of Zhou

清庙之什 First Decade of Hymns of Zhou ·················· (392)

目 录
CONTENTS

清庙 King Wen's Temple ·················· (392)

维天之命 King Wen Deified ·················· (392)

维清 King Wen's Statutes ·················· (393)

烈文 King Cheng's Inaugural Address ·················· (393)

天作 Mount Qi ·················· (394)

昊天有成命 King Cheng's Hymn ·················· (395)

我将 King Wu's Sacrificial Hymn ·················· (396)

时迈 King Wu's Progress ·················· (398)

执竞 Kings Cheng and Kang ·················· (398)

思文 Hymn to the Lord of Corn ·················· (398)

臣工之什 Second Decade of Hymns of Zhou ·················· (400)

  臣工 Husbandry ·················· (400)

  噫嘻 King Kang's Prayer ·················· (401)

  振鹭 The Guest Assisting at Sacrifice ·················· (401)

  丰年 Thanksgiving ·················· (402)

  有瞽 Temple Music ·················· (402)

  潜 Sacrifice of Fish ·················· (404)

  雝 King Wu's Prayer to King Wen ·················· (404)

  载见 King Cheng's Sacrifice to King Wu ·················· (405)

  有客 Guests at the Sacrifice ·················· (406)

  武 Hymn to King Wu Great and Bright ·················· (407)

闵予小子之什 Third Decade of Hymns of Zhou ·················· (408)

  闵予小子 Elegy on King Wu ·················· (408)

目 录
CONTENTS

　　访落 King Cheng's Ascension to the Throne ……………(408)

　　敬之 King Cheng's Consultation ……………………(409)

　　小毖 King Cheng's Self-Criticism ……………………(410)

　　载芟 Cultivation of the Ground ……………………(411)

　　良耜 Hymn of Thanksgiving ……………………(413)

　　丝衣 Supplementary Sacrifice ……………………(414)

　　酌 The Martial King ……………………(415)

　　桓 Hymn to King Wu ……………………(416)

　　赉 King Wu's Hymn to King Wen ……………………(416)

　　般 The King's Progress ……………………(417)

鲁颂 Hymns of Lu ……………………(418)

　　駉 Horses ……………………(418)

　　有駜 The Ducal Feast ……………………(420)

　　泮水 The Poolside Hall ……………………(421)

　　閟宫 Hymn to Marquis of Lu ……………………(424)

商颂 Hymns of Shang ……………………(431)

　　那 Hymn to King Tang ……………………(431)

　　烈祖 Hymn to Ancestor ……………………(432)

　　玄鸟 The Swallow ……………………(433)

　　长发 The Rise of Shang ……………………(434)

　　殷武 Hymn to King Wu Ding ……………………(437)

国 风

BOOK OF SONGS

周 南

Songs Collected South of the Capital, Modern Shaanxi and Henan

关 雎

Cooing and Wooing*

关关①雎鸠②，　关关和唱的鱼鹰，　　By riverside a pair
在河之洲。　　在河中小洲之上。　　Of turtledoves are cooing;
窈窕淑女，　　美丽善良的姑娘啊，　There is a maiden fair
君子好逑。　　是君子追求的对象。　whom a young man is wooing.

参差荇菜，　　长长短短的荇菜，　　Water flows left and right
左右流③之。　左左右右地采摘。　　Of cresses here and there;
窈窕淑女，　　美丽善良的姑娘啊，　The youth yearns day and night
寤寐求之。　　想她想到梦里来。　　For the maiden so fair.

求之不得，　　追求不到那姑娘，　　His yearning grows so strong,
寤寐思服。　　却是醒也思梦也想。　He cannot fall asleep,
悠哉悠哉，　　想念她啊想念她，　　But tosses all night long,
辗转反侧。　　翻来覆去到天亮。　　So deep in love, so deep!

参差荇菜，　　长长短短的荇菜，　　Now gather left and right
左右采之。　　左左右右地采摘。　　Cress long or short and tender!

---

①关关：雌雄两鸟的和鸣声。②雎鸠(jūjiū)：一种水鸟，相传这种鸟雌雄间的爱情很专一。③流：顺着水流之势而择取。

* The young man made acquaintance with the maiden in spring when turtledoves were cooing (Stanza 1), wooed her in summer when cress floated on water (Stanza 2) and yearned for her until they were engaged in autumn when cress was gathered (Stanza 4) and married in winter when cresses were cooked (Stanza 5).

窈窕淑女，　　美丽善良的姑娘啊，　　O lute, play music light
琴瑟友之。　　弹琴鼓瑟把她爱。　　For the fiancée so slender!

参差荇菜，　　长长短短的荇菜，　　Feast friends at left and right
左右芼①之。　　左左右右地采摘。　　On cresses cooked tender!
窈窕淑女，　　美丽善良的姑娘啊，　　O bells and drums, delight
钟鼓乐之。　　敲钟打鼓取悦她。　　The bride so sweet and slender!

葛　覃　　　　　　　Home-Going of the Bride*

葛②之覃③兮，　　葛藤长长，　　The vines outspread and trail
施④于中谷，　　缠蔓山沟里，　　In the midst of the vale.
维叶萋萋。　　叶子密层层。　　Their leaves grow lush and sprout;
黄鸟于飞，　　轻飞是黄莺，　　Yellow birds fly about
集于灌木，　　落入灌木丛，　　And perch on leafy trees.
其鸣喈喈。　　叽叽叫不停。　　O how their twitters please!

葛之覃兮，　　葛藤长长，　　The vines outspread and trail
施于中谷，　　缠蔓山沟里，　　In the midst of the vale.
维叶莫莫。　　叶子密层层。　　Their leaves grow lush on soil,
是刈⑤是濩⑥，　　割煮忙又忙，　　So good to cut and boil
为𫄨⑦为绤⑧，　　织成粗布和细布，　　And make cloth coarse or fine.
服之无斁⑨。　　穿在身上多舒畅。　　Who wears it likes the vine.

---

①芼(mào)：采摘。②葛：一种多年生蔓草，可以用来织布。③覃(tán)：延长。④施(yì)：蔓延。⑤刈(yì)：割。⑥濩(huò)：煮。⑦𫄨(chī)：细葛布。⑧绤(xì)：粗葛布。⑨斁(yì)：厌恶。

* Going back to her parents' home was an important event for a bride after her wedding.

言告师氏，	向我保姆告个假，	I tell Mother-in-law
言告言归。	我要回娘家。	Soon I will homeward go.
薄污①我私②，	洗了我的内衣，	I'll wash my undershirt
薄浣③我衣。	洗了我的外褂，	And rinse my outerskirt.
害浣害④否？	还要洗啥，不要洗啥？	My dress cleaned, I'll appear
归宁⑤父母。	就要回家见爹妈。	Before my parents dear.

卷 耳⑥ — Mutual Longing*

采采卷耳，	采啊采啊采卷耳，	Wife: "I gather the mouse-ear
不盈顷筐。	总是不满小浅筐。	With a basket to fill.
嗟我怀人，	一心想着远行人，	I miss my husband dear
寘⑦彼周行⑧。	把筐放在大路旁。	And leave it empty still."

陟⑨彼崔嵬⑩，	登上石山高又险，	Man: "The hill I'm climbing up
我马虺隤⑪！	我的马儿腿发软。	Has tried and tired my horse.
我姑酌彼金罍，	先把酒壶来倒满，	I'll drink my golden cup
维以不永怀。	好让心儿静又安。	So as to gather force.

陟彼高冈，	攀上山梁陡又狭，	"The height I'm climbing up
我马玄黄⑫！	我的马儿眼发花。	Has dizzied my horse in strife.

---

①污：洗涤。②私：内衣。③浣(huàn)：洗涤。④害(hé)：何，哪一个。⑤归宁：回家问候父母。⑥卷耳：一种植物，嫩苗可以吃，也可以药用。⑦寘(zhì)：放。⑧周行(háng)：大道。⑨陟(zhì)：登。⑩崔嵬(cuīwéi)：高山。⑪虺隤(huītuí)：疲惫难行。⑫玄黄：指因病而变色，眼花。

* A wife was longing for the return of her husband while he was longing for her on his homeward way.

| 我姑酌彼兕觥， | 先把酒杯来倒满， | I drink my rhino cup |
| 维以不永伤。 | 好让心儿免悲伤。 | Lest I'd think of my wife. |

陟彼砠①矣，	艰难登上土石山，	"I climb the rocky hill;
我马瘏②矣，	我的马儿要累倒，	My wornout horse won't go.
我仆痡③矣！	我的仆人要累病。	My servant's very ill.
云何吁矣！	这种忧伤何时了。	O how great is my woe!"

樛　木　　　　　　Married Happiness*

南有樛木④，	南山有棵弯弯树，	Up crooked Southern trees
葛藟⑤纍之。	野葛都来攀缘它，	Are climbing creepers' vines;
乐只君子，	这样快乐的君子，	On lords whom their wives please,
福履⑥绥之！	上天降福赐给他。	Quiet happiness shines.

南有樛木，	南山有棵弯弯树，	The crooked Southern trees
葛藟荒⑦之。	野葛都来遮掩它。	Are covered by grapevines;
乐只君子，	这样快乐的君子，	On lords whom their wives please,
福履将之！	上天降福保佑他。	Greater happiness shines.

南有樛木，	南山有棵弯弯树，	Round crooked Southern trees
葛藟萦之。	野葛都来缠绕它。	Are twining creepers' vines;
乐只君子，	这样快乐的君子，	On lords whom their wives please,
福履成之！	上天降福成全他。	Perfect happiness shines.

---

①砠(jū)：有土的石山。②瘏(tú)：劳累过度。③痡(fū)：疲病。④樛(jiū)木：树木向下弯曲。⑤葛藟(lěi)：野葛。⑥福履：福禄。⑦荒：掩盖。

* A wife was to her lord as the vine was to the tree.

螽 斯　　　　　　Blessed with Children*

螽①斯②羽③，	螽儿的翅膀，	Insects in flight,
诜诜兮④。	密密地排。	Well you appear.
宜尔子孙，	你多子多孙啊，	It is all right
振振⑤兮。	兴旺无法量。	To teem with children dear.
螽斯羽，	螽儿的翅膀，	Insects in flight,
薨薨⑥兮。	翁翁地响。	How sound your wings!
宜尔子孙，	你多子多孙啊，	It is all right
绳绳兮。	绵延无限长。	To have children in strings.
螽斯羽，	螽儿的翅膀，	Insects in flight,
揖揖⑦兮。	群集会聚。	You feel so warm.
宜尔子孙，	你多子多孙啊，	It is all right
蛰蛰⑧兮。	团聚真欢畅。	To have children in swarm.

桃 夭　　　　　　The Newly-Wed*

桃之夭夭⑨，	桃树茂盛枝杈嫩，	The peach tree beams so red;
灼灼⑩其华。	开的花儿红又粉。	How brilliant are its flowers!

---

① 螽(zhōng)：蝗虫的一种。② 斯：的。③ 羽：翅膀。④ 诜诜(shēnshēn)：和顺的声音。
⑤ 振振(zhēnzhēn)：众多的样子。⑥ 薨薨(hōnghōng)：繁多的样子。⑦ 揖揖(jíjí)：聚集。⑧ 蛰蛰(zhízhí)：集和。⑨ 夭夭：树因为年轻而长得茂盛。⑩ 灼灼：红红的。

* The poet wished the family to be blessed with as many children as a swarm of insects.

* Under the Zhou dynasty (1121-255 B.C.) young people were married in spring when the peach tree was in flower. This was the first nuptial song in Chinese history, in which the beauty of the bride was compared to that of peach blossoms.

| 之子①于归， | 这个姑娘要出嫁， | The maiden's getting wed, |
| 宜其室家。 | 和顺对待夫家人。 | Good for the nuptial bowers. |

桃之夭夭，	桃树茂盛枝权嫩，	The peach tree beams so red;
有蕡②其实。	结的果儿红又润。	How plentiful its fruit!
之子于归③，	这个姑娘要出嫁，	The maiden's getting wed;
宜其家室。	和顺对待夫家人。	She's the family's root.

桃之夭夭，	桃树茂盛枝权嫩，	The peach tree beams so red;
其叶蓁蓁④。	长的叶儿绿又肥。	Its leaves are lush and green.
之子于归，	这个姑娘要出嫁，	The maiden's getting wed;
宜其家人。	和顺对待夫家人。	On household she'll be keen.

兔　罝　　　　　　　The Rabbit Catcher*

肃肃兔罝⑤，	严严实实结兔网，	Well set are rabbit nets;
椓⑥之丁丁。	木桩敲得当当响。	On the pegs go the blows.
赳赳武夫，	赳赳武夫真勇猛，	The warrior our lord gets
公侯干城⑦。	公侯把他做屏障。	Protects him from the foes.

| 肃肃兔罝， | 严严实实结兔网， | Well set are rabbit nets, |
| 施于中逵⑧。 | 放在大路正中央。 | Placed where crossroads appear. |

---

① 之子：这个姑娘。② 蕡(fén)：大。③ 于归：出嫁。④ 蓁蓁(zhēnzhēn)：繁盛的样子。⑤ 罝(jū)：网。⑥ 椓(zhuó)：敲打。⑦ 干城：城墙，屏障。⑧ 中逵：大路。

* This was a song in praise of a rabbit catcher, fit to be a warrior and compeer of the lord. It set forth the influence of the lord as so powerful and beneficial that individuals of the lowest rank might be made fit to occupy the highest positions.

赳赳武夫，	赳赳武夫真勇猛，	The warrior our lord gets
公侯好仇①。	公侯把他做伴当。	Will be his good compeer.

肃肃兔罝，	严严实实结兔网，	Well set are rabbit nets,
施于中林。	放在树林正中央。	Amid the forest spread.
赳赳武夫，	赳赳武夫真勇猛，	The warrior our lord gets
公侯腹心。	公侯心腹守四方。	Serves him with heart and head.

芣苢   Plantain Gathering*

采采芣苢②，	鲜亮亮的车前子呀，	We gather plantain seed.
薄言采之。	快呀快呀采摘它。	Let's gather it with speed!
采采芣苢，	鲜亮亮的车前子呀，	We gather plantain ears.
薄言有之。	快呀快呀收起它。	Let's gather them with cheers!

采采芣苢，	鲜亮亮的车前子呀，	We gather plantain seed.
薄言掇之。	快呀快呀拾取它。	Let's rub it out with speed!
采采芣苢，	鲜亮亮的车前子呀，	We gather plantain ears.
薄言捋之。	快呀快呀捋取它。	Pull by handfuls with cheers!

采采芣苢，	鲜亮亮的车前子呀，	We gather plantain seed.
薄言袺③之。	翻过衣襟装起它。	Let's fill our skirts with speed!

---

① 仇(qiú)：伴当，搭档。② 芣苢(fúyǐ)：车前子，叶可食用，实可药用。③ 袺(jié)：手执衣襟以承物。

* This song was sung by women while gathering plantain seed which was thought to be favorable to child-bearing and difficult labors.

采采芣苢，　　鲜亮亮的车前子呀，　　We gather plantain ears.
薄言襭①之。　提起衣襟兜满它。　　Belt up full skirts with cheers!

汉　广　　　　　　　　　　　A Woodcutter's Love*

南有乔木②，　南方有棵高高树，　　The tallest Southern tree
不可休息。　　树下少荫不可休。　　Affords no shade for me.
汉有游女，　　汉江有个好游女，　　The maiden on the stream
不可求思。　　枉费心思不可求。　　Can but be found in dream.
汉之广矣，　　汉江之水广又宽，　　For me the stream's too wide
不可泳思。　　游过好比登天难。　　To reach the other side
江之永矣，　　好似汉江长又长，　　As River Han's too long
不可方③思。　航行不能用小舫。　　To cross its current strong.

翘翘错薪，　　丛丛柴草长得高，　　Of the trees in the wood
言刈其楚。　　割柴最好割荆条。　　I'll only cut the good.
之子于归，　　有个姑娘要出嫁，　　If she should marry me,
言秣④其马。　先把马儿来喂饱。　　Her stable-man I'd be.
汉之广矣，　　汉江之水广又宽，　　For me the stream's too wide
不可泳思。　　游过好比登天难。　　To reach the other side
江之永矣，　　好似汉江长又长，　　As River Han's too long
不可方思。　　航行不能用小舫。　　To cross its current strong.

---

① 襭(xié)：翻动衣襟以承物。② 乔木：高大的树木。③ 方：舫，小舟。④ 秣(mò)：用草喂马。

* The legend said that there was a Goddess on the River Han. Here the woodcutter compared the maiden he loved to the inaccessible Goddess.

翘翘错薪，	丛丛柴草长得高，	Of the trees here and there
言刈其蒌①。	割柴最好割芦蒿。	I'll only cut the fair.
之子于归，	有个姑娘要出嫁，	If she should marry me,
言秣其驹。	先把马驹来喂饱。	Her stable-boy I'd be.
汉之广矣，	汉江之水广又宽，	For me the stream's too wide
不可泳思。	游过好比登天难。	To reach the other side
江之永矣，	好似汉江长又长，	As River Han's too long
不可方思。	航行不能用小舫。	To cross its current strong.

汝坟

A Wife Waiting

遵②彼汝坟③，	沿着汝水走堤岸，	Along the raised bank green
伐其条枚④。	先砍树枝再砍干。	I cut down twigs and wait.
未见君子，	没有见到我君子，	My lord cannot be seen;
惄⑤如调⑥饥。	忧似忍饥在晨朝。	I feel a hunger great.
遵彼汝坟，	沿着汝水走堤岸，	Along the raised bank green
伐其条肄。	砍那新生树枝条。	I cut fresh sprigs and spray.
既见君子，	已经见到我君子，	My lord can now be seen,
不我遐弃。	幸未曾把我远抛。	But soon he'll go away.
鲂鱼赪⑦尾，	鲂鱼尾红因疲劳，	"I'll leave your red-tailed fish:

---

① 蒌(lóu)：多长在水边的一种植物，叶嫩时可食，老时可为薪。② 遵：沿着。③ 坟：河堤。④ 枚：树干。⑤ 惄(nì)：忧思。⑥ 调(zhōu)：整个早晨。⑦ 赪(chēng)：赤色。

* A wife tried to dissuade her lord from leaving her again by cooking for him a red-tailed fish to show the unfed flame of her heart.

王室如燬①，	王朝多难如火烧。	The kingdom is on fire."
虽则如燬，	虽然多难如火烧，	"If you leave as you wish，
父母孔迩。	父母供奉莫忘掉。	Who'll take care of your sire?"

麟之趾　　　　　　　　The Good Unicorn*

麟之趾，	麟的脚趾不踏生物，	The unicorn will use its hoofs to tread on none
振振公子。	好比仁厚的公子。	Just like our Prince's noble son.
于嗟麟兮！	值得赞美的麟啊！	Ah! they are one.
麟之定，	麟的额头不顶生灵，	The unicorn will knock its head against none
振振②公姓。	好比仁厚的公孙。	Just like our Prince's grandson.
于嗟麟兮！	值得赞美的麟啊！	Ah! they are one.
麟之角，	麟的头角不触万物，	The unicorn will fight with its corn against none
振振公族。	好比仁厚的公族。	Just like our Prince's great-grandson.
于嗟麟兮！	值得赞美的麟啊！	Ah! they are one.

① 燬(huǐ)：火烧。② 振振(zhēnzhēn)：仁厚的样子。

* The unicorn was a fabulous animal, the symbol of all goodness and benevolence, having the body of a deer, the tail of an ox, the hoofs of a horse, one horn in the middle of the forehead. Its hoofs were mentioned because it did not tread on any living thing, not even on live grass; its head because it did not butt with it; and its horn because the end of it was covered with flesh, to show that the creature, while able for war, would have peace. This song celebrated the goodness of the offspring of King Wen (1184–1134 B. C.), founder of the Zhou dynasty.

召 南

Songs Collected South of Zhao, Modern Henan

鹊 巢

The Magpie's Nest*

维鹊有巢，	喜鹊树上有个巢，	The magpie builds a nest,
维鸠①居之。	斑鸠飞来居住它。	Where comes the dove in spring.
之子于归，	这个姑娘要出嫁，	The bride comes fully-drest,
百两御之。	百辆车子迎接她。	Welcomed by cabs in string.

维鹊有巢，　喜鹊树上有个巢，　The magpie builds a nest,
维鸠方②之。　斑鸠飞来占住它。　Where dwells the dove in spring.
之子于归，　这个姑娘要出嫁，　The bride comes fully-drest,
百两将之。　百辆车子恭送她。　Escort'd by cabs in string.

维鹊有巢，　喜鹊树上有个巢，　The magpie builds a nest,
维鸠盈之。　斑鸠飞来占满它。　Where lives the dove in spring.
之子于归，　这个姑娘要出嫁，　The bride comes fully-drest,
百两成之。　百辆车子成就她。　Celebrated by cabs in string.

采 蘩

The Sacrifice*

于以采蘩？　什么地方采白蒿？　Gather southernwood white

---

① 鸠：斑鸠，占住其他鸟巢的一种鸟。② 方：占有。

* The newly-wed were compared to magpie and dove or myna. The bride came escorted and welcomed by cabs and the wedding was celebrated by cabs.

* This song narrates the industry of the chambermaids assisting the prince in sacrificing.

于沼于沚。	水中小洲和湖沼。	By the pools here and there.
于以用之?	什么地方能用到?	Employ it in the rite
公侯之事。	公侯祭祀他祖考。	In our prince's affair.

于以采蘋，	什么地方采白蒿?	Gather southernwood white
于涧之中。	幽深山涧能找到。	In the vale by the stream.
于以用之?	什么地方能用到?	Employ it in the rite
公侯之宫。	公侯祭祀他祖庙。	Under the temple's beam.

被①之僮僮②，	首饰佩戴得整齐，	Wearing black, gloosy hair,
夙夜在公。	早晚参加祭祀礼。	We're busy all the day.
被之祁祁③，	首饰佩戴得华丽，	With disheveled hair
薄言还归。	祭祀完毕回家去。	At dusk we go away.

草　虫

The Grasshoppers*

喓喓④草虫，	蟋蟀喓喓叫，	Hear grassland insects sing
趯趯⑤阜螽⑥。	蚱蜢蹦蹦跳。	And see grasshoppers spring!
未见君子，	没有见君子，	When my lord is not seen,
忧心忡忡⑦。	心绪乱如搅。	I feel a sorrow keen.
亦既见止，	如果已经相见了，	When I see him downhill
亦既觏⑧止，	如果已经相聚了，	And meet him by the rill,

---

① 被(bì):首饰。② 僮僮:盛大。③ 祁祁(qíqí):繁盛的样子。④ 喓喓(yāoyāo):虫叫的声音。⑤ 趯趯(tìtì):跳跃。⑥ 阜螽(zhōng):蚱蜢。⑦ 忡忡(chōngchōng):心跳。⑧ 觏(gòu):相会。

* A wife was longing for her lord from autumn when grasshoppers sang, to spring when fern was gathered, and to summer when herb was gathered.

我心则降。	我心平静不焦躁。	My heart would then be still.

陟彼南山，	登到南山上，	I go up southern hill;
言采其蕨。	要去采蕨菜。	Of ferns I get my fill.
未见君子，	没有见君子，	When my lord is not seen,
忧心惙惙①。	心里愁得慌。	I feel a grief more keen.
亦既见止，	如果已经相见了，	When I see him downhill
亦既觏止，	如果已经相聚了，	And meet him by the rill,
我心则说。	我心欢乐多舒畅。	My heart with joy would thrill.

陟彼南山，	登到南山上，	I go up southern hill;
言采其薇。	要去采薇菜。	Of herbs I get my fill.
未见君子，	没有见君子，	When my lord is not seen,
我心伤悲。	心里悲得凄。	I feel a grief most keen.
亦既见止，	如果已经相见了，	When I see him downhill
亦既觏止，	如果已经相聚了，	And meet him by the rill,
我心则夷②。	我心安详多欣喜。	My heart would be serene.

采 蘋　　　　　Sacrifice before Wedding*

于以采蘋？	什么地方采蘋草？	Where to gather duckweed?
南涧之滨。	南山溪水边。	In the brook by south hill.
于以采藻？	什么地方采浮藻？	Where to gather pondweed?

---

①惙惙(chuòchuò)：惶惑。②夷：平。

* According to ancient custom, the bride-to-be should gather duckweed and offer it as sacrifice in the temple three months before her wedding.

| 于彼行潦①。 | 沟水积水边。 | Between the brook and rill. |

于以盛之？	什么东西装盛它？	Where to put what we've found?
维筥及筐②。	圆篓和方筐。	In baskets square or round.
于以湘③之？	什么器具蒸煮它？	Where to boil what we can?
维锜④及釜。	三脚没脚釜。	In the tripod or pan.

于以奠之？	什么地方祭献它？	Where to put offerings?
宗室牖⑤下。	宗室窗子下。	In the temple's both wings.
谁其尸⑥之？	什么人来主祭啊？	Who offers sacrifice?
有齐⑦季女。	斋戒小女娃。	The bride-to-be so nice.

甘　棠　　　　　　　　The Duke of Zhao*

蔽芾⑧甘棠，	茂盛的棠梨树，	O leafy tree of pear!
勿翦勿伐，	不剪不砍它，	Don't clip or make it bare,
召伯所茇⑨。	召伯曾停留在树下。	For once our Duke lodged there.

蔽芾甘棠，	茂盛的棠梨树，	O leafy tree of pear!
勿翦勿败，	不剪不折它，	Don't break its branches bare,
召伯所憩。	召伯曾歇息在树下。	For once our Duke rested there.

---

① 行潦(háng lǎo)：流动的水沟，积水。② 筥(jǔ)：圆竹器。③ 湘：烹煮。④ 锜(qí)：三足的釜。⑤ 牖(yǒu)：窗子。⑥ 尸：主持。古代祭祀时被当做神的人。⑦ 齐：斋，斋戒。⑧ 蔽芾(fèi)：茂盛。⑨ 茇(bá)：草舍，这里指在树下休息。

* The Duke of Zhao was a principal adherent of King Wen. The love of the people for the memory of the Duke of Zhao made them love the tree beneath which he had rested.

蔽芾甘棠，	茂盛的棠梨树，	O leafy tree of pear!
勿翦勿拜，	不剪不弯它，	Don't bend its branches bare,
召伯所说①。	召伯曾住宿在树下。	For once our Duke halted there.

行　露　　　　　　　　　　　　I Accuse*

厌浥②行露。	道上的露水湿漉漉，	The path with dew is wet;
岂不夙夜，	难道清早不走路，	Before dawn off I set;
谓行多露？	就怕道上的湿露？	I fear nor dew nor threat.

谁谓雀无角？	谁说雀儿没有角，	Who says in sparrow's head
何以穿我屋？	怎么会啄穿我的屋？	No beak can pierce the roof?
谁谓女无家？	谁说你未娶妻已成家，	Who says the man's not wed?
何以速我狱？	怎么要送我去监狱？	He jails me without proof.
虽速我狱，	就是送我去监狱，	He can't wed me in jail;
室家③不足。	强迫结婚无道理。	I'm jailed to no avail.

谁谓鼠无牙？	谁说老鼠没有牙？	Who says in the rat's head
何以穿我墉？	怎么会打通我的墙。	No teeth can pierce the wall?
谁谓女无家？	谁说你未娶妻已成家？	Who says the man's not wed?
何以速我讼？	怎么逼我上公堂。	He brings me to judge's hall.
虽速我讼，	就算逼我上公堂，	Though brought to judge's hall.
亦不女从。	我也不会顺从你。	I will not yield at all.

---

① 说(shuì)：税，住宿，休息。②厌浥(yèyì)：被露水沾湿。③ 室家：成室成家，结婚。
* A young woman resisted an attempt to force her to marry a married man and she argued her cause though put in jail and brought to the judge's hall.

羔羊　　　　　　　　　　Officials in Lamb Furs*

羔羊之皮，	羔羊皮做袄，	In lamb and sheep skins drest,
素丝五纰①。	白丝交错缝。	With their five braidings white,
退食自公，	退朝吃饭在公家，	They come from court to rest
委蛇委蛇②。	步履神态全从容。	And swagger with delight.

羔羊之革，	羔羊革做袄，	In sheep and lamb skins drest,
素丝五緎。	白丝交错缝。	With five seams of silk white,
委蛇委蛇，	步履神态全从容，	They swagger, come to rest
自公退食。	退朝吃饭也在公。	And take meals with delight.

羔羊之缝③，	羔羊皮做袄，	In lamb and sheep furs drest,
素丝五总。	白丝交错缝。	With their five joinings white,
委蛇委蛇，	步履神态全从容，	They take their meals and rest
退食自公。	退朝吃饭也在公。	And swagger with delight.

殷④其雷　　　　　　　　Why Not Return?*

| 殷其雷， | 隆隆的雷声， | The thunder rolls away |
| 在南山之阳。 | 就在南山的阳坡。 | O'er southern mountain's crest. |

---

① 五纰(tuó)：丝线交错缝制。② 委蛇(yí)：从容自得。③ 缝：革。④ 殷(yǐn)：雷声。

* It was said that this song was a satire on those officials who did nothing but swagger, take meals and rest without delight.

* A young wife was longing for the return of her husband absent on pubic service.

何斯违斯①？	为什么又要离开这里？	Why far from home do you stay,
莫敢或遑②。	不敢稍有停留。	Not daring take a rest?
振振君子，	诚实忠厚的君子，	Brave lord for whom I yearn,
归哉归哉！	归来啊归来吧！	Return, return!

殷其雷，	隆隆的雷声，	The thunder rolls away
在南山之侧。	在南山的旁边。	By southern mountain's side.
何斯违斯？	为什么又要离开这里？	Why far from home do you stay,
莫敢遑息。	不敢稍事歇息。	Not daring take a ride?
振振君子，	诚实忠厚的君子，	Brave lord for whom I yearn,
归哉归哉！	归来啊归来吧！	Return, return!

殷其雷，	隆隆的雷声，	The thunder rolls away
在南山之下，	在南山的下边。	At southern mountain's foot.
何斯违斯？	为什么又要离开这里？	Why far from home do you stay
莫敢遑处。	不敢稍作闲处。	As if you'd taken root?
振振君子，	诚实忠厚的君子，	Brav lord for whom I yearn,
归哉归哉，	归来啊归来吧！	Return, return!

摽③有梅　　　　　　　　　　An Old Maid*

摽有梅，	梅子纷纷落地，	The fruits from mume-tree fall,
其实七兮。	还有七成在树。	One-third of them away.

---

① 违斯：离开此地。② 遑(huáng)：闲暇。③ 摽(biào)：落下。

* According to ancient custom, young people should be married in spring. When mume fruit fell, it was summer and maidens over twenty might get married without courtship.

求我庶①士，	追求我的士子们，	If you love me at all,
迨②其吉兮！	不要误了好日子。	Woo me a lucky day!

摽有梅，	梅子纷纷落地，	The fruits from mume-tree fall,
其实三兮。	还有三成在树。	Two-thirds of them away.
求我庶士，	追求我的士子们，	If you love me at all,
迨其今兮！	今天就是好日子。	Woo me this very day!

摽有梅，	梅子纷纷落地，	The fruits from mume-tree fall,
顷筐塈③之。	要用筐来收取了。	Now all of them away.
求我庶士，	追求我的士子们，	If you love me at all,
迨其谓之！	姑娘就等你开口。	You need not woo but say.

小　星

The Starlets*

嘒④彼小星，	小星微微闪着光，	Three or five stars shine bright
三五在东。	三三五五在东方。	Over the eastern gate.
肃肃宵征，	急急夜里来赶路，	We make haste day and night,
夙夜在公。	为了公事早晚忙。	Busy early and late.
寔命不同！	实在命运不一样。	Different is our fate.

嘒彼小星，	小星微微闪着光，	The starlets shed weak light
维参与昴。	参星靠在昴星旁。	With the Pleiades o'erhead.
肃肃⑤宵征，	急急夜里来赶路，	We make haste day and night,

---

① 庶：众多。② 迨：及时。③ 塈(jì)：收取。④ 嘒(huì)：微光。⑤ 肃肃：急速匆忙。

* This was a complaint of petty officials who should get up by starlight and go to bed by starlight.

抱衾与裯。　　被子帐子自己扛。　　Carrying sheets of bed:
寔命不犹!　　真是人人比我强。　　No other way instead.

　　　　　　　江有汜　　　　　　　　A Merchant's Wife②

江有汜①，　　大江也有水分流，　　Upstream go you
之子归，　　　夫君归来是时候。　　To wed the new
不我以。　　　他不亲近我，　　　　And leave the old,
不我以，　　　他不亲近我，　　　　You leave the old:
其后也悔。　　他的懊悔在后头。　　Regret foretold.

江有渚，　　　大江也有小水洲，　　Downstream go you
之子归，　　　夫君归来是时候。　　To wed the new
不我与。　　　他不同我聚，　　　　And forsake me.
不我与，　　　他不好我聚，　　　　You forsake me;
其后也处!　　他的忧愁在后头。　　Rueful you'll be.

江有沱②，　　大江也会有支流，　　Bystream go you
之于归，　　　夫君归来是时候。　　To wed the new
不我过。　　　他不到我处，　　　　And desert me.
不我过，　　　他不到我处，　　　　You desert me.
其啸也歌。　　以哭当歌在后头。　　Woeful you'll be.

---

① 汜(sì)：由主流分出而后汇合的河流。② 沱(tuó)：江的支流。

* This was the complaint of a woman deserted by her husband who went upstream and downstream for commerce.

野有死麕

A Deer Killer and a Jadelike Maiden*

野有死麕①，	打死的獐子在郊野，	An antelope is killed
白茅包之。	白茅草包起它。	And wrapped in white afield.
有女怀春，	有个姑娘动了心，	A maid for love does long,
吉士②诱之。	小伙子趁机讨好她。	Tempted by a hunter strong.

林有朴樕③，	树林里伐倒小树，	He cuts down trees amain
野有死鹿，	野地里躺着死鹿。	And kills a deer again.
白茅纯④束。	白茅草搓绳一起捆。	He sees the white-drest maid
有女如玉。	有个姑娘美如玉。	As beautiful as jade.

"舒而脱脱⑤兮！	缓缓地慢慢来，	"O soft and slow, sweetheart,
无感我帨⑥兮！	别碰得我围裙动，	Don't tear my sash apart!"
无使尨⑦也吠！"	别惹得那狗儿叫。	The jadelike maid says, "Hark!
		Do not let the dog bark!"

何彼襛矣

The Princess' Wedding*

何彼襛⑧矣？	怎么那样绚艳繁盛，	Luxuriant in spring

---

① 麕(jūn)：獐鹿。② 吉士：男子的美称。③ 朴樕(sù)：小树。④ 纯(tún)束：捆扎。
⑤ 脱脱(duìduì)：慢慢地。⑥ 帨(shuì)：围裙。⑦ 尨(máng)：多毛狗。⑧ 襛(nóng)：繁盛的样子。

* A hunter killed a deer, wrapped it in white rushes and offered it as present to a beautiful maiden. The last stanza described their lovemaking implicitly.
* This song described the marriage in 683 B. C. of the granddaughter of King Ping (769-719 B. C) and the son of the Marquise of Qi. The silken thread forming a fishing line might allude to the newly-wed forming a happy family.

唐棣之华。	像郁李的花一样。	As plum flowers o'er water,
曷不肃雝,	多么雍容又大方,	How we revere the string
王姬之车。	那是王姬的花车。	Of cabs for the king's daughter!

何彼秾矣?	怎么那么绚艳繁盛?	Luxuriant in spring
华如桃李。	盛放的桃李般的漂亮。	As the peach flowers red,
平王之孙,	那是平王的孙女,	The daughter of the king
齐侯之子。	齐侯儿子是新郎。	To a marquis' son is wed.

其钓维何?	用什么钓鱼最适宜?	We use the silken thread
维丝伊缗①。	用丝麻搓合成钓绳。	To form a fishing line.
齐侯之子,	那是齐侯的儿郎,	The son of marquis is wed
平王之孙。	平王的孙女结婚姻。	To the princess divine.

驺　虞　　　　　　　　　　A Hunter*

彼茁者葭②,	丛生的芦苇真茁壮,	Abundant rushes grow along;
壹发五豝③。	一箭射中五头大猪上,	One arrow hits one boar among.
于嗟乎驺④虞!	好样的猎人啊!	Ah! what a hunter strong!

彼茁者蓬,	丛生的蓬蒿真茁壮,	Abundant reeds along the shores,
壹发五豵⑤。	一箭射中五只小猪,	One arrow scares five boars.
于嗟乎驺虞!	好样的猎人啊!	Ah! what a hunter one adores!

---

① 缗(mín):绳。② 葭(jiā):芦苇。③ 豝(bā):母猪。④ 驺(zōu)虞:猎人。⑤ 豵(zōng):小猪。

* This was a song sung during the hunting season in spring.

邶　风

Songs Collected in Bei, Modern Hebei

柏　舟

Depression*

泛①彼柏舟，	柏木船儿顺水流，	Like cypress boat
亦泛其流。	飘飘荡荡不停休。	Mid-stream afloat,
耿耿②不寐，	心内不安难入眠，	I cannot sleep
如有隐忧。	如有烦恼在心头。	In sorrow deep.
微我无酒，	不是家中没有酒，	I won't drink wine,
以敖以游。	遨游也难消我愁。	Nor roam nor pine.
我心匪鉴③，	我心并非是明镜，	Unlike the brass
不可以茹④。	不是所有都留影。	Where images pass,
亦有兄弟，	我兄我弟全都在，	On brothers I
不可以据。	依靠信任都不行。	Cannot rely.
薄言往愬，	正要去向其诉说，	When I complain,
逢彼之怒。	他们却在发雷霆。	I meet disdain.
我心匪石，	我心不能石头般，	Have I not grown
不可转也。	哪能随人来翻转。	Firm as a stone?
我心匪席，	我心难把芦席比，	Am I as flat
不可卷也。	哪能任人翻卷起。	As level mat?

---
① 泛(fàn)：随水流动。② 耿耿：烦躁不安的样子。③ 鉴：镜子。④ 茹：容纳，含影。

* This song may be interpreted either as complaint of a man or of a woman. Some say it was the forerunner of *Departure in Sorrow* by Qu Yuan (340–278 B. C.).

| 威仪棣棣①， | 堂正雍容有威仪， | My mind is strong: |
| 不可选②也。 | 不能退避受挑剔。 | I've done no wrong. |

忧心悄悄③，	忧愁烦恼备煎熬，	I'm full of spleen,
愠于群小。	小人憎恨也不少。	Hated by the mean;
觏④闵⑤既多，	遭逢痛苦既已多，	I'm in distress,
受侮不少。	忍受侮辱更不少。	Insulted no less;
静言思之，	细细想起这些事，	Thinking at rest,
寤辟有摽。	捶胸顿足心如搅。	I beat my breast.

日居月诸⑥，	太阳啊月亮啊，	The sun and moon
胡迭而微⑦？	为何总有无光时？	Turn dim so soon,
心之忧矣，	心里忧愁忘不了，	I'm in distress
如匪澣衣。	如同没洗脏衣服。	Like dirty dress.
静言思之，	细细想起这些事，	Silent think I:
不能奋飞。	不能奋翅高飞翔。	Why can't I fly?

绿　衣　　　　　My Green Robe*

绿兮衣⑧兮，	绿色衣啊绿色衣，	My upper robe is green;
绿衣黄里⑨。	绿色外衣黄色里。	Yellow my lower dress
心之忧矣，	心里忧伤心忧伤啊，	My sorrow is so keen;

---

① 棣棣：堂堂正正，雍容闲雅。② 选：指责挑剔。③ 悄悄：忧愁的样子。④ 觏(gòu)：遭遇。⑤ 闵(mǐn)：忧患。⑥ 诸：语气助词，无实义。⑦ 微：昏暗无光。⑧ 衣：上衣。⑨ 里：上衣的衬里。

* This was the first elegy in which a widower missed his deceased wife who had made the green robe and yellow dress for him.

| 曷维其已! | 何时才能够停止。 | When will end my distress? |

绿兮衣兮, 绿色衣啊绿色衣, My upper robe is green;
绿衣黄裳①, 绿色外衣黄裙裳。 Yellow my dress with dots.
心之忧矣, 心里忧伤心忧伤啊, My sorrow is so keen;
曷维其亡! 何时才能够遗忘。 How can it be forgot?

绿兮丝兮, 绿色丝啊绿色丝, The silk is green that you,
女所治兮。 你曾亲手所缝制。 Old mate, dyed all night long;
我思古人②, 想我亡故的贤妻啊, I miss you, old mate, who
俾③无訧兮。 使我平生少过失。 Kept me from doing wrong.

绨兮绤兮, 葛布不论粗和细啊, The linen coarse or fine
凄其以风。 穿在身上凉凄凄。 Is cold when blows the breeze.
我思古人, 想我亡故的贤妻啊, I miss old mate of mine,
实获我心。 真正是合我心意。 Who put my mind at ease.

燕 燕　　　　　　　A Farewell Song*

燕燕于飞, 燕子飞来飞去, A pair of swallows fly
差④池其羽。 羽翅参差不齐。 With their wings low and high.

---

① 裳:下衣。② 古人:故人,指已死去的妻子。③ 俾(bǐ):使。④ 差(cī)池:不整齐。

* This was the first farewell song in Chinese history, written by Duchess Zhuang Jiang whose beauty was described in Poem "The Duke's Bride" and who bore no children but brought up the son of Duchess Dai Wei, who became Duke Huan of Wei and was murdered by his half brother on the 16th day of the 3rd moon in 719 B. C. In this farewell song the duchess related her grief at the departure of Duchess Dai Wei, obliged to return to her native State of Chen after her son's death. The "late lord" here refers to their husband.

之子于归，	我的妹子要远嫁，	You go home in your car;
远送于野。	送到郊外要分手。	I see you off afar.
瞻望弗及，	眺望踪影不能见，	When your car disappears,
泣涕如雨。	涕泪如雨落纷纷。	Like rain fall down my tears.
燕燕于飞，	燕子飞来飞去，	A pair of swallows fly;
颉之颃①之。	上下相随呢喃唱。	You go home with a sigh.
之子于归，	我的妹子要远嫁，	When they fly up and down,
远于将之。	远远相送道路长。	I see you leave the town.
瞻望弗及。	眺望踪影不能见，	When your car disappears,
伫立以泣。	呆立流泪心悲伤。	I stand there long in tears.
燕燕于飞，	燕子飞来飞去，	A pair of swallows fly,
下上其音。	鸣声呢喃时翻飞。	Their songs heard far and nigh.
之子于归，	我的妹子要远嫁，	You go to your home state;
远送于南。	送她远嫁去南方。	I see you leave south gate.
瞻望弗及，	眺望踪影不能见，	When your car disappears.
实劳我心。	思念不已心悲伤。	Deeply grieved, I shed tears.
仲②氏任③只，	二妹诚实且可靠，	My faithful sister dear
其心塞渊。	思虑沉稳远深长。	With feeling e'er sincere,
终温且惠，	心性温和又恭顺，	So gentle and so sweet,
淑慎其身。	为人谨慎又善良。	So prudent and discreet!
先君之思，	如此安排是先君，	The thought of our late lord
以勖④寡人⑤。	以此勉慰我忧伤。	Strikes our sensitive chord.

---

① 颉颃(jiéháng)：上下飞舞。② 仲：排行第二。③ 任：信赖可靠。④ 勖(xù)：勉励。
⑤ 寡人：寡德之人。

日　月　　　　　　　　　　　　　　Sun and Moon

日居月诸，	太阳啊月亮啊，	Sun and moon bright,
照临下土。	光辉普照大地上。	Shed light on earth!
乃如之人兮！	怎么能有这样的人，	This man in sight
逝不古处。	会把古道全相忘。	Without true worth
胡能有定？	心内妄念何以止，	Has set his mind
宁不我顾？	为何竟然把我忘。	To be unkind.
日居月诸，	太阳啊月亮啊，	Sun and moon bright,
下土是冒①。	光辉普照大地上。	Cast shade with glee!
乃如之人兮！	怎么能有这样的人，	This man in sight
逝不相好。	义断情绝不来往。	Would frown at me.
胡能有定？	心内妄念何以止，	He's set his mind
宁不我报？	为何让我空相望。	To leave me behind.
日居月诸，	太阳啊月亮啊，	Sun and moon bright
出自东方。	闪烁光辉出东方。	Rise from the east.
乃如之人兮！	怎么能有这样的人，	This man in sight
德音无良。	胡言乱语丧天良。	Is worse than beast.
胡能有定？	心内妄念何以止，	His mind is set
俾也可忘。	使我难于把他忘。	All to forget.

---

① 冒：覆盖。

* This song was the complaint of a wife abandoned by her husband.

日居月诸，	太阳啊月亮啊，	Sun and moon bright
东方自出。	东方升起天下亮。	From east appear.
父兮母兮！	唤罢父亲喊母亲啊，	Can I requite
畜①我不卒。	夫君养我不久长。	My parents dear?
胡能有定？	心内妄念何以止，	My mind not set,
报我不述！	待我全无道理讲。	Can I forget?

终 风　　　　　　　　The Violent Wind

终风②且暴，	狂风吹得大又急，	The wind blows violently;
顾我则笑。	见了我就笑嘻嘻。	He looks and smiles at me.
谑浪笑敖，	对我戏谑又讪笑，	With me he seems to flirt;
中心是悼！	我的心里生烦恼。	My heart feels deeply hurt.

终风且霾③，	狂风大作尘飞扬，	The wind blows dustily;
惠然肯来？	难得他能来光顾。	He's kind to come to me.
莫往莫来，	如他不来往，	Should he nor come nor go.
悠悠我思！	我又总是把他想。	How would my yearning grow!

终风且曀④，	整天刮风又阴天，	The wind blows all the day;
不日有曀。	不见太阳黑沉沉。	The clouds won't fly away.
寤言不寐，	翻来覆去睡不着，	Awake, I'm ill at ease.
愿言则嚏⑤。	想得使他打喷嚏。	Would he miss me and sneeze!

---

① 畜：养育。② 终风：整天刮风。③ 霾(mái)：阴尘。④ 曀(yì)：阴沉。⑤ 嚏(tì)：打喷嚏。

* This is the description of a feminine mind after a man's flirtation with her.

曀曀其阴,	黑黑沉沉天阴阴,	In gloomy cloudy sky
虺虺其雷。	轰轰隆隆正打雷。	The thunder rumbles high.
寤言不寐,	翻来覆去睡不着,	I cannot sleep again.
愿言则怀。	但愿他也能想我。	O would he know my pain!

击 鼓　　　　　　　　Complaint of a Soldier*

击鼓其镗①,	敲击战鼓镗镗响,	The drums are booming out;
踊跃用兵②。	士兵踊跃练刀枪。	We leap and bound about.
土国城漕,	别人修路筑城墙,	We build walls high and low,
我独南行。	独我从军到南方。	But I should southward go.

从孙子仲,	跟随将军孙子仲,	We follow Sun Zizhong
平③陈与宋。	交好盟国陈与宋。	To fight with Chen and Song.
不我以归,	驻守南方不能归,	I cannot homeward go;
忧心有忡。	我心伤悲有苦痛。	My heart is full of woe.

爰居爰处?	在哪儿住啊在哪儿歇?	Where stop and stay our forces
爰丧其马?	在哪儿失了我的马?	When we have lost our horses?
于以求之?	去往哪里寻找它?	Where can we find them, please?
于林之下。	树林大树下。	Buried among the trees.

"死生契阔④",	"生死永远不分离",	Meet or part, live or die;

---

① 镗:击鼓的声音。② 兵:兵器。③ 平:和好,交好。④ 契阔:契合疏阔。

* A soldier of the State of Wei repined over his separation form his family after the war made on the State of Chen in 718 B. C.

与子成说①。	我曾与你相盟定。	We made oath, you and I.
执子之手，	当时握着你的手，	When can our hands we hold
与子偕老。	发誓到死不分离。	And live till we grow old?

于嗟阔兮，	可叹啊，如今相隔太遥远，	Alas! so long we've parted,
不我活兮！	我们不能重相聚。	Can I live broken-hearted?
于嗟洵兮，	可叹啊，如今离别太长久，	Alas! the oath we swore
不我信②兮！	我们不能守誓言。	Can be fulfilled no more.

凯 风   Our Mother*

凯风③自南，	和风吹来自南方，	From the south blows the breeze
吹彼棘心④。	吹在酸枣树苗上。	Amid the jujube trees.
棘心夭夭，	酸枣树苗还正小，	The trees grow on the soil;
母氏劬⑤劳。	母亲辛苦又勤劳。	We live on mother's toil.

凯风自南，	和风吹来自南方，	From the south blows the breeze
吹彼棘薪。	吹在酸枣枝条上。	On branches of the trees.
母氏圣善，	母亲明理又善良，	Our mother's good to sons;
我无令人⑥。	我们兄弟不像样。	We are not worthy ones.

| 爰有寒泉， | 寒泉清冷把暑消， | The fountain's water runs |
| 在浚之下。 | 源在浚城之下绕。 | To feed the stream and soil. |

---

① 成说：约定，成约。② 信：伸。③ 凯风：和风。④ 棘心：小酸枣树。⑤ 劬(qú)：辛勤。⑥ 令人：善人，好样的。

* Seven sons blamed themselves for the unhappiness of their mother in her state of widowhood.

有子七人，　儿子七个不算少，　Our mother's seven sons
母氏劳苦。　母亲依旧独勤劳。　Are fed by her hard toil.

睍睆①黄鸟，　美丽黄鸟，　　　The yellow birds can sing
载好其音。　婉转和鸣。　　　To comfort us with art.
有子七人，　空有七子，　　　We seven sons can't bring
莫慰母心。　不能安慰慈母心。　Comfort to mother's heart

雄　雉　　　　　　　　　My Man in Service*

雄雉②于飞，　雄雉展翅飞远方，　The male pheasant in flight
泄泄③其羽。　拍拍翅膀真舒畅。　Wings its way left and right.
我之怀矣，　想念无止境，　　　O dear one of my heart!
自诒④伊阻⑤！　独留空忧伤。　　　We are so far apart.

雄雉于飞，　雄雉展翅飞远方，　See the male pheasant fly;
下上其音。　上下翻飞自鸣唱。　Hear his song low and high.
展⑥矣君子，　诚实我君子，　　　My man is so sincere.
实劳我心！　牵挂心难放。　　　Can I not miss him so dear?

瞻彼日月，　眼看日月向人催，　Gazing at moon or sun,
悠悠我思！　忧愁思念更悠长。　I think of my dear one.
道之云远，　道路相隔太遥远，　The way's a thousand li.
曷云能来？　何时回到我身旁？　How can he come to me?

---

①睍睆(xiànhuǎn)：美丽，漂亮。②雉：野鸡。③泄泄(yìyì)：慢慢舒展。④诒(yí)：留。⑤阻：忧伤。⑥展：诚实。

* A wife deplored the absence of her husband in service and celebrated his virtue.

百尔①君子，	所谓君子都一样，	If he is really good,
不知德行。	没有道德与修养。	He will do what he should.
不忮②不求，	如若不妒且又不贪，	For nothing would he long.
何用不臧③？	走到哪里都顺畅。	Will he do anything wrong?

匏有苦叶　　　　　Waiting for Her Fiance*

匏④有苦叶，　　葫芦叶子味道苦，　　The gourd has leaves which fade;
济有深涉。　　　济水深处也能渡。　　The stream's too deep to wade.
深则厉⑤，　　　水深漫着衣裳行，　　If shallow leap
浅则揭⑥。　　　水浅提起衣裳过。　　And strip if deep!

有弥济盈，　　　茫茫白水济河满，　　See the stream's water rise;
有鷕⑦雉鸣。　　野鸡吆吆声不断。　　Hear female pheasant's cries.
济盈不濡轨，　　水满不过半轮高，　　The stream wets not the axle straight;
雉鸣求其牡。　　雌鸡把那雄鸡叫。　　The pheasant's calling for her mate.

雝雝⑧鸣雁，　　雁鸣声声真相和，　　Hear the song of wild geese;
旭日始旦。　　　初升太阳照济河。　　See the sun rise in glee.
士如归妻，　　　你若有心来娶我，　　Come before the streams freeze
迨冰未泮⑨。　　莫等封冰早过河。　　If you will marry me.

招招舟子，　　　船夫摇摇把船摆，　　I see the boatman row

---

① 百尔：众多。② 忮(zhì)：损人，害人。③ 臧(zāng)：顺利。④ 匏(páo)：葫芦。⑤ 厉：以衣涉水。⑥ 揭(qì)：提起衣裳渡水。⑦ 鷕(wěi)：野鸡的叫声。⑧ 雝雝(yōngyōng)：雁鸣声。⑨ 泮(pàn)：冰化成水。

* A maiden was waiting at the ferry for her fiance to come across the stream.

人涉卬①否。	别人过河我等待。	Across but I will wait;
人涉卬否，	别人过河我等待，	With others I won't go:
卬须我友。	等个人儿过河来。	I will wait for my mate.

谷　风　　　　　　　　　A Rejected Wife*

习习谷风②，	呼呼吹来山谷风，	Gently blows eastern breeze
以阴以雨。	又是阴天又是雨。	With rain 'neath cloudy skies.
黾③勉同心，	同心合意过日子，	Let's set our mind to please
不宜有怒。	不要对我发脾气。	And let no anger rise!
采葑采菲，	采了萝卜和蔓菁，	Who gathers plants to eat
无以下体？	为何根茎全抛弃。	Should keep the root in view.
德音莫违，	往日恩情休忘记，	Do not forget what's meet
及尔同死。	说好到死不分离。	And me who'd die with you!

行道迟迟，	踏上去路慢腾腾，	Slowly I go my way;
中心有违。	心里有恨难移步。	My heart feels sad and cold.
不远伊迩，	只是几步不算远，	You go as far to say
薄送我畿④。	只望送我到门坎。	Goodbye as the threshold.
谁谓荼苦，	谁说荼菜味道苦，	Is lettuce bitter? Nay,
其甘如荠。	它的味比荠菜甜。	To me it seems e'en sweet.
宴尔新昏，	你的新婚多快乐，	Feasting on wedding day,
如兄如弟。	好比亲兄和亲弟。	You two looks as brothers meet.

---

① 卬(áng)：我。② 谷风：从山谷吹来的风。③ 黾(mǐn)勉：辛勤功劳。④ 畿(jī)：门坎。

* This was the plaint of a wife rejected and supplanted by another whom she addressed in lines 5–6 of the 3rd stanza.

泾以渭浊，	泾水因为渭水浑，	The by-stream is not clear,
湜湜①其沚。	泾水停下也能清。	Still we can see its bed.
宴尔新昏，	你的新婚多快乐，	Feasting your new wife dear,
不我屑以。	不屑跟我再亲近。	You treat the old as dead.
毋逝我梁，	不要放开我鱼梁，	Do not approach my dam,
毋发我笱。	不要打开我鱼筐。	Nor move my net away!
我躬不阅，	自己尚且不能容，	Rejected as I am,
遑②恤③我后？	身后事儿何遑想？	What more have I to say?

就其深矣，	河水深了，	When the river was deep,
方④之舟之，	用船用筏来渡它。	I crossed by raft or boat;
就其浅矣，	河水浅了，	When 't was shallow, I'd keep
泳之游之。	浮着游着来渡它。	Myself aswim or afloat.
何有何亡，	往日家产有或无，	I would have spared no breath
黾勉求之。	尽心尽力去操持。	To get what we did need;
凡民⑤有丧，	左邻右舍有急难，	Wherever I saw death,
匍匐救之。	奔走扶助不拖延。	I would help with all speed.

不我能慉⑥，	不再爱我本不怨，	You loved me not as mate;
反以我为雠。	反而把我当仇人。	Instead you gave me hell.
既阻⑦我德⑧，	一片好心被你拒，	My virtue caused you hate
贾⑨用⑩不售⑪。	好似卖不出的货物。	As wares which did not sell.
昔育⑫恐育鞫⑬，	从前日子太潦倒，	In days of poverty

---

①湜湜(shíshí)：水清澈见底。②遑：哪有空闲。③恤：忧念。④方：用筏子渡河。⑤民：左邻右舍的人。⑥慉(xù)：爱。⑦阻：非难，拒绝。⑧德：德惠，情意。⑨贾(gǔ)：卖。⑩用：中用的货物。⑪不售：卖不出去。⑫育：生活。⑬鞫(jū)：贫困潦倒。

及尔颠覆。	相互扶持已度过。	Together we shared woe
既生既育，	现在生活更好转，	Now in prosperity
比予于毒。	却把我比大毒虫。	I seem your poison slow.

我有旨蓄，	我有干菜和腌菜，	I've vegetables dried
亦以御冬。	可以用来过冬天。	Against the winter cold.
宴尔新昏，	你们新婚很快乐，	Feast them with your new bride,
以我御穷。	用我来抵御困穷。	Not your former wife old.
有洸①有溃，	又是动粗又发怒，	You beat and scolded me
既诒我肄②。	全家数我最辛苦。	And gave me only pain.
不念昔者，	从前恩情你不念，	The past is gone, I see,
伊余来墍③！	我新来时亦爱浓。	And no love will remain.

式　微　　　　　　　　　　　　　　　Toilers*

式微④式微，	天色昏啊天将黑，	It's near dusk, lo!
胡不归？	为什么却不回？	Why not home go?
微⑤君之故，	不是因为君主的缘故，	It is for you
胡为乎中露？	为什么全身遭受露水？	We're wet with dew.

式微式微，	天色昏啊天将黑，	It's near dusk, lo!
胡不归？	为什么却不回？	Why not home go？

---

① 洸(guāng)，溃(kuì)：原指水激荡的样子，喻指人发怒动粗的样子。② 肄：辛苦的事情。③ 墍(xì)：爱。④ 微(式微的微)：通"昧"，此处指天色昏黄，夜幕将临。⑤ 微(微君之故)：非，不是。

* This was a plaint of toilers in the service of the marquis of Wei.

微君之躬，	不是因为君主的身体，	For you, O Sire,
胡为乎泥中？	为什么全身沾满着泥水。	We toil in mire.

旄 丘　　　　　　　　　Refugees*

旄丘①之葛兮，	葛藤长在山坡上，	The high mound's vines appear
何诞之节兮？	为何枝节那么长？	So long and wide.
叔兮伯兮，	叔叔啊伯伯啊，	O uncles dear,
何多日也？	为何好久不帮忙。	Why not come to our side?

何其处也？	在哪里安顿啊？	Why dwell you thereamong
必有与也。	一定有帮助的人。	For other friends you make?
何其久也？	为何等这么久啊？	Why stay so long?
必有以也。	一定有它的原因。	For who else' sake?

狐裘蒙戎。	身穿狐裘毛纷乱，	Furs in a mess appear;
匪车不东。	坐着车子不向东。	Eastward goes not your cart.
叔兮伯兮！	叔叔啊伯伯啊，	O uncles dear,
靡所与同。	我们感情不相通。	Don't you feel sad at heart?

琐兮尾②兮！	我们渺小又卑贱，	So poor and base appear
流离之子。	沦落流亡乞人怜。	We refugees.
叔兮伯兮！	叔叔啊伯伯啊，	O uncles dear,
褎③如充耳。	趾高气扬听不见。	Why don't you listen, please?

---

① 旄丘：前高后低的土山。② 尾：微。③ 褎(xiù)：微笑。

* It was said that this was a complaint of the refugees in the State of Wei.

简 兮　　　　　　　　　　A Dancer*

简①兮简兮，	威武啊,气昂昂啊,	With main and might
方将万舞②。	看那万舞要开场。	Dances the ace.
日之方中，	太阳正在头顶上,	Sun at its height,
在前上处。	瞧他正在前面站。	He holds his place.
硕人俣俣③,	高高个子好身材,	He dances long
公庭万舞。	公堂面前跳万舞。	With might and main.
有力如虎，	扮成力士力如虎,	Like tiger strong
执辔如组④。	拿着缰绳如丝带。	He holds the rein.
左手执龠⑤，	拿着管儿是左手,	A flute in his left hand,
右手秉翟⑥。	舞着雉羽是右手。	In his right a plume fine,
赫如渥⑦赭⑧，	脸儿红得像赭石,	Red-faced, he holds command,
公言锡爵。	大人赏赐一杯酒。	Given a cup of wine.
山有榛，	高高山上有榛栗,	Hazel above,
隰⑨有苓。	低田湿地长苦苓。	Sweet grass below.
云谁之思?	柔肠百结思念谁?	Who is not sick for love
西方美人。	来自西方的美人。	Of the dancing Beau?

---

① 简:形容威容的姿态。② 万舞:古时一种用于朝廷、宗庙、山川祭祀仪式上的舞蹈,由文舞与武舞宽合。③ 俣俣(yǔyǔ):大而美。④ 组:宽丝带。⑤ 龠(yuè):可以吹的一种乐器,似是排箫的前身。⑥ 翟(dí):野鸡尾。⑦ 渥(wò):厚重。⑧ 赭(zhě):赤褐色。⑨ 隰(xí):湿地。

* It was said that this was a censure against the State of Wei for not giving offices equal to their merit to its men of worth but employing them as dancers.

| 彼美人兮！ | 那个美人啊， | Who is not sick for love |
| 西方之人兮！ | 正是来自方啊！ | Of the Western Beau? |

泉　水　　　　　　　　　　　Fair Spring*

毖①彼泉水，	涓涓泉水流不息，	The bubbling water flows
亦流于淇。	最后流到淇水里。	From the spring to the stream.
有怀于卫，	想起卫国我故乡，	My heart to homeland goes;
靡日不思。	没有一天不惦记。	Day and night I seek to dream.
娈彼诸姬，	诸位姬姓好姐妹，	I'll ask my cousins dear
聊与之谋。	姑且和她共商议。	How I may start from here.

出宿于泲②，	出门住宿在泲滨，	I will lodge in one place,
饮饯于祢。	喝酒饯行在祢城。	Take my meal in another,
女子有行③，	姑娘出嫁到远方，	And try to find the trace
远父母兄弟。	离开兄弟和爹娘。	How I parted from mother.
问我诸姑，	临行问候众姑姑，	I'll ask about aunts dear
遂及伯姊。	还有大姐别忘记。	On my way far from here.

出宿于干，	出门住宿在干地，	I'll lodge in a third place
饮饯于言。	喝酒饯行在言城。	And dine in a fourth one.
载脂载舝④，	涂好轴油安好键，	I'll set my cab apace;
还车言迈。	转车回家走得快。	With axles greased 'twill run.

---

① 毖(bì)：水流的样子。② 泲(jǐ)：与后面的祢、干、言，都是卫国的地名。③ 行：出嫁。④ 舝(xiá)：车轴上的金属键。

* A daughter of the House of Wei, married in another State, expressed her longing to revisit Wei.

遄①臻②于卫，　　只想快快回卫国，　　I'll hasten to go home.
不瑕有害？　　　回去看看又何妨？　　Why should I not have come?

我思肥泉，　　　想到那肥泉，　　　　When I think of Fair Spring,
兹之永叹。　　　不免长声叹。　　　　How can I not heave sighs!
思须与漕，　　　想到须与漕，　　　　Thoughts of my homeland bring
我心悠悠。　　　心里长思念。　　　　Copious tears to my eyes.
驾言出游，　　　驾车外出游，　　　　I drive to find relief
以写我忧。　　　以此解我愁。　　　　And drown my homesick grief.

北　门　　　　　　　　　　　　　　A Petty Official*

出自北门　　　　走出北门来，　　　　Out of north gate
忧心殷殷③。　　　心里忧愁意深深。　　Sadly I go.
终窭④且贫，　　　一直鄙陋又贫困，　　I'm poor by fate.
莫知我艰。　　　无人知道我艰难。　　Who knows my woe?
已焉哉！　　　　算了吧，　　　　　　Let it be so!
天实为之，　　　老天这样的安排，　　Heaven wills this way.
谓之何哉！　　　又有什么好说的。　　What can I say?

王事适⑤我，　　　王事派给我，　　　　I am busy about
政事一埤⑥益我。　公事加给我。　　　　Affairs of royalty.
我入自外，　　　我从外面回家来，　　When I come from without,

---

① 遄(chuán)：快速地。② 臻(zhēn)：到。③ 殷殷：忧愁的样子。④ 窭(jù)：鄙陋不能备礼。⑤ 适：派给。⑥ 埤(bī)：使。

* An officer of Wei set forth his hard lot and his silence under it in submission to Heaven.

室人交遍讁①我。	家人全都责备我。	I'm blamed by family.
已焉哉!	算了吧,	So let it be!
天实为之,	老天这样的安排,	Heaven wills this way.
谓之何哉!	又有什么好说的。	What can I say?

王事敦②我,	王事逼迫我,	I am busier about
政事一埤遗我。	公事加给我。	Public affairs, but oh!
我入自外,	我从外面回家,	When I come from without,
室人交遍摧③我。	家人全都讽刺我。	I'm given blow on blow.
已焉哉!	算了吧,	Let it be so!
天实为之,	老天这样的安排,	Heaven wills this way.
谓之何哉!	又有什么好说的。	What can I say?

北 风　　　　　　　　The Hard Pressed*

北风其凉,	北风吹得冷,	The cold north wind does blow
雨雪其雱④。	大雪下得猛。	And thick does fall the snow.
惠而⑤好我,	我和我朋友,	To all my friends I say:
携手同行。	握手一起走。	"Hand in hand let us go!
其虚⑥其邪⑦?	还能再磨蹭吗?	There's no time for delay;
既⑧亟只且⑨!	情况很紧急啦!	We must hasten our way."

---

① 讁(zhé):责难,埋怨。② 敦(duī):逼迫。③ 摧:讽刺。④ 雱(pāng):下大雪的样子。⑤ 惠而:仁爱相从。⑥ 虚:舒。⑦ 邪:徐。⑧ 既:已经。⑨ 只且(jū):语气助词。

* The hard-pressed people left the State of Wei in consequence of the prevailing oppression and misery. The first two lines in all the stanzas are a metaphorical description of the miserable condition of the State. Foxes and crows were both creatures of evil omen.

北风其凉,	北风吹得响,	The sharp north wind does blow
雨雪其雱。	大雪白茫茫。	And heavy falls the snow.
惠而好我,	我和我朋友,	To all my friends I say
携手同归①。	握手一起走。	"Hand in hand let's all go!
其虚其邪?	还能再磨蹭吗?	There's no time for delay;
既亟只且!	情况很紧急啦!	We must hasten our way."
莫赤匪狐,	没有红的不是狐狸,	Red-handed foxes glow;
莫黑匪乌。	没有黑的不是乌鸦。	Their hearts are black as crow.
惠而好我,	我和我朋友,	To all my friends I say
携手同车。	握手同车走。	"In my cart let us go!
其虚其邪?	还能再磨蹭吗?	There's no time for delay;
既亟只且!	情况很紧急啦!	We must hasten our way."

静 女 A Shepherdess*

静②女其姝③,	娴静的姑娘惹人爱,	A maiden mute and tall
俟我于城隅。	约我城角楼上来。	Trysts me at corner wall.
爱④而不见,	暗地里藏着不见我,	I can find her nowhere;
搔首踟蹰⑤。	让我抓耳挠腮又徘徊。	Perplexed, I scratch my hair.
静女其娈⑥,	娴静的姑娘真美丽,	The maiden fair and mute

---

① 同归:一起到有德的地方去。② 静:娴静,端正庄重。③ 姝:美丽。④ 爱:故意隐藏起来。⑤ 踟蹰(chíchú):徘徊的样子。⑥ 娈(luán):漂亮,美好。

* This was the first in Chinese song which the poet showed his participation in the feeling of things.

贻我彤管。	送我彤管有用意。	Gives me a grass-made lute.
彤管有炜①，	彤管红红好光彩，	Playing a rosy air,
说怿②女美。	我是喜欢姑娘的美。	I'm happier than e'er.

自牧归荑，	送我白茅牧场采，	Coming back from the mead.
洵③美且异。	确实美丽不平凡，	She gives me a rare reed,
匪女之为美，	不是草儿太美丽，	Lovely not for it's rare:
美人之贻。	美人所赠心甜蜜。	It's given by the fair.

新　台　　　　　　　　　　The New Tower

新台有泚④，	新台照水倒影明，	How bright is the new tower
河水弥弥⑤。	河水涨得与岸平。	On brimming river deep!
燕婉⑥之求，	只说嫁个美少年，	Of youth she seeks the flower,
籧篨⑦不鲜。	嫁个蛤蟆不像人。	Not loathsome toad to keep.

新台有洒⑧，	新台近水建得高，	How high is the new tower
河水浼浼⑨。	河水涨满浪滔滔。	On tearful river deep!
燕婉之求，	只说嫁个美少年，	Of youth she seeks the flower,
籧篨不殄⑩。	嫁个蛤蟆不得了。	No stinking toad to keep.

---

① 炜(wěi)：红色鲜明有光泽。② 说怿(yuè yì)：喜爱。③ 洵(xún)：确实，真的。④ 泚(cǐ)：鲜明的样子。⑤ 弥弥：水盛大的样子。⑥ 燕婉：安详和顺。⑦ 籧篨(qúchú)：蟾蜍，癞蛤蟆。⑧ 洒(cuǐ)：高峻的样子。⑨ 浼浼(měiměi)：水涨平岸。⑩ 不殄(tiǎn)：没福相。

* This was a satire against Duke Xuan of Wei who took his eldest son's bride as his own and built a new tower by the Yellow River to welcome her in 699 B.C. Here the toad and the hunchback refer to the duke and the flower of youth to his eldest son.

鱼网之设，	架起渔网为打鱼，	A net for fish is set;
鸿①则离②之。	谁想打个癞蛤蟆。	A toad is caught instead.
燕婉之求，	只说嫁个美少年，	The flower of youth she'll get,
得此戚施③。	嫁个蛤蟆怎么办。	Not a hunchback to wed.

二子乘舟　　　　　　Two Sons in a Boat*

二子乘舟，	两位公子去坐船，	My two sons take a boat;
泛泛④其景。	飘飘荡荡去得远。	Downstream their shadows float.
愿言思子，	思念他们啊，	I miss them when they're out;
中心养养⑤。	心里忧愁不定当。	My heart is tossed about.

二子乘舟，	两位公子去坐船，	My two sons take a boat;
泛泛其逝。	飘飘荡荡去不还。	Far, far away they float.
愿言思子，	思念他们啊，	I think of them so long.
不瑕有害？	该不会遭逢祸殃？	Would no one do them wrong!

---

① 鸿:指蛤蟆。② 离:罹难,遭遇。③ 戚施(yī):癞蛤蟆。④ 泛泛:飘荡。⑤ 养养:忧愁的样子。

* Duke Xuan of Wei who had taken his eldest son's bride as his own plotted to get rid of this son by sinking his boat, but his younger brother, aware of this design, insisted on going in the same boat with him, and their mother, worried, wrote this song.

鄘风

Songs Collected in Yong, Modern Shandong

柏 舟

A Cypress Boat*

泛彼柏舟，	柏木船儿飘荡，
在彼中河。	在那河水中央。
髧①彼两髦②，	那人头发分两旁，
实维我仪③。	真是我的好对象。
之④死矢⑤靡它。	发誓到死无他心！
母也天只！	娘啊，天啊！
不谅人只！	我的心啊怎么就不体谅！

A cypress boat
Midstream afloat.
Two tufts of hair o'er his forehead,
He is my mate to whom I'll wed.
I swear I won't change my mind till I'm dead.
Heaven and mother,
Why don't you understand another?

泛彼柏舟，	柏木船儿飘荡，
在彼河侧。	在那河水边上。
髧彼两髦，	那人头发分两旁，
实维我特⑥。	和我天生是一双。

A cypress boat
By riverside afloat.
Two tufts of hair o'er his forehead,
He is my only mate to whom I'll wed.

---

① 髧(dàn)：头发下垂的样子。② 髦(máo)：把头发分成两股。③ 仪：配偶，对象。
④ 之：到。⑤ 矢：誓。⑥ 特：配偶。

* This song of a determined woman was mistaken for that of a chaste widow.

之死矢靡慝①。	发誓到死不变心！	I swear I won't change my mind though dead.
母也天只，	娘啊，天啊，	Heaven and mother,
不谅人只！	我的心啊怎么就不体谅！	Why don't you understand another?

墙有茨　　　　　　　　Scandals*

墙有茨②，	墙上蒺藜草，	The creepers on the wall
不可扫也。	不可把它扫。	Cannot be swept away.
中冓③之言，	宫廷悄悄话，	Stories of inner hall
不可道也。	不可向外道。	Should not be told by day.
所可道也？	如果向外道，	What would have to be told
言之丑也。	说了让人臊。	Is scandals manifold.
墙有茨，	墙上蒺藜草，	The creepers on the wall
不可襄④也。	不可尽除掉。	Cannot be rooted out.
中冓之言，	宫中悄悄话，	Scandals of inner hall
不可详⑤也。	不可仔细讲。	Should not be talked about.
所可详也？	如果仔细讲，	If they are talked of long,
言之长也。	要说话太长。	They'll be an endless song.

---

① 慝(tè)：改变。② 茨(cí)：蒺藜草。③ 中冓(gòu)：宫闱内室。④ 襄：除去。⑤ 详：细说。

* After the death of Duke Xuan of Wei, the beautiful duchess had illicit connections with his son and gave birth to three sons and two daughters, the youngest daughter being Baroness Mu of Xu who wrote the Poem "Patriotic Baroness Mu of Xu". These connections raised scandals in the inner hall of the ducal palace.

墙有茨，	墙上蒺藜草，	The creepers on the wall
不可束也。	不能都捆束。	Cannot be together bound.
中冓之言，	宫中悄悄话，	Scandals of inner hall
不可读也。	不可宣扬它。	Should not be spread around.
所可读也？	如果要宣扬，	If spread from place to place,
言之辱也。	说来是耻辱。	They are shame and disgrace.

君子偕老

Duchess Xuan Jiang of Wei*

君子偕老，	宣公和你同到老，	She'd live with her lord till old,
副①笄②六珈③。	首饰玉簪镶珠宝。	Adorned with gems and gold.
委委佗佗，	体态庄重又从容，	Stately and full of grace,
如山如河，	思如河深体如崇，	Stream-like, she went her pace.
象服④是宜。	身上华服很合适。	As a mountain she'd dwell;
子之不淑⑤，	你的德行不贤淑，	Her robe became her well.
云如之何！	还能让人如何讲。	Raped by the father of her lord,
		O how could she not have been bored!

玼⑥兮玼兮，	真鲜艳啊又绚丽，	She is so bright and fair
其之翟⑦也。	绣着雉纹的翟衣。	In pheasant-figured gown.
鬒⑧发如云，	黑发如云真正美，	Like cloud is her black hair,
不屑髢⑨也。	不必用那假发佩。	No false locks but her own.

---

① 副：古代女人的首饰。② 笄(jī)：簪子。③ 珈：首饰名，又称步摇。④ 象服：画袍，是王后之服。⑤ 不淑：不幸。⑥ 玼(cǐ)：玉色鲜明。⑦ 翟(dí)：翟衣，祭服，绣绘有翟雉之形。⑧ 鬒(zhěn)：黑发。⑨ 髢(dí)：假发。

* This was a portrait of the beautiful Duchess Xuan of Wei. The first stanza described her arrival at the new tower (See Poem "The New Tower").

玉之瑱①也，	美玉耳环垂两边，	Her earrings are of jade,
象之揥②也。	象牙簪子插发间，	Her pin ivory-made.
扬③且之皙也。	额头宽广又白皙。	Her forehead's white and high,
胡然而天也，	莫非尘世有天仙，	Like goddess from the sky.
胡然而帝也。	莫非帝子降人间。	

瑳④兮瑳兮，	真美丽啊真明艳，	She is so fair and bright
其之展也⑤，	轻薄细纱做礼服。	In rich attire snow-white.
蒙彼绉絺⑥。	罩上蝉翼般纹衣，	O'er her fine undershirt
是绁袢⑦也；	夏天穿着白内衣。	She wears close-fitting skirt.
子之清扬，	你的眉目清且秀，	Her eyes are bright and clear;
扬且之颜也。	额头丰满又白净。	Her face will facinate.
展⑧如之人兮，	的的确确这个人，	Alas! fair as she might appear,
邦之媛也。	倾城倾国的美女啊。	She's a raped beauty of the State.

桑　中　　　　　　　　　　Trysts*

爰采唐⑨矣？	什么地方把那兔丝子采，	"Where gather golden thread?"
沫之乡矣。	在那沫邑的郊外。	"In the fields over there."
云谁之思？	想念的那人儿是谁？	"Of whom do you think ahead?"
美孟⑩姜矣。	美丽的姜家大姑娘。	"Jiang's eldest daughter fair.

---

① 瑱(tiàn)：垂在两耳旁的玉。② 揥(tì)：发插类的首饰。③ 扬：眉宇间开阔方正。
④ 瑳(cuō)：玉色洁白鲜明。⑤ 展也：夏天的礼服。⑥ 绉絺(chī)：细葛布。⑦ 绁袢(xièbàn)：夏天穿的白色内衣。⑧ 展：诚然，的确。⑨ 唐：兔丝子草。⑩ 孟：兄弟姐妹中排行最长的人。

* It was possible that this song was constructed to deride the licentiousness that prevailed in the State of Wei.

期我乎桑中，	约我等待在桑田，	She did wait for me 'neath mulberry,
要我乎上宫，	邀我相会在上宫，	In upper bower tryst with me
送我乎淇之上矣。	淇水边上长相送。	And see me off on River Qi."

爰采麦矣？	什么地方把那麦穗采？	"Where gather golden wheat?"
沬之北矣。	在那沬邑的北边。	"In northern fields o'er there."
云谁之思？	想念的那人儿是谁？	"Whom do you long to meet?"
美孟弋矣。	美丽的弋家大姑娘。	"Yi's eldest daughter fair.
期我乎桑中，	约我等待在桑田，	She did wait for me 'neath mulberry,
要我乎上宫，	邀我相会在上宫，	In upper bower tryst with me
送我乎淇之上矣。	淇水边上长相送。	And see me off on River Qi."

爰采葑矣？	什么地方把那芜菁采？	"Where gather mustard plant?"
沬之东矣。	在那沬邑的东边。	"In eastern fields o'er there."
云谁之思？	想念的那人儿是谁？	"Who does your heart enchant?"
美孟庸矣。	美丽的庸家大姑娘。	"Yong's eldest daughter fair.
期我乎桑中，	约我等待在桑田，	She did wait for me 'neath mulberry,
要我乎上宫，	邀我相会在上宫，	In upper bower tryst with me
送我乎淇之上矣。	淇水边上长相送。	And see me off on River Qi."

鹑之奔奔　　　　　　　　　　Misfortune*

| 鹑①之奔奔②， | 雌鹑跟着雄鹑飞， | The quails together fly; |

---

① 鹑(chún)：鹌鹑。② 奔奔：雌雄同处同飞。

* The beautiful Duchess Xuan Jiang of Wei (See Poems "The New Tower", "Two Sons in a Boat", "Scandals", "Duchess Xuan Jiang of Wei") was first raped by Duke Xuan of Wei (master) and then by his son (brother). She was not so fortunate as quails and magpies which have a faithful mate.

鹊之彊彊①。	雌鹊跟着雄鹊飞。	The magpies sort in pairs.
人之无良，	这个男人不善良，	She takes an unkind guy
我以为兄。	为啥当他是兄长。	For brother unawares.

鹊之彊彊，	雌鹊跟着雄鹊飞；	The magpies sort in pairs;
鹑之奔奔，	雌鹑跟着雄鹑飞。	The quails together fly.
人之无良，	这个男人不善良，	For master unawares
我以为君。	为啥当他是君王。	She takes an unkind guy.

定之方中　　　　　　　　Duke Wen of Wei*

定②之方中③，	营室星儿正当中，	At dusk the four stars form a square;
作于楚宫。	十月修建楚邱宫。	It's time to build a palace new.
揆④之以日，	确定方向察日影，	The sun and shade determine where
作于楚室。	建筑房屋兴工程。	To build the Palace at Chu,
树之榛栗，	种上榛树还有栗，	To plant hazel and chestnut trees,
椅桐梓漆，	更有椅桐和梓漆，	Fir, yew, plane, cypress. When cut down,
爰伐琴瑟。	长成砍伐作琴瑟。	They may be used to make lutes to please
		The ducal crown.

升彼虚矣，	登上那个旧城址，	The duke ascends the ruined wall
以望楚矣。	远眺楚邱的位置。	To view the site of capital
望楚与堂，	望见楚邱与堂邑，	And where to build his palace hall.

---

① 彊彊(jiàngjiàng)：同"奔奔"。② 定：星名，又名营室。③ 方中：正当中的位置。
④ 揆(kuí)：测量。

* After the defeat and death of Duke Yi of Wei in 659 B. C., Duke Wen succeeded him, moved the capital to Cao and built a new palace in Chu. As he was diligent and sympathetic with the people, the State of Wei became prosperous under his reign.

景山①与京②。	大山高岗全相集。	He then surveys the mountain's height
降观于桑，	下来观察种桑地，	And comes down to see mulberries.
卜云其吉，	占卜都说大吉祥，	The fortune-teller says it's right
终塞渊焉允③臧。	于是选中这福地。	And the duke is pleased with all these.

灵雨既零，	好雨知时水如泉，	After the fall of vernal rain
命彼倌④人。	命令那个驾车员，	The duke orders his groom to drive
星言夙驾，	从早到晚把车赶，	His horse and cab with might and main.
说⑤于桑田。	把车停歇在桑田。	At mulberry fields they arrive;
匪直⑥也人，	不只关心把农劝，	To farmers he is good indeed
秉心塞渊⑦，	诚心为国谋深远，	He wishes husbandry to thrive
骍⑧牝⑨三千。	骏马繁殖到三千。	And three thousand horses to breed.

蝃蝀　　　　　　　　　　Elopement*

蝃蝀⑩在东，	东方出彩虹，	A rainbow rose high in the east;
莫之敢指。	没人敢指点它。	None dared to point to it at least.
女子有行⑪，	姑娘要出嫁，	I went to wed like others
远父母兄弟。	远远离开父母兄弟家。	And left my parents and my brothers.

---

① 景山：大山。② 京：高冈。③ 允：真正。④ 倌(guān)人：管理车马的小臣。⑤ 说(shuì)：通税，休息，停止。⑥ 匪直：不但。⑦ 塞渊：笃实深远。⑧ 骍(lái)：高大的马。⑨ 牝(pìn)：母马。⑩ 蝃蝀(dìdōng)：彩虹。⑪ 行：出嫁。

* This was said to be a protest of Duchess Xuan Jiang against Duke Xuan of Wei who raped her (See Poem "The New Tower"). A rainbow was regarded by ancient people as an emblem of improper connections between man and woman, and it was held unlucky to point to a rainbow in the east. The clouds bringing fresh showers to thirsting flowers were compared to love-making.

朝隮①于西，	早上虹云在西边，	The morning clouds rose in the west;
崇朝②其雨。	整个早上在下雨。	The day with rain would then be blest.
女子有行，	姑娘要出嫁，	I went to wed another
远兄弟父母。	远远离开父母兄弟家。	When I left my father and mother.
乃如之人也，	她是这样的人儿啊！	Did I know I'd be raped by such a man
怀昏姻也，	一心想着要出嫁。	Who would do whatever he can!
大无信也，	不听媒妁之美言，	He is a faithless mate.
不知命也。	父母之命也不依。	Is it my fault or fate?

相 鼠　　　　　　　　　　The Rat*

相鼠有皮，	看看老鼠还有皮，	The rat has skin, you see?
人而无仪③。	这个人却没威仪。	Man must have decency.
人而无仪，	人要如果没威仪，	If he lacks decency,
不死何为？	不死还能干什么？	Worse than death it would be.
相鼠有齿，	看看老鼠还有齿，	The rat has teeth, you see?
人而无止④。	这个人却没节制。	Man must have dignity.
人而无止，	人要如果没节制，	If he lacks dignity,
不死何俟？	不死还在等什么？	For what but death waits he?
相鼠有体，	看看老鼠还有体，	The rat has limbs, you see?

---

①隮(jī)：彩云。②崇朝：整个早晨。③仪：威仪，使人尊敬的仪表。④止：言行适当，有所节制。

* This was a satire against the ruling class of the State of Wei who, without propriety, was not equal to a rat.

人而无礼。	这个人却不守礼。	Man must have propriety.
人而无礼。	人要如果不守礼法，	Without propriety,
胡不遄①死？	还不如快些就去死。	It's better dead to be.

干旄

Betrothal Gifts*

孑孑②干③旄，	旗杆上牛尾饰的旗，	The flags with ox-tail tied
在浚之郊。	树立在浚邑的郊区。	Flutter in countryside.
素丝纰④之，	白丝线把旗边缝，	Adorned with silk bands white,
良马四之。	四匹良马做前驱。	Four steeds trot left and right.
彼姝者子，	那位贤德的才俊。	What won't I give and share
何以畀⑤之？	拿什么送给他啊？	With such a maiden faire?

孑孑干旟，	旗杆上隼鸟纹饰的旗帜，	The falcon-banners fly
在浚之都。	树立在浚邑的都市。	In the outskirts nearby.
素丝组之，	白丝线把旗边缝，	Adorned with ribbons white,
良马五之。	五匹良马做前驱。	Five steeds trot left and right.
彼姝者子，	那位贤德的才俊，	What won't I give and send
何以予之？	拿什么赠与他啊。	To such a good fair friend?

孑孑干旌，	旗杆上五色鸟羽饰的旗帜，	The feathered streamers go down
在浚之城。	树立在浚邑的城区。	All the way to the town.

---

① 遄(chuán)：快速地。② 孑孑(jiéjié)：特出的。③ 干：旗杆。④ 纰(pí)：把旗的边上用线缝好。⑤ 畀(bì)：给予。

* This song described how a young lord sent betrothal gifts to his fiancee.

素丝祝①之，	白丝线把旗边缝，	Bearing rolls of silk white,
良马六之。	六匹良马做前驱。	Six steeds trot left and right.
彼姝者子，	那位贤德的才俊，	What and how should I say
何以告之？	拿什么忠言以相告啊？	To her as fair as May?

载 驰

Patriotic Baroness Mu of Xu*

载驰载驱，	赶着马儿快些走，	I gallop while I go
归唁②卫侯。	回来吊问我卫侯。	To share my brother's woe.
驱马悠悠③，	赶着马儿路悠悠，	I ride down a long road
言至于漕。	走到漕邑城门楼。	To my brother's abode.
大夫跋涉，	许国大夫匆忙来，	The deputies will thwart
我心则忧。	让我心里添忧愁。	My plan and fret my heart.

既不我嘉④，	对我做法都摇头，	"Although you say me nay,
不能旋反。	可我不能往回走。	I won't go back the other way.
视尔不臧⑤，	你的想法不算好，	Conservative are you
我思不远。	我的做法近可求。	While farsight'd is my view?

既不我嘉，	对我做法都反对，	"Although you say me nay,
不能旋济。	决不渡河再回头。	I won't stop on my way.

① 祝：连结。② 唁(yàn)：吊问失国。③ 悠悠：路途遥远。④ 嘉：好，赞同。⑤ 臧：好。

* Baroness Mu of Xu, daughter of Duchess Xuan Jiang (See Poem "Scandals") of Wei, complained that the deputies of Xu did not allow her to go back to Wei to condole with her brother Duke Wen on the desolation of his State after the death of Duke Dai in 659 B.C., and to appeal to a mighty State on its behalf. It was contrary, however, to the rules of propriety for a lady in her position to return to her native State, so she picked toad lilies which might, it was said, assuage her sorrow.

视尔不臧，	你的想法不算好，	Conservative are you,
我思不闷①。	我的计划有理由。	I can't accept your view."

陟彼阿丘，	登上那个高山岗，	I climb the sloping mound
言采其蝱，	采些贝母慰忧伤。	To pick toad-lilies round.
女子善怀，	女人虽然多想法，	Of woman don't make light!
亦各有行。	各有理由和主张。	My heart knows what is right.
许人尤之，	许国大夫反对我，	My countrymen put blame
众稚且狂。	真是幼稚又愚妄。	On me and feel no shame.

我行其野，	我正行走原野上，	I go across the plains;
芃芃②其麦。	麦苗油油长得旺。	Thick and green grow the grains.
控③于大邦，	奔告大国来帮忙，	I'll plead to mighty land,
谁因谁极！	靠着谁来救危亡。	Who'd hold out helping hand.
大夫君子，	大夫君子众人们，	"Deputies, don't you see
无我有尤。	不要再把我阻挡。	The fault lies not with me?
百尔所思，	你们纵有好计策，	Whatever may think you,
不如我所之！	不如我去走一趟。	It's not so good as my view."

---

①闷(bì)：闭塞，止息。② 芃芃(péngpéng)：草木茂盛的样子。③ 控：求告。

诗经 Book of Poetry

卫 风

Songs Collected in Wei, Modern Henan

淇 奥

Duke Wu of Wei*

瞻彼淇奥①，	看那淇水转弯处，	Behold by riverside
绿竹猗猗②。	绿竹婀娜真茂密。	Green bamboos in high glee.
有匪君子，	文雅风流美君子，	Our duke is dignified
如切③如磋④，	如经切磋玉骨器，	Like polished ivory
如琢⑤如磨⑥。	雕琢玉石美如许。	And stone or jade refined.
瑟兮僩⑦兮，	庄严啊威武，	With solemn gravity
赫兮咺⑧兮。	威仪啊磊落。	And elevated mind,
有匪君子，	这个文雅的君子，	The duke we love a lot
终不可谖⑨兮！	教人记住不能忘。	Should never be forgot.

瞻彼淇奥，	看那淇水转弯处，	Behold by riverside
绿竹青青，	绿竹青青真茂密。	Bamboos with soft green shade.
有匪君子，	文雅风流美君子，	Our duke is dignified
充耳琇莹，	耳充宝石真晶莹，	When crowned with strings of jade

①奥:弯曲处。②猗猗:长而美。③切:治骨曰切。④磋:治象牙曰磋。⑤琢:治玉曰琢。⑥磨:治石曰磨。⑦僩(xiàn):宽大、威武。⑧咺(xuān):威仪。⑨谖(xuān):忘记。

* This song was written in praise of Duke Wu who ruled the State of Wei in 811–751 B. C. The duke cultivated the principles of government. The people increased in number, and others flocked to the State. In 770 B. C. when King You of Zhou was killed by a barbarian tribe, the duke led his army to the rescue of Zhou and rendered such great service against the enemy that King Ping appointed him a minister of the royal court.

会弁如星。	帽缝美玉如明星。	As bright as stars we find.
瑟兮侗兮，	庄严啊威武，	With solemn gravity
赫兮咺兮。	威仪啊磊落。	And elevated mind,
有匪君子，	这个文雅的君子，	The duke we love a lot
终不可谖兮！	教人记住不能忘。	Should never be forgot.

瞻彼淇奥，	看那淇水转弯处，	Behold by riverside
绿竹如箦①。	绿竹郁郁真茂密。	Bamboos so lush and green.
有匪君子，	文雅风流美君子，	Our duke is dignified
如金如锡，	才学精深如金锡，	With gold-or tin-like sheen.
如圭如璧。	品行洁美如圭璧。	With his sceptre in hand,
宽兮绰兮，	宽厚啊温文啊，	He is in gentle mood;
猗重较②兮。	靠倚在车旁。	By his chariot he'd stand;
善戏谑兮，	谈笑风趣易接近，	At jesting he is good,
不为虐兮。	不骄不躁不刻薄。	But he is never rude.

考 槃　　　　　　　　　　　A Happy Hermit*

考③槃④在涧，	快乐啊溪水旁，	By riverside unknown
硕人之宽⑤。	贤人心舒畅。	A hermit builds his cot.
独寐寤言，	独睡独醒独自说，	He sleeps, wakes, speaks alone;
永矢弗谖。	这样的乐趣永不忘。	Such joy won't be forgot.

---

① 箦(zé)：密密层层的样子。② 重较：古时车厢横木两端伸出的弯木。③ 考：成就。
④ 槃(pán)：快乐。⑤ 宽：放松。

* It was said that this song was directed against Duke Zhuang of Wei, who did not walk in the footsteps of his father Duke Wu, and by his neglect of his duties led men of worth to withdraw from public lire into retirement.

考槃在阿，	快乐啊山坡上，	By mountainside unknown
硕人之薖①。	贤人多惬意。	A hermit will not fret.
独寐②寤③歌，	独睡独醒独歌唱，	He sleeps, wakes, sings alone:
永矢弗过。	这样的乐趣永难忘。	A joy never to forget.

考槃在陆，	快乐啊平地上，	On wooded land unknown
硕人之轴④。	贤人在徜徉。	A hermit lives, behold!
独寐寤宿，	独睡独醒独自卧，	He sleeps, wakes, dwells alone
永矢弗告。	这样的快乐不张扬。	A joy ne'er to be told.

硕 人　　　　The Duke's Bride

硕人其颀⑤，	有个美人身颀秀，	The buxom lady's big and tall,
衣锦褧⑥衣。	锦衣外面布衣罩。	A cape o'er her robe of brocade.
齐侯之子，	她是齐侯的女儿，	Her father, brothers, husband all
卫侯之妻，	卫侯的妻子，	Are dukes or marquis of high grade.
东宫之妹，	太子的妹妹，	
邢侯之姨，	邢侯的小姨子，	
谭公维私⑦。	谭公是她的妹夫。	

| 手如柔荑， | 手指像茅草的嫩芽， | Like lard congealed her skin is tender, |
| 肤如凝脂， | 皮肤像凝冻的白脂， | Her fingers like soft blades of reed; |

---

①薖(guō)：快乐。②寐：睡觉。③寤：醒来。④轴：放心，舒畅。⑤颀(qí)：身段修长而健美。⑥褧(jiǒng)：罩袍，披风。⑦私：古代女子称姊姐的丈夫曰私。

* This was the first description of a beautiful lady in Chinese poetry. The beautiful lady was married to Duke Zhuang of Wei who reigned in 757–735 B. C. but she bore no children and brought up Duke Huan who was murdered by his half-brother in 718 B. C. (See Poem "A Farewell Song")

领如蝤蛴①，	脖颈像白而长的蝤蛴，	Like larva white her neck is slender,
齿如瓠犀②，	牙齿像整齐的瓠瓜子，	Her teeth like rows of melon-seed,
螓③首蛾眉，	前额方正眉细弯。	Her forehead like a dragonfly's,
巧笑倩兮，	轻巧笑时酒窝显，	Her arched brows curved like a bow.
美目盼兮。	四顾望时眼波转。	Ah! dark on white her speaking eyes,
		Her cheeks with smiles and dimples glow,

硕人敖敖，	有个美人身颀秀，	The buxom lady goes along;
说④于农郊。	车子停歇在近郊。	She passes outskirts to be wed.
四牡有骄，	四匹雄马气势骄，	Four steeds run vigorous and strong,
朱帻⑤镳镳，	马勒绸带红绸飘，	Their bits adorned with trappings red.
翟茀⑥以朝。	雉羽蔽车来上朝。	Her cab with pheasant-feathered screen
大夫夙退，	大夫可以早退朝，	Proceeds to the court in array.
无使君劳。	不教君主多辛劳。	Retire, officials, from the scene!
		Leave duke and her without delay!

河水洋洋，	黄河流水浩洋洋，	
北流活活，	向北流去哗哗响，	The Yellow River wide and deep
施罛⑦濊濊，	渔网撒向水中央，	Rolls northward its jubilant way.
鳣鲔发发，	鳣鱼鲔鱼全入网，	When nets are played out, fishes leap
葭菼⑧揭揭⑨。	芦苇荻梗长正旺。	And splash and throw on reeds much spray.

---

① 蝤蛴(qiúqí)：天牛的幼虫，身体长而白。② 瓠犀(hùxī)：葫芦籽，洁白而整齐。③ 螓(qín)：像蝉而比蝉小的一种虫，额头方正。④ 说(shuì)：停止。⑤ 朱帻(fén)：系在马衔两边用来装饰的红绸。⑥ 翟茀(dífú)：用山鸡毛装饰的车子。⑦ 罛(gū)：渔网。⑧ 葭菼(jiātǎn)：荻苇。⑨ 揭揭(jiējiē)：高高上扬的样子。

庶姜孽孽①，	从嫁的姜女盛妆忙，	Richly-dressed maids and warriors keep
庶士有朅②。	护送的武士气宇轩昂。	Attendance on her bridal day.

氓　　　　　A Faithless Man*

氓③之蚩蚩④，	那人满脸笑嘻嘻，	A man seemed free from guile;
抱布贸丝，	抱着布匹来换丝。	In trade he wore a smile.
匪来贸丝，	不是真的来换丝，	He'd barter cloth for thread;
来即我谋。	前来找我谈婚事。	No, to me he'd be wed.
送子涉淇，	送你渡过淇水去，	I saw him cross the ford,
至于顿丘。	直到顿丘才分手。	But gave him not my word.
匪我愆⑤期，	不是我要误婚期，	I said by hillside green:
子无良媒。	是你没有请良媒。	"You have no go-between.
将⑥子无怒，	求你不要生我气，	Try to find one, I pray.
秋以为期。	清秋时节是佳期。	In autumn be the day."
乘彼垝⑦垣，	登上坍坏残城墙，	I climbed the wall to wait
以望复关。	眺望你在的复关。	To see him pass the gate.
不见复关，	没有看见那复关，	I did not see him pass;
泣涕涟涟。	伤心落泪涕涟涟。	My tears streamed down, alas!
既见复关，	已经看到那复关，	When I saw him pass by,
载笑载言。	转眼就是笑开颜。	I'd laugh with joy and cry.

---

① 孽孽(nièniè)：盛妆的样子。② 朅(qiè)：英武敏健的样子。③ 氓(méng)：野民，村民。④ 蚩蚩(chīchī)：憨厚嘻嘻的样子。⑤ 愆(qiān)：错过，失约。⑥ 将(qiāng)：请。⑦ 垝(guǐ)：毁坏。

* A wonan who had been seduced into an improper connection, now cast off, related and bemoaned her sad case.

尔卜尔筮， 你已卜卦又请筮， Both reed and tortoise shell
体无咎言①。 还好没有不吉话。 Foretold all would be well.
以尔车来， 打发你车来一趟， "Come with your cart," I said,
以我贿②迁。 把我嫁妆一齐装。 "To you I will be wed."

桑之未落， 桑树叶儿还未落， How fresh were mulberries
其叶沃若。 润泽繁盛又新鲜。 With their fruit on the trees!
于嗟鸠兮， 小小斑鸠鸟儿啊， Beware, O turtledove,
无食桑葚！ 不要去吃那桑葚儿。 Eat not the fruit of love!
于嗟女兮， 年纪青青姑娘啊， It will intoxicate.
无与士耽③！ 不要太爱男人啊。 Do not repent too late!
士之耽兮， 男人若是爱恋深， Man may do what he will;
犹可说④也； 可以停止以脱身。 He can atone it still.
女之耽兮， 姑娘若是恋爱深， No one will e'er condone
不可说也。 永无休止难脱身。 The wrong a woman's done.

桑之落矣， 桑树叶儿落下来， The mulberries appear
其黄而陨。 干黄憔悴顿飘零。 With yellow leaves and sear.
自我徂尔， 自从来到你们家， E'er since he married me,
三岁食贫。 三年贫困度苦寒。 I've shared his poverty.
淇水汤汤， 淇水浩浩又荡荡， Deserted, from him I part;
渐车帷裳。 湿了一半车帷帐。 The flood has wet my cart.
女也不爽⑤， 我的感情没变样， I have done nothing wrong;
士贰⑥其行。 你的行为不一样。 He changes all along.
士也罔极⑦， 男人心思不可猜， He's fickle to excess,

---

① 咎言：不吉利的言辞。② 贿(huì)：财物，嫁妆。③ 耽(dān)：沉湎。④ 说：脱，解脱。
⑤ 爽：差错，过失。⑥ 贰：前后言行不一。⑦ 极：准则。

二三其德。	三心二意无德行。	Capricious, pitiless.

三岁为妇,	三年媳妇不算短,	Three years I was his wife
靡室劳矣,	全家活儿一人担。	And led a toilsome life.
夙兴夜寐,	早起晚睡已习惯,	Each day I early rose
靡有朝矣。	日日夜夜忙不完。	And late I sought repose.
言既遂①矣,	生活渐渐顺了心,	But he founld fault with me
至于暴矣。	脾气慢慢成暴残。	And treated me cruelly.
兄弟不知,	兄弟不知这些事,	My brothers who didn't know
咥②其笑矣。	看见我时展笑颜。	Let their jeers at me go.
静言思之,	细细想想这些事,	Mutely I ruminate
躬自悼矣。	只能一人独伤怨。	And I deplore my fate.

及尔偕老,	原想和你同到老,	I'd live with him till old;
老使我怨。	现实让我心满怨。	My grief was not foretold.
淇则有岸,	淇水宽宽也有岸,	The endless stream has shores;
隰③则有泮④。	漯河阔阔也有边。	My endless grief e'er pours.
总角⑤之宴,	记得童年多欢乐,	When we were girl and boy,
言笑晏晏⑥。	说说笑笑无愁烦。	We'd talk and laugh with joy.
信誓旦旦,	山盟海誓两相愿,	He pledged to me his troth.
不思其反⑦。	回忆这些是枉然。	Could he forget his oath?
反是不思,	别想从前多喜欢,	He's forgot what he swore.
亦已焉哉!	一切不再是从前。	Should I say any more?

---

① 遂:安定,顺心。② 咥(xì):带有讥讽的笑。③ 隰(xí):水名,又称漯河。④ 泮(pàn):岸。⑤ 总角:小孩子的发型。指童年。⑥ 晏晏:融洽,快乐。⑦ 反(不思其反的反):反复,变心。

竹　竿

		A Lovesick Fisherman
籊籊[①]竹竿，	钓鱼竹竿细又长，	With long rod of bamboo
以钓于淇。	当年垂钓淇水上。	I fish in River Qi.
岂不尔思？	难道旧游不曾想？	Home, how I long for you,
远莫致之。	道路遥遥难回乡。	Far-off a thousand li!
泉源在左，	泉水源头在左边，	At left the Spring flows on;
淇水在右。	淇河流水向右边。	At right the River clear.
女子有行，	姑娘自从出嫁后，	To wed they saw me gone,
远兄弟父母。	远离父母兄弟前。	Leaving my parents dear.
淇水在右。	淇河流水向右边，	The River clear at right,
泉源在左。	泉水源头在左边。	At left the Spring flows on.
巧笑之瑳[②]，	巧妙笑时齿鲜白，	O my smiles beaming bright
佩玉之傩[③]。	佩玉摇动声连连。	And ringing gems are gone!
淇水滺滺，	淇水流长悠悠流，	The long, long River flows
桧楫松舟。	桧树做楫松做舟。	With boats of pine home-bound.
驾言出游，	只好驾车来出游，	My boat along it goes.
以写我忧。	聊以解除我心忧。	O let my grief be drowned!

---

① 籊籊(tì tì)：长而细的样子。② 瑳(cuō)：玉色鲜白。③ 傩(nuó)：有节奏。

* A daughter of the House of Wei, married in another state, expressed her longing to revisit the scenes of her youth, where she had rambled in elegant dress between River Qi and the Spring. It was said that the daughter was Baroness Mu of Xu （See Poem "Patriotic Baroness Mu of Xu"）.

芄 兰　　　　　　　　A Widow in Love*

芄兰之友，	芄兰的枝，	The creeper's pods hang like
童子佩觿①，	童子佩带象牙锥。	The young man's girdle spike.
虽则佩觿，	虽然佩戴象牙锥，	An adult's spike he wears;
能不我知。	才能低下我知道。	For us he no longer cares.
容②兮遂兮！	摇摇摆摆装得像，	He puts on airs and swings
垂带悸③兮！	带子似的下垂样。	To and fro tassel-strings.

芄兰之叶，	芄兰的叶，	The creeper's leaves also swing;
童子佩韘④。	童子佩带象牙玦。	The youth wears archer's ring.
虽则佩韘，	虽然佩戴象牙玦，	An archer's ring he wears;
能不我甲。	才能不把我超越。	For us he no longer cares.
容兮遂兮，	摇摇摆摆装得像，	He puts on airs and swings
垂带悸兮！	带子似的下垂样。	To and fro tassel-strings.

河　广　　　　　　　　The River Wide*

| 谁谓河广？ | 谁说黄河太宽广？ | Who says the River's wide? |

---

① 觿(xī)：用象骨制作,形状如锥的解结用具。② 容：形状像。③ 悸：带子下垂的样子。④ 韘(shè)：用象骨制作的射箭用具,戴于右手拇指上,俗称扳指。

* It was said that the conceited youth alluded to Duke Hui of Wei who murdered his elder brother and succeeded to the State in 718 B. C. (See Poem "A Farewell Song")

* This song was said to be written by a daughter of Xuan Jiang who longed to see her son, Duke Xiang of Song.

一苇杭之。	一束芦苇可以航。	A reed could reach the other side.
谁谓宋远？	谁说宋国太遥远？	Who says Song's far-off? Lo!
跂①予望之。	踮起脚来可以望。	I could see it on tiptoe.

谁谓河广？	谁说黄河太宽广？	Who says the River's wide?
曾不容刀。	难容一只小船荡。	A boat could reach the other side.
谁谓宋远？	谁说宋国太遥远？	Who says Song's far away?
曾不崇朝②。	走到宋国一早上。	I could reach it within a day.

伯 兮　　　　　　　　　　My Lord*

伯③兮朅④兮，	夫君啊，多英武，	My lord is brave and bright,
邦之桀兮。	是国家的英雄。	A hero in our land,
伯也执殳⑤，	夫君拿着殳杖，	A vanguard in King's fight,
为王前驱。	为君王当先锋。	With a lance in his hand.

自伯之东，	自从夫君走向东，	Since my lord eastward went,
首如飞蓬。	我的头发乱蓬蓬。	Like thistle looks my hair.
岂无膏沐⑥，	难道没有脂和油，	Have I no anointment?
谁适为容！	为谁打扮为谁容？	For whom should I look fair?

其雨其雨，	总是觉得该下雨，	Let it rain, let it rain!
杲杲⑦出日。	一轮太阳高高挂。	The sun shines bright instead.

---

① 跂(qǐ)：踮起脚尖。② 崇朝：整个早上。③ 伯：周代妇女称丈夫为伯。④ 朅(qiè)：威武健壮。⑤ 殳(shū)：古代的一种兵器。⑥ 膏沐：化妆用的油脂。⑦ 杲杲(gǎogǎo)：太阳出来火红光亮的样子。

* A wife mourned over the protracted absence of her lord on the King's service around 706 B. C. This was considered as the earliest song of a wife longing for her husband in service.

| 愿言思伯， | 一心只把夫君想， | I miss my lord in vain, |
| 甘心首疾。 | 想得心疼头也痛。 | Heedless of aching head. |

焉得谖①草？	哪儿去找忘忧草，	Where's the Herb to Forget?
言树②之背③。	把它栽到北堂好。	To plant it north I'd start.
愿言思伯，	一心只把夫君想，	Missing my lord, I fret:
使我心痗④。	病驻心头忘不了。	It makes me sick at heart.

有　狐　　　　　　　A Lonely Husband*

有狐绥绥⑤，	有只狐狸独自走，	Like lonely fox he goes
在彼淇梁。	在那淇水桥头上。	On the bridge over there.
心之忧矣，	我的心里直发愁，	My heart sad and drear grows:
之子无裳。	这人裙裳也没有。	He has no underwear.

有狐绥绥，	有只狐狸缓缓走，	Like lonely fox he goes
在彼淇厉⑥。	在那淇水摆渡口。	At the ford over there.
心之忧矣，	我的心里直发愁，	My heart sad and drear grows:
之子无带。	这人衣带也没有。	He has no belt to wear.

有狐绥绥，	有只狐狸慢慢走，	Like lonely fox he goes
在彼淇侧。	在那淇水旁边头。	By riverside o'er there.
心之忧矣，	我的心里直发愁，	My heart sad and drear grows:

---

① 谖(xuān)草：忘忧草。② 树：栽种。③ 背：北堂。④ 痗(mèi)：病痛。⑤ 绥绥(suísuí)：慢慢独自行走。⑥ 厉：水深处的渡口。

* It was said that in this song a woman expressed her desire for a husband, for through the misery and desolation of the State of Wei, many, both men and women, were left unmarried or had lost their partners.

之子无服。	这人衣衫也没有。	He has no dress whate'er.

木 瓜

Gifts*

投①我以木瓜，	姑娘送我用木瓜，	She throws a quince to me;
报之以琼琚②。	我用琼琚报答她。	I give her a green jade
匪报也，	琼琚哪能报答，	Not in return, you see,
永以为好也。	是想永远相好啊。	But to show acquaintance made.

投我以木桃，	姑娘送我用红桃，	She throws a peach to me;
报之以琼瑶。	我用琼瑶报答她。	I give her a white jade
匪报也，	琼瑶哪能报答，	Not in retrun, you see,
永以为好也。	是想永远相好啊。	But to show friendship made.

投我以木李，	姑娘送我用木李，	She throws a plum to me;
报之以琼玖。	我用琼玖报答她。	I give her jasper fair
匪报也，	琼玖哪能报答，	Not in return, you see,
永以为好也。	是想永远相好啊。	But to show love fore'er.

---

① 投：男女互相投赠东西，是民间一种求爱的方式。② 琼琚(jū)、琼瑶、琼玖：美玉。
* This song referred to an interchange of courtesies between a lover and his mistress.

王风 — Songs Collected around the Capital, Modern Henan

黍离 — The Ruined Capital*

彼黍离离①，	看那黍子成行盛茂，	The millet drops its head;
彼稷之苗。	看那高粱正发新苗。	The sorghum is in sprout.
行迈靡靡②，	就要远行难迈步，	Slowly I trudge and tread;
中心摇摇③。	无限忧愁在心头。	My heart is tossed about.
知我者谓我心忧，	知道我的人说我心里烦忧，	Those who know me will say My heart is sad and bleak;
不知我者谓我何求。	不知道我的人说我有什么要求。	Those who don't know me may Ask me for what I seek.
悠悠苍天，	遥远的苍天啊，	O boundless azure sky,
此何人哉！	这是谁造成的啊。	Who's ruined the land and why?

彼黍离离，	看那黍子成行盛茂，	The millet drops its head;
彼稷之穗。	看那高粱正抽早穗。	The sorghum in the ear.
行迈靡靡，	就要远行难迈步，	Slowly I trudge and tread;
中心如醉。	心中恍惚如醉酒。	My heart seems drunk and drear

---

① 离离：长得一行一行茂盛的样子。② 靡靡：行走迟缓的样子。③ 摇摇：心神不安，忧伤的样子。

* In 769 B. C. King Ping of the Zhou dynasty removed the capital to the east and from this time the kings of Zhou sank nearly to the level of the princes of the States. An official seeing the desolation of the old capital wrote this song expressing his melancholy.

知我者谓我心忧，	知道我的人说我心里烦忧，	Those who know me will say My heart is sad and bleak;
不知我者谓我何求。	不知道我的人说我有什么要求。	Those who don't know me may Ask me for what I seek.
悠悠苍天，	遥远的苍天啊，	O boundless azure sky,
此何人哉!	这是谁造成的啊。	Who's ruined the land and why?

彼黍离离，	看那黍子成行盛茂，	The millet drops its head;
彼稷之实。	看那高粱正在结实。	The sorghum is in grain.
行迈靡靡，	就要远行难迈步，	Slowly I trudge and tread;
中心如噎①。	心口如噎真难受。	My heart seems choked with pain.
知我者谓我心忧，	知道我的人说我心里烦忧，	Those who know me will say My heart is sad and bleak;
不知我者谓我何求。	不知道我的人说我有什么要求。	Those who don't know me may Ask me for what I seek.
悠悠苍天，	遥远的苍天啊，	O boundless azure sky,
此何人哉!	这是谁造成的啊。	Who's ruined the land and why?

君子于役　　　　　　　　My Man Is Away*

君子于役②，	夫君在服劳役，	My man's away to serve the State;
不知其期。	不知他的归期。	I can't anticipate
曷至③哉?	什么时候回来?	How long he will there stay

---

① 噎(yē)：气阻不顺。② 役：服劳役。③ 至：回家。

* This song expressed the feeling of a wife on the prolonged absence of her husband on service and her longing for his return.

鸡栖于埘①，	鸡已纷纷飞上窝，	Or when he'll be on homeward way.
日之夕矣，	太阳也已下山了，	The sun is setting in the west;
羊牛下来。	牛羊纷纷下山岗。	The fowls are roosting in their nest;
		The sheep and cattle come to rest.
君子于役，	夫君在服劳役，	To serve the State my man's away.
如之何勿思!	怎么能够不想他。	How can I not think of him night and day?
君子于役，	夫君在服劳役，	

不日不月。	没有准期要回来。	My man's away to serve the State;
曷其有佸②？	什么时候能团圆？	I can't anticipate When we'll again have met.
鸡栖于桀③；	鸡已纷纷歇木桩，	The sun's already set;
日之夕矣，	太阳也下山了，	The fowls are roosting in their nest;
羊牛下括④。	牛羊纷纷下山坡。	The sheep and cattle come to rest.
君子于役，	夫君在服劳役，	To serve the State my man's away.
苟无饥渴？	但愿不要饿肚肠。	Keep him from hunger and thirst, I pray.

君子阳阳　　　　　　　　What Joy*

| 君子阳阳⑤， | 君子走来喜洋洋， | My man sings with delight; |

---

① 埘(shí)：鸡窝。② 佸(huó)：会和，团圆。③ 桀：木桩。④ 括：到来。⑤ 阳阳：快乐。

* It was said that this song showed the husband's satisfaction and his wife's joy on his return.

左执簧，	左手拿着笙簧，	In his left hand a flute of reed,
右招我由房①。	右手招我去游逛。	He calls me to sing with his right,
其乐只且!	快乐心花放。	What joy indeed!

君子陶陶②，	君子走来乐陶陶，	My man dances in delight;
左执翿③，	左手拿着羽旄扬，	In his left hand a feather-screen,
右招我由敖。	右手招我去游遨。	He calls me to dance with his right.
其乐只且!	快乐心花放。	What joy foreseen!

扬之水　　　　　　　　　　　In Garrison*

扬④之水，	激扬的河水啊，	Slowly the water flows;
不流束薪。	成捆的柴草漂不走。	Firewood can't be carried away.
彼其之子，	那个人啊，	You're afraid of your foes;
不与我戍⑤申。	不和我去驻申地。	Why don't you in garrison stay?
怀哉怀哉!	想念啊想念，	How much for home I yearn!
曷月予还归哉?	哪月我才能回去啊？	O when may I return?

扬之水，	激扬的河水啊，	Slowly the water flows;
不流束楚。	成捆的荆条漂不走。	No thorn can be carried away.
彼其之子，	那个人啊，	You're afraid of your foes;

---

① 由房：游戏玩耍。② 陶陶：和乐。③ 翿(dào)：羽毛做的舞具。④ 扬：水流激荡。⑤ 戍：驻防。

* The troops of Zhou murmured against the lords who kept them on duty in the State of Shen, modern Nanyang. The water which flows so slowly and whose power is too weak to carry away firewood or thorn or rushes may allude to the Kingdom of Zhou, too weak to defend its frontiers.

不与我戍甫。	不和我去驻甫地。	Why don't you in army camps stay?
怀哉怀哉!	想念啊想念,	How much for home I yearn!
曷月予还归哉?	哪月我才能回去啊?	O when may I return?

扬之水,	激扬的河水啊,	Slowly the water flows;
不流束蒲。	成捆的蒲草漂不走。	Rushes can't be carried away.
彼其之子,	那个人啊,	You're afraid of your foes;
不与我戍许。	不和我去驻许地。	Why don't you in army tents stay?
怀哉怀哉!	想念啊想念,	How much for home I yearn?
曷月予还归哉?	哪月我才能回去啊?	O when may I return?

中谷有蓷　　　　　　Grief of a Deserted Wife*

中谷有蓷①,	谷中长着益母草,	Amid the vale grow mother-worts;
暵②其干矣!	枝干枯槁将折断。	They are withered and dry.
有女仳③离,	离弃之女伤心肝,	There's a woman her lord deserts.
嘅④其叹矣。	感慨伤心又长叹。	O hear her sigh!
嘅其叹矣,	感慨伤心又长叹,	O hear her sigh!
遇人之艰难矣!	嫁个贤人可真难。	Her lord's a faithless guy.

中谷有蓷,	谷中长着益母草,	Amid the vale grow mother-worts;
暵其脩⑤矣。	蓷菱枯槁将发烂。	They are scorched and dry.
有女仳离,	离弃之女伤心肝,	There's a woman her lord deserts.

---

① 蓷(tuī): 益母草。② 暵(hàn): 干枯。③ 仳(pǐ): 离弃。④ 嘅(kǎi): 叹息。⑤ 脩: 干肉,代指干。

* This song was expressive of pity for a deserted wife.

条其歗①矣。	伤心不禁长声叹。	O hear her cry!
条其歗矣,	伤心不禁长声叹,	O hear her cry!
遇人之不淑矣!	嫁个男人是祸患。	She has met a bad guy.

中谷有蓷,	谷中长着益母草,	Amid the vale grow mother-worts;
暵其湿矣。	根枝枯槁将朽坏。	They are now drowned and wet.
有女仳离,	离弃之女伤心肝,	There's a woman her lord deserts.
啜其泣矣。	伤心呜咽尽泣哭。	See her tears jet!
啜其泣矣,	伤心呜咽尽泣哭,	See her tears jet!
何嗟及矣!	后悔莫及空长叹!	It's too late to regret.

兔爰　　　　　　　　Past and Present*

有兔爰爰②,	兔子自由自在,	The rabbit runs away,
雉离③于罗。	野鸡落入网来。	The pheasant in the net.
我生之初,	在我幼年生活时,	In my earliest day
尚无为;	尚无繁重劳役忙。	For nothig did I fret;
我生之后,	我生活一段时日后,	In later years of care
逢此百罹。	遭逢千百种灾殃。	All evils have I met.
尚寐,	还是睡觉吧,	O I would sleep fore'er.
无吪④!	不动不声张。	

有兔爰爰,	兔子自由自在,	The rabbit runs away,
雉离于罦⑤。	野鸡触入网中。	The pheasant in the snare.

---

① 歗(xiào):痛声。② 爰爰:自由自在行走的样子。③ 离:罹难,落入网中。④ 吪(é):说话。⑤ 罦(fú):网。

* The present referred to the time of King Ping (718–696 B. C.). The rabbit was said to be of a crafty nature while the pheasant to be bold and determined and easily snared.

我生之初，	在我幼年生活时，	In my earliest day
尚无造①；	尚无劳役重繁忙。	For nothing did I care;
我生之后，	我生活一段时日后，	In later years of ache
逢此百忧。	遭逢千百种愁伤。	I'm in grief and despair.
尚寐，	还是睡觉吧，	I'd sleep and never wake.
无觉!	不醒无声响。	

有兔爰爰，	兔子自由自在，	The rabbit runs away,
雉离于罿②。	野鸡陷入网中。	The pheasant in the trap.
我生之初。	在我幼年生活时，	In my earliest day
尚无庸③；	尚无辛劳苦奔忙。	I lived without mishap;
我生之后，	我生活一段时日后，	But in my later year
逢此百凶。	遭逢千百种凶险。	All miseries appear.
尚寐，	还是睡觉吧，	I'd sleep and never hear.
无聪!	不听犹死状。	

葛藟　　　　　　　　　　A Refugee*

绵绵葛藟，	长长的野葛茎，	Creepers spread all the way
在河之浒。	在河边上生。	Along the river clear.
终远兄弟，	离别兄弟们，	From brothers far away,
谓他人父。	称呼他人为父。	I call a stranger "father dear."
谓他人父，	称呼他人为父，	Though called "dear father," he

---

① 造：造作。② 罿(tóng)：网。③ 庸：劳役。

* A refugee mourned over his lot, unpitied by man and woman, old and young. The growth of creepers on the soil proper to them was presented by the refugee in contrast to his own position, torn from his family and proper soil.

亦莫我顾!	也没有人对我照顾。	Seems not to care for me.

绵绵葛藟,	长长的野葛茎,	Creepers spread all the way
在河之涘。	在河边上生。	Beside the river clear.
终远兄弟,	离别兄弟们,	From brothers far away,
谓他人母。	称呼他人为娘。	I call a stranger "mother dear."
谓他人母,	称呼他人为娘,	Though called "dear mother," she
亦莫我有!	也没有人对我亲近。	Seems not to cherish me.

绵绵葛藟,	长长的野葛茎,	Creepers spread all the way
在河之漘①。	在河边上生。	Beyond the river clear.
终远兄弟,	离别兄弟们,	From brothers far away,
谓他人昆②。	称呼他人为兄。	I call a stranger "brother dear."
谓他人昆,	称呼他人为兄,	Though called "dear brother," he
亦莫我闻!	也没有人对我怜悯。	Seems not to pity me.

采 葛   One Day When I See Her Not*

彼采葛兮。	那人正在采葛啊。	To gather vine goes she.
一日不见,	一天不见她,	I miss her whom I do not see,
如三月兮。	好像过去三个月。	One day seems longer than months three.

彼采萧③兮。	那人正在采青蒿啊。	To gather reed goed she.

---

① 漘(chún):同浒、涘,水边。② 昆:兄长。③ 萧:青蒿。

* It has become proverbial that a short absence from the lover seems to be long, and longer the more she is dwelt upon.

一日不见，	一天不见她，	I miss her whom I do not see,
如三秋①兮。	好像过去九个月。	One day seems long as seasons three.

彼采艾兮。	那人正在采艾啊。	To gather herbs goes she.
一日不见，	一天不见她，	I miss her whom I do not see,
如三岁兮。	好像过去了三年。	One day seems longer than years three.

大 车　　　　　　　　　　To Her Captive Lord *

大车槛槛②，	大车经过声槛槛，	Rumbling your cart,
毳③衣如菼④。	车毡有似芦苇花。	Reedlike your gown,
岂不尔思？	难道是我不想你？	I miss you in my heart.
畏子不敢。	怕你犹豫心不敢。	How dare I make it known?

大车啍啍⑤，	大车驶过慢吞吞，	Rattling your cart,
毳衣如璊⑥。	车毡有似红玉色。	Reddish your gown,
岂不尔思？	难道是我不想你？	I miss you in my heart.
畏子不奔。	怕你犹豫不相奔。	How dare I have it shown?

榖⑦则异室，	活着不能住一起，	Living, we dwell apart;
死则同穴。	死去同埋一个圹。	Dead, the same grave we'll share.
谓予不信，	别不相信我的话，	Am I not true at heart?

---

① 秋：一个秋天三个月。三秋即九个月。② 槛槛(kǎnkǎn)：车行走的声音。③ 毳(cuì)：车上蔽风雨的毡子。④ 菼(tǎn)：初生的芦苇花。⑤ 啍啍(tūntūn)：车缓慢而笨重的声音。⑥ 璊(mén)：赤色的玉。⑦ 榖：活着。

* This song was said to be written by the beautiful Lady of Peach Blossom, whose lord became a captive of the prince of Chu.

有如皦①日。　青天太阳来做证。　By the bright sun I swear.

丘中有麻　　　　　　　　　　To Her Lover*

丘中有麻，　土丘上面种苎麻，　Hemp on the mound I see.
彼留子嗟。　住在留地的名子嗟。Who's there detaining thee?
彼留子嗟，　住在留地的名子嗟，Who's there detaining thee?
将②其来施③。愿他高兴走来吧。　From coming jauntily to me?

丘中有麦，　土丘上面种大麦，　Wheat on the mound I'm thinking of.
彼留子国。　住在留地的名子国。Who detains thee above?
彼留子国，　住在留地的名子国，Who detains thee above
将其来食。　愿他快快来进食。　From coming with me to make love?

岳中有李，　土丘上面种李树，　On the mound stands plum tree.
彼留之子。　居住留地的好儿郎。Who's there detaining thee?
彼留之子，　居住留地的好儿郎，Who's there detaining thee
贻我佩玖。　送我美玉永难忘。　From giving girdle gems to me?

---

① 皦(jiǎo)：光明。② 将：请愿。③ 施施：高兴的样子。

* A woman longed for the presence of her lover who, she thought, was detained from her by another woman.

郑 风

Songs Collected in Zheng, Modern Henan

缁 衣

A Good Wife*

缁①衣之宜兮，	黑衣正合适啊，	The black-dyed robe befits you well;
敝，予又改为兮！	破了我又替你改制。	When it's worn out, I'll make another new.
适子之馆②兮，	到你的客舍里啊，	You go to work in your hotel;
还，予授子之粲兮！	回来我给你备食饭。	Come back, I'll make a meal for you.

缁衣之好兮，　　黑衣真美好啊，　　The black-dyed robe becomes you well;
敝，予又改造兮！　破了我又替你改造。When it's worn out, I'll get another new.
适子之馆兮，　　　到你的客舍里啊，　You go to work in your hotel;
还，予授子之粲兮！回来我给你备食馔。Come back, I'll make a meal for you.

缁衣之席③兮，　　黑衣真宽大啊，　　The black-dyed robe does suit you well;

---

① 缁(zī)：黑色。② 馆：客舍。③ 席：宽大。

* It was said that this song was expressive of the wife's regard that was due to the virtue and ability of her lord.

敝,予又改作兮! 破了我又替你改做。When it's worn out, you'll have another new.
适子之馆兮, 到你的客舍里啊, You go to work in your hotel;
还,予授子之粲兮! 回来我给你备佳饭。Come back, I'll make a meal for you.

将仲子　　　　　　　　　　Cadet My Dear*

将①仲子兮,　　请求仲子啊,　　　Cadet my dear,
无逾我里,　　　不要翻入我闾里,　Don't leap into my hamlet, please,
无折我树杞。　　不要攀折我家的杞。Nor break my willow trees!
岂敢爱之?　　　难道我是爱惜它,　Not that I care for these;
畏我父母。　　　只怕我父母要说话。It is my parents that I fear.
仲可怀也,　　　仲子叫我牵挂,　　Much as I love you, dear,
父母之言,　　　可是父母的话,　　How can I not be afraid
亦可畏也!　　　也让我有些害怕。　Of what my parents might have said!

将仲子兮,　　　请求仲子啊,　　　Cadet my dear,
无逾我墙,　　　不要跨过我院墙,　Don't leap over my wall, please,
无折我树桑。　　不要攀折我家的桑。Nor break my mulberries!
岂敢爱之?　　　难道我是爱惜它,　Not that I care for these;
畏我诸兄。　　　只怕我兄长要说话。It is my brothers that I fear.
仲可怀也,　　　仲子叫我牵挂,　　Much as I love you, dear,

---

① 将(qiāng):请求。
* A woman begged her lover not to excite the suspicions and remarks of her parents and others.

诸兄之言，	可是兄长的话，	How can I not be afraid
亦可畏也！	也让我有些害怕。	Of what my brothers might have said!

将仲子兮，	请求仲子啊，	Cadet my dear,
无逾我园，	不要翻进我后园，	Don't leap into my garden, please,
无折我树檀。	不要攀折我家的檀。	Nor break my sandal trees!
岂敢爱之？	难道我是爱惜它，	Not that I care for these;
畏人之多言。	只怕我邻居要说话。	It is my neighbors that I fear.
仲可怀也，	仲子叫我牵挂，	Much as I love you, dear,
人之多言，	可是邻居的话，	How can I not be afraid
亦可畏也！	也让我有些害怕。	of what my neighbors might have said!

叔于田　　　　　　　The Young Cadet*

叔于田[①]，	叔在打猎，	The young cadet to chase has gone;
巷无居人。	大街小巷没有人。	It seems there's no man in the town.
岂无居人？	街巷怎会无人？	Is it true there's none in the town?
不如叔也，	谁都不如叔啊，	It's only that I cannot find
洵美且仁！	那么美好又慈仁。	Another hunter so handsome and kind.

[①] 田：打猎。

* It was said that the young cadet referred to the younger brother of Duke Zhuang of Zheng who succeeded Duke Wu in 742 B. C.

叔于狩①，	叔在冬天打猎，	The young cadet's gone hunting in the wood.
巷无饮酒。	街巷没有人喝酒。	In the town there's no drinker good.
岂无饮酒？	街巷怎会无人喝酒？	Is it true there's no drinker good?
不如叔也，	谁都不如叔啊，	In the town no drinker of wine
洵美且好！	那么善良又清秀。	Looks so handsome and fine.
叔适野，	叔在郊外打猎，	The young cadet has gone to countryside;
巷无服马②。	街巷没有人驾马。	In the town there's none who can ride.
岂无服马？	街巷怎会无人驾马？	Is it true there's none who can ride?
不如叔也，	谁都不如叔啊，	I cannot find among the young and old
洵美且武！	那么俊美又英武。	Another rider so handsome and bold.

大叔于田

Hunting*

叔于田，	大叔在打猎，	Our lord goes hunting in the land,
乘乘③马。	四匹马儿拉着车。	Mounted in his cab with four steeds.

---

①狩：冬天打猎。②服马：用马驾车。③乘乘(chēngshèng)马：乘坐四匹马拉的车。前乘字指乘坐，后乘字指四匹马拉的车。

* This was the earliest description of hunting in Chinese poetry.

执辔①如组，	手握缰绳如丝带，	He waves and weaves the reins in hand;
两骖②如舞。	两匹边马像舞蹈。	Two outside horses dance with speed.
叔在薮③，	叔在泽地草边，	Our lord goes hunting in grass land;
火烈具举。	几处猎火齐烧。	The hunters' torches flame in a ring.
襢裼④暴虎⑤，	赤膊空拳捉猛虎，	He seizes a tiger with bared hand
献于公所。	献给公爵去。	And then presents it to the king.
将⑥叔无狃⑦，	请叔不要再这样，	Don't try, my lord, to do it again
戒其伤女。	小心它会伤害你。	For fear you may get hurt with pain!
叔于田，	大叔在打猎，	Mounted in his chariot and four,
乘乘黄。	四匹黄马拉着车儿。	Hunting afield our lord does go.
两服上襄，	中间两马并驾前，	The inside horses run before;
两骖雁行。	外面边马如雁行。	Two on the outside follow in a row.
叔在薮，	叔在湖地草边，	Our lord goes to the waterside;
火烈具扬。	一片猎火高扬。	The hunters' torches blaze up high.
叔善射忌，	叔是射箭神手，	He knows not only how to ride
又良御忌。	赶车技术高超。	But also shoot with his sharp eye.
抑磬控忌，	一会儿勒马不进，	He runs and stops his steeds at will
抑纵送⑧忌。	一会儿马蹄奔放。	And shoots his arrows with great skill.
叔于田，	大叔在打猎，	Mounted in cab and four steeds fine,
乘乘鸨⑨。	四匹花马拉着车儿。	Our lord goes hunting in the lands.

---

① 辔(pèi)：马缰绳。② 骖(cān)：四匹马中外面的两匹马。③ 薮(sǒu)：沼泽丛林。
④ 襢裼(tǎnxī)：赤膊。⑤ 暴虎：空手打虎。⑥ 将(qiāng)：请。⑦ 无狃(niǔ)：不要习
以为常，不在意。⑧ 纵送：一面射箭，一面追赶野兽。⑨ 鸨(bǎo)：毛色黑白相杂的马。

两服齐首，	中间两马齐并头，	Two on the inside have their heads in a line;
两骖如手。	外面边马如两手。	Two on the outside follow like two hands.
叔在薮，	叔在湖地草边，	To waterside our lord does go;
火烈具阜①。	一片猎火高照。	The hunters' fire spreads everywhere.
叔马慢忌，	叔的马儿慢悠闲，	His grey and yellow steeds go slow;
叔发罕忌。	叔的弓箭发得少。	The arrows he shoots become rare.
抑释掤②忌，	把箭放在箭袋里，	Aside his quiver now he lays
抑鬯③弓忌。	把弓放在弓袋里。	And returns his bow to the case.

清 人　　　　　　　　　Qing Warriors*

清人在彭，	清地的兵驻彭庄，	Qing warriors stationed out,
驷介④旁旁⑤。	四马披甲真强壮。	Four mailed steeds run about.
二矛重英，	两矛饰着重缨络，	Two spears adorned with feathers red,
河上乎翱翔。	河边闲游又翱翔。	Along the stream they roam ahead.
清人在消，	清地的兵驻消地，	Qing warriors stationed on the shore
驷介麃麃⑥。	四马披甲雄骁骁。	Look martial in their cab and four.
二矛重乔⑦，	两矛披着野鸡毛，	Two spears with pheasant's feathers red,

---

① 阜：旺盛。② 掤(bīng)：箭筒盖子。③ 鬯(chàng)：装弓的袋子。④ 驷介：四匹马披甲驾车。⑤ 旁旁：强盛的样子。⑥ 麃麃(biāobiāo)：威武的样子。⑦ 乔：野鸡毛。

* This was a satire against Duke Wen who ruled in the State of Zheng (662–627 B. C.) but manoeuvred uselessly an army of Qing on the frontier.

河上乎逍遥。河边闲游多逍遥。 Along the stream they stroll ahead.

清人在轴， 清地的兵驻轴地， Qing warriors stationed on the stream
驷介陶陶。 四马披甲如风跑。 Look proud in their cab and mailed team.
左旋右抽， 车子左转右抽刀， Driver at left, spearsman at right,
中军①作好。将军武姿真是好！ The general shows his great delight.

羔裘

Officer in Lamb's Fur*

羔裘如濡②， 羊羔皮袍光又润， His fur of lamb is white
洵直且侯③。真是舒直又美好。 As the man is upright.
彼其之子， 那个人啊， The officer arises
舍命不渝。 舍弃性命不改变。 Unchanged in a crisis.

羔裘豹饰， 羊羔皮袍饰豹皮， With cuffs of leopard-skin,
孔武有力。 显得英武又有力。 The fur of lamb he's in
彼其之子， 那个人啊， Makes him look strong and bold;
邦之司直。 掌管司法很正直。 To the right he will hold.

羔裘晏④兮，羊羔皮袍真鲜明， His fur of lamb is bright
三英⑤粲兮。三道镶饰真美丽。 With three stripes left and right.
彼其之子， 那个人啊， The officer stands straight,
邦之彦⑥兮。国中的才士文采异。A hero of the State.

---

① 中军：军中的统帅。② 濡：湿滑润泽。③ 侯：美好。④ 晏：鲜明的样子。⑤ 英：袍子上的饰纹。⑥ 彦：士的美称。

* This song celebrated some officer of Zheng for his elegant appearance and integrity.

遵大路　　　　　　　　　　Leave Me Not*

遵大路兮，　　沿着大路走啊，　　I hold you by the sleeve
掺①执子之祛兮！拉着你的袖啊。　　Along the public way.
无我恶兮，　　不要厌弃我啊，　　O do not hate and leave
不寁②故也！　　不要这么快抛弃　　A mate of olden day!
　　　　　　　　旧情啊。

遵大路兮，　　沿着大路走啊，　　I hold you by the hand
掺执子之手兮，拉着你的手啊。　　Along the public road.
无我魗③兮，　　不要嫌弃我啊，　　Don't think me ugly and
不寁好也！　　不要这么快抛弃　　Leave your former abode!
　　　　　　　　相好啊。

女曰鸡鸣　　　　　　　　A Hunter's Domestic Life*

女曰："鸡鸣。"女人说耳听鸡叫了，The wife says, "Cocks crow, hark!"
士曰："昧旦④。"男人说天才刚刚亮。The man says, "It's still dark."
"子兴⑤视夜，　你且起床看夜空，"Rise and see if it's night;
明星⑥有烂。" 启明星儿闪闪亮。 The morning star shines bright."
"将翱将翔，　请你快起来遨游啊，"Wild geese and ducks will fly;

---

① 掺(shǎn)：执，拉着。② 寁(jié)：很快。③ 魗(chóu)：丑。④ 昧旦：天色将亮未亮的时候。⑤ 兴：起来。⑥ 明星：启明星。

* A woman entreated her lover not to cast her off.

* A wife sent her husbnd from her side to his hunting and expressed her affection for him.

弋凫与雁。"	射野鸭子也射雁。	I'll shoot them down from high."

"弋言加①之，	射中鸭雁正正好，	"At shooting you are good;
与子宜②之。	给你烹了做佳肴。	I'll dress the game as food.
宜言饮酒，	应该用来饮美酒，	Together we'll drink wine
与子偕老。	与你一起相偕老。	And live to ninety-nine.
琴瑟在御③，	你弹琴来我鼓瑟，	With zither by our side,
莫不静好。"	多么宁静又美好。	In peace we shall abide."

"知子之来④之，	知道你真关心我，	"I know your wifely care;
杂佩以赠之。	送你杂佩表我爱。	I'll give you pearls to wear.
知子之顺之，	知道你真体贴我，	I know you will obey;
杂佩以问⑤之。	送你杂佩表谢意。	Can pearls and jade repay?
知子之好之，	知道你真喜欢我，	I know your steadfast love;
杂佩以报之。"	送你杂佩表同心。	I value nothing above."

有女同车　　　　　　　　　　Lady Jiang*

有女同车，	有个同车的姑娘，	A lady in the cab with me
颜如舜华⑥。	脸儿美如木槿花。	Looks like a flower from a hedge-tree.
将翱将翔，	我们一起遨游，	She goes about as if in flight;
佩玉琼琚。	身戴佩环是美玉。	Her girdle-pendants look so bright.

---

①加：射中。②宜：肴。③御：协奏。④来：关怀。⑤问：慰问。⑥舜华：同"舜英"，木槿花。

* It was said that this was a praise of the newly-wed Lady Jiang.

彼美孟姜，	美丽的孟家大姑娘，	O Lady Jiang with pretty face,
洵美且都①！	确实美丽又文雅。	So elegant and full of grace!

有女同行，	有个同行的姑娘，	The lady together with me
颜如舜英。	脸儿美如木槿花。	Walks like a blossoming hedge-tree.
将翱将翔，	我们一起游玩，	She moves about as if in flight;
佩玉将将。	身戴佩环响叮叮。	Her girdle-pendants tinkle light.
彼美孟姜，	美丽的孟家大姑娘，	O Lady Jiang with pretty face,
德音不忘！	美好品德永明光。	Can I forget you so full of grace?

山有扶苏　　　　　　　　　　A Joke*

山有扶苏，	山上有扶木，	Uphill stands mulberry
隰有荷华。	洼地有荷花。	And lotus in the pool.
不见子都，	没有看见漂亮的子都，	The handsome I don't see;
乃见狂且②。	却看见一个轻狂小伙子。	Instead I see a fool.

山有桥松，	山上有高松，	Uphill stands a pine-tree
隰有游龙③。	洼地有荭草。	And in the pool leaves red.
不见子充，	没有看见漂亮的子充，	The pretty I don't see;
乃见狡童。	却看见一个狡猾的小伙子。	I see the sly instead.

---

① 都：闲雅。② 且(jū)：狂童。③ 游龙：荭草。

* A woman mocked her lover as a sly fool.

萚 兮　　　　　　　　　　Sing Together*

萚①兮萚兮，	枯树枝啊枯树叶，	Leaves sear, leaves sear,
风其吹女。	大风把你吹飘荡。	The wind blows you away.
叔兮伯兮，	老三啊老大啊，	Sing, cousins dear,
倡②予和女。	你来领唱我来和。	And I'll join in your lay.

萚兮萚兮，	枯树枝啊枯树叶，	Leaves sear, leaves sear,
风其漂女。	大风把你吹纷扬。	The wind wafts you away.
叔兮伯兮，	老三啊老大啊，	Sing, cousins dear,
倡予要女。	你来起头我来和。	And I'll complete your lay.

狡 童　　　　　　　　　A Handsome Guy*

彼狡童兮，	那个小伙子太狡猾，	You handsome guy
不与我言兮。	不再肯和我说话。	Won't speak to me words sweet.
维③子之故，	因为你的缘故啊，	For you I sigh
使我不能餐兮！	让我茶饭咽不下。	And can nor drink nor eat.

| 彼狡童兮， | 那个小伙子太狡猾， | You handsome guy |
| 不与我食兮。 | 不再和我同吃饭。 | Won't eat with me at my request. |

---

① 萚(tuò)：枯树枝叶。② 倡：唱。③ 维：因为。

* When leaves wafted in the wind after harvest, a songstress asked her companions to sing and dance together like wafting leaves..
* Some misunderstanding seemed to have arisen between the poetess and her handsome lover.

维子之故，	因为你的缘故啊，	For you I sigh
使我不能息兮！	让我睡觉都不安。	And cannot take my rest.

褰裳　　　　　　　　　　Lift up Your Robe*

子惠思我，	你若爱我想念我，	If you think of me as you seem,
褰①裳涉溱。	提起衣裳渡溱河。	Lift up your robe and cross that stream!
子不我思，	你若变心不想我，	If you don't love me as you seem,
岂无他人？	难道无人爱我。	Can I not find another one?
狂童之狂也且！	你这人儿太狂妄。	Your foolishness is second to none.

子惠思我，	你若爱我想念我，	If you think of me as you seem,
褰裳涉洧。	提起衣裳过洧河。	Lift up your gown and cross this stream!
子不我思，	你若变心不想我，	If you don't love me as you seem,
岂无他士？	难道无人爱我。	Can I not find another mate?
狂童之狂也且！	你这人儿太狂妄。	Your foolishness is really great.

丰　　　　　　　　　　　Lost Opportunity*

子之丰②兮，	你的容貌丰润啊，	You looked plump and plain

---

① 褰(qiān)：提起。② 丰：丰满。

* A woman sang to her lover who would not lift up his robe and cross the stream to meet her.
* A woman regretted that she had not kept her promise and wished that her lover would come again.

俟我乎巷兮。	等候我在里巷啊。	And waited for me in the lane.
悔予不送兮!	后悔我没和你走啊。	Why did I not go with you?
		I complain.

子之昌①兮,	你的体魄多魁伟啊,	You looked strong and tall
俟我乎堂兮。	等候我在堂屋啊。	And waited for me in the hall.
悔予不将兮!	后悔我没同你行啊。	I regret I did not return your call.

衣锦褧衣,	穿着锦衣罩单衣,	Over my broidered skirt
裳②锦褧裳。	穿着锦裙罩单裙。	I put on simple shirt.
叔兮伯兮,	大叔大伯啊,	O Sir, to you I say:
驾予与行③!	驾车载我一起走。	Come in your cab and let us drive away!

裳锦褧裳,	穿着锦裙罩单裙,	I put on simple shirt
衣锦褧衣。	穿着锦衣罩单衣。	Over my broidered skirt.
叔兮伯兮,	大叔大伯啊,	O Sir, I say anew:
驾予与归④!	驾车载我一同归。	Come in your cab and take me home with you!

东门之墠　　　　A Lover's Monologue*

|东门之墠⑤,|东门外面地平坦,|At eastern gate on level ground|

---

① 昌:魁伟。② 裳(cháng)下裙。③ 行:出嫁。④ 归:出嫁。⑤ 墠(shàn):平坦的场地。

* A woman thought of her lover and complained that he did not come to her though his house was very near, at the eastern gate of the capital of Zheng.

茹藘①在阪②。	茜草长在山坡上。	There are madder plants all around.
其室则迩，	她的房屋近咫尺，	My lover's house is very near,
其人甚远。	她的人儿远天涯。	But far away he does appear.

东门之栗，	东门外面栗树下，	'Neath chestnut tree at eastern gate
有践③家室。	那有成排的村落。	Within my house in vain I wait.
岂不尔思？	难道我不想念你，	How can I not think of my dear?
子不我即④！	你却不与我亲近。	Why won't he come to see me here?

风　雨　　　　　　　　Wind and Rain*

风雨凄凄，	风凄凄雨冷冷，	The wind and rain are chill;
鸡鸣喈喈，	喈喈鸡鸣不住声。	The crow of cocks is shrill.
既见君子，	终于见到了君子，	When I've seen my man best,
云胡不夷⑤。	怎么会不高兴。	Should I not feel at rest?

风雨潇潇，	风凄凄雨潇潇，	The wind whistles with showers;
鸡鸣胶胶，	胶胶鸡鸣不停叫。	The cocks crow dreary hours.
既见君子，	终于见到了君子，	When I've seen my dear one,
云胡不瘳⑥。	病怎么会还不好。	With my ill could I not have done?

风雨如晦⑦，	风雨黑天暗地，	Gloomy wind and rain blend;
鸡鸣不已，	鸡鸣还是不已。	The cocks crow without end.

---

① 茹藘(rúlú)：茜草。② 阪(bǎn)：土坡。③ 践：房屋排列整齐。④ 即：靠近。⑤ 夷：平，舒坦。⑥ 瘳(chōu)：病愈。⑦ 晦：昏暗不明的样子。

* This described the joy of a lonely wife on seeing her husband's return in wind and rain.

| 既见君子， | 终于见到了君子， | When I have seen my dear, |
| 云胡不喜。 | 怎么会不欢喜。 | How full I feel of cheer! |

子　衿　　　　　　　　　To a Scholar*

青青子衿①，	青青的你的衣衫，	Student with collar blue,
悠悠我心。	长长挂在我的心间。	How much I long for you!
纵我不往，	即使我不能去到你那里，	Though to see you I am not free,
子宁不嗣②音？	你怎么也不给我个音讯。	O why don't you send word to me?

青青子佩，	青青的你的佩带，	Scholar with belt-stone blue,
悠悠我思。	长长印在我的心间。	How long I think of you!
纵我不往，	即使我不能去到你那里，	Though to see you I am not free,
子宁不来？	你怎么也不来到我这里。	O why don't you come to see me?

挑兮达兮，	我徘徊不安啊，	I'm pacing up and down
在城阙③兮。	在这城楼之上。	On the wall of the town.
一日不见，	一天看不见你，	When to see you I am not free,
如三月兮！	就像隔了三个月啊。	One day seems like three months to me.

---

① 衿(jīn)：衣领。② 嗣：寄。③ 城阙：城楼上。
* A woman longed for her lover.

扬之水　　　　　　　　　Believe Me*

扬之水，	舒缓的河水，	Wood bound together may
不流束楚。	一捆荆条漂不起。	Not be carried away.
终鲜兄弟，	既然没有兄弟，	We have but brethren few;
维予与女。	只有我和你。	There're only I and you.
无信人之言，	不要听信别人的话，	What others say can't be believed,
人实迋①女。	人家是在哄骗你。	Or you will be deceived.

扬之水，	舒缓的河水，	A bundle of wood may
不流束薪。	一捆柴草流不去。	Not be carried away.
终鲜兄弟，	既然没有兄弟，	We have but brethren few;
维予二人。	只有我你二人。	There are only we two.
无信人之言，	不要听信别人的话，	Do not believe what others say!
人实不信。	人家的话不能相信。	Untrustworthy are they.

出其东门　　　　　　　　My Lover in White*

出其东门，	走出东城门，	Outside the eastern gate
有女如云。	姑娘多如云。	Like clouds fair maidens date.
虽则如云，	虽然多如云，	Though they are fair as cloud,
匪我思存。	不是意中人。	My love's not in the crowd.

---

① 迋(guàng)：哄骗。

* A woman asserted good faith to her husband and protested against people who would make them doubt each other. A bundle of firewood might allude to a couple well united.

* A man praised his lover in white, contrasted with beautiful maidens dating outside the eastern gate of the capital of Zheng.

缟①衣綦②巾，　白衣青巾人，　　Dressed in light green and white,
聊乐我员。　　是我梦中人。　　Alone she's my delight.

出其闉闍③，　走出外城郭，　　Outside the outer gate
有女如荼。　　姑娘如花多。　　Like blooms fair maidens date.
虽则如荼，　　虽然如花多，　　Though like blooms they are fair,
匪我思且④。　不能打动我。　　The one I love's not there.
缟衣茹藘，　　白衣红巾人，　　Dressed in scarlet and white,
聊可与娱。　　是我梦中人。　　Alone she gives me delight.

野有蔓草　　　　　　The Creeping Grass*

野有蔓草，　　郊外野草蔓延，　Afield the creeping grass
零露漙⑤兮。　露水滴落浓浓。　With crystal dew o'erspread,
有美一人，　　有一位美人啊，　There's a beautiful lass
清扬婉兮。　　眉清目秀好容颜。With clear eyes and fine forehead.
邂逅⑥相遇，　不约而巧遇，　　When I meet the clear-eyed,
适我愿兮。　　正合我的心愿。　My desire's satisfied.

野有蔓草，　　郊外野草蔓延，　Afield the creeping grass
零露瀼瀼⑦。　露水滴落晶莹。　With round dewdrops o'erspread,
有美一人，　　有一位美人啊，　There's a beautiful lass

---

① 缟(gǎo)：白色。② 綦(qí)：青色。③ 闉闍(yīndū)：城外曲城的重门。④ 且(zhù)：往。⑤ 漙(tuán)：露多。⑥ 邂逅：不期而遇。⑦ 瀼瀼(ráng ráng)：露多。

* This song described the love-making of a young man and a beautiful lass amid the creeping grass o'erspread with morning dew.

婉如清扬。	眉清目秀有风情。	With clear eyes and fine forehead.
邂逅相遇，	不约而巧遇，	When I meet the clear-eyed,
与子偕臧。	我们两心相悦。	Amid the grass let's hide!

溱洧

Riverside Rendezvous*

溱与洧，	溱水和洧水，	The Rivers Zhen and Wei
方涣涣兮。	正在哗哗淌。	Overflow on their way.
士与女，	小伙儿和姑娘，	The lovely lad and lass
方秉蕳①兮。	手握兰草香。	Hold in hand fragrant grass.
女曰："观乎？"	姑娘说："去看看吧？"	"Let's look around," says she;
士曰："既且。"	小伙子说："已经看过了，"	"I've already," says he.
"且往观乎。	"再去看看也好。	"Let us go there again!
洧之外，	洧水的边上，	Beyond the River Wei
洵訏②且乐。"	地方宽敞人快乐。"	The ground is large and people gay."
维士与女，	男女相伴，	Playing together then,
伊其相谑，	你说说我笑笑，	They have a happy hour;
赠之以勺药。	送你一把芍药。	Each gives the other peony flower.
溱与洧，	溱水和洧水，	The Rivers Zhen and Wei
浏其清矣。	清澈能见底。	Flow crystal-clear;
士与女，	小伙儿和姑娘，	Lad and lass squeeze their way

---

① 蕳(jiān)：兰草。② 訏(xū)：大。

* It was the custom of the State of Zheng for young people to meet and make love by the riverside on the festive day of the third lunar month in spring.

殷①其盈矣。	拥拥攘攘多热闹。	Through the crowd full of cheer.
女曰:"观乎?"	姑娘说:"去看看吧?"	"Let's look around," says she;
士曰:"既且。"	小伙子说:"已经看过了,"	"I've already," says he.
"且往观乎,	"再去看一下也好。	"Let us go there again!
洧之外,	洧水的边上,	Beyond the River Wei
洵讦于且乐。"	地方宽敞人喜悦。"	The ground is large and people gay."
维士与女,	男女相伴,	Playing together then,
伊其相谑,	你说说我笑笑,	They have a happy hour;
赠之以勺药。	送你一把芍药。	Each gives the other peony flower.

---

① 殷:众多。

齐　风

Songs Collected in Qi, Modern Shandong

鸡　鸣

A Courtier and His Wife*

"鸡既鸣矣，	"听见鸡叫了，	"Wake up!" she says, "Cocks crow.
朝①既盈矣。"	朝堂上的人该满了。"	The court is on the go."
"匪鸡则鸣，	"不是鸡在叫，	"It's not the cock that cries,"
苍蝇之声。"	那是苍蝇闹。"	He says, "but humming flies."
"东方明矣，	"看见东方亮了，	"The east is brightening;
朝既昌②矣。"	朝堂上的人该从了。"	The court is in full swing."
"匪东方则明，	"不是东方亮了，	"It's not the east that's bright
月出之光。"	是月亮发出的光。"	But the moon shedding light."
"虫飞薨薨③，	"虫飞嗡嗡嗡，	"See buzzing insects fly.
甘与子同梦。"	我愿和你同入梦。"	It's sweet in bed to lie.
"会④且归矣，	朝会都要散啦，	But courtiers will not wait;
无庶予子憎。"	别因我而被人憎。"	None likes you to be late."

---

① 朝：朝堂。② 昌：盛多。③ 薨薨（hōnghōng）：虫子成群飞鸣声。④ 会：朝会。

* This was a dialogue between a courtier and his wife. It was said that the dialogue might refer to the marquess of Qi (934–894 B. C.) and the marchioness.

还　　　　　　　　　　　　Two Hunters*

子之还①兮，	你真轻捷啊，	How agile you appear!
遭我乎峱②之间兮。	遇逢我在峱山间。	Amid the hills we meet.
并驱从③两肩④兮，	并排驱赶两只兽，	Pursuing two boars, compeer,
揖我谓我儇⑤兮。	你作揖夸我好身手。	You bow and say I'm fleet.
子之茂⑥兮，	你真壮健啊，	How skilful you appear!
遭我乎峱之道兮。	遇逢我在峱山道上。	We meet halfway uphill.
并驱从两牡兮，	并排驱赶两公兽，	Driving after two males, compeer,
揖我谓我好兮。	你作揖夸我好样的。	You bow and praise my skill.
子之昌兮，	你真强壮啊，	How artful you appear!
遭我乎峱之阳兮。	遇逢我在峱山南边。	South of the hill we meet.
并驱从两狼兮，	并排驱赶两只狼，	Pursuing two wolves, compeer,
揖我谓我臧兮。	作揖夸我好良善良。	You bow and say my art's complete.

---

① 还（xuán）：轻捷的样子。② 峱（náo）：齐国山名，在今山东省。③ 从：追逐。④ 肩：三岁的兽。⑤ 儇（xuān）：灵利。⑥ 茂：健美，强壮。

* This was the compliments interchanged by two hunters of Qi. Some critics said that this was a specimen of admirable satire, through which the boastful manners of the people of Qi were clearly exhibited.

著　　　　　　　　　　The Bridegroom*

俟①我于著②乎而，　等我就在门屏间，　He waits for me between the door and screen,
充耳以素乎而，　　　冠垂白丝挂耳边。　His crown adorned with ribbons green
尚之以琼华③乎而！　添加上红玉更明显。Ended with gems of beautiful sheen.

俟我于庭乎而，　　　等我就在院子间，　He waits for me in the court with delight,
充耳以青乎而，　　　冠垂青丝在耳边。　His crown adorned with ribbons white
尚之以琼莹乎而！　　添加上红玉更美艳。Ended with gems and rubies bright.

俟我于堂乎而，　　　等我就在堂屋间，　He waits for me in inner hall,
充耳以黄乎而，　　　冠垂黄丝在耳边。　His crown adorned with yellow ribbons all
尚之以琼英乎而！　　添加上红玉更光鲜。Ended with gems like golden ball.

---

①俟：等待。②著：门屏间。③琼华：美玉，下"琼莹"、"琼英"同。

* A bride described her first meeting with the bridegroom who should wait for her arrival first at the door, then in the court and at last in the inner hall, according to ancient nuptial ceremony.

东方之日　　　　　　　　Nocturnal Tryst*

东方之日兮，	东方的太阳啊，	The eastern sun is red;
彼姝①者子，	那个美丽的姑娘，	The maiden like a bloom
在我室兮。	在我的房间啊。	Follows me to my room.
在我室兮，	在我的房间啊，	The maiden in my room
履我即兮。	伴我意浓情长。	Follows me to the bed.
东方之月兮，	东方的月亮啊，	The eastern moon is bright;
彼姝者子，	那个美丽的姑娘，	The maiden I adore
在我闼②兮。	在我的门旁啊。	Follows me out of door.
在我闼兮，	在我的门旁啊，	The maiden out of door
履我发兮。	随我情浓意长。	Leaves me and goes out of sight.

东方未明　　　　　　　　A Tryst before Dawn*

东方未明，	东方没有亮，	Before the east sees dawn,
颠倒衣裳。	颠颠倒倒穿衣裳。	You put on clothes upside down.
颠之倒之，	穿反了，穿倒了，	O upside down you put them on,
自公召之。	公爷紧急要召见。	For orders come from ducal crown.
东方未晞③，	东方没有光，	Before the east is bright,

---

① 姝(shū)：美女。② 闼(tà)：门。③ 晞(xī)：破晓的时候。

* The maiden came to the tryst like the eastern sun and left her lover like the eastern moon.

* A toiler complained of the early rise before dawn and the disorder brought by the order of the duke and the supervisor.

颠倒裳衣。	颠颠倒倒穿衣裳。	You take the left sleeve for the right.
倒之颠之，	穿反了，穿倒了，	You put in left sleeve your right arm,
自公令之。	公爷命令心急慌。	For orders bring disorder and alarm.

| 折柳樊圃， | 攀折柳条编园篱， | Don't leave my garden fence with willow tree; |
| 狂夫①瞿瞿②。 | 狂妄监工眼盯着。 | Do not stare at my naked body, please. |

| 不能辰夜， | 白昼黑夜难分清， | You either come too late at night, |
| 不夙则莫。 | 不是凌晨即暮昏。 | Or leave me early in twilight. |

南 山

Incest*

To Duke Xiang of Qi

南山崔崔，	巍巍南山势高峻。	The southern hill is great;
雄狐绥绥③。	雄狐慢慢寻雌狐。	A male fox seeks his mate.
鲁道有荡④，	鲁国大道势平坦，	The way to Lu is plain;

---

① 狂夫：指狂妄的监工。② 瞿瞿(qùqù)：惊惧怒视的样子。③ 绥绥：求偶相随的样子。④ 荡：平坦。

* This was a satire against Duke Xiang of Qi and Duke Huan of Lu. In 708 B. C. Duke Huan married a daughter of Qi, known as Wen Jiang. There was an improper affection between her and her brother, Duke Xiang; and on his succession to Qi, the couple visited him. The consequences were incest between the brother and sister, the murder of the husband and a disgraceful connection, long continued, between the guilty pair. In the first stanza, the great southern hill alluded to the great State of Qi and the male fox seeking his mate alluded contemptuously to Duke Xiang seeking his sister who was going to wed Duke Huan of Lu. In the second stanza, the shoes and strings of gems made in pairs alluded to the union of man and wife. In the third stanza, the ground well prepared for hemp alluded to the preparations for marriage between Duke Huan and Wen Jiang. In the last stanza, the splitting of firewood was a formality in contracting a marriage during the Zhou dynasty.

齐子由归。	齐国女子从此嫁。	Your sister with her train
既曰归止，	既然已经嫁出去，	Goes to wed Duke of Lu.
曷又怀止？	为什么还要想着她？	Why should you go there too?

葛屦五两①，	葛鞋排列排成双，	The shoes are made in pairs
冠绥②双止。	帽带一对双垂下。	And strings of gems she wears.
鲁道有荡，	鲁国大道势平坦，	The way to Lu is plain;
齐子庸止。	齐国女子从此嫁。	Your sister goes to reign
既曰庸止，	既然已经嫁出去，	And wed with Duke of Lu.
曷又从止？	为什么还要盯着她？	Why should you follow her too?

To Duke Huan of Lu

蓺麻如之何？	怎么想要种大麻？	For hemp the ground is ploughed and dressed
衡从其亩。	田亩横纵有其法。	From north to south, from east to west.
取妻如之何？	青年怎么娶妻子？	When a wife comes to your household,
必告父母。	必先告诉父母家。	Your parents should be told.
既曰告止，	已经告诉父母家，	If you told your father and mother,
曷又鞠③止？	为什么还要放纵她？	Should your wife go back to her brother?

析薪如之何？	怎么劈柴砍木头？	How is the firewood split?
匪斧不克。	不用斧头不能做。	An axe can sever it.
取妻如之何？	迎娶妻子靠什么？	How can a wife be won?
匪媒不得。	没有媒人得不到。	With go-between it's done.

---

① 五两：排列成双。② 绥(ruí)：帽带。③ 鞠(jú)：放纵。

| 既曰得止， | 已经娶到妻子了， | To be your wife she's vowed; |
| 曷又极^①止？ | 为什么还要放任她？ | No incest is allowed. |

甫　田　　　　　　　　　Missing Her Son*

无田甫^②田，	不要耕种主家大田，	Don't till too large a ground,
维莠^③骄骄。	只有狗尾草长得高。	Or weed will spread around.
无思远人，	不要想念远方的人，	Don't miss one far away,
劳心忉忉^④。	想念使人更心伤。	Or you'll grieve night and day.

无田甫田，	不要耕种主家大田，	Don't till too large a ground,
维莠桀桀。	只有狗尾草长得旺。	Or weed overgrows around.
无思远人，	不要想念远方的人，	Don't miss the far-off one,
劳心怛怛^⑤。	想念使人更悲伤。	Or your grief won't be done.

婉兮娈兮，	清秀啊漂亮啊，	My son was young and fair
总角丱^⑥兮。	两束小辫像羊角。	With his two tufts of hair.
未几见兮，	不久没有见到他，	Not seen for a short time,
突而弁^⑦兮？	突然戴上成人帽。	He's grown up to his prime.

---

① 极：放任到了极点。② 甫：大。③ 莠：狗尾草。④ 忉忉(dāodāo)：忧伤的样子。
⑤ 怛怛(dádá)：悲伤的样子。⑥ 丱(guàn)：小孩子梳两个辫子，也叫总角。⑦ 弁
(biàn)：帽子。

* It was said that song was written for Wen Jiang of Qi （See the preceding poem）
missing her son who became Duke Zhuang of Lu at the age of thirteen.

卢 令

Hunter and Hounds*

卢①令令，　　猎狗颈铃响当当，
其人美且仁。　那人漂亮好心肠。

The bells of hound
Give ringing sound;
Its master's mind
Is good and kind.

卢重环，　　　猎狗颈铃带双环，
其人美且鬈②。那人漂亮头发卷。

The good hound brings
Its double rings;
Its master's hair
Is curled and fair.

卢重鋂③，　　猎狗颈铃是双铃，
其人美且偲④。那人漂亮又多才。

The good hound brings
Its triple rings;
Its master's beard
Is deep revered.

敝笱

Duchess Wen Jiang of Qi*

敝笱⑤在梁，　破鱼篓在鱼梁上，
其鱼鲂鳏。　　鲂鱼鳏鱼在游荡。
齐子归止，　　齐国的女子回国去，
其从如云。　　前呼后拥云一样。

The basket is worn out
And fishes swim about.
The duchess comes with crowd,
Capricious like the cloud.

敝笱在梁，　　破鱼篓在鱼梁上，

The basket is worn out;

---

① 卢：猎狗。② 鬈(quán)：头发卷曲。③ 鋂(méi)：一大环套两个小环。④ 偲(cāi)：多才。⑤ 笱(gǒu)：鱼篓。

* This was a description of a handsome hunter. It was said that this was a satire against Duke Xiang's wild addiction to handsome to the detriment of public interest.

* The worn-out basket unable to catch fish alluded to Duke Huan of Lu unable to control the bold licentious conduct of his wife Wen Jiang in returning to the State of Qi(See Note on Poem "Incest").

其鱼鲂鲔。	鳊鱼鲢鱼意洋洋。	Bream and tench swim about.
齐子归止,	齐国的女子回国去,	The duchess comes like flower,
其从如雨。	前呼后拥像雨一样。	Inconstant like the shower.

敝笱在梁,	破鱼篓在鱼梁上,	The basket is worn out;
其鱼唯唯①。	鱼儿游来又游往。	Fish swim freely about.
齐子归止,	齐国的女子回国去,	Here comes Duke of Qi's daughter,
其从如水。	前呼后拥像水一样。	Changeable like water.

载 驱　　　　Duke of Qi and Duchess of Lu*

载驱薄薄②,	车马快走拍拍响,	The duke's cab drives ahead
簟③茀④朱鞹⑤。	竹席车帘红皮帐。	With screens of leather red;
鲁道有荡,	鲁国大路真平坦,	The duchess starts her way
齐子发夕。	齐女夜归把车上。	Before the break of day.

四骊⑥济济,	四匹黑马多强壮,	The duke's steeds run amain;
垂辔沵沵⑦。	缰绳垂下多舒畅。	Soft looks their hanging rein.
鲁道有荡,	鲁国大路真平坦,	The duchess speeds her way
齐子岂⑧弟。	齐女乘车天将亮。	At the break of the day.

---

① 唯唯:鱼儿相随游行的样子。② 薄薄:车马走得很快的声音。③ 簟(diàn):竹席。④ 茀(fù):车帘。⑤ 朱鞹(kuò):红色的去毛的兽皮。⑥ 骊(lí):黑色的马。⑦ 沵沵(nǐnǐ):柔和舒畅,指驾技高。⑧ 岂(kǎi)弟:天刚亮。

* This was a satire against the open shamelessness of Duchess of Wen Jiang of Lu in her meeting with her brother, Duke Xiang of Qi. The merry-making might allude to their love-making (See Note on Poem "Incest").

汶水汤汤，	汶水涨得汪洋洋，	The river flows along;
行人彭彭。	路上行人熙攘攘。	Travellers come in throng.
鲁道有荡。	鲁国大路真平坦，	Duke and duchess meet by day
齐子翱翔。	齐女在此闲游逛。	And make merry all the way.
汶水滔滔，	汶水流得浩荡荡，	The river's overflowed
行人儦儦①。	路上行人跄跄跄。	With travellers in crowd.
鲁道有荡，	鲁国大路真平坦，	Duke and duchess all day
齐子游敖。	齐女在此自遨荡。	Make merry all the way.

猗 嗟　　　　　　　　The Archer Duke

猗嗟②昌兮！	啊呀，真精壮啊。	Fairest of all,
颀而长兮！	身材高而长啊。	He's grand and tall,
抑若扬兮！	额头丰满真漂亮啊。	His forehead high
美目扬兮！	眼睛上扬真明亮啊。	With sparkling eye;
巧趋跄③兮！	步伐多矫健啊。	He's fleet of foot
射则臧兮！	射箭多熟练啊。	And skilled to shoot.
猗嗟名兮！	啊呀，真漂亮啊。	His fame is high
美目清兮！	眼目真清澈啊。	With crystal eye;
仪既成兮！	仪容已成就啊。	In brave array

---

① 儦儦(biāobiāo)：人多的样子。② 猗(yī)嗟：赞叹的语气词。③ 趋跄(qiàng)：行走矫健有节奏。

* This song referred to Duke Zhuang of Lu, son of Duchess Wen Jiang and nephew of Duke Xiang of Qi.

终日射侯①,	整日射箭靶啊。	He shoots all day;
不出正②兮!	不出正中心啊。	Each shot a hit,
展③我甥兮!	真是个好外甥啊。	No son's so fit.

猗嗟娈兮!	啊呀,真美好啊。	He's fair and bright
清扬婉兮!	眼睛清澈明媚啊。	With keenest sight;
舞则选④兮!	舞姿多出色啊。	He dances well;
射则贯⑤兮!	射箭中靶心啊。	Each shot will tell;
四矢反⑥兮!	四箭中一点啊。	Four shots right go;
以御乱兮!	用来抵御叛乱啊。	He'll quell the foe.

---

① 侯:箭靶。② 正:箭靶正中心。③ 展:真正的。④ 选:合节拍。⑤ 贯:射中而穿透。
⑥ 反:复,一次次。

魏 风

Songs Collected in Wei, Modern Shanxi

葛 屦

A Well-Drest Lady and Her Maid*

| 纠纠①葛屦， | 缠缠绕绕编草鞋， | In summer shoes with silken lace, |
| 可②以履霜？ | 如何用它踩秋霜？ | A maid walks on frost at quick pace. |

| 掺掺③女手， | 纤纤细细姑娘手， | By slender fingers of the maid |
| 可以缝裳？ | 如何能够缝衣裳？ | Her mistress' beautiful attire is made. |

| 要④之襋⑤之， | 缝好衣纽缝衣领， | The waistband and the collar fair |
| 好人服之。 | 贵人试穿新衣裳。 | Are ready now for her mistress to wear. |

好人提提⑥，	贵人走路好傲慢，	The lady moves with pride;
宛然左辟，	都闪左边把路让。	She turns her head aside
佩其象揥⑦。	象牙簪子头上戴。	With ivory pins in her hair.
维是褊心，	真是偏心不公平，	Against her narrow mind
是以为刺。	因此讽刺把歌唱。	I'll use satire unkind.

---

① 纠纠：缠绕。② 可(hé)：何，怎么。③ 掺掺(xiānxiān)：纤细瘦弱。④ 要(yāo)：衣纽。⑤ 襋(jí)：衣领。⑥ 提提：傲慢的样子。⑦ 揥(tì)：簪子。

* This was a satire against a well-dressed lady and a praise of her sewing maid.

| 汾沮洳 | | A Scholar Unknown* |

彼汾沮洳①，	汾水岸边湿地上，	By riverside, alas!
言采其莫②。	采那里的莫菜忙。	A scholar gathers grass.
彼其之子，	那个采摘莫菜的人，	He gathers grass at leisure,
美无度。	美得难衡量。	Careful beyond measure,
美无度，	美得难衡量，	Beyond measure his grace,
殊异乎公路③。	管公家车的将军比不上。	Why not in a high place?

彼汾一方，	汾水河岸斜坡旁，	By riverside picks he
言采其桑。	采那里的饲蚕桑。	The leaves of mulberry.
彼其之子，	那个采摘蚕桑的人，	Amid the leaves he towers
美如英。	美得如花放。	As brilliant as flowers.
美如英，	美得如花放，	Such brilliancy and beauty,
殊异乎公行④。	管公家战车的将军比不上。	Why not on official duty?

彼汾一曲，	汾水曲曲水湾浜，	By riverside he trips
言采其藚⑤。	采那里的泽泻香。	To gather the ox-tips.
彼其之子，	那个采摘泽泻的人，	His virtue not displayed
美如玉。	美得如玉样。	Like deeply buried jade.
美如玉，	美得如玉样，	His virtue once appears,

---

① 沮洳(jùrù)：低湿地。② 莫：酸模，可以食用。③ 公路：管公家车子的将军。④ 公行：管公家战车的将军。⑤ 藚(xù)：泽泻，可以入药。

* This was a criticism of the State of Wei where only wealthy lords could be high officials while brilliant scholars could only gather grass and leaves without any official duty.

殊异乎公族①。管公家属车的将军比不上。He would surpass his peers.

园有桃　　　　　　　A Scholar Misunderstood*

园有桃，	园中有桃树，	Fruit of peach tree
其实之殽②。	桃子可以吃。	Is used as food.
心之忧矣，	心里很忧伤，	It saddens me
我歌且谣。	只能唱歌谣。	To sing and brood.
不知我者，	不了解我的人，	Who knows me not
谓我"士也骄。	说士人太骄傲。	Says I am proud.
彼人是哉，	那个人说的对吗，	He's right in what?
子曰何其！"	你说又能怎么样？	Tell me aloud.
心之忧矣，	心里忧伤啊，	I'm full of woes
其谁知之？	谁能了解我？	My heart would sink,
其谁知之，	谁能了解我，	But no one knows,
盖亦勿思！	还是不要去想它。	For none will think,

园有棘，	园中有枣树，	Of garden tree
其实之食。	枣子可以吃。	I eat the date.
心之忧矣，	心里很忧伤，	It saddens me
聊以行国。	只能去游荡。	To roam the state.
不知我者，	不了解我的人，	Who knows me not

---

① 公族：管公家属车的将军。② 殽：肴，指可以吃。

* This was another criticism of the State of Wei where unemployed poor scholars used peach and date as food.

谓我"士也罔极①。	说士人太偏激。	Says I am queer.
彼人是哉,	那个人说的对吗,	He's right in what?
子曰何其!"	你说又能怎么样?	O let me hear!
心之忧矣,	心里忧伤啊,	I'm full of woes;
其谁知子?	谁能了解我?	My heart would sink.
其谁知之,	谁能了解我,	But no one knows,
盖亦勿思!	还是不要去想它。	For none will think.

陟 岵②　　　　　A Homesick Soldier*

陟彼岵②兮,	登上那座青山啊,	I climb the hill covered with grass
瞻望父兮。	眺望家中父亲啊。	And look towards where my parents stay.
父曰:"嗟!	父亲好像正在说:"唉,	My father would say, "Alas!
予子行役,	我的儿子在服役。	My son's on service far away;
夙夜无已。	日日夜夜不停歇。	He cannot rest night and day.
上慎旃③哉,	还是千万小心啊,	O may he take good care
犹来无止!"	可以回来不停留。"	To come back and not remain there!"
陟彼屺④兮,	登上那座秃山啊,	I climb the hill devoid of grass
瞻望母兮。	眺望家中母亲啊。	And look towards where my parents stay.

---

① 罔极:无正中之道。② 岵(hù):有草木的山。③ 旃(zhān):之,助词。④ 屺(qǐ):没有草木的山。

* A young soldier on service solaced himself with the thought of home.

母曰:"嗟!	母亲好像正在说:"唉,	My mother would say, "Alas!
予季行役,	我的小儿子在服役,	My youngest son's on service far away;
夙夜无寐。	日日夜夜无安眠。	He cannot sleep well night and day.
上慎旃哉,	还是千万小心啊,	O may he take good care
犹来无弃!"	可以回来不放弃。"	To come back and not be captive there!"

陟彼冈兮,	登上那座山岗啊,	I climb the hilltop green with grass
瞻望兄兮。	眺望家中兄长啊。	And look towards where my brothers stay.
兄曰:"嗟!	兄长好像正在说:"唉,	My eldest brother would say, "Alas!
予弟行役,	我的弟弟在服役,	My youngest brother is on service far away;
夙夜必偕①。	日日夜夜与在人军营里。	He stays with comrades night and day.
上慎旃哉,	还是要小心啊,	O may he take good care
犹来无死!"	可以回来不世弃。"	To come back and not be killed there!"

十亩之间　　　　　　　　　Gathering Mulberry*

十亩之间兮，一块桑园十亩大啊，Among ten acres of mulberry

---

① 偕：与行伍的兄弟们一起。

* This was a song sung by a planter of mulberry trees to a lass after the gathering of mulberries.

桑者闲闲兮。	采桑人儿真悠闲啊。	All the planters are free.
行与子还兮。	我要与你同回去啊。	Why not come back with me?
十亩之外兮，	一块桑园十多亩啊，	Beyond ten acres of mulberry
桑者泄泄①兮。	采桑人儿真自在啊。	All the lasses are free.
行与子逝兮。	我要与你同回去啊。	O come away with me!

伐　檀

The Woodcutter's Song*

坎坎②伐檀兮，	砍伐檀树满山响啊，	Chop, chop our blows on elm-trees go;
寘③之河之干④兮，	把它放在河岸上啊。	On rivershore we pile the wood.
河水清且涟⑤猗。	河水清澈起波澜啊。	The clear and rippling waters flow.
不稼⑥不穑⑦，	不耕种啊不收获，	How can those who nor reap nor sow
胡取禾三百廛⑧兮？	凭什么有禾三百束啊？	Have three hundred sheaves of corn in their place?
不狩⑨不猎，	不上山啊去打猎，	How can those who nor hunt nor chase
胡瞻尔庭有县貆兮？	为什么你的庭内挂貆肉啊？	Have in their courtyard badgers of each race?

---

① 泄泄(yìyì)：轻松自在的样子。② 坎坎：砍伐木头的声音。③ 寘：置，安放。④ 干：河岸。⑤ 涟：风吹形成的水纹。⑥ 稼：种庄稼。⑦ 穑(sè)：收庄稼。⑧ 廛(chán)：束。⑨ 狩(shòu)：冬天打猎。

* This was a satire against those idle and greedy lords of the State.

彼君子兮，	那些君子大人啊，	Those lords are good
不素餐①兮！	全都是在白吃饭啊！	Who do not need work for food!

坎坎伐辐兮，	砍伐檀树制车辐啊，	Chop, chop, our blows for wheel-spokes go；
寘之河之侧兮，	把它放在河边上啊。	By riverside we pile the wood.
河水清且直猗。	河水清激又顺直啊。	The clear and even waters flow.
不稼不穑，	不耕种啊不收获，	How can those who nor reap nor sow
胡取禾三百亿②兮？	凭什么有禾三百束啊？	Have three millions of sheaves in their place?
不狩不猎，	不上山啊去打猎，	How can those who nor hunt nor chase
胡瞻尔庭有县特③兮？	为什么你的庭内挂兽肉啊？	Have in their courtyard games of each race?
彼君子兮，	那些君子大人啊，	Those lords are good
不素食兮！	全都是在白吃饭啊！	Who need no work to eat their food!

坎坎伐轮兮，	砍下檀树做车轮啊，	Chop, chop our blows for the wheels go；
置之河之漘④兮，	把它放在河边上啊。	At river brink we pile the wood.
河水清且沦⑤猗。	河水清激起微澜啊。	The clear and dimpling waters flow.

---

①素餐：白吃饭，不劳而食。②亿：束。③特：野兽。④漘(chún)：河岸。⑤沦：水上的微波。

不稼不穑，	不耕种啊不收获，	How can those who nor reap nor sow
胡取禾三百囷①兮？	凭什么有禾三百囷啊？	Have three hundred ricks of corn in their plaee?
不狩不猎，	不上山啊去打猎，	How can those who nor hunt nor chase
胡瞻尔庭有县鹑兮？	为什么你的庭内挂着鹌鹑肉啊？	Have in their courtyard winged games of each race?
彼君子兮，	那些君子大人啊，	Those lords are good
不素飧②兮。	全都是在白吃饭啊！	Who do not have to work for food!

硕③鼠

Large Rat*

硕鼠硕鼠，	大老鼠啊大老鼠，	Large rat, large rat,
无食我黍！	不要吃我种的黍。	Eat no more millet we grow!
三岁贯④女，	三年辛苦养活你，	Three years you have grown fat;
莫我肯顾。	你却没有顾及我。	No care for us you show.
逝⑤将去⑥女，	发誓从此离开你，	We'll leave you now, I swear,
适⑦彼乐土。	到那理想乐土去。	For a happier land,
乐土乐土，	乐土啊乐土，	A happier land where
爰得我所！	才是我的好归处！	We may have a free hand.
硕鼠硕鼠，	大老鼠啊大老鼠，	Large rat, large rat,

---

① 囷(qūn)：捆。② 飧(sūn)：晚餐。③ 硕：大。④ 贯：养活。⑤ 逝：发誓。⑥ 去：离开。⑦ 适：往，到。

* The large rat was symbolic of the corrupt official and the happier land or state was a Utopia of the peasants.

无食我麦！	不要吃我种的麦。	Eat no more wheat we grow!
三岁贯女，	三年辛苦养活你，	Three years you have grown fat;
莫我肯德。	你却没有些感激。	No kindness to us you show.
逝将去女，	发誓从此离开你，	We'll leave you now, I swear,
适彼乐国。	到那理想乐国去。	For a happier state,
乐国乐国，	乐国啊乐国，	A happier state where
爰得我直①！	才能劳而有所获！	We can decide our fate。

硕鼠硕鼠，	大老鼠啊大老鼠，	Large rat, large rat,
无食我苗！	不要吃我种的苗。	Eat no more rice we grow!
三岁贯女，	三年辛苦养活你，	Three years you have grown fat;
莫我肯劳②。	却没有些慰劳。	No rewards to our labor go.
逝将去女，	发誓从此离开你，	We'll leave you now, I swear,
适彼乐郊。	到那理想乐郊去。	For a happier plain,
乐郊乐郊，	乐郊啊乐郊，	A happier plain where
谁之永号！	抒发郁闷长长呼号！	None will groan or complain.

---

① 直：价值。② 劳：慰劳。

唐　风

Songs Collected in Tang, Modern Shanxi

蟋　蟀

The Cricket*

蟋蟀在堂，	蟋蟀已经入堂屋，	The cricket chirping in the hall,
岁聿其莫①。	一年就要过完了。	The year will pass away.
今我不乐，	今天我不及时乐，	The present not enjoyed at all,
日月其除②。	时光将去不复返。	We'll miss the passing day.
无已大康③，	不要过分地行乐，	Do not enjoy to excess
职④思其居⑤。	常思地位和责任。	But do our duty with delight!
好乐无荒，	寻乐不能荒正业，	We'll enjoy ourselves none the less
良士瞿瞿⑥。	良士警惕事变化。	If we see those at left and right.

蟋蟀在堂，	蟋蟀已经入堂屋，	The cricket chirping in the hall,
岁聿其逝⑦。	一年就要结束了。	The year will go away.
今我不乐，	今天我不及时乐，	The present not enjoyed at all,
日月其迈⑧。	时光将逝不复还。	We'll miss the bygone day.
无已大康，	不要过分地行乐，	Do not enjoy to excess
职思其外。	常思地位和责任。	But only to the full extent!
好乐无荒，	寻乐不能荒正业，	We'll enjoy ourselves none the less

---

① 莫：暮，晚。② 除：流逝，过去。③ 大康：安乐康泰。④ 职：常。⑤ 居：所处的地位，所处之事。⑥ 瞿瞿：警惕四顾的样子。⑦ 逝：过去。⑧ 迈：消逝。

* We might see in this song the cheerfulness and discretion of the people of Jin and their tempered enjoyment at fitting seasons.

良士蹶蹶①。	良士努力勤做事。	If we are diligent.

蟋蟀在堂，	蟋蟀已经入堂屋，	The cricket chirping by the door，
役车其休。	服役的车儿停下了。	Our cart stands unemployed.
今我不乐，	今天我不及时乐，	The year will be no more
日月其慆②。	时光将永不再来。	With the days unenjoyed.
无已大康。	不要过分地行乐，	Do not enjoy to excess
职思其忧。	常思谋事多有忧。	But think of hidden sorrow!
好乐无荒，	寻乐不能荒正业，	We'll enjoy ourselves none the less
良士休休③。	良士安然心坦荡。	If we think of tomorrow.

山有枢　　　　　　　　　Why Not Enjoy?＊

山有枢，	山上有枢树，	Uphill you have elm-trees；
隰有榆。	洼地有榆树。	Downhill you have elms white.
子有衣裳，	你有上衣和下裙，	You have dress as you please.
弗曳④弗娄⑤。	不穿也不著。	Why not wear it with delight?
子有车马，	你有车辆和马匹，	You have horses and car.
弗驰弗驱。	不驾也不赶。	Why don't you take a ride?
宛⑥其死矣，	要是一天死去了，	One day when dead you are，
他人是愉。	别人一定很高兴。	Others will drive them with pride.

---

① 蹶蹶(guìguì)：敏捷奋进的样子。② 慆(tāo)：逝去。③ 休休：安然自得的样子。
④ 曳(yè)：拖。⑤ 娄：提。⑥ 宛：枯萎。

＊ This was a satire on the folly of not enjoying the good things and letting death put them into the hands of others.

山有栲，	山上有栲树，	Uphill you've varnish trees;
隰有杻。	洼地有杻树。	Downhill trees rooted deep.
子有廷①内，	你有庭院和内室，	You have rooms as you please.
弗洒弗扫。	不洒水也不扫地。	Why not clean them and sweep?
子有钟鼓，	你有大钟和大鼓，	You have your drum and bell.
弗鼓弗考②。	不打也不敲。	Why don't you beat and ring?
宛其死矣，	要是一天死去了，	One day when tolls your knell,
他人是保③。	别人一定来占有。	Joy to others they'll bring.

山有漆，	山上有漆树，	Uphill you've chestnut trees;
隰有栗。	洼地有栗树。	Downhill trees with deep root.
子有酒食，	你有酒和菜，	You have wine as you please.
何不日鼓瑟。	何不每天弹琴瑟。	Why not play lyre and lute
且以喜乐，	就这样求欢乐，	To be cheerful and gay
且以永日。	就这样度时日。	And to prolong your bloom?
宛其死矣，	要是一天死去了，	When you are dead one day,
他人入室。	别人一定进堂屋。	Others will enter your room.

扬之水　　　　　　　　　　Our Prince*

扬之水，	舒缓不息的河水，	The clear stream flows ahead
白石凿凿④。	河水中白石鲜明。	And the white rocks out stand.

---

① 廷：庭院。② 考：打击。③ 保：占有。④ 凿凿：鲜明的样子。

* The prince referred to the uncle of Marquis Zhao of Jin, who was raised by a rebellious party to displace the Marquis in 73 B. C. The rocks were symbolic of the conspirators and the speaker was an adherent of the conspiracy who bad heard the secret order to conspire against Marquis Zhao of Jin.

素衣朱襮①，	身着素净的红领征衣，	In our plain dress with collars red,
从子于沃。	大家相送你到曲沃。	We follow you to eastern land.
既见君子，	已经看到君子了，	Shall we not rejoice since
云何不乐？	怎不内心喜若狂。	We have seen our dear prince?

扬之水，	舒缓不息的河水，	The clear stream flows ahead
河水中白石皓皓。	河水中白石晧洁。	And naked rocks out stand.
素衣朱绣，	身着素净的红领征衣，	In plain dress with sleeves broidered red,
从子于鹄。	大家相送你到鹄邑。	We follow you to northern land.
既见君子，	已经看到君子了，	How can we feel sad since
云何其忧？	又有何值得去忧伤。	We have seen our dear prince?

扬之水，	舒缓不息的河水，	The clear stream flows along the border;
白石粼粼②。	河水中白石清澄。	Wave-beaten rocks stand out.
我闻有命，	我听说将有命令，	We've heard the secret order,
不敢以告人。	如何敢把它告诉别人。	But nothing should be talked about.

椒 聊③　　　　　The Pepper Plant*

椒聊之实，	串串花椒的种子，	The fruit of pepper plant
蕃衍盈升。	繁多得超过一升。	Is so luxuriant.

---

① 襮(bó)：绣有图案的衣领。② 粼粼：清澈澄明的样子。③ 椒聊：花椒的种子多成串。

* The productive pepper plant referred to a reproductive or fertile woman. That is the reason why a woman's bedroom was called pepper chamber in Chinese.

彼其之子，	那个妇人子孙多，	The woman there
硕大无朋①。	魁梧高大无人能比。	Is large beyond compare.
椒聊且!	像一串串花椒啊，	O pepper plant, extend
远条②且!	香味悠远啊。	Your shoots without end!
椒聊之实，	串串花椒的种子，	The pepper plant there stands;
蕃衍盈匊③。	繁多得超过一捧。	Its fruit will fill our hands.
彼其之子，	那个妇人子孙多，	The woman here
硕大且笃。	魁梧高大忠实敦厚。	Is large without a peer.
椒聊且!	像一串串花椒啊，	O pepper plant, extend
远条且!	香味悠远啊。	Your shoots without end!

绸 缪　　　　　　　　　A Wedding Song*

绸缪④束薪，	捆好柴薪，	The firewood's tightly bound
三星⑤在天。	参星在天上。	When in the sky three stars appear.
今夕何夕，	今夜是什么日子?	What evening's coming round
见此良人?	能看到这个好人。	For me to find my bridegroom here!
子兮子兮，	你啊你啊，	O he is here! O he is here!
如此良人何?	像你这样的好人该怎么办啊?	What shall I not do with my dear!

---

① 无朋:无比。② 远条:长远,悠远。③ 匊(jū):两手合捧。④ 绸缪(chóumóu):缠绵,捆好。⑤ 三星:指参星。

* The firewood or hay or thorns tightly bound alluded to husband and wife well united. The first stanza should be sung by the bride, the second by the guests and the third by the bridegroom.

绸缪束刍①，　捆好青草，　　　　The hay is tightly bound
三星在隅。　　参星在屋角。　　　When o'er the house three stars
　　　　　　　　　　　　　　　　　　　appear.

今夕何夕，　　今夜是什么日子？　What night is coming round
见此邂逅②？　能够不约而遇。　　To find this couple here!
子兮子兮，　　你啊你啊，　　　　O they are here! O they are here!
如此邂逅何？　像这样不约而遇该　How lucky to see this couple dear!
　　　　　　　　怎么办啊？

绸缪束楚，　　捆好荆条，　　　　The thorns are tightly bound
三星在户。　　参星在门上。　　　When o'er the door three stars
　　　　　　　　　　　　　　　　　　　appear.

今夕何夕，　　今夜是什么日子？　What midnight's coming round
见此粲者③？　能看到这个美人。　For me to find my beauty here!
子兮子兮，　　你啊你啊，　　　　O she is here! O she is here!
如此粲者何？　像你这样的美人该　What shall I not do with my dear?
　　　　　　　　怎么办啊？

杕　杜　　　　　　　　　　　　A Wanderer

有杕④之杜，　孤独的赤棠，　　　A tree of russet pear
其叶湑湑⑥。　叶子繁茂。　　　　Has leaves so thickly grown.
　　　　　　　　　　　　　　　　　Alone I wander there

---

① 刍(chú)：青草。② 邂逅：不约而遇。③ 粲者：指前面说的"良人"。④ 杕(dì)：特立的样子。⑤ 杜：赤棠。⑥ 湑湑(xǔxǔ)：繁茂的样子。

* This was the lament of a beggar deprived of his brothers and relatives or forsaken by them.

独行踽踽①，	孤独地行走，	With no friends of my own.
岂无他人？	难道没有别人？	Is there no one
		Who would of me take care?
不如我同父②。	不像我同族的兄弟亲。	But there is none
嗟行之人，	独行叹息的人，	Like my own father's son.
胡不比③焉？	为什么没有人做伴？	O wanderer, why are there few
人无兄弟，	人要是没有兄弟，	To sympathize with you?
胡不佽④焉？	谁与他同甘共苦？	Can yon not find another
		To help you like a brother?
有杕之杜，	孤独的赤棠，	A tree of russet pear
其叶菁菁。	叶子茂盛。	Has leaves so lushly grown.
独行睘睘⑤，	孤独地行走，	Alone I loiter there
岂无他人？	难道没有别人？	Without a kinsman of my own.
不如我同姓。	不像我同族的兄弟亲。	Is there no one
嗟行之人，	独行叹息的人，	Who would take care of me?
胡不比焉？	为什么没有人做伴？	But there is none
人无兄弟，	人要是没有兄弟，	Like my own family.
胡不佽焉？	谁与他同甘共苦？	O loiterer, why are there few
		To sympathize with you?
		Can you not find another
		To help you like a brother?

羔裘　　　　　　An Unkind Lord in Lamb's Fur*

羔裘豹祛⑥，	羊皮袍子豹皮袖，	Lamb's fur and leopard's cuff,
自我人居居⑦。	对人傲慢态度差。	To us you are so rough.

---

① 踽踽(jǔjǔ)：孤独的样子。② 同父：同一个祖父的兄弟。③ 比：辅助。④ 佽(cì)：帮助。⑤ 睘睘(qióngqióng)：孤独的样子。⑥ 祛(qū)：袖子。⑦ 居居：同"裾裾"，恶劣。

* The people of some lord complained of his hard treatment of them.

岂无他人？	难道没有其他大人，	Can't we find another chief
维子之故！	只是与你念及情谊。	Who would cause us no grief?

羔裘豹褎①，	羊皮袍子豹皮袖，	Lamb's fur and leopard's cuff,
自我人究究。	对人傲慢态度差。	You ne'er give us enough.
岂无他人？	难道没有其他大人，	Can't we find another chief
维子之好！	只是念及你我旧交！	Who would assuage our grief?

鸨 羽

The Peasants' Complaint*

肃肃②鸨羽，	鸨鸟展翅沙沙响，	Swish, swish sound the plumes of wild geese;
集③于苞④栩。	停在丛生柞树上。	They can't alight on bushy trees.
王事靡盬⑤，	国王的差事无休止，	We must discharge the king's affair.
不能蓺⑥稷黍，	不能回家种稷黍。	How can we plant our millet with care?
父母何怙⑦？	靠什么养活父母？	On what can our parents rely?
悠悠苍天！	悠远的苍天啊，	O gods in boundless, endless sky,
曷其有所？	什么时候才能回家乡？	When can we live in peace? I sigh.

---

① 褎(xiù)：袖子。② 肃肃：鸨鸟展翅飞的声音。③ 集：群鸟停歇在树上。④ 苞：丛生。
⑤ 盬(gǔ)：停歇。⑥ 蓺(yì)：种植。⑦ 怙(hù)：依靠。

* The men of Jin called out to warfare by the king's order mourned over the consequent suffering of their parents and longed for their return to their ordinary agricultural pursuits.

肃肃鸨翼，	鸨鸟展翅沙沙响，	Swish, swish flap the wings of wild geese;
集于苞棘。	停在丛生枣树上。	They can't alight on jujube trees.
王事靡盬，	国王的差事做不完，	We must discharge the king's affair.
不能蓺黍稷，	不能回家种黍稷。	How can we plant our maize with care?
父母何食？	父母靠什么吃饭？	On what can our parents live and rely?
悠悠苍天！	悠远的苍天啊，	O gods in boundless, endless sky,
曷其有极？	什么时候才能结束？	Can all this end before I die?
肃肃鸨行，	鸨鸟展翅沙沙响，	Swish, swish come the rows of wild geese;
集于包桑。	停在丛生桑树上。	They can't alight on mulberries.
王事靡盬，	国王的差事永忙繁，	We must discharge the king's affair.
不能蓺稻粱，	不能回家种稻粱。	How can we plant our rice with care?
父母何尝？	父母用何去果腹？	What can our parents have for food?
悠悠苍天！	悠远的苍天啊，	O Heaven good, O Heaven good!
曷其有常？	什么时候才能得安康？	When can we gain a livelihood?

无 衣　　　　　　　　　　To His Deceased Wife*

岂曰无衣七兮？　怎么说我没有七套　　Have I no dress?
　　　　　　　　衣裳？　　　　　　You made me seven.
不如子之衣，　　只是不像你的衣裳，　I'm comfortless,
安且吉兮！　　　舒适又漂亮。　　　　Now you're in heaven.

岂曰无衣六兮？　怎么说我没有六套　　Have I no dress?
　　　　　　　　衣裳？　　　　　　You made me six.
不如子之衣，　　只是不像你的衣裳，　I'm comfortless
安且燠①兮！　　舒服又暖和。　　　　As if on pricks.

有杕之杜　　　　　　　　　The Russet Pear Tree*

有杕之杜，　　一棵孤伶的赤棠，　　A lonely tree of russet pear
生于道左。　　长在路的左旁。　　　Stands still on the left of the way.
彼君子兮，　　那个君子人啊，　　　O you for whom I care,
噬②肯适我？　可会来到我这边？　　Won't you come as I pray?
中心好之，　　心中那么喜欢他，　　In my heart you're so sweet.
曷饮食之？　　怎不备好酒菜款　　　When may I give you food to eat?
　　　　　　　待他？

有杕之杜，　　一棵孤伶的赤棠，　　A lonely tree of russet pear

---

① 燠(yù)：暖和。② 噬(shì)：何，怎么。

* The speaker was thinking of his deceased wife who had made his dress for him.

* The russet pear tree was said to be symbolic of a lonely woman longing for her lover.

生于道周①。	长在路的右旁。	Stands still on the road's right-hand side.
彼君子兮，	那个君子人啊，	O you for whom I care,
噬肯来游？	可会逛到我这边。	Won't you come for a ride?
中心好之，	心中那么喜欢他，	In my heart you're so sweet.
曷饮食之？	怎不备好酒菜款待他？	When may I give you food to eat?

葛　生

An Elegy*

葛生蒙②楚，	葛藤缠绕荆条，	Vine grows o'er the thorn tree;
蔹③蔓于野。	白蔹蔓延荒郊。	Weeds in the field o'erspread.
予美亡此，	我爱的人逝这里，	The man I love is dead.
谁与独处！	谁让我一个人孤独自守。	Who'd dwell alone with thee?

葛生蒙棘，	葛藤缠绕枣树，	Vine grows o'er jujube tree;
蔹蔓于域④。	白蔹蔓延荒郊。	Weeds o'er the graveyard spread.
予美亡此，	我爱的人逝这里，	The man I love is dead.
谁与独息！	谁让我一个人独自息睡。	Who'd stay alone with thee?

---

① 周：右。② 蒙：覆盖。③ 蔹(liǎn)：白蔹，一种植物，根可以药用。④ 域：坟地。

* This was the first elegy in Chinese poetry. A widow mourned the death of her husband killed in the war waged by Duke Xian of Jin (reigned 675–650 B.C.). The vine supported by the tree might be suggestive of the widow's own desolate, unsupported condition or descriptive of the battleground where her husband had met his death.

角枕粲兮，	牛角枕鲜明啊，	How fair the pillow of horn
锦衾烂兮。	锦绣被绚烂啊。	And the embroidered bed!
予美亡此，	我爱的人逝这里，	The man I love is dead.
谁与独旦。	谁让我一个人独守到天亮。	Who'd stay with thee till morn?

夏之日，	夏天的日长，	Long is the summer day;
冬之夜。	冬天的夜长。	Cold winter night appears.
百岁之后，	百年以后，	After a hundred years
归于其居①！	我要与他相会在坟场。	In the same fomb we'd stay.

冬之夜，	冬天的夜长，	The winter night is cold;
夏之日。	夏天的日长。	Long is the summer day.
百岁之后，	百年以后，	When I have passed away,
归于其室②！	我要与他墓中相依傍。	We'll be in same household.

采 苓③　　　　　　　　　　Rumor*

采苓采苓，	采甘草啊采甘草，	Could the sweet water plant be found
首阳之颠。	在首阳山顶找。	On the top of the mountain high?
人之为④言，	别人说的假话，	The rumor going round,
苟⑤亦无信。	真的不要相信。	If not believed can't fly.

---

① 居：坟墓。② 室：坟坑。③ 苓：甘草。④ 为：伪，假的。⑤ 苟：真的。

* This was directed against Duke Xian of Jin who killed his son on believing rumors. Rumors should no more be believed than water plants could be found on the top of the mountain.

舍旃舍旃①，	放弃它放弃它，	Put it aside, put it aside
苟亦无然。	那些全都不可靠。	So that it can't prevail.
人之为言，	别人的话，	The rumor spreading far and wide
胡得焉!	能得到什么呢?	Will be of no avail.
采苦采苦，	采苦菜啊采苦菜，	Could bitter water plant be found
首阳之下。	在首阳山下找。	At the foot of the mountain high?
人之为言，	别人说的假话，	The rumor going round
苟亦无与②。	真的不要赞同。	Is what we should deny.
舍旃舍旃，	放弃它放弃它，	Put it aside, put it aside
苟亦无然。	那些全都不可靠。	So that it can't prevail.
人之为言，	别人的话，	The rumor spreading far and wide
胡得焉!	能得到什么呢?	Will be of no avail.
采葑采葑，	采芜菁啊采芜菁，	Could water plants be found
首阳之东。	在首阳山东找。	East of the mountain high?
人③之为言，	别人说的假话，	The rumor going round,
苟亦无从。	真的不要听从。	If disregarded, will die.
舍旃舍旃，	放弃它放弃它，	Put it aside, put it aside
苟亦无然。	那些全都不可靠。	So that it can't prevail.
人之为言!	别人的话，	The rumor spreading far and wide
胡得焉!	能得到什么呢?	Will be of no avail.

---

① 旃(zhān):之,代指假话。② 与:理会。③ 人:听从。

秦 风

Songs Collected in Qin, Modern Shaanxi

车 邻

Lord Zhong of Qin*

有车邻邻①，	有车走过响辚辚，	The cab bells ring;
有马白颠，	有马额顶是白色。	Dappled steeds neigh.
未见君子，	没有看见君子人，	"Let ushers bring
寺人②之令。	只是宦官传命令。	In friends so gay!"

阪有漆，	山坡种漆树，	There're varnish trees uphill
隰有栗。	洼地种栗树。	And chestnuts in lowland.
既见君子，	已经见到君子人，	Friends see Lord Zhong sit still
并坐鼓瑟。	和他并坐来弹瑟。	Beside lute-playing band.
"今者不乐，	"今天不及时行乐，	"If we do not enjoy taday,
逝者其耋③！"	转眼就会变老翁。"	At eighty joy will pass away."

阪有桑，	山坡种桑树，	There're mulberries uphill
隰有杨。	洼地种杨树。	And willows in lowland.
既见君子，	已经见到君子人，	Friends see Lord Zhong sit still
并坐鼓簧。	和他并坐吹笙簧。	Beside his music band.

---

① 邻邻：辚辚声。② 寺人：宦官。③ 耋(dié)：八十岁。

* This song celebrated the pleasures of Lord Zhong of Qin, who, made a great officer of the court by King Xuan in 826 B. C., began to turn Qin from a barbarian state to a music-loving civilized one, which unified China and founded the Empire of Qin in 221 B. C.

"今者不乐，	"今天不及时行乐，	"If we do not enjoy today,
逝者其亡！"	转眼就会死去。"	We'll regret when life ebbs away."

驷 驖①   Winter Hunting*

驷驖孔阜②，	四匹肥马毛色黑，	Holding in hand six reins
六辔在手。	六根缰绳握在手。	Of four iron-black steeds,
公之媚子③，	公爷宠爱的那人，	Our lord hunts on the plains
从公于狩。	跟从公爷去打猎。	With good hunters he leads.
奉④时辰牡⑤，	供奉应时的野兽，	The male and female preys
辰牡孔硕。	肥大的野兽到处有。	Have grown to sizes fit.
公曰左之，	公爷命令车向左，	"Shoot at the left!" he says;
舍拔⑥则获。	一箭射中那猎物。	Their arrows go and hit.
游于北园，	游猎在北园，	He comes to northern park
四马既闲。	四马驾车很熟练。	With his four steeds at leisure;
輶⑦车鸾镳⑧，	轻车鸾铃马衔镳，	Long-and short-mouthed hounds bark
载猃⑨歇骄⑩。	众犬车马间。	In the carriage of pleasure.

---

① 驷驖(tiě)：四匹黑马。② 阜：肥大。③ 媚子：宠爱的人。④ 奉：供奉，敬献。⑤ 辰牡：应时的公兽。⑥ 舍拔：射箭。⑦ 輶(yóu)车：轻车。⑧ 镳(biāo)：马嚼子两端露出嘴外的部分。⑨ 猃(xiǎn)：长嘴猎狗。⑩ 歇骄：短嘴猎狗。

* This song celebrated the growing opulence of Duke Xiang, grandson of Lord Zhong of Qin, as seen in his hunting in 769 B. C.

小 戎①   A Lord on Expedition*

小戎俴②收，	小兵车又小车厢，	His chariot finely bound,
五楘③梁辀④。	五皮革穿铜环绕车毂。	Crisscrossed with straps around,
游环胁驱⑤，	活动的环圈控制骖马，	Covered with tiger's skin,
阴靷⑥鋈⑦续。	革带穿铜环使骖马就范。	Driven by horses twin;
文茵⑧畅⑨毂⑩，	虎皮垫铺在长毂车上，	His steeds controlled with reins
驾我骐⑪馵⑫。	驾车的青马后腿白色。	Through slip rings like gilt chains;
言念君子，	我想念那君子人啊，	I think of my lord dear
温其如玉。	温和得像玉一样。	Far-off on the frontier;
在其板屋，	他从军住在板木屋，	He's pure as jade and plain.
乱我心曲。	想他想得我心里乱。	O my heart throbs with pain.
四牡孔阜，	四匹雄马真肥大，	His four fine steeds there stand;
六辔在手。	六根缰绳拿在手。	He holds six reins in hand.
骐馏⑬是中，	两匹赤身黑鬣的服马在中间，	The insides have black mane,
騧⑭骊是骖。	两匹黄身黑嘴的骖马在两边。	Yellow the outside twain.

① 小戎:小兵车。② 俴(jiàn):浅。③ 五楘(mù):五束连络的皮革。④ 梁辀(zhōu):弯曲如船的车辕。⑤ 胁驱:驾马的用具。⑥ 阴靷(yǐn):系骖马的革带。⑦ 鋈(wù):白铜环。⑧ 文茵:虎皮垫。⑨ 畅:长。⑩ 毂(gǔ):车轮中的圆木,中有圆孔,可以插轴。⑪ 骐:青黑色的马。⑫ 馵(zhù):后左足白色的马。⑬ 馏(liú):赤身黑鬣的马。⑭ 騧(guā):黄身黑嘴的马。

* The wife of a Qin lord absent on an expedition against the western tribes who killed King You of Zhou in 771 B.C., gave a glowing description of his chariot, steeds and weapons and expressed her regret at his absence.

龙盾①之合，	画龙的盾牌双双合在车前面，	Dragon shields on two wings,
鋈以觼軜②。	银环把骖马的内缰绳来串联。	Buckled up as with strings.
言念君子，	我想念的那君子人啊，	I think of my lord dear
温其在邑。	温和在邑可以为友。	So good on the frontier.
方何为期，	什么时候才能回来啊，	When will he come to me?
胡然我念之。	叫我怎么不想他啊。	Can I be yearning-free?

俴驷③孔群④，	薄金甲的四匹马多威风，	How fine his team appears!
厹⑤矛鋈錞⑥。	三隅矛杆套装着白银镦。	How bright his trident spears!
蒙伐⑦有苑⑧，	盾牌上画着鸟羽纹，	His shield bears a carved face;
虎韔⑨镂膺⑩。	刻金的虎皮弓囊雕刻纹。	In tiger's skin bow-case
交韔二弓，	两弓交错在弓囊中，	With bamboo frames and bound
竹闭⑪绲⑫縢⑬。	竹制弓檠绳索捆。	With strings, two bows are found.

言念君子，	我想念那君子人啊，	I think of my dear mate,
载寝载兴。	早起晚睡不安宁。	Rise early and sleep late.
厌厌⑭良人，	那温良文静的人啊，	My dear, dear one,
秩秩德音。	明慧有礼贤德行。	Can I forget the good you've done?

---

①龙盾：画有龙形的盾。②觼軜(juénà)：有舌环穿过骖马的皮带，使内辔固定。③俴驷：披薄金甲的四匹马。④孔群：很合群。⑤厹(qiú)矛：三棱锋刃的矛。⑥鋈錞(wùduì)：用白铜镀矛柄底的金属套。⑦伐：盾牌。⑧苑：文彩。⑨虎韔(chàng)：用虎皮做的弓囊。⑩镂膺：刻纹。⑪闭：弓檠。⑫绲(gǔn)：绳。⑬縢：缠束。⑭厌厌：安静的样子。

蒹葭①   Where Is She? *

蒹葭苍苍，	初生的芦苇色青苍，	Green, green the reed,
白露为霜。	夜来白露凝成霜。	Frost and dew gleam
所谓伊人，	所说的那个人，	Where's she I need?
在水一方。	在水的那一方。	Beyond the stream.
溯洄②从之，	逆水而上去找她，	Upstream I go;
道阻且长；	道路崎岖长又长，	The way's so long.
溯游③从之，	顺流而下去寻她，	And downstream, lo!
宛在水中央。	仿佛在那水中央。	She's thereamong.

蒹葭萋萋，	芦苇长得很茂盛，	White, white the reed,
白露未晞④。	路上白露还未干。	Dew not yet dried.
所谓伊人，	所说的那个人，	Where's she I need?
在水之湄⑤。	在那水草滩。	On the other side.
溯洄从之，	逆水而上去找她，	Upstream I go;
道阻且跻；	道路崎岖难攀登，	Hard is the way.
溯游从之，	顺流而下去寻她，	And downstream, lo!
宛在水中坻⑥。	仿佛在那水中沙滩。	She's far away.

蒹葭采采，	芦苇长得连成片，	Bright, bright the reed,
白露未已。	路上白露没有干。	With frost dews blend.

---

①蒹葭:初生的芦苇。②溯洄:逆流而上。③溯游:顺流而下。④晞(xī):干。⑤湄(méi):水草相杂的地方。⑥坻(chí):水中的小高地。

* This was said to be the first symbolic love song in Chinese poetry.

所谓伊人，	所说的那个人，	Where's she I need?
在水之涘①。	在水的那一岸。	At river's end.
溯洄从之，	逆水而上去找她，	Upstream I go;
道阻且右；	道路崎岖弯又弯，	The way does wind.
溯游从之，	顺流而下去寻她，	And downstream, lo!
宛在水中沚②。	仿佛在那水中小洲。	She's far behind.

终 南   Duke Xiang of Qin*

终南何有？	终南山上长什么？	What's on the southern hill?
有条③有梅。	有山楸树有红梅。	There're mume trees and white firs.
君子至止，	君子来到这里住，	Our lord comes and stands still,
锦衣狐裘。	穿着锦衣和狐裘。	Wearing a robe and furs.
颜如渥丹，	面目丰满又红润，	Vermillion is his face.
其君也哉！	真是尊贵好君王。	O what majestic grace!

终南何有？	终南山上长什么？	What's on the southern hill?
有纪④有堂⑤。	有杞树又有赤棠。	There are trees of white pears.
君子至止，	君子来到这里住，	Our lord comes and stands still;
黻⑥衣绣裳。	穿着锦衣和绣裳。	A broidered robe he wears.
佩玉将将，	佩戴美玉响叮响，	His gems give tinkling sound.

---

① 涘(sì)：水边。② 沚(zhǐ)：水中的沙洲。③ 条：小楸树。④ 纪：杞树。⑤ 堂：赤棠树。⑥ 黻(fú)：绣着青黑色。

* This song celebrated the dignity of Duke Xiang of Qin, the first of Qin lords recognized as a prince of the kingdom, who, wearing the black ducal robe conferred by King Ping in 769 B.C. after his victory over the western tribes who had killed King You in 771 B.C., passed by the Southern Mountain 25 killometres south of the capital (modern Xi'an) on his homeward way to Qin.

寿考不忘！　　祝你长寿永安康。　　Long live our lord black-gowned!

黄　鸟　　　　　　　　　Burial of Three Worthies*

交交①黄鸟，	黄鸟交交叫，	The golden orioles flew
止于棘。	停在枣树上。	And lit on jujube tree.
谁从②穆公？	谁从穆公去陪葬？	Who's buried with Duke Mu?
子车奄息。	子车氏叫奄息的人。	The eldest of the three.
维此奄息，	这个奄息，	This eldest worthy son
百夫之特③。	才德百人比不上。	Could be rivaled by none.
临其穴，	走近他的墓穴，	Coming to the graveside,
惴惴其栗。	浑身战栗心里慌。	Who'd not be terrified?
彼苍者天，	那苍天啊，	O good Heavens on high,
歼④我良人！	杀我的好人！	Why should the worthy die?
如可赎兮，	如果可以赎他的命啊，	If he could live again,
人百其身！	人愿意死百次来抵偿。	Who not have been slain?

交交黄鸟，	黄鸟交交叫，	The golden oriole flew
止于桑。	停在桑树上。	And lit on mulberry.
谁从穆公？	谁从穆公去陪葬？	Who's buried with Duke Mu?
子车仲行。	子车氏叫仲行的人。	The second of the three.
维此仲行，	这个仲行，	The second worthy son
百夫之防⑤。	才德百人难能比。	Could be equalled by none.

① 交交：黄鸟鸣叫的声音。② 从：从死，陪葬。③ 特：杰出。④ 歼：灭亡，杀害。
⑤ 防：抵挡。

* The three worthies were buried alive together with 174 others in the same grave with Duke Mu of Qin in 620 B. C. They were not so free as the golden oriole.

临其穴，	走近他的墓穴，	Coming to the graveside,
惴惴其栗。	浑身战栗心里慌。	Who'd not be terrified?
彼苍者天，	那苍天啊，	O good Heavens on high,
歼我良人！	杀我的好人！	Why should the worthy die?
如可赎兮，	如果可以赎他的命啊，	If he could live again,
人百其身！	人愿意死百次来抵偿。	Who would not have been slain?

交交黄鸟，	黄鸟交交叫，	The golden oriole flew
止于楚。	停在荆条上。	And lit on the thorn tree.
谁从穆公？	谁从穆公去陪葬？	Who's buried with Duke Mu?
子车鍼虎。	子车氏叫鍼虎的人。	The youngest of the three.
维此鍼虎，	这个鍼虎，	The youngest worthy son
百夫之御①。	才德百人没他强。	Could be surpassed by none.
临其穴，	走近他的墓穴，	Coming to the graveside,
惴惴其栗。	浑身战栗心里慌。	Who'd not be terrified?
彼苍者天，	那苍天啊，	O good Heavens on high,
歼我良人！	杀我的好人！	Why should the worthy die?
如可赎兮，	如果可以赎他的命啊，	If he could live again,
人百其身！	人愿意死百次来抵偿。	Who would not have been slain?

晨　风　　　　　　　　　　The Forgotten*

鴥②彼晨风③，	晨风鸟飞得急，	The falcon flies above
郁彼北林。	北林树长得密。	To the thick northern wood.

---

① 御:抵挡。② 鴥(yù):鸟儿疾飞的样子。③ 晨风:鸟名。

* A wife told her grief because of the absence of her husband and his forgetfulness of her.

未见君子，	没有见到君子人，	While I see not my love,
忧心钦钦①。	我的心里多忧伤。	I'm in a gloomy mood.
如何如何？	为什么啊为什么，	How can it be my lot
忘我实多！	把我忘得无踪影！	To be so much forgot?

山有苞栎，	山上栎树丛生，	The bushy oaks above
隰有六驳。	洼地多长榆树。	And six elm-trees below.
未见君子，	没有见到君子人，	While I see not my love,
忧心靡乐。	我的心里不快乐。	There is no joy I know.
如何如何？	为什么啊为什么，	How can it be my lot
忘我实多！	把我忘得无踪影！	To be so much forgot?

山有苞棣，	山上郁李丛生，	The sparrow-plums above
隰有树檖。	洼地长着山梨。	Below trees without leaf.
未见君子，	没有见到君子人，	While I see not my love,
忧心如醉，	我的心里如酒醉。	My heart is drunk with grief.
如何如何？	为什么啊为什么，	How can it be my lot
忘我实多！	把我忘得无踪影！	To be so much forgot?

无 衣　　　　　　　　Comradeship*

岂曰无衣？	谁说没有衣服穿，	Are you not battle-drest?
与子同袍。	你与我同穿长袍。	Let's share the plate for breast!
王于兴师，	国王要起兵，	We shall go up the line.

① 钦钦：忧愁的样子。

* This was the song sung by Duke Ai of Qin when he despatched five hundred chariots to the rescue of the State of Chu besieged by Wu in 505 B. C.

修我戈矛，	修理我的戈与矛，	Let's make our lances shine!
与子同仇。	与你同对仇人。	Your foe is mine.

岂曰无衣？	谁说没有衣服穿，	Are you not battle-drest?
与子同泽①。	你与我同穿汗衫。	Let's share the coat and vest!
王于兴师，	国王要起兵，	We shall go up the line.
修我矛戟，	修理我的矛与戟，	Let's make our halberds shine!
与子偕作！	与你一起作战。	Your job is mine.

岂曰无衣？	谁说没有衣服穿，	Are you not battle-drest?
与子同裳。	你我同穿战裙。	Let's share the kilt and the rest!
王于兴师，	国王要起兵，	We shall go up the line.
修我甲兵，	修理我的盔甲和刀枪，	Let's make our armour shine!
与子偕行！	与你一起前行。	We'll march your hand in mine.

渭　阳

Farewell to Duke Wen of Jin*

我送舅氏，	我给舅舅送行，	I see my uncle dear
曰至渭阳。	送到渭水的北边。	Off north of River Wei.
何以赠之？	拿什么送给他？	What's the gift for one I revere?
路车乘黄。	黄马大车表我心。	Golden cab on the way.

我送舅氏，	我给舅舅送行，	I see my uncle dear

---

① 泽：贴身穿的汗衫。

* This song was sung by Duke Kang of Qin in 635 B. C. while, heir-apparent of Qin, he escorted his uncle into the State of Jin where he became the famous Duke Wen after nineteen years' refuge in Qin.

悠悠我思①。	想念我的娘亲。	Off and think of my mother.
何以赠之?	拿什么送给他?	What's the gift for one she and I revere?
琼瑰②玉佩。	美玉琼瑶表我心。	Jewels and gems for her brother.

权　舆　　　　　　　　　　Not As Before*

於!我乎,	唉!我啊,	Ah me! Where is my house of yore?
夏屋③渠渠④,	当初大碗盛得满。	Now I've not a great deal
今也每食无余,	现在每顿都吃光。	To eat at every meal.
于嗟乎!	唉呀,	Alas!
不承权舆⑤!	不能去跟当初比啊。	I can't live as before.

於!我乎,	唉!我啊,	Ah me!
每食四簋⑥。	当初每顿四大盆。	Where are my dishes four?
今也每食不饱,	现在每顿填不饱。	Now hungry I feel at every meal.
于嗟呼!	唉呀,	Alas!
不承权舆。	不能去跟当初比啊。	I can't eat as before.

---

① 悠悠我思:指思念母亲。② 琼瑰:美玉。③ 夏屋:一种大的食器。④ 渠渠:盛,满。
⑤ 权舆:当初,开始的时候。⑥ 簋(guǐ):一种食器。

* This song was said to be a complaint against Duke Kang of Qin who was not so hospitable as Lord Zhong (in Poem "Lord Zhong of Qin") and Duke Mu of Qin.

陈 风

Songs Collected in Chen, Modern Henan

宛 丘

A Religious Dancer*

子之汤①兮，	你的舞姿飘荡啊，	In the highland above
宛丘②之上兮。	在宛丘的上面啊。	A witch dances with swing.
洵有情兮，	我诚有深情啊，	With her I fall in love;
而无望③兮。	却徒然无望啊。	Hopeless, I sing.
坎其击鼓，	咚咚咚把鼓敲响，	She beats the drum
宛丘之下。	在宛丘的下面啊。	At the foot of highland.
无冬无夏，	不分冬夏舞不停，	Winter and summer come,
值④其鹭羽。	摇着鹭鸶的羽毛。	She dances plume in hand.
坎其击缶，	当当当把缶敲响，	She beats a vessel round
宛丘之道。	在宛丘的路上啊。	On the way to highland.
无冬无夏，	不分冬夏舞不停，	Spring or fall comes around,
值其鹭翿⑤。	舞着鹭鸶的羽毛。	She dances fan in hand.

---

① 汤：荡，飘荡。② 宛丘：四边高、中间低的土山。③ 望：指望，盼头。④ 值：持，拿着。
⑤ 翿(dào)：一种带羽毛的舞具。

* This song described the pleasure-seeking of the people of Chen in the capital where there was a mound in the highland, favorite resort of pleasure-seekers.

东门之枌①		Secular Dancers*

东门之枌，	东门外的白榆树，	From white elms at east gate
宛丘之栩②。	宛丘上的柞树。	To oak-trees on the mound
子仲之子，	子仲家的姑娘，	Lad and lass have a date;
婆娑③其下。	大树下起舞。	They dance gaily around.

榖旦④于差⑤，	选择一个好日子，	A good morning is chosen
南方之原。	去到南边的平原上。	To go to the south where,
不绩其麻，	不纺手中麻，	Leaving the hemp unwoven,
市也婆娑。	闹市舞一场。	They dance at country fair.

榖⑥旦于逝，	大好时光要结束，	They go at morning hours
越以鬷迈。	你我屡屡总相遇。	Together to highland.
视尔如荍⑦，	看你美如荆葵花，	Lasses look like sunflowers,
贻我握椒。	送我一束香花椒。	A token of love in hand.

衡 门		Contentment*

衡门之下，	支起横木即是门，	Beneath the door of single beam
可以栖迟。	横木之下来栖身。	You can sit and rest at your leisure;

---

① 枌(fén)：白榆树。② 栩：柞树。③ 婆娑：舞蹈。④ 榖旦：好日子。⑤ 差：选择。
⑥ 鬷(zōng)：总，屡次。⑦ 荍(qiáo)：荆葵。

* This song described wanton associations of the young people of Chen. The mound at the eastern gate was a favorite resort of pleasure-seekers.

* This showed that one might enjoy oneself and forget one's hunger, be satisfied with fish of smaller note and be happy with a wife though she were not of a noble family.

泌之洋洋，	泌水荡漾漾，	Beside the gently flowing stream
可以乐饥①。	快乐慰饥肠。	You may drink to stay hunger with pleasure.

岂其食鱼，	难道想要吃鱼，	If you want to eat fish,
必河之鲂？	一定要吃黄河里的鳊鱼？	Why must you have bream as you wish?
岂其娶妻，	难道想要娶妻，	If you want to be wed,
必齐之姜？	一定要娶齐国姜家女？	Why must you have Qi the nobly bred?

岂其食鱼，	难道想要吃鱼，	If you want to eat fish,
必河之鲤？	一定要吃黄河里的鲤鱼？	Why must you have carp as you wish?
岂其娶妻，	难道想要娶妻，	If you want to be wed,
必宋之子？	一定要娶宋国子家大姑娘？	Why must you have Song the highly bred?

东门之池　　　　　　　　　To a Weaving Maiden*

东门之池，	东门外的池塘，	At eastern gate we could
可以沤②麻。	可以沤麻制衣裳。	Steep hemp in river long.
彼美淑姬，	端庄美丽的姑娘，	O maiden fair and good,

---

① 乐饥：乐而忘饥。② 沤(òu)：长时间泡。

* The stalks of the hemp had to be steeped, preparatory to getting the threads or filaments from them so that the maiden might weave clothes.

可与晤歌。	可以和她对唱。	To you I'll sing a song.

东门之池，	东门外的池塘，	At eastern gate we could
可以沤纻①。	可以沤纻做衣裳。	Steep nettle in the creek.
彼美淑姬，	端庄美丽的姑娘，	O maiden fair and good,
可与晤语。	可以和她倾情肠。	To you I wish to speak.

东门之池，	东门外的池塘，	At eastern gate we could
可以沤菅②。	可以沤菅。	Steep in the moat rush-rope.
彼美淑姬，	端庄美丽的姑娘，	O maiden fair and good,
可与晤言。	和她叙话心花放。	On you I hang my hope.

东门之杨　　　　　　　　　　A Date*

东门之杨，	东门外的杨树，	On poplars by east gate
其叶牂牂③。	叶子沙沙响。	The leaves are rustling light.
昏以为期，	约定在黄昏的时候，	At dusk we have a date;
明星煌煌。	长庚星闪闪发光。	The evening star shines bright.

东门之杨，	东门外的杨树，	On poplars by east gate
其叶肺肺④。	叶子哗哗响。	The leaves are shivering.
昏以为期，	约定在黄昏的时候，	At dusk we have a date;

---

① 纻：苎麻。② 菅(jiān)：菅草。③ 牂牂(zāngzāng)：风吹树叶的声音。④ 肺肺(pèi)：同"牂牂"。

* The rustling poplar leaves and the evening star hinted at the lovers before their love-making and the shivering leaves and the morning star at the couple after their love-making.

| 明星晢晢①， | 长庚星灼灼发光。 | The morning star is quivering. |

墓 门   The Evil-Doing Usurper*

墓门有棘，	墓门旁边有枣树，	The thorn at burial gate
斧以斯②之。	挥动斧头把它砍。	Should soon be cut away;
夫也不良，	那人不是好东西，	The usurper of the State
国人知之。	全国的人都知道。	Should be exposed to the day;
知而不已，	知道他坏还不改，	If he's exposed too late,
谁昔③然矣！	由来已久这样坏。	He'll still do what he may.

墓门有梅，	墓门旁有酸梅树，	At burial gate there's jujube tree,
有鸮④萃⑤止。	猫头鹰来栖上面。	On which owls perch all the day long;
夫也不良，	那人不是好东西，	The usurper from evil is not free.
歌以讯⑥之。	想用作歌劝谏他。	Let's warn him by a song!
讯予不顾，	劝谏他也不愿改，	But he won't listen to our plea,
颠倒思予！	是非好歹也不分。	For he takes right for wrong.

---

① 晢晢(zhézhé)：明亮的样子。② 斯：砍掉。③ 谁昔：畴昔，从前。④ 鸮(xiāo)：猫头鹰。⑤ 萃(cuì)：集。⑥ 讯：谏，劝谏。

* This was a satirical song directed against Tuo of Chen, a brother of Duke Huan (743-706 B.C.), upon whose death Tuo killed his eldest son and got possession of the State of Chen, but was killed by its neighboring State the year after. The thorn and the owl were both things of evil omen, and were employed here to introduce the evil-doing usurper. The legend went that this song was sung by a mulberry-gathering woman to ward off an official's attempt to rape her.

防①有鹊巢　　　　　　　　Riverside Magpies*

防有鹊巢，	堤岸上怎么会有鹊巢，	By riverside magpies appear;
邛②有旨苕③。	山丘上怎么会有水草。	On hillock water grasses grow.
谁侜④予美，	谁在欺骗我的爱人，	Believe none who deceives, my dear,
心焉忉忉⑤。	我的心里很苦恼。	Or my heart will be full of woe.
中唐⑥有甓⑦，	庭道上怎么会有瓦片，	How can the court be paved with tiles
邛有旨鹝⑧。	山丘上怎么会有水草。	Or hillock spread with water grass?
谁侜予美，	谁在欺骗我的爱人，	Believe, my dear, none who beguiles,
心焉惕惕。	我的心里真烦恼。	Or I'll worry for you, alas!

　　月　出　　　　　　　　　　The Moon*

月出皎⑨兮，	月儿出来明亮亮啊，	The moon shines bright;
佼⑩人僚兮，	照着美人多漂亮啊。	My love's snow-white.
舒窈纠⑪兮。	安闲的步子娇窕的影啊，	She looks so cute.

---

① 防：堤岸。② 邛(qióng)：山丘。③ 苕(tiáo)：水草。④ 侜(zhōu)：欺骗。⑤ 忉忉(dāodāo)：苦恼。⑥ 唐：朝庭前的大路。⑦ 甓(pì)：砖瓦。⑧ 鹝(yì)：绶草。⑨ 皎：洁白明亮。⑩ 佼：美好。⑪ 窈纠(yǎojiǎo)：身姿苗条，行步舒缓的样子。

* This song might speak of the separation between lovers effected by evil tongues or refer to Duke Xuan of Chen (691-647 B.C.) who believed slanderers.

* This was the first song in Chinese poetry describing the poet's love for a beauty in moonlight.

劳心悄①兮。	我的心儿多忧伤。	Can I be mute?

月出皓兮,	月儿出来皓亮亮啊,	The bright moon gleams;
佼人懰②兮,	照着美人多俏丽啊。	My dear love beams.
舒忧受③兮。	安闲的步子婀娜的啊,	Her face so fair,
劳心慅④兮。	我的心儿多忧伤啊。	Can I not care?

月出照兮,	月儿出来高高照啊,	The bright moon turns;
佼人燎兮,	照着美人多鲜亮啊。	With love she burns.
舒夭绍⑤兮。	安闲的步子轻盈的行啊,	Her hands so fine,
劳心惨兮。	我的心儿多忧愁啊。	Can I not pine?

株　林⑥　　　　　　　　　The Duke's Mistress*

胡为乎株林?	为什么去株林?	"Why are you going to the Wood?
从夏南⑦!	去找夏南。	To see the fair lady's son?"
匪适株林,	其实不是去株林,	"I'm going to its neighborhood
从夏南!	是为了找夏南。	To see the son of the fair one.

驾我乘马,	骑上我的大马,	"I'll drive to the countryside

---

① 悄:深忧烦恼。② 懰(liǔ):娇美。③ 忧受:从容不迫,婀娜多姿的样子。④ 慅(cǎo):忧愁的样子。⑤ 夭绍:体态轻盈柔美的样子。⑥ 株林:夏姬的住处。⑦ 夏南:夏姬的儿子。表面上说是看夏南,其实是看夏姬。

*This song was directed against the intrigue of Duke Ling of Chen （reigned 612–598 B. C.）with the beautiful Lady Xia. The duke went to the wood in the countryside to tryst with her under the pretext of visiting her son Xia Nan, by whom he was killed in 598 B. C.

说于株野。	在株林停下。	And take a short rest there;
乘我乘驹，	骑上我的骏马，	I'll change my horse and ride
朝食于株。	赶到株林食早饭。	To breakfast with the fair."

泽 陂①　　　　　A Bewitching Lady*

彼泽之陂，	那池塘的堤岸，	By poolside over there
有蒲与荷。	长有蒲草伴荷花。	Grow reed and lotus bloom.
有美一人，	有一个美人儿，	There is a lady fair
伤如之何！	忧伤得怎么办！	Whose heart is full of gloom.
寤寐②无为，	日夜相思没办法，	She does nothing in bed;
涕泗滂沱。	眼泪鼻涕一把把。	Like streams her tears are shed.

彼泽之陂，	那池塘的堤岸，	By poolside over there
有蒲与蕑③。	长有蒲草伴莲花。	Grow reed and orchid bloom.
有美一人，	有一个美人儿，	There is a lady fair
硕大且卷④。	身材高大发饰美！	Heart-broken, full of gloom.
寤寐无为，	日夜相思没办法，	Tall and with a curled head,
中心悁悁⑤，	心中忧郁难打发。	She does nothing in bed.

彼泽之陂，	那池塘的堤岸，	By poolside over there
有蒲菡萏⑥。	长有蒲草伴荷花。	Grow reed and lotus thin.

---

① 陂(bēi)：堤岸。② 寤寐：醒着和睡着。③ 蕑(jiān)：莲。④ 卷(quán)：鬈，发饰美。
⑤ 悁悁(yuānyuān)：忧郁的样子。⑥ 菡萏(hàndàn)：荷花。

* It was said that this song described the bewitching Lady Xia mourning over the death of Duke Ling of Chen and her son Xia Nan killed by King Zhuang of Chu in 598 B. C. (See Poem "The Duke's Mistress").

有美一人，	有一个美人儿，	There is a lady fair
硕大且俨①。	身材高大貌端庄！	Tall and with double chin.
寤寐无为，	日夜相思没办法，	She does nothing in bed,
辗转伏枕。	翻来覆去空烦恼。	Tossing about her head.

---

① 俨(yǎn)：神态庄重的样子。

桧　风

Songs Collected in Gui, Modern Henan

羔　裘

The Last Lord of Gui*

羔裘逍遥，	游玩时穿着羔裘，	You seek amusement in official dress;
狐裘以朝。	公堂上穿着狐裘。	You hold your court in sacrificial gown.
岂不尔思？	难道我不想你吗？	How can we not think of you in distress?
劳心忉忉。	想你想得我心伤。	O how can our heavy heart not sink down?
羔裘翱翔，	游逛时穿着羔裘，	You find amusement in your lamb's fur dress;
狐裘在堂。	朝堂上穿着狐裘。	In your fox's fur at court you appear.
岂不尔思？	难道我不想你吗？	How can we not think of you in distress?
我心忧伤。	担心国事我忧伤。	O how can our heart not feel sad and drear?
羔裘如膏，	羔裘如膏脂润泽，	You appear in your greasy dress

---

* The lamb's fur was used for official dress, but the lord of Gui wore it while seeking amusement; the fox's fur was used for sacrificial dress, but the lord wore it at court. This showed that the lord neglected state affairs and that was the reason why the State of Gui was extinguished by the State of Zheng in 769 B. C.

日出有曜①。	太阳出来闪耀耀。	Which glistens in the sun.
岂不尔思?	难道我不想你吗?	How can we not think of you in distress?
中心是悼。	想你想得我哀伤。	We are heart-broken at the wrong you've done.

素 冠　　　　　　　　　　The Mourning Wife*

庶②见素冠兮,	有幸再看见戴白帽的人啊,	The deceased's white cap seen,
棘③人栾栾④兮。	见他又黑又瘦弱嶙峋啊。	His worn-out face so lean,
劳心慱慱⑤兮。	心中悲痛啊。	I feel a sorrow keen.

庶见素衣兮,	有幸再看见穿白衣的人啊,	Seeing my lord's white dress,
我心伤悲兮。	我的心中伤痛啊。	I become comfortless;
聊与子同归兮。	誓愿与你同归去啊。	I would share his distress.

庶见素韠⑥兮,	有幸再看见穿白裙的人啊,	I see his white cover-knee,
我心蕴结兮。	我的心中长郁闷啊。	Sorrow is knotted on me,
聊与子如一兮。	誓愿与你同患难啊。	One with him I would be!

---

① 有曜:在太阳的照耀下。② 庶:幸,希望。③ 棘:瘠,瘦弱。④ 栾栾(luánluán):瘦瘠的样子。⑤ 慱慱(tuántuán):忧伤的样子。⑥ 韠(bì):蔽膝,裙。

* It was said that mourners should wear white cap, white dress and white cover-knee since then.

隰有苌①楚　　　　　　The Unconscious Tree*

隰有苌楚，　　洼地长羊桃，　　In lowland grows the cherry
猗傩②，其枝。　枝叶多妖娆。　　With branches swaying in high glee.
夭③之沃沃④，　细嫩又美好，　　Why do you look so merry?
乐⑤子⑥之无知！美你无知无烦恼。I envy you, unconscious tree.

隰有苌楚，　　洼地长羊桃，　　In lowland grows the cherry
猗傩其华。　　花朵多俊俏。　　With flowers blooming in the breeze.
夭之沃沃，　　细嫩又美好，　　Why do you look so merry?
乐子之无家！　美你无家真逍遥。I envy you quite at your ease.

隰有苌楚，　　洼地长羊桃，　　In lowland grows the cherry
猗傩其实。　　果实多美妙。　　With fruit overloading the tree.
夭之沃沃，　　细嫩又美好，　　Why do you look so merry?
乐子之无室。　美你无家无妻小。I envy you from cares so free.

匪　风　　　　　　　　　Nostalgia*

匪风发兮，　　那风儿吹动啊，　The wind blows a strong blast;

---

① 苌(cháng)楚：羊桃，猕猴桃。② 猗傩(nuó)：枝叶柔弱，花实附枝，随风而舞的样子。③ 夭：草木初生嫩美的样子。④ 沃沃：光泽润滑的样子。⑤ 乐：喜爱，羡慕。⑥ 子：指苌楚。

* The speaker, groaning under the oppression of the government, wished he were an unconscious tree.

*This song spoke of King Ping's removal to the east as a result of the barbarian invasion in 769 B. C. when the State of Gui, the poet's homeland, was extinguished by Duke Wu of Zheng (770—743 B. C.).

匪车偈①兮。	那车子开得快啊，	The carriage's running fast.
顾瞻周道，	回头看看那大道，	I look to homeward, way.
中心怛②兮。	心中多么忧伤啊。	Who can my grief allay?

匪风飘兮，	那风儿飘动啊，	The whirlwind blows a blast;
匪车嘌③兮。	那车子摇动啊。	The cab runs wild and fast.
顾瞻周道，	回头看看那大道，	Looking to backward way,
中心吊兮。	心中多么悽惶啊。	Can I not pine away?

谁能亨④鱼？	谁能够烹煮鲜鱼？	Who can boil fish?
溉⑤之釜鬵⑥。	把锅儿洗干净。	I'll wash their boiler as they wish.
谁将西归？	谁要将向西边去？	Who's going west?
怀之好音。	请他报个平安回家乡。	Will he bring words at my request?

---

①偈(jié)：疾驰的样子。②怛(dá)：悲伤。③嘌(piāo)：飘摇不定。④亨：烹，煮。⑤溉(kài)：洗。⑥鬵(xín)：大锅。

曹 风

Songs Collected in Cao, Modern Shandong

蜉 蝣①

The Ephemera*

蜉蝣之羽，	蜉蝣的羽啊，	The ephemera's wings
衣裳楚楚。	像鲜亮的衣裳。	Like morning robes are bright.
心之忧矣，	我的心里忧伤，	Grief to my heart it brings;
于我归处！	究竟归处何方！	Where will it be at night?

蜉蝣之翼，	蜉蝣的翅膀，	The ephemera's wings
采采衣服。	像明亮的衣服。	Like rainbow robes are bright.
心之忧矣，	我的心里忧伤，	Grief to my heart it brings;
于我归息！	究竟归息何方！	Where will it rest by night?

蜉蝣掘阅②，	蜉蝣掘洞飞出，	The ephemera's hole
麻衣如雪。	洁白如雪麻衣服。	Like robe of hemp snow-white.
心之忧矣，	我的心里忧伤，	It brings grief to my soul:
于我归说③！	究竟归宿何方！	Where may I go tonight?

---

① 蜉蝣(fúyóu)：虫名，羽极薄而有光泽，多朝生暮死。② 掘阅：即掘穴，掘土而出。
③ 说(shuì)：税，歇息。

* This was directed against Duke Zhao of Cao (reigned 661—651 B.C.) occupied with frivolous pleasures and oblivious of important matters. The small State of Cao was extinguished by Duke Jing of Song in 487 B.C.

候　人① Poor Attendants*

彼候人兮，	那个恭候迎宾的小官啊，	Holding halberds and spears,
何②戈与祋③。	扛着长戈和长棍。	The attendants escort
彼其之子，	他们那些人啊，	The rich three hundred peers,
三百赤芾④。	三百多穿着大红蔽膝的人。	Wearing red cover-knee in court.
维鹈⑤在梁，	只是鹈鸟在鱼梁上，	The pelicans catch fish
不濡其翼。	没有打湿它的翅膀。	Without wetting their wings;
彼其之子，	他们那些人啊，	The peers have what they wish,
不称其服。	不配他们的好衣裳。	But they're unworthy things.
维鹈在梁，	只是鹈鸟在鱼梁上，	The pelicans catch fish
不濡其咮⑥。	没有沾湿它的喙。	Without wetting their beak;
彼其之子，	他们那些人啊，	The peers do what they wish,
不遂其媾⑦。	不配他们的高官厚禄。	Unworthy of favor they seek.
荟兮蔚⑧兮，	云雾弥漫啊，	At sunrise on south hill

---

① 候人：修路迎宾的官。② 何：荷，扛着。③ 祋(duì)：殳，一种兵器。④ 赤芾(fú)：红蔽膝，大夫朝服的一部分。⑤ 鹈(tí)：水鸟名。⑥ 咮(zhòu)：鸟喙。⑦ 媾(gòu)：厚禄。⑧ 荟蔚(huìwèi)：云雾弥漫的样子。

* This was directed against Duke Gong of Cao who had three hundred worthless peers but only one hundred diligent attenndants in his court and who was impolite to Duke Wen of Jin in 641 B. C.

南山朝㈎①。	南山早上升彩虹。	The attendants still wait;
婉兮娈兮，	柔婉啊娇美啊，	Their hungry daughters feel ill,
季女斯饥。	幼小的女儿忍着饥。	Weeping their bitter fate.

鸤 鸠②　　　　　An Ideal Ruler*

鸤鸠在桑，	布谷鸟筑巢桑树间，	The cuckoo in the mulberries
其子七兮。	它的儿子有七个啊。	Breeds seven fledglings with ease.
淑人君子，	善良的君子人啊，	An ideal ruler should take care
其仪一兮。	他仪容端庄是一样啊。	To deal with all men fair and square.
其仪一兮，	他仪容端庄是一样啊，	If he treats all men fair and square,
心如结兮。	忠心耿耿如石坚啊。	He would be good beyond compare.
鸤鸠在桑，	布谷鸟筑巢桑树间，	The cuckoo in the mulberries
其子在梅。	它的儿子在梅树上。	Breeds fledglings in mume trees.
淑人君子，	善良的君子人啊，	An ideal ruler should be fair and bright,
其带伊丝。	他的带子镶边用白丝。	His girdle hemmed with silk white.
其带伊丝，	他的带子镶边用白丝，	If he's as bright as silken hems,

---

① 朝㈎(jī)：彩虹。② 鸤鸠(shījiū)：布谷鸟。

* An ideal ruler was celebrated by way of contrast with the rulers of the State of Cao.

其弁①伊骐②。	玉饰皮帽镶青丝。	He'd be adorned with jade and gems.
鸤鸠在桑，	布谷鸟筑巢桑树间，	The cuckoo in the mulberries
其子在棘。	它的儿子在酸枣树上。	Breeds fledglings in the jujube trees.
淑人君子，	善良的君子人啊，	An ideal ruler should be polite;
其仪不忒。	他的威仪不改变。	Whatever he does should be right.
其仪不忒，	他的威仪不改变，	If he is right as magistrate,
正③是四国。	四国模范的榜样。	He'd be a model for the state.
鸤鸠在桑，	布谷鸟筑巢桑树间，	The cuckoo in the mulberries
其子在榛。	它的儿子在榛树上。	Breeds fledglings in the hazel trees.
淑人君子，	善良的君子人啊，	Ruler should be a good magistrate
正是国人。	国人敬仰好榜样。	To help the people of the state.
正是国人，	国人敬仰好榜样，	If he helps people to right the wrong,
胡不万年！	何不祈祝他寿无疆。	May he live ten thousand years long!

下　　泉　　　　　　　　　　The Capital*

冽④彼下泉，	冰冷的泉水向下流，	The bushy grass drowned by

---

① 弁(biàn)：帽子。② 伊骐：青黑色的马，指青黑色。③ 正：法则，榜样。④ 冽(liè)：寒冷。

* The bushy grass and plants drowned in cold water might allude to the small State of Cao drowned in misery which made the writer think of the capital of Zhou and of its prosperity.

浸彼苞稂①。	淹那丛生的莠草根。	Cold water flowing down,
忾②我寤叹，	我醒来只有叹息，	When I awake, I sigh
念彼周京。	想念那周朝的京城。	For our capital town.

冽彼下泉，	冰冷的泉水向下流，	The southernwood drowned by
浸彼苞萧。	浸那丛生的蒿草根。	Cold water flowing down,
忾我寤叹，	我醒来只有叹息，	When I awake, I sigh
念彼京周。	想念那周朝的京城。	For our municipal town.

冽彼下泉，	冰冷的泉水向下流，	The bushy plants drowned by
浸彼苞蓍③。	淹那丛生的蓍草根。	Cold water flowing down,
忾我寤叹，	我醒来只有叹息，	When I awake, I sigh
念彼京师。	想念那周朝的京城。	For our old royal town.

芃芃④黍苗，	蓬蓬勃勃的黍苗，	Where millet grew in spring,
阴雨膏⑤之。	雨水来润泽它们。	Enriched by happy rain;
四国⑥有王⑦，	四方诸侯上朝来，	The state ruled by the wise king,
郇⑧伯劳之。	郇伯一一来慰劳。	The toilers had their grain.

---

① 稂(láng)：狗尾草。② 忾(xì)：叹息。③ 蓍(shī)：草名,古人用来占筮。④ 芃芃(péngpéng)：草木茂盛的样子。⑤ 膏：滋润。⑥ 四国：四方诸侯之国。⑦ 有王：有周天子。⑧ 郇(xún)伯：郇国的国君。

豳 风

Songs Collected in Bin, Modern Shaanxi

七 月

Life of Peasants

七月流火①，	七月里火星偏向西，	In seventh moon Fire Star west goes;
九月授衣。	九月里女工缝衣裳。	In ninth to make dress we are told.
一之日②觱发③,	十一月里起寒风，	In eleventh moon the wind blows;
二之日栗烈④。	十二月里风刺骨。	In twelfth the weather is cold.
无衣无褐⑤，	没有长袍和短袄，	We have no warm garments to wear.
何以卒岁？	怎么才能度冬天？	How can we get through the year?
三之日于耜⑥，	正月里修理家具，	In the first moon we mend our plough with care;
四之日举趾⑦。	二月里下地去春耕。	In the second our way afield we steer.
同我妇子，	叫我妻子和儿女，	Our wives and children take the food
馌⑧彼南亩，	把饭送到田地头，	To southern fields; the *overseer*
田畯⑨至喜。	田官看了心喜欢。	says, "Good!"

---

① 流火：火星向西下行。② 一之日：周历的正月，夏历的十一月。二之日、三之日以此类推。③ 觱发(bìbō)：寒风吹动的声音。④ 栗烈：凛烈。⑤ 褐(hè)：粗布衣服。⑥ 耜(sì)：耒耜，犁的一种。⑦ 举趾：举足下田耕地。⑧ 馌(yè)：给耕地的人送饭到地头。⑨ 田畯(jùn)：田官，监督奴隶们劳动的人。

* This was a description of the life of the peasants in Bin, where the first settlers of the House of Zhou dwelt for nearly five centuries from 1796 to 1325 B. C.

诗经 Book of Poetry

七月流火，	七月里火星偏向西，	In seventh moon Fire Star west goes;
九月授衣。	九月里妇女们发寒衣。	In ninth we make dress all day long.
春日载阳①，	春天太阳暖洋洋，	By and by warm spring grows
有鸣仓庚②。	黄莺枝头声声啼。	And golden orioles sing their song.
女执懿③筐，	姑娘们提着深竹筐，	The lasses take their baskets deep
遵④彼微行⑤，	沿着小路向前走，	And go along the small pathways
爰求柔桑。	采呀采呀采嫩桑。	To gather tender mulberry leaves in heap.
春日迟迟⑥，	春天日子渐渐长，	When lengthen vernal days,
采蘩祁祁⑦。	采摘白蒿忙又忙。	They pile in heaps the southernwood.
女心伤悲，	姑娘们心里暗悲伤，	They are in gloomy mood.
殆⑧及⑨公子同归⑩。	怕与公子强抢回。	For they will say adieu to maidenhood.

七月流火，	七月里火星偏向西，	In seventh moon Fire Star west goes;
八月萑⑪苇。	八月里割苇好收藏。	In eighth we gather rush and reed.
蚕月⑫条桑⑬，	三月里剪枝条桑，	In silkworm month with axe's blow
取彼斧斨⑭。	拿起斧子去砍伐。	We cut mulberry sprigs with speed.
以伐远扬⑮，	高枝长条砍干净，	We lop off branches long and high
猗彼女桑。	攀着短枝摘嫩桑。	And bring young tender leaves in.

---

① 载阳：开始暖和。② 仓庚：黄鹂。③ 懿(yì)筐：深筐。④ 遵：沿着。⑤ 微行(hàng)：小路。⑥ 迟迟：春日渐长的样子。⑦ 祁祁：采蘩的人很多的样子。⑧ 殆：怕。⑨ 及：与。⑩ 同归：强行带走去做妾婢。⑪ 萑(huán)苇：芦苇。⑫ 蚕月：夏历三月是养蚕之月，所以称三月为蚕月。⑬ 条桑：修剪桑枝。⑭ 斨(qiāng)：柄孔方的斧叫斨。⑮ 远扬：长得又长又高的桑枝。

七月鸣鵙①，	七月里伯劳树上叫，	In seventh moon we hear shrikes cry;
八月载绩②。	八月里纺麻又织布。	In eighth moon we begin to spin.
载玄载黄，	染成黑色染成黄，	We use a bright red dye
我朱孔阳③，	我染出红色最漂亮，	And a dark yellow one
为公子裳。	为那公子做件衣裳。	To color robes of our lord's son.

四月秀④葽⑤，	四月里远志结子，	In fourth moon grass begins to seed;
五月鸣蜩。	五月里蝉鸣不止。	In fifth cicadas cry.
八月其获，	八月里庄稼收割，	In eighth moon to reap we proceed;
十月陨箨⑥。	十月里落叶飘飞。	In tenth down come leaves dry.
一之日于貉，	十一月上山打貉。	In eleventh moon we go in chase
取彼狐狸，	取那狐狸剥下皮，	For wild cats and foxes fleet
为公子裘。	做件皮袄给公子。	To make furs for the sons of noble race.

二之日其同，	十二月里大聚会，	In the twelfth moon we meet
载缵⑦武功⑧。	继续打猎练武功。	And manoeuvre with lance and sword.
言私其豵⑨，	小猪自己留下来，	We keep the smaller boars for our reward
献豜⑩于公。	大猪送到公府去。	And offer larger ones o'er to our lord.

---

① 鵙(jué)：鸟名，又叫伯劳。② 绩：织麻。③ 孔阳：很鲜亮。④ 秀：植物不开花而结实。⑤ 葽(yāo)：草名，远志。⑥ 箨(tuò)：草木落下的枝叶皮等。⑦ 缵：继续。⑧ 武功：武事，打猎。⑨ 豵(zōng)：小野猪。⑩ 豜(jiān)：大野猪。

五月斯螽①动股，	五月里斯螽弹动腿，	In fifth moon locusts move their legs;
六月莎②鸡振羽。	六月里蝈蝈抖翅膀。	In sixth the spinner shakes its wings.
七月在野，	七月蟋蟀在田野，	In seventh the cricket lays its eggs;
八月在宇，	八月屋檐底下唱。	In eighth under the eaves it sings.
九月在户，	九月跳进房门来，	In ninth it moves indoors when chilled;
十月蟋蟀入我床下。	十月在我床下藏。	In tenth it enters under the bed.
穹窒③熏鼠，	塞住漏洞熏老鼠，	We clear the corners, chinks are filled, We smoke the house and rats run in dread.
塞向④墐⑤户。	堵上北窗封好门，	We plaster northern window and door
嗟我妇子，	感叹我的妻子和儿女，	And tell our wives and lad and lass;
曰为改岁⑥，	眼看就要过年了，	The old year will soon be no more.
入此室处。	住进这屋里避风寒。	Let's dwell inside, alas!
六月食郁及薁⑦，	六月吃李和葡萄，	In sixth moon we've wild plums and grapes to eat;

---

① 斯螽(zhōng)：蚱蜢。② 莎(suō)鸡：虫名，纺织娘。③ 穹窒(qióngzhì)：室中洞隙加以堵塞。④ 向：北窗。⑤ 墐(jìn)：用泥土涂抹。⑥ 改岁：过年。⑦ 薁(yù)：野葡萄。

七月亨葵及 菽。	七月煮葵苗烧豆汤。	In seventh we cook beans and mallows nice.
八月剥枣，	八月打下大红枣，	In eighth moon down the dates we beat;
十月获稻；	十月收割稻米香。	In tenth we reap the rice
为此春酒，	用来酿春酒，	And brew the vernal wine,
以介①眉寿②。	喝来祝长寿。	A cordial for the oldest-grown.
七月食瓜，	七月吃瓜果，	In seventh moon we eat melon fine;
八月断③壶④，	八月摘葫芦，	In eighth moon the gourds are cut down.
九月叔苴。	九月拣芝麻。	In ninth we gather the hemp-seed;
采荼薪樗，	采苦菜砍些柴，	Of fetid tree we make firewood;
食⑤我农夫。	养活我们农夫们。	We gather lettuce to feed Our husbandmen as food.
九月筑场⑥圃，	九月修好打谷场，	In ninth moon we repair the threshing-floor;
十月纳禾稼，	十月庄稼要进仓，	In tenth we bring in harvest clean;
黍稷重穋⑦，	谷子高粱早晚熟，	The millet sown early and late are put in store,
禾麻菽麦。	粟麻豆麦一起藏。	And wheat and hemp, paddy and bean.
嗟我农夫！	嗟叹我们农夫，	There is no rest for husbandmen:
我稼既同①，	庄稼刚刚收完，	Once harvesting is done, alas!
上入执宫功：	还要服役修宫房：	We're sent to work in lord's house then.
昼尔于茅，	白天割来茅草，	By day for thatch we gather reed and grass;
宵尔索绹②，	晚上搓好绳子。	

---

①介：祈求。②眉寿：高寿的人眉毛长，所以称高寿的人为眉寿。③断：摘下。④壶：葫芦。⑤食(sì)：养活。⑥场：打谷场。⑦重穋(lù)：庄稼后熟叫重，先熟叫穋。

亟其乘屋，	急忙去修屋顶，	At night we twist them into ropes,
其始播百谷；	开春又要种谷。	Then hurry to mend the roofs again,
二之日凿冰冲冲	十二月凿冰冲冲响，	For we should not abandon the hopes
三之日纳于凌阴③。	正月里把冰窖冰藏。	Of sowing in time our fields with grain.
四之日其蚤④，	二月里起早来祭祀，	In the twelfth moon we hew out ice;
献羔祭韭。	献上韭菜和羔羊。	In the first moon we store it deep. In the second we offer early sacrifice Of garlic, lamb and sheep.
九月肃霜，	九月里天高气清爽，	In ninth moon frosty is the weather;
十月涤场⑤。	十月里清扫打谷场。	In tenth we sweep and clear the threshing-floor.
朋酒斯飨，	两壶美酒可飨，	We drink two bottles of wine together
曰杀羔羊，	再杀佐酒羔羊。	And kill a lamb before the door.
跻⑥彼公堂，	登上台阶进公堂，	Then we go up To the hall where
称⑦彼兕觥⑧，	高高举起牛角杯，	We raise our buffalo-horn cup
万寿无疆!	同声高唱寿无疆。	And wish our lord to live fore'er.

① 同：收齐集中。② 绹(táo)：绳子。③ 凌阴：冰窖。④ 蚤：早晨。⑤ 涤场：一年农事完毕，打扫场圃。⑥ 跻：登上。⑦ 称：举杯。⑧ 兕觥(sìgōng)：兕牛角制成的酒器。

鸱 鸮①   A Mother Bird*

鸱鸮鸱鸮，   猫头鹰啊猫头鹰，   Owl, owl, you've

既取我子，   你已经抓走我的小鸟，   taken my young ones away.
无毁我室。   就不是要再毁我的巢。   Do not destroy my nest!
恩斯勤斯，   辛勤养护我的宝小鸟，   With love and pain I toiled all day
鬻②子之闵③斯！ 为了养它我又累又乏。   To hatch them without rest.
迨天之未阴雨， 等着天晴无阴雨，   Before it is going to rain,
彻彼桑土，   剥下桑树根上皮，   I gather roots of mulberry
绸缪④牖户⑤。   修补窗子和门户。   And mend my nest with might and main
今女下民，   现在你们树下的人，   Lest others bully me.
或敢侮予！   还有谁敢来欺侮。

予手拮据⑥，   我的手儿已疲劳，   My claws feel sore
予所捋荼，   我却还要采茅草，   From gathering reeds without rest;
予所蓄租⑦，   再去忙着贮存草。   I put them up in store
予口卒瘏⑧，   我的嘴巴累坏了，   Until my beak feels pain to mend my nest.
曰予未有室家！ 我的窝儿没修好。

---

① 鸱鸮(chīxiāo)：猫头鹰。② 鬻(yù)：养育。③ 闵：怜恤，疾病。④ 绸缪：缠缚，修补。⑤ 牖户：指鸟窝。⑥ 拮据：劳累过度，脚爪麻木。⑦ 租(jū)：干茅草。⑧ 卒瘏(tú)：劳累致病。

* This was the first fable in Chinese poetry.

予羽谯谯①，	我的羽毛渐稀少，	Sparse is my feather
予尾翛翛②。	我的尾巴已枯焦。	And torn my tail;
予室翘翘③，	我的窝儿还晃摇，	My nest is tossed in stormy
风雨所漂摇，	风吹雨打多飘摇，	weather;
予维音哓哓④！	吓得我啊大声叫。	I cry and wail td no avail.

东　山

Coming Back from the Eastern Hills*

我徂⑤东山，	自我远征到东山，	To east hills sent away,
慆慆⑥不归。	长久不能回来。	Long did I there remain.
我来自东，	我从东方回来，	Now on my westward way,
零雨⑦其濛。	小雨迷濛落下来。	There falls a drizzling rain.
我东曰归，	听说将自东方归，	Knowing I'll be back from the east,
我心西悲。	想到西方心悲伤。	My heart yearns for the west.
制彼裳衣⑧，	缝制家常的衣裳，	Fighting no more at least,
勿士行枚⑨。	再不衔枚把兵当。	I'll wear a farmer's vest.
蜎蜎⑩者蠋⑪，	蠕动的毛毛虫，	Curled up as silkworm crept
烝⑫在桑野。	趴在那桑树上。	On the mulberry tree,
敦⑬彼独宿，	蜷缩的人独自睡，	Beneath my cart alone I slept.
亦在车下。	独自睡在战车下。	O how it saddened me!

---

① 谯谯(qiáoqiáo)：羽毛稀疏的样子。② 翛翛(xiāoxiāo)：羽毛枯焦的样子。③ 翘翘(qiáoqiáo)：摇晃，危险的样子。④ 哓哓(xiāoxiāo)：惊恐的叫声。⑤ 徂：往。⑥ 慆慆(tāotāo)：时间长久。⑦ 零雨：下得又慢又细的小雨。⑧ 裳衣：普通人所着的服装。⑨ 行枚：衔枚，为了行军时不发出声音。⑩ 蜎蜎(yuānyuān)：蠕动的样子。⑪ 蠋(zhú)：毛虫。⑫ 烝：久，留，多。⑬ 敦：蜷曲成一团。

* The Duke of Zhou put down a rebellion in the east after 1125 B.C.

我徂东山，	我远征到东山，	To east hills sent away,
慆慆不归。	长久不能回来。	Long did I there remain.
我来自东，	我从东方回来，	Now on my westward way,
零雨其濛。	小雨迷濛落下来。	There falls a drizzling rail.
果臝①之实，	瓜蒌结藤子儿大，	The vine of gourd may clamber
亦施于宇。	子儿结在屋檐下。	The wall and eave all o'er;
伊威②在室，	土鳖儿在屋里爬，	I may find woodlice in my chamber
蠨蛸③在户。	蜘蛛结网门上挂。	And cobwebs across the door;
町疃④鹿场，	鹿在野外回旋，	I may see in paddock deer-track
熠⑤耀宵行⑥。	萤火虫儿光闪闪。	And glow-worms' fitful light.
不可畏也？	家园荒凉不可怕，	Still I long to be back
伊可怀也？	它是多么让人牵挂。	To see such sorry sight.

我徂东山，	我远征到东山，	To east hills sent away,
慆慆不归。	长久不能回来。	Long did I there remain.
我来自东，	我从东方回来，	Now on my westward way,
零雨其濛。	小雨迷濛落下来。	There falls a drizzling rain.
鹳⑦鸣于垤⑧，	老鹳在墩上不停叫，	The cranes on ant-hill cry;
妇叹于室。	我妻在屋里不停叹。	My wife in cottage room
洒扫穹窒；	打扫屋子塞鼠洞，	May sprinkle, sweep and sigh
我征聿至⑨。	行人离家不远了。	For my returning home.
有敦瓜苦，	有只葫芦团又团，	The gourd may still hang high
烝在栗薪。	撂在柴堆没有管。	Beside the chestnut tree.

---

①果臝(luǒ)：植物名，瓜蒌。②伊威：虫名，土鳖。③蠨蛸(xiāoshāo)：蜘蛛。④町疃(tīngtuǎn)：野外。⑤熠(yì)耀：萤光发光的样子。⑥宵行：萤火虫。⑦鹳(guàn)：鸟名，似鹤。⑧垤(dié)：土堆。⑨聿至：即将到。

自我不见，	从我不见这些事，	O three years have gone by
于今三年。	直到今天已三年。	Since last she was with me.
我徂东山，	我远征到东山，	To east hills sent away,
慆慆不归。	长久不能回来。	long did I there remain.
我来自东，	我从东方回来，	Now on my westward way,
零雨其濛。	小雨迷濛落下来。	There falls a drizzling rain.
仓庚于飞，	记得那天黄鹂飞，	The oriole takes flight
熠耀其羽。	羽毛闪闪映阳光。	with glinting wings outspread.
之子于归，	这个姑娘要出嫁，	I remember on horse bright
皇驳①其马。	马儿有红也有黄。	My bride came to be wed.
亲结其缡②，	娘为女儿结佩巾，	Her sash by her mother tied,
九十其仪③。	多种仪式真堂皇。	She should observe the rite.
其新孔嘉，	想想新娘真是美，	Happy was I to meet my bride;
其旧如之何？	久别重逢会怎样？	How happy when my wife's in sight!

破 斧　　　　　　　With Broken Axe*

既破我斧，	我的斧子破了，	With broken axe in hand
又缺我斨④，	我的斨子缺口。	And hatchet, our poor mates
周公东征，	周公向东讨伐，	Follow our duke from eastern land;
四国⑤是皇⑥。	四国得到安匡。	We've conquered the four States.

---

① 驳：红白相杂。② 缡(lí)：古代妇女的佩巾，出嫁时母亲为她结戴佩巾。③ 仪：仪式。④ 斨(qiāng)：斧柄方孔的叫斨。⑤ 四国：四方之国。⑥ 皇：匡正。

* In 1125 B. C. the Duke of Zhou undertook an expedition against the four eastern States ruled by his own brothers Guan and Cai and Yan and the son of the last king of Shang. The battles were so fierce that many axes and hatchets were broken, and it took him three years to put down the rebellion.

哀我人斯，	我们战士多辛劳啊，	Alas! those who are not strong
亦孔之将。	立下的功劳真不少。	Cannot come along.

既破我斧，	我的斧子破了，	With broken axe in hand
又缺我锜①。	我的凿子缺口。	And chisel, our poor mates
周公东征，	周公向东讨伐，	Follow our duke from eastern land;
四国是吪②。	四国得到教化。	We've controlled the four States.
哀我人斯，	我们战士多辛劳啊，	Alas! those who do not survive!
亦孔之嘉。	立下的功劳得好评。	Lucky those still alive.

既破我斧，	我的斧子破了，	With broken axe in hand
又缺我銶③。	我的铁锹缺口。	And halberd, our poor mates
周公东征，	周公向东讨伐，	Follow our duke from eastern land
四国是遒④。	四国得到安定。	We've ruled o'er the four States.
哀我人斯，	我们战士多辛劳啊，	Alas! those who are dead!
亦孔之休。	立下的功劳值得夸。	Lucky, let's go ahead.

伐 柯⑤ An Axe-Handle*

伐柯如何？	怎么去砍那斧柄？	Do you know how to make
匪斧不克，	没有斧子怎能行。	An axe-handle? With an axe keen.
取妻如何？	怎么去娶那妻子？	Do you know how to take
匪媒不得。	没有媒人怎能行。	A wife? Just ask a go-between.

---

① 锜(qí)：凿子。② 吪(é)：教化。③ 銶(qiú)：铁锹。④ 遒(qiú)：安定。⑤ 柯：斧柄。

* It was said that this song was sung by a bridegroom to his unmarried friends. That was the reason why a go-between was called a handlemaker in China.

伐柯伐柯，　　砍斧柄啊砍斧柄　　When a handle is hewed,
其则不远。　　它的法则在近旁。　The pattern should not be far.
我觏之子，　　我遇见这个姑娘，　When a maiden is wooed,
笾①豆②有践③。她把餐具列成行。　See how many betrothal gifts there are.

九　罭④   The Duke's Return*

九罭之鱼，　　捕小鱼的细网，　　In a nine-bagged net
鳟鲂。　　　　捉住了鳟与鲂。　　There are breams and red-eyes.
我觏之子，　　我看见这个人，　　See ducal coronet
衮衣⑤绣裳。　穿着龙袍绣裳。　　And gown on which the broidered dragon flies.

鸿飞遵渚，　　大雁沿着沙滩飞，　Along the shore the swan's in flight.
公归无所？　　公爷岂非无归处？　Where will our duke alight?
于女信⑥处。　暂在这里住两宿。　He stops with us only tonight.
鸿飞遵陆，　　大雁沿着大陆飞，　The swan's in flight along the track.
公归不复，　　公爷离去不再回。　Our duke, once gone, will not come back.

---

① 笾(biān)：盛果品的竹器。② 豆：盛肉的木器。③ 践：行列。④ 九罭(yù)：捕小鱼的细网。⑤ 衮(gǔn)衣：绣着龙的礼服。⑥ 信：住两晚叫信。

* The people of the eastern States expressed their admiration of the Duke of Zhou and sorrow at his return to the capital in 1122 B. C.

于女信宿。	请在这里住一会儿。	His soldiers pass the night in bivouac.
是以有衮衣兮！	把龙袍留在这里啊，	Let's keep his broidered gown.
无以我公归兮！	别让公爷回去啊，	May he not leave our town
无使我心悲兮！	别再让我伤悲。	Lest in regret our heart will drown!

狼　跋① —— Like an Old Wolf *

狼跋其胡，	狼向前踩住颔下肉，	The duke can't go ahead
载疐②其尾。	向后退又被大尾绊住。	Nor at his ease retreat.
公孙硕肤③，	公孙心宽又体胖，	He's good to put on slippers red
赤舄④几几⑤。	饰金鞋头多漂亮。	And leave the regent's seat.

狼疐其尾，	狼后退踩住尾巴，	The duke cannot retreat
载跋其胡。	狼前进踩住颔下肉。	Nor with ease forward go.
公孙硕肤，	公孙心宽又体胖，	He's good to leave his seat
德音不瑕。	声名美誉传远方。	And keep his fame aglow.

---

① 跋：兽颔下的垂肉。② 疐(zhì)：踩。③ 硕肤：心宽体胖。④ 赤舄(xì)：以金为饰物的鞋。⑤ 几几：盛装的样子。

* The Duke of Zhou was regent, in 1115 B.C., but he could neither advance nor retreat, for if he should advance, the rumor would spread that he would seize the throne; if he should retreat, the young king would be dethroned. He was like an old wolf which would be hindered by its dewlap in advancing and would tread on its own tail in retreating. The Duke left the regent's seat and restored King Cheng to the throne in 1109 B.C.

小 雅

BOOK OF ODES

鹿鸣之什①

First Decade of Odes

鹿 鸣

To Guests*

呦呦鹿鸣，	小鹿呦呦地鸣叫，	How gaily call the deer
食野之苹②。	野地啃食艾蒿草。	While grazing in the shade!
我有嘉宾，	我有满座的嘉宾，	I have welcome guests here.
鼓瑟③吹笙。	弹奏琴瑟吹箫笙。	Let lute and pipe be played.
吹笙鼓簧，	弹奏琴瑟吹箫笙呀，	Let offerings appear
承筐是将④。	献上礼品满竹筐。	And lute and strings vibrate.
人之好我，	人们喜欢爱戴我呀，	If you love me, friends dear,
示我周行⑤。	给我前路指迷津。	Help me to rule the State.
呦呦鹿鸣，	小鹿呦呦地鸣叫	How gaily call the deer
食野之蒿。	野地啃食青蒿草。	While eating southernwood!
我有嘉宾，	我有满座的嘉宾，	I have welcome guests here
德音孔昭。	品德优秀声望高。	Who give advices good.
视⑥民不恌⑦，	教育民众莫轻薄，	My people are benign;
君子是则是效。	君子学习又仿效。	My lords will learn from you.
我有旨酒，	我有佳肴和美酒呀，	I have delicious wine;

---

① 什(shí)：十。② 苹：蕨蒿。③ 瑟：一种弦乐器，像琴，二十五弦。④ 将：进献。
⑤ 周行(háng)：正道。⑥ 视：示。⑦ 恌(tiāo)：轻佻，奸巧。

* This was a festal ode sung at entertainments to the king's guests from the feudal States. It referred to the time of King Wen (1184—1134 B. C.).

嘉宾式燕①以敖②。	嘉宾共饮同逍遥。	You may enjoy my brew.

呦呦鹿鸣，	小鹿呦呦地鸣叫	How gaily call the deer
食野之芩，	野地啃食野蒿草。	Eating grass in the shade!
我有嘉宾，	我有满座的嘉宾，	I have welcome guests here.
鼓瑟鼓琴。	弹奏琴瑟奏乐调。	Let lute and flute be played.
鼓瑟鼓琴，	弹奏琴瑟奏乐调呀，	Play luate and zither fine;
和乐且湛。③	宾主和乐兴致高。	We may enjoy our best.
我有旨酒，	我有佳肴和美酒，	I have delicious wine
以燕乐嘉宾之心。	希望嘉宾乐逍遥。	To delight the heart of my guest.

四　牡　　　　　　　　　　Loyalty and Filial Piety*

四牡骓骓④，	四匹马儿跑不停，	Four horses forward go
周道倭迟。	大路弯曲又远长。	Along a winding way.
岂不怀归？	我怎能不想回故乡？	How can my homesickness not grow?
王事靡盬⑤，	公家的差事办不完，	But the king's affairs bear no delay.
我心伤悲。	我的心里多悲伤。	My heart is full of woe.

---

① 燕：通"宴"。② 敖：遨游。③ 湛(dān)：过度逸乐。④ 骓骓(fēifēi)，马行不停的样子。
⑤ 盬(gǔ)：止息。

* This was a festal ode complimentary to an officer on his return from an expedition, celebrating the union in him of loyal duty and filial feeling.

四牡騑騑，	四匹马儿跑不停，	Four horses forward go;
啴啴①骆②马。	黑鬃白马气喘急。	They pant and snort and neigh.
岂不怀归？	我怎能不想回故乡？	How can my homesickness not grow?
王事靡盬，	公家的事情没个完，	But the king's affairs bear no delay.
不遑启处③。	别想安居稍休息。	I can't rest flor drive slow.
翩翩者鵻④，	鹁鸪鸟儿翩翩飞，	Doves fly from far and near
载飞载下，	时而高来时而低，	Up and down on their way.
集于苞栩。	落在丛生的栎树上。	They may rest on oaks with their peer,
王事靡盬，	公家的事情没个完，	But the king's affairs bear no delay,
不遑将⑤父。	不能赡养老父亲。	And I can't serve my father dear.
翩翩者鵻，	鹁鸪鸟儿翩翩飞，	Doves fly from far and near
载飞载止，	时而飞来时而止，	High and low on their way.
集于苞杞。	落在丛生杞树枝。	They may perch on trees with their peer.
王事靡盬，	公家的事情没个完，	But the king's affairs bear no delay,
不遑将母。	不能赡养老母亲。	And I can't serve my mother dear.

---

① 啴啴(tāntān)：喘气的样子。② 骆：白身黑鬣(liè)的马。③ 启处：安居休息。
④ 鵻(zhuī)：鹁鸪。⑤ 将：养。

驾彼四骆,	驾着四匹黑鬃马,	I drive black-maned white steed
载骤骎骎①。	马儿飞跑奔前方。	And hurry on my way.
岂不怀归?	我怎能不想回故乡?	Don't I wish to go home with speed?
是用作歌,	于是做了这首歌,	I can't but sing this lay
将母来谂②。	深深怀想我亲娘。	Though I have my mother to feed.

皇皇者华 The Envoy*

皇皇③者华,	花儿色明颜色艳,	The flowers look so bright
于彼原隰④。	开在高低的山坡上。	On lowland and on height.
駪駪⑤征夫,	众多使臣奔波忙,	The envoy takes good care
每怀靡及。	纵有私事也顾不上。	To visit people here and there.

我马维驹⑥,	我的马儿六尺高,	"My ponies have brown manes
六辔如濡⑦。	六条缰绳光润亮。	And smooth are the six reins.
载驰载驱,	一路驾着车马跑,	I ride them here and there,
周⑧爰⑨咨诹⑩。	到处寻访求良策。	Making inquiries everywhere.

| 我马维骐⑪, | 我的马儿黑又青, | "My horses have white manes; |

---

① 骎骎(qīnqīn):马飞跑。② 谂(shěn):思念。③ 皇皇:煌煌,花色明亮。④ 隰(xí):低湿的地方。⑤ 駪駪(shēnshēn):众多的样子。⑥ 驹:本作骄,马高六尺为骄。⑦ 濡:润泽貌。⑧ 周:普遍。⑨ 爰:语助。⑩ 诹(zōu):咨事。⑪ 骐:青黑色的马,其纹路如棋盘。

* This was an ode appropriate to the despatch of an envoy, complimentary to him and suggesting instructions as to the discharge of his duties.

六辔如丝。	六条缰绳如丝洁。	Silken are the six reins.
载驰载驱，	一路驾着车马跑，	I ride them here and there,
周爰咨谋。	到处寻访求良谋。	Seeking counsel everywhere.

我马维骆，	我的白马黑鬃毛，	"My horses have black manes;
六辔沃若。	六条缰绳润光滑。	Glossy are the six reins.
载驰载驱，	一路驾着车马跑，	I ride them here and there,
周爰咨度。	到处寻访做调查。	Seeking advice everywhere.

我马维骃，①	我的马儿黑白配，	"My horses have grey manes;
六辔既均②。	六条缰绳均如一。	Shiny are the six reins.
载驰载驱，	一路驾着车马跑，	I ride them here and there,
周爰咨询。	到处寻访细咨询。	Visiting people everywhere."

常　棣　　　　　　　　　　Brotherhood*

常棣③之华，	常棣开出的花儿，	The blooms of cherry tree,
鄂不④韡韡⑤。	花蒂异常美丽。	How gorgeous they appear!
凡今之人，	当今世上之人，	Great as the world may be,
莫如兄弟。	哪能比得上兄弟。	As brother none's so dear.

死丧之威⑥，	死亡灾丧的威胁，	A dead man will be brought
兄弟孔怀⑦。	兄弟最放在心上。	To brother's mind with woe.

---

① 骃(yīn)：浅黑杂白马。② 均：长短如一。③ 常棣：木名。果实像李子而较小。④ 鄂不：花蒂。⑤ 韡韡(wěiwěi)：光辉。⑥ 威，通"畏"。⑦ 孔怀：很关心。

* This ode came into use at entertainments given at the court to the princes of the same
 surname as the royal House.

原隰裒①矣，	作战丧命于原野，	A lost man will be sought
兄弟求②矣。	唯有兄弟来相寻。	By brothers high and low.
脊令③在原，	若是不幸遇危难，	When a man is in need;
兄弟急难。	也是兄弟来相救。	Like wagtails flying high
每④有良朋，	那些交好的朋友，	To help him brothers speed,
况⑤也永叹。	往往口中空叹惜。	While good friends only sigh.
兄弟阋⑥于墙，	兄弟尽管家里相争，	Brothers quarrel within;
外御其务⑦。	却能同心抵御外辱。	They fight the foe outside.
每有良朋，	那些交好的朋友，	Good friends are not akin;
烝⑧也无戎⑨。	久久也不能相助。	They only stand aside.
丧乱既平，	丧事过去战乱息，	When war comes to an end,
既安且宁。	生活渐渐安且宁。	Peace and rest reappear.
虽有兄弟，	这时虽有亲兄弟，	Some may think a good friend
不如友生⑩。	却又不如友相亲。	Better than brothers dear.
傧尔笾豆⑪，	摆上竹碗和木碗，	But you may drink your fill
饮酒之⑫饫⑬。	痛快畅饮醉一晚。	With dishes in array
兄弟既具⑭，	兄弟既来齐相聚，	And feel happier still
和乐且孺⑮。	相亲相爱乐融融。	To drink with brothers gay.

---

①裒(póu)：聚。②求：相求。③脊令：水鸟名。④每：时常。⑤况：即"贶"，赐给。⑥阋(xì)：相争。⑦务：通"侮"，欺负。⑧烝(zhēng)：久。⑨戎：助。⑩友生：朋友。⑪笾(biān)豆：祭祀或燕享时用来盛食物的器具。笾用竹制，豆用木制。⑫之：是。⑬饫(yù)：满足。⑭具：同"俱"，聚集。⑮孺：中心相爱。

妻子好合，	与妻儿相处融洽，	Your union with your wife
如鼓瑟琴。	像琴瑟一样协调。	Is like music of lutes
兄弟既翕①，	与兄弟相处融洽，	And with brothers your life
和乐且湛②。	那欢乐更加美好。	Has longer, deeper roots.

宜③尔室家	让你的家庭安康，	Delight your family
乐尔妻帑④。	让你的妻儿幸福。	Your wife and children dear.
是究是图，	仔细体会这句话，	If farther you can see,
亶⑤其然乎!	说的一点都不假。	Happiness will be near.

伐 木　　　　　Friendship and Kinship*

伐木丁丁⑥，	伐木铮铮响，	The blows on brushwood go
鸟鸣嘤嘤⑦。	鸟儿嘤嘤叫。	While the songs of the bird
出自幽谷，	飞自幽谷中，	From the deep vale below
迁于乔木。	栖于乔木上。	To lofty trees are heard.
嘤其鸣矣，	嘤嘤是鸟鸣，	Long, long the bird will sing
求其友声。	求其友伴声。	And for an echo wait;
相⑧彼鸟矣，	你看鸟儿鸣嘤嘤，	Even though on the wing,
犹求友声。	是要来把朋友寻。	It tries to seek a mate.
矧⑨伊人矣，	何况我们人与人，	We're more than what it is.
不求友生?	为何不把朋友交?	Can we not seek a friend?
神之听之，	天神若知人友爱，	If gods listen to this,

① 翕(xī):聚合。② 湛(dān):久乐或甚乐。③ 宜:安。④ 帑(nú):子孙。⑤ 亶(dǎn):确实。⑥ 丁丁(zhēngzhēng):刀斧砍树的声音。⑦ 嘤嘤(yīngyīng):鸟鸣声。⑧ 相:视。⑨ 矧(shěn):况。

* This was a festal ode sung at the entertainment of friends, intended to celebrate the duty and value of friendship.

终①和且平。	既保平安又美好。	There is peace in the end.

伐木许许②，	伐木呼呼响，	Heighho, they fell the wood;
酾③酒有藇④。	筛酒甘且醇。	I have strained off my wine.
既有肥羜⑤，	家有小肥羊，	My fatted lamb is good;
以速⑥诸父。	请来叔伯尝。	I'll ask kinsmen to dine.
宁⑦适不来，	为何还不来？	Send them my best regards
微⑧我弗顾。	可别不赏光。	Lest they resist my wishes
於⑨粲洒埽，	屋室扫完多清亮，	Sprinkle and sweep the yards
陈馈⑩八簋⑪。	丰盛食品摆桌上。	And arrange eight round dishes.
既有肥牡⑫，	烹煮一只肥公羊，	Since I have fatted meat,
以速诸舅⑬。	等待长亲来品尝。	I'll invite kinsmen dear.
宁适不来，	为何现在还不来？	Why won't they come to eat?
微我有咎⑭。	莫非我已有过错？	Can't they find pleasure here?

伐木于阪⑮，	树倒在山坡，	On brushwood go the blows;
酾酒有衍⑯。	酒水已满溢。	I have strained off my wine.
笾豆有践⑰，	果品陈列上，	The dishes stand in rows;
兄弟无远。	兄弟别客气。	All brethren come to dine.
民之失德，	人与人失和，	Men may quarrel o'er food,
干餱⑱以愆⑲。	常因饮食缘。	O'er late or early brew.

---

①终：既。②许许：剥木皮的声音。③酾(shī)：用筐滤(lù)酒去掉酒糟。④藇(xù)：甘美。⑤羜(zhù)：五月大小羊。⑥速：召。⑦宁：犹"何"。⑧微：无，勿。⑨於：发声词，犹"爱"。⑩馈：进食品给人叫"馈"。⑪簋(guǐ)：盛食品的器具，圆筒形。⑫牡：指羜之雄性的。⑬诸舅：对异姓长辈的尊称。⑭咎：过错。⑮阪：山坡。⑯衍：水溢的样子。⑰践：陈列的样子。⑱餱(hóu)：干粮。⑲愆(qiān)：过失。

有酒湑①我②，	有酒把酒筛来喝，	Drink good wine if you could,
无酒酤③我。	没酒就把酒来买。	Or o'ernight brew will do.
坎坎④鼓我，	我们咚咚打起鼓，	Let us beat drums with pleasure
蹲蹲⑤舞我。	一起翩翩来起舞。	And dance to music fine.
迨我暇矣，	正好今天有时间，	Whenever we have leisure,
饮此湑矣。	来把美酒喝个足。	Let's drink delicious wine.

天 保　　　　　　　　The Royalty*

天保定尔，	上天保佑你安定，	May Heaven bless our king
亦孔之固。	皇权巩固永不倒。	With great security,
俾尔单厚⑥，	使你国家强且盛，	Give him favor and bring
何福不除⑦？	哪种福气不恩赐？	Him great felicity
俾尔多益，	使你福气日益多，	That he may do more good
以莫不庶。	民富物丰样样齐。	And people have more food.
天保定尔，	上天保佑你安定，	May Heaven bless our king
俾尔戬⑧榖。	给你福气和厚禄。	With perfect happiness,
罄⑨无不宜，	所有事情都适宜，	Make him do everything
受天百禄。	接受上天百种禄。	Right and with great success
降尔遐⑩福，	上天赐你鸿福运，	That he may have his will

---

① 湑(xǔ):澄滤。② 我:语尾助词。③ 酤(gū):买酒。④ 坎坎:击鼓声。⑤ 蹲蹲(cúncún):起舞的样子。⑥ 单厚:大。⑦ 除(chù):施予。⑧ 戬(jiǎn)榖:福禄。⑨ 罄(qìng):尽。⑩ 遐:远。

* This was an ode responsive to any of the five preceding. The guests feasted by the king celebrated his praises and desired for him the blessing of Heaven and his ancestors, whose souls were supposed to appear in the witch.

维日不足。	日日享用也不尽。	And we enjoy our fill.
天保定尔，	上天保佑你安定，	May Heaven bless our king
以莫不兴。	没有什么不兴盛。	With great prosperity
如山如阜，	像是平地隆土丘，	Like hills and plains in spring
如冈如陵。	又像高山的脊背。	Grown to immensity
如川之方至，	就像大河齐汇聚，	Or the o'erbrimming river
以莫不增。	没有可能不增长。	Flowing forever and ever.
吉蠲①为饎②。	案台洁净酒食香，	Offer your wine and rice
是用孝享③。	祭祀祖先齐献上。	From summer, fall to spring
禴④祠烝尝，	春夏秋冬都祭祀，	As filial sacrifice
于公先王。	献给先公与先王。	To your ancestral king
君曰卜尔，	先人承诺赐予你，	Whose soul in the witch appears:
万寿无疆。	福寿无疆万古长。	"May you live long, long years!"
神之吊⑤矣，	上天神灵多善良，	The spirit comes and confers
诒尔多福。	赐你世间许多福。	Many blessings on you
民之质⑥矣，	民众生活之所求，	And on simple laborers
日用饮食。	日常用度及饮食。	But daily food and brew.
群黎百姓，	天下贵族和百姓，	The common people raise
徧为⑦尔德。	受你教化感恩德。	Their voice to sing your praise:
如月之恒；	你如上弦月渐明，	"Like the moon in the sky

---

① 蠲(juān)：涓，清洁。② 饎(xī)：糟，酒食。③ 享：献。④ 禴(yuè)：夏祭。祠：春祭。烝：冬祭。尝：秋祭。⑤ 吊：至。⑥ 质：质朴；诚信。⑦ 为：通"谓"，认为。

如日之升； 你如太阳初上升。 Or sunrise o'er the plain,
如南山之寿， 寿命就像终南山， Like southern mountains high
不骞①不崩。 不会亏减永不崩。 Which never fall or wane
如松柏之茂， 福气就像茂松柏， Or like luxuriant pines,
无不尔或②承。 子孙后代永传承。 May such be your succeeding
　　　　　　　　　　　　　　　　　　lines!"

采　薇　　　　　　　　　A Homesick Warrior*

采薇③采薇， 采呀采呀大巢菜， We gather fern
薇亦作④止⑤。 巢菜新芽新又绿。 Which springs up here.
曰归曰归， 说回家呀说回家， Why not return
岁亦莫⑥止。 转眼又到一年末。 Now ends the year?
靡⑦室靡家， 无室无家谁之过？ We left dear ones
猃狁⑧之故； 都怪作战与猃狁。 To fight the Huns.
不遑⑨启居⑩， 没有闲暇坐下来， We wake all night:
猃狁之故。 还是作战与猃狁。 The Huns cause fright.

采薇采薇， 采呀采呀大巢菜， We gather fern
薇亦柔⑪止。 巢菜叶儿肥又嫩。 So tender here.
曰归曰归， 说回家呀说回家， Why not return?

---

① 骞(qiān)：亏。② 或：语助，无实义。③ 薇：豆科植物，野生，可食。④ 作：生出。⑤ 止：语尾助词。⑥ 莫：通"暮"，岁暮，一年将尽的时候。⑦ 靡：无。⑧ 猃狁(xiǎnyǔn)：一作"狁狁"，民族名。⑨ 遑：退。⑩ 启居：启是小跪；居是安坐。⑪ 柔：是说未老而肥嫩。

* This and the next two epic odes formed a triad, having reference to the same expedition undertaken in the time of King Wen when he was only Duke of Zhou discharging his duty as chief of the region of the west, to the last king of Shang.

心亦忧止。	我的心里多忧愁。	My heart feels drear.
忧心烈烈①，	忧心如焚烈烈烧，	Hard pressed by thirst
载饥载渴。	出征路上饥又渴。	And hunger worst,
我戍②未定，	驻扎的地方没有定，	My heart is burning
靡使归聘③。	谁能替我传家信？	For home I'm yearning.
		Far from home, how
		To send word now?
采薇采薇，	采呀采呀大巢菜，	We gather fern
薇亦刚④止。	巢菜叶儿老且硬。	Which grows tough here.
曰归曰归，	说回家呀说回家，	Why not return?
岁亦阳⑤止。	转眼又到十月间。	The tenth month's near.
王事靡盬，	王室的事情办不完，	The war not won,
不遑启处⑥。	哪有片刻能安闲。	We cannot rest.
忧心孔疚⑦，	忧愁的心情很痛苦，	Consoled by none,
我行不来⑧。	如今有谁来安慰。	We feel distressed.
彼尔⑨维何？	什么花儿最繁盛？	How gorgeous are
维常⑩之华。	是那艳丽的常棣。	The cherry flowers!
彼路⑪斯何？	什么那样高又壮？	How great the car
君子之车。	君子的车马与兵将。	Of lord of ours!
戎车既驾，	战车已经开上路，	It's driven by
四牡⑫业业⑬。	四匹公马高且壮。	Four horses nice.
岂敢定居，	哪里敢于安定居，	We can't but hie

---

① 烈烈：本是火势猛盛的样子，形容忧心如焚。② 戍：驻守。③ 聘：问讯。④ 刚：是说将老而粗硬。⑤ 阳：十月。⑥ 启处：犹"启居"。⑦ 疚：病痛。孔疚：等于说很痛苦。⑧ 来：慰勉。不来，是说无人慰问。⑨ 尔：原作"薾"，花开繁盛。⑩ 常：常棣的简称。⑪ 路：即"辂"，指车的高大。⑫ 牡：指驾车的雄马。⑬ 业业：高大貌。

一月三捷①。	一个月内三转移。	In one month thrice.
驾彼四牡,	驾起了四匹公马,	Driven by four
四牡骙骙②,	那公马强壮有力。	Horses alined,
君子③所依,	将帅们坐在上面,	Our lord before,
小人所腓④。	士兵们以它为遮蔽。	We march behind.
四牡翼翼⑤,	四匹公马并排走,	Four horses neigh,
象弭⑥鱼服⑦。	象牙弓饵鱼皮鞘。	Quiver and bow
岂不日戒?	天天警备无松懈,	Ready each day
狁孔棘⑧。	狁实在太猖狂。	To fight the foe.
昔我往矣,	想我当年离家时,	When I left here,
杨柳依依⑨。	杨柳柔弱随风起。	Willows shed tear.
今我来思,	看我如今回家日,	I come hack now,
雨雪霏霏⑩。	大雪纷纷苦飘零。	Snow bends the bough.
行道迟迟,	一路走得慢腾腾,	Long, long the way;
载渴载饥。	还要忍受饥与渴。	Hard, hard the day.
我心伤悲,	我的心里多悲伤,	Hunger and thirst
莫知我哀!	谁人知道我哀愁。	Press me the worst.
		My grief o'erflows.
		Who knows? Who knows?

出 车

General Nan Zhong and His Wife*

我⑪出我车,	驾上我的战车,	Our chariots run

---

① 捷:抄行小路。② 骙骙(kuíkuí):强壮的样子。③ 君子:指将帅。④ 腓(féi):隐蔽。
⑤ 翼翼:闲习的样子。⑥ 弭(mǐ):弓两端受弦的地方。⑦ 服:盛箭的器具。⑧ 棘:急。
⑨ 依依:杨柳柔弱随风摆动的样子。⑩ 霏霏:雪飞的样子。⑪ 我:诗人代南仲自称。

* General Nan Zhong was the speaker in the first four stanzas and his wife in the last two.

于彼牧①矣。	来到远郊牧地。	To pasture land.
自天子所，	从天子的所在，	The Heaven's Son
谓②我来矣。	奉命来到这里。	Gives me command.
召彼仆夫③，	号召驾车的勇士，	Let our men make
谓之载矣。	叫他们装载武器。	Haste to load cart!
王事多难，	如今王室多难，	The State at stake，
维④其棘⑤矣。	情况已很危机。	Let's do our part!
我出我车，	驾上我的战车，	Out goes my car
于彼郊矣。	来到野郊之地。	Far from the town.
设此旐⑥矣，	挂起龟蛇旗帜，	Adorned flags are
建彼旄⑦矣。	插上漂亮毛羽。	With falcons brown，
彼旟⑧旐斯，	挂起的各种旗子，	Turtles and snakes
胡不旆旆⑨？	为何不迎风飘扬？	They fly in flurry.
忧心悄悄⑩，	我心忧虑重重，	O my heart aches
仆夫况⑪瘁。	战士们无不憔悴。	And my men worry.
王⑫命南仲，	大王命令南仲帅，	Ordered am I
往城于方。	去到北方修城墙。	To build north wall.
出车彭彭⑬，	一行车马众多，	Cars seem to fly；
旂⑭旐央央⑮。	旗帜威武鲜亮。	Flags rise and fall.
天子命我，	天子给我命令，	I'm going forth，

---

① 牧：远郊放牧之地。② 谓：命使。③ 仆夫：御者。④ 维：发语词。⑤ 棘：急。⑥ 旐(zhào)：绘有龟蛇的旗。⑦ 旄(máo)：装在旗杆头的羽毛，这里指装饰着羽毛的旗。⑧ 旟(yǔ)：画鸟隼(sǔn)的旗。⑨ 旆旆(pèipèi)：动摇，飞扬。⑩ 悄悄：忧伤的样子。⑪ 况：甚。⑫ 王：指周宣王。⑬ 彭彭：众盛。⑭ 旂(qí)：龙旗。⑮ 央央：又作"英英"，鲜明。

城彼朔方。	修筑城墙在北方。	Leading brave sons,
赫赫①南仲,	以我南仲之强大,	To wall the north
狁于襄。	必将猃狁扫荡。	And beat the Huns.
昔我往②矣,	当年离家之时,	On parting day
黍稷方华③。	高粱穗花刚吐。	Millet in flower.
今我来④思,	当今归来之日,	On westward way
雨雪载⑤涂⑥。	大雪铺满路途。	It snows in shower.
王事多难,	如今王室多难,	The State at stake,
不遑⑦启居。	不能安居家中。	Can I leave borders?
岂不怀归,	哪能不想回家?	My heart would ache
畏此简书⑧。	怕那告急的文书。	At royal orders.
喓喓⑨草虫⑩,	蝈蝈喓喓地叫,	Hear insects sing;
趯趯⑪阜螽⑫。	蚱蜢趯趯野地跳。	See hoppers spring!
未见君子⑬,	丈夫出征还未归,	My lord not seen,
忧心忡忡⑭。	我心忧伤神摇荡。	My grief is keen.
既见君子,	如今见到他归来,	I see him now;
我心则降⑮。	我的心才肯放下。	Grief leaves my brow.
赫赫南仲,	南仲威名镇四方,	With feats aglow,
薄伐西戎。	讨伐猃狁胜在望。	He's beat the foe.
春日迟迟,	春天的日子漫漫长,	Long, long this spring,

---

① 赫赫:显盛。② 往:指出征时。③ 方华:正开花。④ 来:指伐猃狁后归途中。⑤ 载:满。⑥ 涂:泥泞。⑦ 不遑:不暇。⑧ 简书:写在竹简上的文书,指周王的命令。⑨ 喓喓(yāoyāo):虫声。⑩ 草虫:指蝗,或泛指草间之虫。⑪ 趯趯(tìtì):跳跃。⑫ 阜螽(zhōng):蝗类。⑬ 君子:这里是征夫的眷属称征夫之词。⑭ 忡忡:不安。⑮ 降:悦。

卉①木萋萋。　　路边的草木长茁壮。　　Green, green the grasses.
仓庚喈喈，　　　黄莺鸟儿喈喈叫，　　　Hear orioles sing;
采蘩②祁祁③。　　采蘩的姑娘载满筐。　　See busy lasses!
执④讯⑤获⑥丑⑦，抓获战俘依法处，　　With captive crowd,
薄言还归。　　　作战将士凯旋归。　　　Still battle-drest,
赫赫南仲，　　　大将南仲威名扬，　　　My lord looks proud:
狁于夷⑧。　　从此猃狁难猖狂。　　He's quelled the west.

杕⑨　杜⑩　　　　　　　　　　　A Soldier's Wife*

有杕之杜，　　　棠梨树儿孤零零，　　　Lonely stands the pear tree
有睆⑪其实。　　棠梨果圆艳鲜润。　　　With rich fruit on display.
王事靡盬⑫，　　公家差事没个完，　　　From the king's affairs not free,
继嗣⑬我日。　　回家日子拖又延。　　　He's busy day by day.
日月阳止，　　　日子又已到十月，　　　The tenth moon's drawing near,
女心伤止，　　　家中女人心忧伤。　　　A soldier's wife, I feel drear,
征夫遑⑭止。　　征人何日能还乡。　　　My husband is not here.

有杕之杜，　　　棠梨树儿孤零零，　　　Lonely stands the peat tree;
其叶萋萋。　　　棠梨叶密布成荫。　　　So lush its leaves appear.
王事靡盬，　　　公家差事没个完，　　　From the king's affairs he's not
　　　　　　　　　　　　　　　　　　　　　　　free;

---

①卉(huì): 草的总名。②蘩(fán): 白蒿。③祁祁: 众多。④执: 捕。⑤讯: 审问。⑥获: 就是杀而献其左耳。⑦丑: 指首恶。⑧夷: 平。⑨杕(dì): 孤独貌。⑩杜: 棠梨。⑪睆(huàn): 圆。⑫靡盬(gǔ): 无止息。⑬继嗣: 一延再延。⑭遑: 退。

* This ode was a description of the anxiety and longing of a soldier's wife for his return, the first stanza in autumn, the second in spring and the last two in another autumn.

我心伤悲。	我的心伤悲不息。	My heart feels sad and drear.
卉木萋止,	百花齐开树茂盛,	So lush the plants appear;
女心悲止,	女子在家独悲苦,	A soldier's wife, I feel drear:
征夫归止。	盼望丈夫早归还。	Where is my husband dear?

陟彼北山,	登上北面小山坡,	I gather fruit from medlar tree
言采其杞。	天天来把枸杞采。	Upon the northern hill.
王事靡盬,	公家的事情没个完,	From the king's affairs he's not free;
忧我父母。	担心家中的父母。	Our parents rue their fill.
檀车①幝幝,	檀木车子慢慢赶,	See shabby car appear
四牡痯痯②,	四匹马儿累不堪,	With horses weary and drear.
征夫不远。	征人归期应不远。	My soldier must be near.

匪载匪来③,	无人安慰无人问,	Nor man nor car appear;
忧心孔疚。	让我心忧痛难忍。	My heart feels sad and drear.
期逝④不至,	到了期限人未归,	Alas! you're overdue.
而多为恤。	此事让人更忧懑。	Can I not long for you?
卜筮偕⑤止,	龟草占卜运气佳,	The fortune-tellers say.
会言近止,	相会之日不遥远,	You must be on your way.
征夫迩止。	出征的人儿即返家。	But why should you delay?

---

① 檀车:檀木所造的车。② 痯痯(guǎnguǎn):疲劳的样子。③ 来:慰劳。④ 期逝:归期已过。⑤ 偕:谐。一说是"嘉",吉。

鱼丽①   Fish and Wine*

鱼丽于罶②,	鱼儿落进鱼篓里,	How fish in the basket are fine!
鲿③鲨④。	有黄鲿来有花鲨。	Sand-blowers and yellow-jaws as food.
君子有酒,	君子珍藏陈年酒,	Our host has wine
旨⑤且多。	醇厚味美量又多。	So abundant and good.
鱼丽于罶,	鱼儿落到鱼篓里,	How fish in the basket are fine!
鲂鳢⑥。	有鳊鱼来有草鱼。	So many tenches and breams.
君子有酒,	君子珍藏陈年酒,	Our host has wine:
多且旨。	量又多来味又美。	So good and abundant it seems.
鱼丽于罶,	鱼儿落到鱼篓里,	How fish in the basket are fine!
鰋⑦鲤。	有鲇鱼来有鲤鱼。	So many carps and mud-fish.
君子有酒,	君子珍藏陈年酒,	Our host has wine
旨且有。	味道醇美喝不尽。	As abundant as you wish.
物其多矣,	美酒佳肴真正多,	How abundant the food
维其嘉矣。	味道也是很不错。	So delicious and good!

① 丽(lí):通"罹",遭遇。② 罶(liǔ):鱼网。③ 鲿(cháng):黄颊鱼。④ 鲨:一种小鱼,又名鮀(tuó)。⑤ 旨:味美。⑥ 鳢(lǐ):草鱼。⑦ 鰋(yǎn):鲇(nián)鱼。

* This was an ode used at district entertainments. The domain of the king was divided into six districts of which the more trusted and able officers were presented every third year to the king and feasted. The same thing took place in the States which were divided into three districts. At the former of those entertainments this ode was sung in the first place.

物其旨矣,	美酒佳肴真可口,	How delicious the food at hand
维①其偕矣。	品种也是很齐全。	From the sea and the land!
物其有矣,	美酒佳肴吃不完,	We love the food with reason
维其时矣。	都是时鲜真难得。	For it is all in season.

---

① 维:是。

南有嘉鱼之什

Second Decade of Odes

南有嘉鱼

Southern Fish Fine*

南有嘉鱼，	南方汉江有好鱼，	Southern fish fine
烝①然罩罩②。	摇首摆尾数量多。	Swim to and fro.
君子有酒，	君子有酒醇又美，	Our host has wine;
嘉宾式燕③以乐。	宾客畅饮心无忧。	Guests drink and glow.

南有嘉鱼，	南方汉江有好鱼，	Southern fish fine
烝然汕汕④。	游来游去真逍遥。	Swim all so free.
君子有酒，	君子有酒醇又美，	Our host has wine;
嘉宾式燕以衎⑤。	宾客畅饮乐陶陶。	Guests drink with glee.

南有樛⑥木，	南方有树枝弯弯，	South wood is fine
甘瓠累之。	葫芦藤儿将它缠。	And gourds are sweet.
君子有酒，	君子有酒醇又美，	Our host has wine;
嘉宾式燕绥⑦之。	宾客畅饮心安然。	With cheer guests meet.

| 翩翩者鵻⑧， | 鹁鸪翩翩空中飞， | Birds fly in line |

---

① 烝(zhēng)：众。② 罩：捕鱼工具。罩罩，多貌。③ 燕：通"宴"，宴饮。④ 汕：捕鱼工具，抄网。⑤ 衎(kàn)：乐。⑥ 樛(jiū)木：向下弯曲的树。⑦ 绥：安。⑧ 鵻(zhuī)：鹁鸪，一种短尾的鸟。

* This was a festal ode appropriate to the entertainment of worthy guests, celebrating the generous sympathy of the entertainer.

烝然来思。　成群落在树枝上。　O'er dale and hill.
君子有酒，　君子有酒醇又美，　Our host has wine;
嘉宾式燕又①思。　宾客举杯相敬劝。　Guests drink their fill.

南山有台②　　　　　　　　Longevity*

南山有台，　南山有莎草，　Plants grow on southern hill
北山有莱③。　北山有野藤。　And on northern grows grass.
乐只④君子，　君子真快乐，　Enjoy your fill,
邦家之基。　国家根基牢。　Men of first class.
乐只君子，　君子真快乐，　May you live long
万寿无期！　福寿万古长。　Among the throng!

南山有桑，　南山有桑树，　In south grow mulberries
北山有杨。　北山有白杨。　And in north poplars straight.
乐只君子，　君子真快乐，　Enjoy if you please,
邦家之光。　为国增荣光。　Glory of the State.
乐只君子，　君子真快乐，　May you live long
万寿无疆！　万寿永无疆。　Among the throng!

南山有杞，　南山有杞树，　Plums grow on southern hill;
北山有李。　北山有李树。　On northern medlar trees.
乐只君子，　君子真快乐，　Enjoy your fill,

---

① 又：劝酒。② 台：通"苔"，莎草。③ 莱：草。④ 只：感叹词。

* This was a festal ode where the host proclaimed his complacence in the guests and then supplicated blessings on them one by one.

民之父母。	爱民如父母。	Lord, as you please.
乐只君子,	君子真快乐,	You're people's friend;
德音不已。	美名永传扬。	Your fame's no end.

南山有栲①,	南山有山樗,	Plants grow on southern hill;
北山有杻。	北山有檍树。	On northern tree on tree.
乐只君子,	君子真快乐,	Enjoy your fill
遐不眉②寿。	怎能不长寿?	Of longevity.
乐只君子,	君子真快乐,	You're a good mate
德音是茂。	美名传四方。	Of our good State.

南山有枸,	南山有枸树,	Trees grow on southern hill
北山有楰③。	北山有苦楸。	And on northern hill cold.
乐只君子,	君子真快乐,	Enjoy your fill
遐不黄耇④。	怎能不高寿?	And live till old.
乐只君子,	君子真快乐,	O may felicity
保艾⑤尔后。	后代永安康。	Fall to posterity!

蓼⑥ 萧   Southernwood*

蓼彼萧斯,	香蒿长得高又长,	How long grows southernwood
零露湑⑦兮。	颗颗露珠真清亮。	With dew on it so bright!

---

① 栲(kǎo)、杻(niǔ):栲,指山樗;杻,指檍(yì)树。② 眉:老。③ 楰(yú):鼠梓。④ 黄耇(gǒu):老人。黄,指黄发。耇,指高寿。⑤ 艾:养育。⑥ 蓼(lù):长且大。⑦ 湑(xǔ):清澈。

* The host was the speaker in the first and third stanzas and the guests in the second and last. This ode was sung on occasion of the king's entertaining the feudal princes who had come to his court.

既见君子，	如今见到了天子，	Now I see my men good,
我心写①兮。	我的心情真舒畅。	My heart is glad and light.
燕笑语兮，	举杯畅饮且谈笑，	We talk and laugh and feast;
是以有誉②处兮。	如此这般多快乐。	Of our care we are eased.

蓼彼萧斯，	香蒿长得高又长，	How high grows southernwood
零露瀼瀼③。	颗颗露珠聚叶上。	With heavy dew so bright!
既见君子，	如今见到了天子，	Now we see our lord good
为龙④为光。	这种宠爱多荣光。	Like dragon and sunlight.
其德不爽，	天子盛德无差失，	With impartiality
寿考不忘。	祝他长寿永无疆。	He'll enjoy longevity.

蓼彼萧斯，	香蒿长得高又长，	How green grows southernwood
零露泥泥⑤，	颗颗露珠沾衣裳。	Wet with fallen dew bright!
既见君子，	今天见到了天子，	Now I see my men good.
孔燕⑥岂弟⑦。	心中安乐又欢喜。	Let us feast with delight
宜兄宜弟，	宜为兄长宜为弟，	And enjoy brotherhood,
令德寿岂⑧。	品德高尚心惬意。	Be happy day and night.

蓼彼萧斯，	香蒿长得高又长，	How sweet the southernwood
零露浓浓。	颗颗露珠水汪汪。	In heavy dew does stand!
既见君子，	今天见到了天子，	Now we see our lord good,
鞗⑨革冲冲⑩。	金饰辔头闪闪亮。	Holding the reins in hand.

---

①写：倾吐。②誉：欢乐。③瀼瀼(rǎngrǎng)：盛大的样子。④龙：宠，荣。⑤泥泥：露濡。⑥孔燕：孔，甚。燕，安。⑦岂弟(kǎitì)：和易近人。⑧寿岂：寿而且乐。⑨鞗(tiáo)革：皮革所制的缰绳。⑩冲冲：垂饰的样子。

和①鸾雝雝，　车上铃儿叮当响，　Bells ringing far and near,
万福攸②同。　万福聚于你身上。　We're happy without peer.

湛　露　　　　　　　　　　The Heavy Dew*

湛湛③露斯，　露珠儿颗颗大又圆，　The heavy dew so bright
匪阳不晞④。　不见太阳它不干。　　Is dried up on the trunk.
厌厌⑤夜饮，　夜晚饭饱酒又足，　　Feasting long all the night,
不醉无归。　　不喝尽兴人不还。　　None will retire till drunk.

湛湛露斯，　　露珠儿颗颗大又圆，　The heavy dew is bright
在彼丰草⑥。　沾在茂盛的草叶上。　On lush grass in the dell.
厌厌夜饮，　　夜晚饭饱酒又足，　　We feast long all the night
在宗载考⑦。　同姓家亲祭宗祖。　　Till rings the temple bell.

湛湛露斯，　　露珠儿颗颗大又圆，　Bright is the heavy dew
在彼杞棘⑧。　聚在枸杞和酸枣上。　On date and willow trees.
显⑨允⑩君子，　君子高贵又诚实，　　Our noble guests are true
莫不令德。　　无不美好有德望。　　And good at perfect ease.

其桐其椅，　　那些桐树和椅树，　　The plane and jujube trees
其实离离⑪。　果实沉沉坠枝头。　　Have their fruits hanging down.

---

① 和、鸾：都是指铃铛。② 攸：所。③ 湛湛(zhàn zhàn)：露珠茂盛的样子。④ 晞(xī)：干。⑤ 厌厌：安乐貌。⑥ 丰草：喻同姓诸侯。⑦ 考：成。此指举行宴会。⑧ 杞棘：喻庶姓诸侯。⑨ 显：高贵。⑩ 允：诚实。⑪ 离离：垂下的样子。

* This festal ode was proper to the night entertainment of the feudal princes at the royal court.

岂弟君子，　君子平和又安乐，　Our noble guests will please
莫不令仪。　无不合德有礼貌。　In manner and renown.

彤① 弓　　　　　　　　　The Red Bow*

彤弓弨②兮，　朱红漆弓弦松弛，　Receive the red bow unbent
受言藏之。　请君接受来珍藏。　And have it stored.
我有嘉宾，　我有众多好宾客，　It's a gift I present
中心贶③之。　心中诚意来赞扬。　To guest adored.
钟鼓既设，　钟鼓齐鸣音乐起，　Drums beat and bells ring soon.
一朝飨④之。　大家一同来畅饮。　Let's feast till noon.

彤弓弨兮，　朱红漆弓弦松弛，　Receive the red bow unbent
受言载之。　请君接受来收藏。　Fitt'd on its frame.
我有嘉宾，　我有众多好宾客，　It's a gift I present
中心喜之。　别提心里多欢乐。　To guest of fame.
钟鼓既设，　钟鼓齐鸣音乐起，　Drums beat and bells ring soon.
一朝右⑤之。　宾客一同把酒敬。　Let's drink till noon.

彤弓弨兮，　朱红漆弓弦松弛，　Receive the red bow unbent
受言櫜⑥之。　请军接受放囊中。　Placed in its case.
我有嘉宾，　我有众多好宾客，　It's a gift I present

---

① 彤(tóng)弓：朱弓。② 弨(chāo)：放松弓弦。③ 贶(kuàng)：爱戴。④ 飨：大的饮宴。⑤ 右：通"侑"，劝酒。⑥ 櫜(gāo)：隐藏。

* This festal ode was sung on occasion of a feast given by the king to some prince for the merit he had achieved, and the conferring on him of a red bow, which was the highest testimonial of merit, for red was the color of honor with the dynasty of Zhou.

中心好之。	心中实在很喜爱。	To guest with grace.
钟鼓既设，	钟鼓齐鸣音乐起，	Drums beat and bells ring soon.
一朝酬①之。	互相酬谢意融融。	Let's eat till noon.

菁菁者莪②   Our Lord Visiting the School*

菁菁者莪，	萝蒿长得真茂盛，	Lush, lush grows southernwood
在彼中阿。	在那高高的山岗上。	In the midst of the height.
既见君子③，	如今见到了天子，	Now we see our lord good,
乐且有仪。	心中欢乐有礼仪。	We greet him with delight.

菁菁者莪，	萝蒿长得真茂盛，	Lush, lush grows southernwood
在彼中沚④。	在那水中的小洲上。	In the midst of the isle.
既见君子，	如今见到了天子，	Now we see our lord good,
我心则喜。	心中实在很欢喜。	Our faces beam with smile.

菁菁者莪，	萝蒿长得真茂盛，	Lush, lush grows southernwood
在彼中陵。	在那高高的土山上。	In the midst of the hill.
既见君子，	如今见到了君子，	Now we see our lord good,
锡我百朋⑤。	恩赐给我百串钱。	He gives us shells at will.

---

① 酬(chóu)：主人回敬宾客。② 莪(é)：萝蒿，野草名。③ 君子：指宾客。④ 沚：水中的一块小陆地。⑤ 朋：货币单位。百朋，言财多。

* It was said that this ode celebrated the attention paid by the king to the education of talent. The lush southernwood and the boats were metaphorical of the talented youth of the kingdom, without aim or means of culture until the king provided for their training and furnished them with offices and salary thereafter.

汎汎杨舟，	杨木小舟水上飘，	The boats of willow wood
载沉载浮。	浮浮沉沉随波摇。	Sink or swim east or west.
既见君子，	今天见到了天子，	Now we see our lord good,
我心则休①。	我心欢喜乐陶陶。	Our heart can be at rest.

六 月

General Ji Fu[*]

六月栖栖②，	六月里来心惶惶，	Days in sixth moon are long,
戎车既饬③。	整顿兵车备战忙。	Chariots ready to fight.
四牡骙骙④，	四匹公马长得壮，	All our horses are strong,
载是常⑤服。	日月旌旗插车上。	Flags and banners in flight.
狁孔炽，	猃狁气焰太嚣张，	The Huns come in wild band;
我是用急。	我军形势很紧张。	The danger's imminent.
王于出征，	王命出兵去征讨，	To save our royal land
以匡⑥王国。	以此保卫我家邦。	An expedition's sent.

比物四骊，	四匹黑马强又壮，	My four black steeds are strong,
闲⑦之维则⑧。	训练作战有章法。	Trained with skill and address.

---

①休：欣欣然。②栖栖：忙碌的样子。③饬(chì)：修整。④骙骙(kuíkuí)：强壮的样子。⑤常：画有日月的旗帜。⑥匡：救。⑦闲：调息。⑧则：法。

* This epic ode and the thirteen odes which followed were all referred to the time of King Xuan (826—781 B.C). After Kings Cheng and Kang, the House of Zhou fell into decay. Li, the eighth king from Kang, was so oppressive that the people drove him from the capital, The Huns took advantage of this internal disorder and invaded and ravaged the country till King Xuan succeeded to the throne and despatched against them General Ji Fu, whose successful operations in 826 B. C. were sung by Zhang Zhong, writer of this ode.

维此六月，	在这盛夏六月里，	Days in sixth moon are long;
既成我服。	我的军装已制成。	We've made our battle dress.
我服既成，	我的军装已制成，	Nice battle dress is made;
于三十里。	一日可行三十里。	Each day thirty li's done.
王于出征，	王命出兵去征讨，	Our forces make a raid,
以佐天子。	以此辅佐我国王。	Ordred by Heaven's Son.
四牡脩广，	四匹公马高又大，	My four steeds are strong ones,
其大有颙①。	马首威武气轩昂。	With their heads in harness.
薄伐狁，	快快前去打猃狁，	We fight against the Huns
以奏肤公②。	为国为民立功劳。	In view of great success.
有严③有翼，	将帅威严又恭谨，	Careful and strict we'd be;
共武之服。	供职军旅守边防。	In battle dress we stand.
共武之服，	供职军旅守边防，	In battle dress stand we
以定王国。	安邦定国保我王。	To defend the king's land.
狁匪茹④，	猃狁实力不柔弱，	The Huns cross the frontier;
整⑤居焦获⑥。	聚集驻兵在焦获。	Our riverside towns fall.
侵镐及方，	侵占镐京和丰京，	The invaders come near
至于泾阳。	一直到达泾水边。	North of our capital.
织文鸟章，	旌旗上边绣鹰隼，	Like flying birds we speed,
白旆⑦央央⑧。	燕尾旗边光灿灿。	With silken flags aglow.
元戎十乘，	大型兵车有十辆，	Ten large chariots lead

---

①颙(yóng):大。②肤公:大功。③严:威严。④茹:度量。⑤整:训练军队。⑥焦获:地名。⑦白旆(pèi):旗旗周围燕尾形的旗边。⑧央央:鲜明貌。

以先启行。	当先开路上战场。	The way against the foe.
戎车既安，	兵车行得很安全，	The chariots move along
如轾①如轩②。	时而高昂时低伏。	And proceed high and low.
四牡既佶③，	四匹公马真健壮，	The four horses are strong
既佶且闲。	昂首向前步调齐。	And at high speed they go.
薄伐狁，	快快前去打狁，	We fight against the Huns.
至于大④原。	长驱直入到大原。	As far as northern border.
文武吉甫⑤，	吉甫能文又能武，	Wise Ji Fu leads brave sons
万邦为宪⑥。	他是万民的楷模。	And puts the State in order.
吉甫燕喜，	吉甫设宴喜洋洋，	Ji Fu is feasted here
既多受祉⑦。	天子赏赐福无限。	With his gifts on display.
来归自镐，	镐京归来回到家，	He's back from the frontier,
我行永久。	这次行军时间长。	Having come a long way.
饮御⑧诸友，	举杯饮酒敬朋友，	He entertains his friends
炰鳖⑨脍鲤⑩。	蒸煮团鱼和鲤鱼。	With roast turtles and fish.
侯谁在矣，	都是有谁赴此宴，	The filial Zhang Zhong spends
张仲⑪孝友。	孝敬友善有张仲。	His time there by Ji's wish.

采 芑⑫　　　　　　　General Fang*

薄言采芑，	采苦菜呀采苦菜，	Let's gather millet white

---

① 轾(zhì)：车行向前倾。② 轩：车行向后仰。③ 佶(jí)：强健。④ 大(tài)原：今平凉。⑤ 吉甫：尹吉甫。⑥ 宪：楷模。⑦ 祉：福祉。⑧ 御：进献。⑨ 炰(páo)鳖：清蒸团鱼。⑩ 脍鲤：细切鲤鱼。⑪ 张仲：吉甫之友，其性孝。⑫ 芑(qǐ)：苦菜。

* This epic ode celebrated General Fang who conducted this grand expedition against the tribes of the south in 825 B. C.

于彼新田，	在那两年新垦田，	In newly broken land.
于此菑①亩。	又在一年初垦田。	General Fang will alight
方叔莅止，	方叔受命来此地，	Here to take the command.
其车三千，	带领兵车有三千，	Three thousand cars arrive
师②干③之试。	众多兵士勤操练，	With his great well trained forces.
方叔率止，	都由方叔来统帅。	The general takes a drive
乘其四骐④，	驾着四骐拉的车，	On four black and white horses.
四骐翼翼⑤。	昂首阔步走在前，	Four piebalds in a row
路车有奭⑥，	大车赤红有威严，	Draw chariot red and green，
簟茀⑦鱼服，	上有竹帘和箭袋，	With reins and hooks aglow
钩膺⑧鞗⑨革。	还有缨络和鞗革。	Seal skin and bamboo screen.
薄言采芑，	采苦菜呀采苦菜，	Let's gather millet white
于彼新田，	在那两年新垦田，	In newly broken land.
于此中乡。	又在这块地中央。	General Fang will alight
方叔莅止，	方叔受命来此地，	On the field rein in hand.
其车三千，	带领兵车有三千，	Three thousand cars arrive
旂旐央央。	蛇旗龙旗迎风展，	With flags and banners spread.
方叔率止，	方叔率领向前方。	The general leads the drive
约軝⑩错衡，	车毂缠皮辕饰纹，	In chariot painted red.
八鸾玱玱⑪。	八只銮铃响当当。	Hear eight bells' tinkling sound
服其命服，	按照王命穿服装，	And gems of pendant ring.
朱芾斯皇，	黄朱蔽膝真威风，	See golden girdle round

① 菑(zī)亩：开垦一年的土地。② 师：众。③ 干：盾。④ 骐：有青黑花纹的马。⑤ 翼翼：壮健貌。⑥ 奭(shì)：赭(zhě)红色。⑦ 簟茀(diànfú)：蔽车的竹席。⑧ 膺：马带。⑨ 鞗(tiáo)革：革制的缰绳，末端以金为饰。⑩ 軝(qí)：车毂两端有皮革装饰的部分。⑪ 玱玱(qiāngqiāng)：玉声。

有玱葱珩①。	还有绿玉响玱玱。	His robe conferred by the king.

鴥②彼飞隼，	鹰隼空中急速飞，	Rapid is the hawks' flight:
其飞戾③天，	一飞能够冲云霄，	They soar up to the sky
亦集爰止。	落于树上也从容。	And then here they alight.
方叔莅止，	方叔受命来此地，	General Fang comes nigh;
其车三千，	带领兵车有三千。	Three thousand cars arrive;
师干之试。	众多兵士勤操练，	His well-trained soldiers come.
方叔率止，	都由方叔来统帅。	General Fang leads the drive;
钲④人伐鼓，	打起铙钹敲起鼓，	Men jingle and beat drum.
陈师鞠⑤旅。	集合军队宣誓言。	His forces in array,
显允方叔，	方叔英明有威信，	The general has good fame,
伐鼓渊渊⑥，	鼓声敲得震天响，	Drums rolling on display
振旅阗阗⑦。	整顿军队要出师。	And flags streaming in flame.

蠢尔蛮荆，	小小荆蛮真愚蠢，	You southern savages dare
大邦为雠。	要与大国来为敌。	To invade our great land.
方叔元老，	方叔位重资格深，	Our General Fang is there;
克壮其犹。	熟读兵书有良谋。	At war he's a good hand.
方叔率止，	方叔率领此军队，	The general leads his forces
执讯获丑⑧。	抓获战俘依法治。	To make captives of the crowd.
戎车啴啴，	兵车开动声啴啴，	His chariot drawn by horses
啴啴焞焞⑨，	啴啴焞焞震响天，	Now rumbles now rolls loud

---

① 珩(héng)：佩玉。② 鴥(yù)：疾飞的样子。③ 戾：至。④ 钲(zhāng)人：击鼓传令者。⑤ 鞠：宣告。⑥ 渊渊：鼓声。⑦ 阗阗(tiántián)：击鼓声。⑧ 丑：丑类，对敌人的蔑称。⑨ 焞焞(túntún)：盛大的样子。

如霆如雷。	车马行进声如雷。	Like clap or roll of thunder.
显允方叔，	方叔英明有威信，	General Fang in command
征伐玁狁，	率兵前去讨玁狁，	Puts the Huns down and under
蛮荆来威①。	令他蛮夷畏丧胆。	And southern savage band.

车　攻②　　　　　　　　Great Hunting*

我车既攻，	我的车子很坚固，	Our chariots strong
我马既同③。	我的马儿很齐整。	Have well-matched steeds.
四牡庞庞④，	四匹公马高又大，	Our train is long;
驾言徂⑤东⑥。	驾着车儿向东行。	Eastward it seeds.

田车⑦既好，	我的猎车非常好，	Our chariots good,
四牡孔阜⑧。	四匹公马肥又高。	Four steeds in front,
东有甫草⑨，	东边有片绿草原，	Drive to east wood
驾言行狩。	驾车到那去狩猎。	Where we shall hunt.

之子于苗⑩，	天子出门去打猎，	Our king afield,
选⑪徒⑫嚣嚣。	清点兵马声喧喧。	Flags on display,
建旐⑬设旄⑭，	挂起蛇旗牛尾旗，	With archers skilled

---

① 威：畏。② 攻：坚固。③ 同：齐。④ 庞庞(lónglóng)：躯体充实。⑤ 徂(cú)：往，到。⑥ 东：指东都雒邑，在镐京之东。⑦ 田车：打猎时所乘的车。⑧ 孔阜：很高大肥壮。⑨ 甫草：甫田之草。⑩ 苗：指一般田猎。⑪ 选：读为"算"，点数的意思。⑫ 徒：步卒。⑬ 旐(zhào)：古代一种画有龟蛇图案的旗。⑭ 旄(máo)：旗杆头上用旄牛尾做装饰的旗。

* This epic ode celebrated a great hunting presided over by King Xuan(reigned 826−781 B.C) on occasion of his giving audience to the feudal princes at the eastern capital of Luo after the two victories won by General Ji Fu over the northern tribes in 826 B. C. and by General Fang over the southern tribes in 825 B. C.

搏①兽于敖②。	前去打猎上敖山。	Pursues his prey.
驾彼四牡，	四匹公马驾车行，	He drives four steeds
四牡奕奕。	一时舒缓一时急。	Strong and aglow.
赤芾③金舄④，	红色蔽膝金头靴，	Red-shoed, he leads
会同有绎。	大家会集一起去。	His lords in row.
决⑤拾⑥既佽⑦，	戴上扳指和皮袖，	Strings fit, they choose
弓矢既调。	调好箭矢拉开弓。	Arrows and bows.
射夫既同，	诸侯一同来比赛，	Archers in twos
助我举柴⑧。	拣拾猎物堆如山。	Reap games in rows.
四黄⑨既驾，	四匹黄马驾车行，	Four yellow steeds
两骖⑩不猗⑪。	两边马儿不偏倚。	Run straight and fit.
不失其驰⑫，	驾车之人守法则，	Our chariot speeds,
舍矢如破⑬。	箭一离弦有收获。	Each shot a hit.
萧萧⑭马鸣，	马儿萧萧地鸣叫，	Long, long steeds neigh;
悠悠旆旌。	旌旗迎风悠悠飘。	Flags float and stream.
徒御⑮不惊，	步兵御者都警惕，	Footmen look gay;
大庖不盈。	厨房怎能不丰收。	With smiles cooks beam.

---

①搏："薄"，无意。②敖：地名，和"甫田"相近。③赤芾(fú)：赤色的蔽膝。④金舄(xì)：黄朱色的鞋。⑤决：射箭时钩弦之具，用象骨制成，戴在左手拇指。⑥拾：皮质的套袖，以防衣服阻碍钩弦射箭。⑦佽(cì)：准备好。⑧柴：堆积物，这里指堆积动物的尸首。⑨四黄：四匹黄马。⑩两骖(cān)：左右两侧的马。⑪猗：当作"倚"。"不倚"指方向不偏，和中间两马一致。⑫不失其驰：指御不违法则。御和射相配合，有一定法则。⑬破：射中。⑭萧萧：马长嘶声。⑮徒：指步行者。御，指在车上驾驶者。

之子于征，	那位君子踏上征程，	On backward way
有闻①无声。	兵车隆隆不闻人声。	We hear no noise.
允②矣君子，	那位君子实在可信，	What happy day!
展③也大成！	现在果然大功告成。	How we rejoice!

吉 日　　　　Royal Hunting*

吉日维戊，	良辰吉日是戊时，	On lucky vernal day
既伯④既祷。	又祭祀来又祈祷。	We pray to Steed Divine.
田车既好，	猎车已经准备好，	Our chariots in array,
四牡孔阜。	四匹公马大又肥。	Four horses stand in line.
升彼大阜，	登上那座大土丘，	We come to wooded height
从其群丑⑤。	驱车追赶众禽兽。	And chase the herds in flight.

吉日庚午，	良辰吉日是庚午，	Three days after we pray,
既差⑥我马。	已经选好我的马。	Our chosen steeds appear.
兽之所同⑦，	这里百兽齐相聚，	We chase all kinds of prey:
麀⑧鹿麌麌⑨。	而且母鹿尤其多。	Roebucks, does, stags and deer.
漆⑩沮之从，	从那漆水沮水旁，	We come to riverside
天子之所。	一直赶到狩猎场。	Where Heavens' Son may ride.

---

① 有闻：盲车行马鸣的声音有所闻。无声，言没有人声。二句说归途中队伍严肃。
② 允：信。③ 展：诚。④ 伯：古代军中祭名，马祖。祷，古代马祭。⑤ 丑：众。⑥ 差：择。⑦ 同：聚。⑧ 麀(yōu)鹿：母鹿。⑨ 麌麌(yǔyǔ)：兽群聚貌。⑩ 漆：沮(jū)，古水名，在今陕西省境内。

* This ode celebrated a hunting expedition by King Xuan on a smaller scale, attended by his own officers and within the royal domain.

瞻彼中原，	看那高高的平原，	Look to the plain we choose:
其祁①孔有。	禽兽种类特别多。	There are all kinds of prey,
儦儦②俟俟③，	四散奔逃真热闹，	Here in threes, there in twos,
或群或友。	三五成群一起跑。	Now they rush, now they stay.
悉率左右，	向左赶了向右赶，	We chase from left and right
以燕天子。	以供天子来射猎。	To the royal delight.
既张我弓，	用力拉开我的弓，	See the king bend his bow,
既挟我矢。	我的箭矢放弦上。	Put arrow on the string,
发彼小豝④，	射杀那只小雌猪，	On a boar let it go;
殪⑤此大兕⑥。	再射这只独角牛。	A rhino's killed by the king.
以御宾客⑦，	做成佳肴献宾客，	He invites guests to dine,
且以酌醴⑧。	一起饮酒乐逍遥。	With cups brimful of wine.

---

① 祁：广大。② 儦儦(biāo biāo)：众。③ 俟俟(shì shì)：兽行走的样子。④ 豝(bā)：雌野猪。⑤ 殪(yì)：死。⑥ 兕(sì)：独角野牛。⑦ 宾客：指诸侯。⑧ 醴(lǐ)：甜酒。

鸿雁之什

Third Decade of Odes

鸿　雁①

The Toilers*

鸿雁于飞，	天上大雁飞去了，	Wild geese fly high
肃肃②其羽。	振翅羽毛沙沙响。	With wings a rustling.
之子③于征，	那人被迫去服役，	We toilers hie
劬④劳于野。	病苦劳累田野上。	Afield a-bustling.
爰⑤及矜人⑥，	这些都是可怜人，	Some mourn their fate:
哀此鳏寡！	还有鳏寡无所依。	They've lost their mate.
鸿雁于飞，	天上大雁飞去了，	Wild geese in flight
集于中泽。	成群聚在水泽边。	In marsh alight.
之子于垣⑦，	那人应征去筑墙，	We build town wall
百堵⑧皆作。	至今已有一百丈。	From spring to fall.
虽则劬劳，	虽然病苦又劳累，	We've done our best
其究安宅？	终究何处是定所。	But have no rest.
鸿雁于飞，	天上大雁飞去了，	Wild geese fly high;
哀鸣嗷嗷。	嗷嗷鸣叫放悲声。	They mourn and cry.
维此哲人，	只有这位明理人，	The wise may know

---

①鸿雁：鸿与雁同物异称，或复称为鸿雁。②肃肃：鸟飞时振羽的声音。③之子：这些人，指被征服役者。④劬(qú)：过度劳累。⑤爰：乃。⑥矜人：可怜人。⑦于垣：往筑墙。⑧百堵，一百方丈。

* This was a folk song collected in the countryside and not a festal ode sung in th court.

谓我劬劳。	说我实在很辛劳。	Our toil and pain.
维彼愚人，	那些昏庸糊涂人，	The fool says, "No,
谓我宣骄①。	只会觉我自视高。	Do not complain！"

庭　燎

Early Audience*

夜如何其②？	长夜漫漫待如何？	How goes the night?
夜未央③，	漫漫长夜未过半。	It's at its height.
庭燎④之光。	庭前烛火耀灿灿。	In royal court a hundred torches blaze bright.
君子至止⑤，	王公诸侯要到来，	Before my lords appear,
鸾声将将⑥。	车前铃声响锵锵。	Their ringing bells I'll hear.

夜如何其？	长夜漫漫待如何？	How goes the night?
夜未艾⑦。	漫漫长夜未过半。	It's passed its height.
庭燎晣晣⑧。	庭前烛火光明亮。	In royal court the torches shed a lambent light.
君子至止，	王公诸侯要到来，	Before my lords appear,
鸾声哕哕⑨。	车前铃声响叮当。	Their tinkling bells will come near.

夜如何其？	长夜漫漫待如何？	How goes the night?

---

① 宣骄：骄傲。② 其(jī)：语尾助词。③ 未央：未尽。一说未央即未中，未半。④ 庭燎：在庭院内点燃的火炬。⑤ 止：是语尾助词。⑥ 将将(qiāngqiāng)：锵锵，铃声。⑦ 未艾：未已，犹"未央"。⑧ 晣晣(xīxī)：小明。⑨ 哕哕(huìhuì)：铃声。

* This was a soliloquy of King Xuan, waking now and again in his anxiety not to be late at his morning levee.

诗经 Book of Poetry

夜乡①晨,	转眼就要天亮了。	Morning is near.
庭燎有烜②。	庭前烛火光熠熠。	In royal court is blown out torches' light.
君子至止,	王公诸侯已到来,	Now all my lords appear;
言观其旂。	看到旗帜随风飘。	I see their banners from here.

沔③ 水   Water Flows*

沔彼流水,	河水漫漫向东流,	The waters flow
朝宗于海④。	百川汇聚入大海。	Towards the ocean.
鴥⑤彼飞隼,	鸟儿漫天疾飞舞,	Hawks fly in slow
载飞载止。	时而飞起时而止。	Or rapid motion.
嗟我兄弟,	感慨同姓诸兄弟,	My friends and brothers,
邦人诸友。	还有同邦与朋友。	Alas! don't care
莫肯念乱,	无人顾忌国祸乱,	For their fathers and mothers
谁无父母!	谁无父母任忧怀?	Nor state affair.

沔彼流水,	河水漫漫向东流,	The waters flow
其流汤汤。	水流汤汤真浩荡。	In current strong.
鴥彼飞隼,	鸟儿漫天疾飞舞,	Hawks fly now low
载飞载扬。	时而低飞时高翔。	Now high and long.
念彼不迹⑥,	想到办事不守规,	None play their part

---

①乡:通"向"。②烜(xūn):烟气。③沔(miǎn):水涨满的样子。④朝宗于海:以百川归东海喻百官拜天子。⑤鴥(yù):疾飞的样子。⑥迹:遵循法则办事。

* This ode bewailed the disorder of the times and the general indifference to it, and traced it to the slanderers encouraged by men in power. The first two lines of the last stanza, missing in the original, are supplanted by the translator.

载起载行。	坐立不安心发慌。	But hatch their plot.
心之忧矣，	我心为此而忧愁，	What breaks my heart
不可弭①忘！	无法停止不可忘。	Can't be forgot.

鴥彼飞隼，	鸟儿漫天疾飞舞，	The waters flow
率②彼中陵。	向着山陵急飞翔。	At rising tide.
民之讹③言，	民众谣言纷纷起，	Hawks fly so low
宁莫之惩④。	不能止息实荒唐？	Along hillside.
我友敬⑤矣，	望我朋友要警惕，	Let's put an end
谗言其兴！	谗言兴起须提防。	To talks ill bred,
		Respectful friend,
		Lest slanders spread.

鹤　鸣

The Crane Cries*

鹤鸣于九皋⑥，	鹤在水泽边鸣叫，	In the marsh the crane cries;
声闻于野。	声音响亮遍荒郊。	Her voice is heard for miles.
鱼潜在渊，	鱼儿遂游在深渊，	Hid in the deep fish lies
或在于渚。	有时也去浅水湾。	Or it swims by the isles.
乐彼之园，	那个园林真可爱，	Pleasant a garden's made
爰有树檀，	园中生长有香檀，	By sandal trees standing still
其下维萚⑦。	还有灌木在下边。	And small trees in their shade.

---

① 弭(mǐ)：停止，消除。② 率：循。③ 讹：伪。④ 惩：止。⑤ 敬：儆，警戒。⑥ 皋(gāo)：沼泽。⑦ 萚(tuò)：棘类灌木。

* The garden described in this ode alluded to a State, the crane and sandal trees to manifested talents, the fish and small trees and paper mulberries to undiscovered talents, and stones from another hill to unpolished talents from other States. It was important for a State to discover and employ different talents.

他山①之石,	其他山上的石头,	Stones from another hill
可以为错②。	可以用来琢美玉。	May be used to polish jade.
鹤鸣于九皋,	鹤在水泽边鸣叫,	In the marsh the crane cries;
声闻于天。	声音响亮冲云霄。	Her voice is heard on high.
鱼在于渚,	鱼儿遨游在浅湾,	By the isle the fish lies
或潜在渊。	有时也会入深渊。	Or in tile deep near-by.
乐彼之园,	那个园林真可爱,	Pleasant the garden in our eyes
爰有树檀,	园中生长有香檀,	Where sandal trees stand still
其下维穀③。	还有楮树在下边。	And paper mulberries 'neath them.
他山之石,	其他山上的石头,	Stones from another hill
可以攻玉。	可以用来雕美玉。	May be used to polish gem.

祈 父④　　　　　　　　　To the Minister of War*

祈父!	大司马呀军长官,	O minister of war!
予王之爪牙。	我是大王的爪牙。	We're soldiers of the crown.
胡转予于恤⑤?	什么让我犯忧愁,	Why send us to an expeditionary corps
靡所止居。	居无定所四漂流。	So that we cannot settle down?

---

① 他山:指异国。② 错:琢玉用的粗磨石。③ 穀(gǔ):楮(chǔ)树,可以用来做纸。
④ 祈父:司马,周王的军事长官。⑤ 恤(xù):患。

* The soldiers of the Royal Guard complained of the service imposed on them by the minister of war in 787 B. C. when the royal army had sustained a great defeat from some of the northern tribes and the royal guards were ordered to join the expeditionary force, a duty which did not belong to them.

祈父！	大司马呀军长官，	O minister of war!
予王之爪士。	我是大王的爪牙。	We're guardians' of this land.
胡转予于恤？	什么让我心担忧，	Why send us to an expeditionary corps
靡所厎①止。	无处安身心发愁。	So that we're under endless command?

祈父！	大司马呀军长官，	O minister of war!
亶②不聪。	实在不听民众声，	Why don't you listen to others?
胡转予于恤？	为啥陷我忧患中？	Why send us to an expeditionary corps
有母③之尸④饔⑤。	家中老母无侍奉。	So that we cannot feed out mothers?

白　驹　　　　　　　The White Pony*

皎皎白驹，	整洁干净的小白马，	The pony withe
食我场苗。	在我圃场吃豆苗。	Feeds on the hay.
絷⑥之维⑦之，	我用绳子拴起它，	Tether it tight,
以永今朝。	让这快乐永留存。	Lengthen the joy of the day
所谓⑧伊人，	那个到来的客人	So that its master may
于焉逍遥。	在我这里多逍遥。	At ease here stay.

---

① 厎(zhǐ)：止。② 亶(dǎn)：确实是。③ 母：毋。④ 尸：空。⑤ 饔(yōng)：熟食。⑥ 絷(zhí)：绊马两足。⑦ 维：用绳一头系马勒一头系在树木楹柱等物上。⑧ 谓：望念。

* The host tried to detain the white pony so as to have its master always with him and expressed his regret on the guest's departure.

皎皎白驹，	整洁干净的小白马，	The pony white
食我场藿①。	在我圃场吃新豆。	Feeds on bean leaves.
絷之维之，	我用绳子拴住它，	Tether it tight;
以永今夕。	让这快乐能久长。	Lengthen the joy of the eves
所谓伊人，	那个到来的客人，	So that its master may
于焉嘉客。	是我家的贵宾客。	As guest here stay.
皎皎白驹，	整洁干净的小白马，	The pony white
贲②然来思。	健壮漂亮有光彩。	Brings pleasure here.
尔公尔侯③！	各位公爵与侯爵，	My noble guest so brigbt,
逸豫无期④。	逍遥自在乐无穷。	Be in good cheer.
慎尔优游，	望你好好玩一玩，	Enjoy at ease.
勉尔遁思。	请勿早早就退席。	Don't take leave, please!
皎皎白驹，	整洁干净的小白马，	The pony white
在彼空谷⑤。	在那空旷深谷中。	Feeds on fresh grass.
生刍⑥一束，	脚下有束新嫩草，	My guest gem-bright.
其人如玉。	那人品德真正好。	Leaves, me, ales!
毋金玉尔音，	把你音信当做宝，	O from you let me hear.
而有遐心⑦！	千万莫有疏远心。	So that to me you're near.

黄　鸟　　　　　　　　　　　　　Yellow Birds*

黄鸟黄鸟⑧！	大黄雀呀大黄雀，	O yellow birds, hear phrase.

---

①藿(huò)：初生的豆。②贲(bēn)：饰。贲然，光彩貌。③尔公尔侯：指"伊人"。
④期(qí)：极。⑤空谷：深谷。⑥生刍：青草，用来喂白驹。⑦遐心：疏远之心。
⑧黄鸟：比剥削者。

* The speaker who had withdrawn to another State found his expectations of the people there disappointed and proposed to return to his homeland.

无集于榖①!	不要停在楮树上，	Don't settle on the trees.
无啄我粟。	不要吃我的小米。	Don't eat my paddy grain.
此邦之人，	这个邦国的人民，	The people here won't deign
不我肯榖②。	跟我一点不友好。	To treat foreigners well.
言旋③，言归，	还是赶快回去吧，	I will go back and dwell
复我邦族。	回到自己的邦族。	In my family cell.
黄鸟黄鸟!	大黄雀呀大黄雀，	O yellow birds, hear please.
无集于桑!	不要停在桑树上，	Don't perch on mulberries.
无啄我梁!	不要啄我的高粱。	Don't eat my sorghum grain.
此邦之人，	这个邦国的人民，	The people here won't deign
不可与明④。	一点都不明事理。	To come and understand.
言旋，言归，	还是赶快回去吧，	I will go back offhand
复我诸兄。	回到哥哥那里去。	To my dear brethren's land.
黄鸟黄鸟!	大黄雀呀大黄雀，	O yellow birds, hear please.
无集于栩⑤!	不要停在橡树上，	Don't settle on oat-trees.
无啄我黍!	不要啄我的黍米。	Don't eat my millet grain.
此邦之人，	这个邦国的人民，	The people here won't deign
不可与处。	实在不好来相处。	To let me live at ease.
言旋，言归，	还是赶快回去吧，	So I'll go back again
复我诸父⑥。	跟我父辈在一起。	To my dear uncles' plain.

---

① 榖(hǔ)：即楮(chǔ)木，皮可造纸。② 榖：亲善。③ 旋：还。④ 明：明晓道理。⑤ 栩(xǔ)：即橡树。⑥ 诸父：指同姓的长辈。

我行其野　　　　　　　A Rejected Husband*

我行其野，	独自走在旷野上，	I go by countryside
蔽芾①其樗②。	臭椿树叶新生出。	With withered trees o'erspread.
昏姻之故，	因为婚姻的缘故，	With you I would reside
言就尔居。	与你居住在一起。	For to you I was wed.
尔不我畜③，	如今你不再养我，	Now you reject my hand,
复我邦家。	只好回到我家邦。	I'll go back to my land.

我行其野，	独自走在旷野上，	I go by countryside
言采其蓫④。	一边采摘羊蹄菜。	with sheep's foot overspread.
昏姻之故，	只因婚姻的缘故，	I'll sleep by your bedside
言就尔宿。	跟你同住一间屋。	For to you I was wed.
尔不我畜⑤，	如今你不再养我，	Now you reject my hand,
言归斯复。	我也只好把家还。	I'll go back to homeland.

我行其野，	独自走在旷野上，	I go by countryside
言采其葍。	一边采摘恶野菜。	With pokeweed overspread.
不思旧姻，	你不顾念旧婚姻，	You drove husband outside,
求尔新特⑥。	一心只把新人求。	To another you'll wed.
成⑦不以富，	并不因为她富有，	I can't bear your disdain,
亦祇⑧以异。	只是新鲜感难挡。	So I go back with pain.

---

① 蔽芾(fèi)：树叶初生的样子。② 樗(chū)：臭椿。③ 畜：养。④ 蓫(zhú)：一种野菜，又名羊蹄菜。⑤ 葍(fú)：一种有臭味的野菜。⑥ 新特：外婚，新的配偶。⑦ 成：诚的假借字。⑧ 祇(zhǐ)：即只仅仅。

* A husband rejected by his wife returned to his own homeland.

斯　干　　　　　　　　　　　　Installation*

秩秩①斯干②，　　山涧泉水清清流，　The stream so clean,
幽幽南山③。　　　终南山上林幽幽。　Mountains so long,
如竹苞④矣，　　　就像竹苞稠密长，　Bamboo so green,
如松茂矣。　　　　又如青松叶繁茂。　Lush pines so strong.
兄及弟矣，　　　　都是手足亲兄弟，　O brothers dear,
式相好矣，　　　　相亲相爱意相容，　Do love each other.
无相犹⑤矣。　　　莫要欺诈相为敌。　Make no scheme here
　　　　　　　　　　　　　　　　　　Against your brother.

似⑥续妣⑦祖，　　续继先祖的功德，　Inherit all from fathers' tombs,
筑室百堵⑧，　　　筑成房屋近百间，　Build solid wall
西南其户⑨。　　　有向西的有向南。　And hundred rooms
爰居爰处，　　　　全家都来此居住，　North, south, east, west
爰笑爰语。　　　　有说有笑乐融融。　Where you may walk,
　　　　　　　　　　　　　　　　　　And sit and rest,
　　　　　　　　　　　　　　　　　　And laugh and talk.

约之阁阁⑩，　　　板子捆得真结实，　The frames' well bound
椓⑪之橐橐⑫。　　用力夯土声声响。　For earth they pound.
风雨攸⑬除，　　　能挡风来能避雨，　Nor wind nor rain,

---

①秩秩：水流的样子。②干：涧，古通用。③南山：即终南山。④苞：植物丛生稠密的样子。⑤犹：欺诈。⑥似：同"嗣"。⑦妣：亡母。⑧堵：方丈为"堵"。⑨西南其户：古人堂寝的制度，有正户有侧户，正户南向，侧户东西向。⑩阁阁：结实整齐。⑪椓(zhuó)：击。⑫橐橐(tuótuó)：敲击的声音。⑬攸：语助词。

* This ode was probably made for a festival on the completion and dedication of a palace, of which there was a description with good wishes for the builder and his posterity.

鸟鼠攸去，　　鸟雀老鼠也不惧，　　Nor bird nor mouse
君子攸芋①。　　大家一起来居住。　　Could spoil in vain
　　　　　　　　　　　　　　　　　Your noble house.

如跂②斯翼，　　房屋屹立如君子，　　As man stands right,
如矢斯棘，　　棱角整饬如箭矢，　　As arrow's straight,
如鸟斯革③，　　房瓴上翘如鸟翼，　　As birds in flight
如翚④斯飞，　　展开双翅欲起飞，　　Spread wings so great,
君子攸跻⑤。　　君子举足登新室。　　'Tis the abode
　　　　　　　　　　　　　　　　　Fit for our lord.

殖殖⑥其庭，　　庭院宽敞又平整，　　Square is the hall
有觉⑦其楹，　　楹柱高大又直正。　　With pillars tall.
哙哙⑧其正，　　正寝宽敞又明亮，　　The chamber's bright,
哕哕⑨其冥，　　暗处幽晦微有光。　　The bedroom's deep.
君子攸宁。　　君子住着多安宁。　　Our lord at night
　　　　　　　　　　　　　　　　　May rest and sleep.

下莞⑩上簟⑪，　　下铺蒲草上铺席，　　Bamboo outspread
乃安斯寝。　　高枕安卧无烦忧。　　On rush-mat bed
乃寝乃兴，　　君子睡醒起身后，　　Where one may rest
乃占我梦。　　请人来占梦中事。　　Or lie awake
吉梦维何？　　怎样才算吉祥梦？　　Or have dreams blest
维熊维罴⑫，　　梦见大熊和小熊，　　Of bear or snake.
维虺⑬维蛇。　　还有虺虫和蛇虫。

---

① 芋：覆盖。② 跂(qǐ)：踮起脚跟。③ 革：鸟翅。④ 翚(huī)：雉名。⑤ 跻(jī)：升。
⑥ 殖殖：平正貌。⑦ 觉：高大。⑧ 哙哙(kuài kuài)：犹"快快"，形容堂殿的轩豁宽明。
⑨ 哕哕(huì huì)：幽晦。⑩ 莞(guān)：莞席。⑪ 簟(diàn)：苇或竹织成的席。⑫ 罴
(pí)：兽名，似熊而高大。⑬ 虺(huī)：四脚蛇蜥蜴类。

大人①占之：	请来太卜来占梦，	Witches divine
"维熊维罴，	"梦见大熊和小熊，	The bear's a sign
男子之祥。	就会生个男娃娃。	Of newborn son
维虺维蛇，	若是梦到虺和蛇，	And the snake's one
女子之祥。"	生个女娃也不差。"	Of daughter fine.
乃生男子，	若是生个男娃娃，	When a son's blest,
载寝之床，	把他放在床榻上，	In bed he's laid,
载衣之裳，	衣服小被包裹着，	In robe he's drest
载弄之璋②。	珍贵玉璋递手上。	And plays with jade.
其泣喤喤③，	哭声就像敲钟鼓，	His cry is loud,
朱芾④斯皇，	红色祭服真辉煌，	Of crown he's proud,
室家君王⑤。	以后一定做君王。	He'll lord o'er crowd.
乃生女子，	如是生下个女娃，	When daughter's blest,
载寝之地，	让她安寝在地上，	She's put aground,
载衣之裼⑥，	把她包在襁褓中，	In wrappers drest,
载弄之瓦⑦。	给她纺锤来玩弄。	She'll play with spindle round.
无非⑧无仪，	遵守礼仪性无邪，	She'd do nor wrong nor good
唯酒食是议，	饭菜酒食会调理，	But care for wine and food;
无父母诒⑨罹。	不给父母添烦忧。	She'd cause her parents dear
		Nor woe nor fear.

---

① 大人：指太卜。② 璋：玉器，形似半圭。③ 喤喤：小儿哭声。④ 芾(fú)：亦作"韨"，古时祭服，以熟治的兽皮制成，着在腹前，遮蔽至膝部，形似今时的围裙。⑤ 君王：诸侯和天子。⑥ 裼(tì)：又名襁衣，就是婴儿的被。⑦ 瓦：指古人纺线时所用的陶锤。⑧ 无非：无违。⑨ 诒：通"贻"，给予。

无 羊　　　　　The Herdsmen's Song*

谁谓尔无羊？	谁说你家没有羊？	Who says you have no sheep?
三百维①群。	一群就是三百只。	There're three hundred in herd.
谁谓尔无牛？	谁说你家没有牛？	Have you no cows to keep?
九十其犉②。	膘肥体壮九十头。	Ninety cattle's low is heard.
尔羊来思，	你的羊儿过来时，	Your sheep don't strive for corn;
其角濈濈③。	头上犄角挨犄角。	They're at peace horn to horn.
尔牛来思，	你的牛儿过来时，	When your cattle appears,
其耳湿湿④。	两只耳朵摇啊摇。	You see their frapping ears.
或降于阿⑤，	有的聚在山坡上，	Some cattle go downhill;
或饮于池，	有的饮水在池边，	Others drink water clear.
或寝或讹⑥。	有的睡觉有的动。	Some move; others lie still.
尔牧来思，	你的牧人都来了，	When your herdsmen appear,
何⑦蓑何笠，	背着蓑衣和斗笠，	They bear hats of bamboos
或负其餱。	干粮袋子也带上。	And carry food and rice.
三十维物⑧，	三十头牛毛一色，	Cattle of thirty hues
尔牲则具。	祭祀之用可齐备。	Are fit for sacrifice.
尔牧来思，	你的牧人都来了，	Then come your men of herds

① 维：为。这句是说以三百羊为一群。② 犉(rún)：七尺的牛。以上言牛羊之多。③ 濈濈(jí)：一作"戢戢"，聚集。④ 湿湿：耳动貌。⑤ 阿：丘陵。⑥ 讹：动。⑦ 何：同"荷"，指肩上担东西。⑧ 物：牛的毛色。

* This ode was supposed to celebrate the largeness and condition of King Xuan's flocks and herds, with an auspice of the prosperity of the kingdom.

以薪以蒸①，	一路捡枝备柴薪，	With large and small firewood
以雌以雄②。	还会猎得兽雌雄。	And male and female birds.
尔羊来思，	你的羊儿过来了，	Your sheep appear so good:
矜矜兢兢，	战战兢兢相依靠，	Fat, they don't run away;
不骞③不崩。	也没减少也不逃。	Tame, they don't go astray.
麾④之以肱，	挥动胳膊来指挥，	At wave of arms, behold!
毕⑤来既升。	一起全都进圈牢。	They come back to the fold.
牧人⑥乃梦，	牧官夜间来做梦，	Then dreams the man of herds
众维鱼矣，	梦里蝗虫变为鱼，	Of locusts turned to fishes.
旐维旟矣。	还有旐旗换旟旗。	Tortoise and snake to birds.
大人占之：	占梦先生来占卜，	The witch divines our wishes:
众维鱼矣，	蝗虫变成许多鱼，	The locust turned to fish
实维丰年。	来年一定大丰收。	Foretells a bumper year;
旐维旟矣，	旐旗旟旗也不赖，	The snakes turned, as we wish,
室家溱溱⑦。	家室繁荣人兴旺。	To greater household dear.

---

① 蒸：细小的柴薪。② 雌、雄：指捕得的鸟兽，如雌兔之类。③ 骞(qiān)：亏损。崩，溃散。④ 麾：指挥。⑤ 毕：既，尽。⑥ 牧人：官名，掌畜牧。上文的"牧"指一般放牧牛羊的人，与此不同。⑦ 溱溱(zhēn zhēn)：众多貌。

节南山之什　　Fourth Decade of Odes

节南山　　To Grand Master Yin*

节①彼南山，	雄伟高峻终南山，	South Mountain's high;
维石岩岩。	岩石磊磊真壮观。	Crags and jags tower.
赫赫师②尹，	威风凛凛的尹太师，	Our people's eye
民具尔瞻。	使得民众齐仰望。	Looks to your power.
忧心如惔③，	心中忧愁如烈火，	We're in distress
不敢戏谈。	不敢随便来戏谈。	For state affair.
国既卒斩，	国运就此到尽头，	It's in a mess.
何用不监？	上天为何不开眼？	Why don't you care?
节彼南山，	雄伟高峻终南山，	South Mountain's high,
有实④其猗。	山上野草密又长。	Rugged here and there.
赫赫师尹，	威风凛凛的尹太师，	In people's eye:
不平谓何？	国政混乱怎奈何？	You're as unfair.
天方荐⑤瘥⑥，	上天降灾又降疫，	Distress and woes

---

① 节：高峻貌。② 师：官名，太师的简称，太师是三公中最尊贵的。③ 惔(tán)：炎的借字，忧心如火之意。④ 实：满。猗，长。⑤ 荐：重，再。⑥ 瘥(cuó)：病，包括疾疫饥馑等灾患。

* This was a lamentation over the miserable state of the kingdom caused by Grand-Master Yin and King You who reigned 780－770 B. C. and after whose death there took place the removal of the royal residence to the eastern capital-the great event in the history of the Zhou dynasty.

丧乱弘多。	丧乱灾祸何其多。	Fall without end.
民言无嘉，	民众口中无好话，	Our grievance grows;
憯①莫惩嗟。	还不赶快惩戒他。	But you won't mend.

尹氏大师，	尹姓的大国师，	Master Yin stands
维周之氐②。	是周国的根石。	Pillar of State.
秉国之均③，	掌握国之权柄，	With power in hands
四方是维，	维系四方宁安。	You rule our fate.
天子是毗④，	辅佐天子朝政，	On you rely
俾民不迷。	引导百姓前行。	People and crown.
不吊⑤昊天，	上天如此不善，	Heaven on high!
不宜空⑥我师⑦。	别让民众犯难。	You've false renown.

弗躬弗亲，	大王执政不亲躬，	Is what you do
庶民弗信。	民众如何信任。	Worthy of trust?
弗问弗仕，	不咨询也不察看，	We don't think you
勿罔⑧君子。	莫把君子相欺骗。	Have used men just.
式⑨夷式已，	纠正坏事停止干，	You put the mean
无小人殆。	小人也要离他远。	In a high place.
琐琐⑩姻亚，	碌碌无为的亲戚，	Let all your kin
则无膴⑪仕。	不要再给他恩宠。	Fall in disgrace!

昊天不佣⑫，	上天真是不公平，	Heaven unfair

---

① 憯(cǎn)：曾，尚。② 氐(dǐ)：同"柢"，树根。③ 均：同"钧"，本是制陶器的模子下面的车盘，这里指治国政权。④ 毗(pí)：辅佐。⑤ 不吊：不善。⑥ 空：穷。⑦ 师：众。⑧ 罔：欺。⑨ 式：语助词。⑩ 琐琐：计谋褊(biǎn)浅。⑪ 膴(wǔ)：厚。⑫ 佣：均。

降此鞠讻①。	降此大灾和病乱。	And pitiless
昊天不惠,	上天真是不仁慈,	Sends man to scare;
降此大戾②。	降下深重的罪难。	We're in distress.
君子如届,	如果君子能到来,	Send us men just
俾民心阕③。	民愤一定能平息。	To bring us rest,
君子如夷,	君子一身正气在,	Worthy of trust;
恶怒是违④。	众人恶怒即消除。	We're not distressed.
不吊昊天,	老天不惜人性命,	Great Heaven, lo!
乱靡有定。	祸乱一直不平定。	Troubles ne'er cease.
式月⑤斯生,	一月更比一月甚,	Each month they grow;
俾民不宁。	使得百姓不安宁。	We have no peace.
忧心如酲⑥,	忧心忡忡如醉昏,	We're grieved at heart.
谁秉国成⑦?	国家法规有谁行?	Who rule and reign,
不自为政,	不肯亲自来执政,	State set apart?
卒⑧劳百姓。	徒使百姓受劳累。	We toil with pain.
驾彼四牡,	驾着四匹公马,	I drive my four
四牡项⑨领。	公马脖颈肥大。	Steeds in harness.
我瞻四方,	放眼望向四方,	I look before
蹙蹙⑩靡所骋。	没有可去的地方。	And see distress.
方茂尔恶,	当你恶意增长,	On evil day.

① 鞠讻:大灾、无凶。② 戾(lì):恶。③ 阕(què):息。④ 违:去除。⑤ 月:通"刖",摧折。⑥ 酲(chéng):病酒。⑦ 国成:国政的成规。⑧ 卒:"瘁"字的假借,病。⑨ 项:大。领,颈。⑩ 蹙蹙(cùcù):拘束不得舒展的意思。

相尔矛矣。	就像箭矛刀枪。	You wield your spear.
既夷既怿①，	当你平息怒气，	When you are gay,
如相酬矣。	就像互酬酒浆。	You drink with cheer.

昊天不平，	老天怨愤心不平，	Heaven's unjust;
我王不宁。	我王辗转心难宁。	Our king's no rest.
不惩其心，	不是自省以正心，	To our disgust
覆②怨其正。	反而怨人恨谏诤。	Alone you're blest.

家父③作诵④，	家父作了这首诗，	I sing to lay
以究⑤王讻。	举发王室的凶徒。	Evil deeds bare
式讹⑥尔⑦心，	只望王心能感化，	So that you may
以畜万邦。	抚养四方万民仰。	Mind state affair.

正　月

Lamentation*

正月⑧繁霜，	四月里来霜露重，	In frosty moon
我心忧伤。	我心实在很忧伤。	My heart is grieved.
民之讹言⑨，	市井民间传谣言，	Rumors spread soon
亦孔⑩之将。	已经一发不可收。	Can't be believed.
念我独兮，	想到只有我担忧，	I stand alone;
忧心京京⑪。	心里更是很难受。	My grief won't go.

---

① 夷、怿(yì)：怨解。② 覆：反。③ 家父：或作"嘉父"，本篇的作者。④ 诵：诗。⑤ 究：举发。⑥ 讹：同"吪(é)"，变化。⑦ 尔：指周王。⑧ 正月：夏历四月。⑨ 讹言：谣言。⑩ 孔：甚。将：大。⑪ 京京：忧不能止。

* This was a lamentation over the miseries of the kingdom caused by King You's employment of worthless men and his indulgence of his favorite Lady Shi of Bao.

哀我小心， 可怜心细忧愁多， With cares I groan
瘉①忧以痒。 心情不悦身受伤。 And ill I grow.

父母生我， 父母既然生下我， Why wasn't I born
胡俾我瘉。 为何又要遭此祸。 Before or after?
不自我先， 来得不早也不晚， I suffer scorn
不自我后， 正好由我来承受。 From people's laughter.
好言自口， 好言出自人之口， Good words or bad
莠言②自口。 坏话也凭人口出。 Are what they say.
忧心愈愈③， 心中忧愁似患病， My heart feels sad,
是以有侮。 由此招来人欺侮。 Filled with dismay.

忧心惸惸④， 我的心里很忧愁， My heart feels grieved;
念我无禄⑤。 想来确是我不幸。 Unlucky am I.
民之无辜， 百姓实在很无辜， People deceived,
并其臣仆。 要被抓去充奴仆。 Slaves and maids cry.
哀我人斯， 这些人们真可怜， Alas for me!
于何从禄? 怎样才能得安生? Can I be blest?
瞻乌爰止， 快看群乌来往飞， The crow I see,
于谁之屋? 它要飞向谁的屋? Where can it rest?

瞻彼中林， 你且看那树林中， See in the wood
侯⑥薪侯蒸。 交错缠蔓细柴草。 Branch large or small.
民今方殆， 民众今日陷危困， For livelihood

---

① 瘉(shǔ):痒。② 莠言:丑言。③ 愈愈:犹"瘐瘐(yǔyǔ)",病。④ 惸惸(qióngqióng):孤独的样子。⑤ 无禄:不幸。⑥ 侯:犹"维"。

视天梦梦①，	心恨老天眼不睁。	We suffer all.
既克有定，	等到老天醒过来，	Dark is the sky.
靡人弗胜。	没人能够违天命。	Who'll make it clear?
有皇②上帝，	请问尊贵的上帝，	Heavens on high
伊谁云憎？	谁是祸首最可憎？	Cause hate and fear.
谓山盖③卑，	人说高山已成丘，	The hills said low
为冈④为陵。	乃是山脊仍高耸？	Are mountains high.
民之讹言，	民间流行的谣言。	Why don't we go
宁⑤莫之惩。	竟然总是不能禁？	Against the lie?
召彼故老，	快把元老召集来，	About our dream,
讯之占梦。	又请占卜解吉凶。	What do they know?
具曰"予圣"，	谁都自称是高手，	Though wise they seem
谁知乌之雌雄！	怎能分辨雌与雄！	They can't tell male
谓天盖高？	谁人说天高又高？	From female crow.
不敢不局⑥。	还是不敢不弯腰。	To what avail?
谓地盖厚？	谁人说地十分厚？	High are the skies;
不敢不蹐⑦。	还是只能小步走。	Down I must bow.
维号斯言，	应该大声宣此言，	Thick the earth lies;
有伦⑧有脊。	以此教人学道理。	I must walk slow.
哀今之人，	可怜今天的民众，	Though what I say
胡为虺蜴？	就像虺蜴东西逃。	Has no mistakes,

---

① 梦梦：不明。② 有皇：犹"皇皇"，大。③ 盖：读为"盍"，犹"何"。下同。④ 冈：山脊。
⑤ 宁：乃。⑥ 局：或作"跼(jú)"，屈曲不伸。⑦ 蹐(jí)：小步。⑧ 伦：理。脊，引作"迹"，
道理。

		Men of today
瞻彼阪田①，	看那远山坡上田，	Bite me like snakes.
有菀其特。	草儿茂盛苗独特。	See rugged field
天之扤②我，	上天把我使劲摇，	Where lush grows grain.
如不我克③，	唯恐未将我压倒。	How can I yield
彼④求我则，	朝廷想要征用我，	To might and main?
如不我得。	似乎很怕得不到。	I was sought after
执我仇仇⑤，	结果待我很冷淡，	But couldn't be got.
亦不我力。	我要出力他不要。	With pride and laughter
		They use me not.

		Laden with cares,
心之忧矣，	我的心里忧愁，	My heart seems bound.
如或结之。	就像纠缠不解。	The state affairs
今兹之正⑥，	如今这个朝政，	In woe are drowned.
胡然厉⑦矣？	为何如此糟糕？	The flames though high
燎⑧之方扬，	田火刚刚燃起，	May be put out.
宁或灭之？	难道就要熄灭？	The world's lost by
赫赫宗周⑨，	堂堂一个周朝，	Fair Lady Bao.
褒姒威之！	竟然灭于褒姒！	

终⑩其永怀⑪，	我总如此忧愁，	Long grieved my heart,
又窘阴雨。	连连遭遇阴雨。	I meet hard rain.
其车既载，	把车装得满满，	Loaded your cart,
乃弃尔辅。	却把夹板丢掉。	No wheels remain.

---

① 阪田：山坡上的田。② 扤(wù)：摇动。③ 克：制胜。④ 彼：指周王。⑤ 仇仇：缓持。⑥ 正：政。⑦ 厉：恶。⑧ 燎：放火烧草木。⑨ 宗周：指镐京。⑩ 终：既。⑪ 永怀：长忧。

载输①尔载，	等到货物坠落，	O'erturned 'twill lie;
将②伯助予！	才有辅佐需要。	For help you'd cry.

无弃尔辅，	不要丢掉车夹板，	Keep your wheel-aid
员③于尔辐。	它能使你车子牢。	And spoke well-made.
屡顾尔仆，	常常照顾赶车人，	Show oft concern
不输尔载。	货物才能保存好。	For driver good
终逾绝险，	这样就能渡难关，	Lest he o'erturn
曾是不意！	这个道理没想到！	Your cart of wood.
		You may get o'er
		Difficulties,
		But not before
		You thought of this.

鱼在于沼④，	鱼儿遨游在池沼，	
亦匪克乐。	但它未必很逍遥，	
潜虽伏矣，	有时会藏在深渊，	
亦孔之炤。	可能也被人看到。	
忧心惨惨，	神情不安心惶惶，	Fish in the pool
念国之为虐。	国之残暴难以忘。	Knows no delight.
		Deep in water cool
		They're still in sight.
		Saddened, I hate
		Evils of the state.

彼有旨酒，	他家备有醇美酒，	
又有佳肴。	又有美味和佳肴。	
洽比⑤其邻，	常和邻居相往来，	
昏姻孔云⑥。	又和亲戚相交好。	
念我独兮，	想我孤单无依靠，	They have' wine sweet
忧心慇慇。	真是忧心焚难熬。	And viands good,
		So they can treat
		Their kin and neighborhood.

① 输：堕。② 将(qiāng)：请。③ 员：增益，加大。④ 沼(zhǎo)：明白。⑤ 比：亲近。
⑥ 云：周旋。

佌佌①彼有屋，	小人也有房屋，	In loneliness I feel distress.
蔌蔌②方有谷。	丑人也有五谷。	The poor have houses small;
民今之无禄，	百姓却无收入，	Their food is coarse.
天夭③是椓。	上天降的灾殃。	Woes on them fall;
哿④矣富人，	富人过得欢快，	They've no resource.
哀此惸独。	穷人哀伤孤独。	Happy the rich class;
		But the poor, alas!

十月之交　　　　　　　President Huang Fu*

十月⑤之交，	十月之初日月交，	In the tenth month the sun and moon
朔日辛卯。	本月初一是辛卯，	Cross each other on the first day.
日有食之，	白天太阳有日食，	The sun was then eclipsed at noon,
亦孔之丑。	可能会有大灾祸。	An evil omen, people say.
彼月而微⑥，	晚上月亮昏天光，	The moon became then small;
此日而微。	白天太阳无光芒。	The sun became not bright.
今此下民，	如今天下的百姓，	The people one and all
亦孔之哀。	心中实在很忧伤。	Are in a wretched plight.
日月告凶，	日月显示凶亡兆，	Bad omen, moon and sun
不用其行。	没有遵循常规道。	Don't keep their proper way.

---

① 佌佌(cǐcǐ)：小。② 蔌蔌(sùsù)：陋貌。③ 夭：灾祸。④ 哿(gě)：喜乐。⑤ 十月：夏历八月。交，月终与月初相交之日。⑥ 微：晦暗不明。

* This political ode was the lamentation of an officer over the prodigies, celestial and terrestrial, betokening the ruin of Zhou. He expounded the true causes of these and named the chief culprit Huang Fu.

四国无政，	全国上下无善政，	In the states evil's done;
不用其良。	选人治国不贤良。	The good are kept away.
彼月而食，	晚上出现了月食，	The eclipse of the moon
则维其常。	这事多么的正常。	Is not uncommon thing;
此日而食，	白天出现了日食，	That of the sun at noon
于何不臧！	无奈坏事突然降！	Will dire disaster bring.

烨烨①震电，	天上烨烨闪雷电，	Lightning flashes, rolls thunder,
不宁不令。	震得苍生不安宁。	There is nor peace nor rest.
百川沸腾，	江河百川都沸腾，	The streams bubble from under;
山冢②崒崩。	山崩地裂震天响。	Crags fall from mountain-crest.
高岸为谷，	高山凹陷成峡谷，	The heights become deep vale;
深谷为陵。	深谷耸立变山峰。	Deep vales turn into height.
哀今之人，	可叹当今执政者，	Men of this time bewail:
胡憯③莫惩！	不知畏惧无忌惮。	What to do with such plight?

皇父④卿士，	执政卿士是皇父，	Huang Fu presides over the state;
番维司徒，	有番在下做司徒。	Fan the interior,
家伯维宰，	还有宰官是加伯，	Jia Bo is magistrates;
仲允膳夫，	仲允管厨是膳夫。	Zhong Yong is minister.
棸子内史，	棸子当的是内史，	Zou records worthy deeds;
蹶维趣马，	蹶氏负责把马牧。	Of stable Qui takes care.
楀维师氏，	楀氏师氏察朝政，	Yu is captain of steeds;

---

① 烨烨(yèyè)：打雷闪电的样子。② 冢(zhǒng)：山顶。③ 憯(cǎn)：同"惨"。④ 皇父(fǔ)、棸(zōu)子、蹶(guì)、楀(jǔ)：皆为姓氏。

艳妻①煽方处。	褒姒势力正鼎盛。	All flatter Lady Bao the fair.

抑②此皇父，	皇父这个卿士呀，	Oh, this Huang Fu would say
岂曰不时？	怎能说他的不是。	He's done all by decree.
胡为我作，	为何派我服劳役	But why drive me away
不即我谋？	一点不和我商量？	Without consulting me?
彻③我墙屋，	把我房屋都拆除，	Why move my house along
田卒汙④莱。	让我田亩都荒芜。	And devastate my land?
曰"予不戕⑤，	还说"我没伤害你，	Has he done nothing wrong?
礼则然矣。"	礼制本来就如此。"	The law is in his hand.

皇父孔圣，	皇父自谓为大圣，	Huang Fu says he is wise
作都于向⑥。	选择向地来建都。	And builds the capital.
择三有事⑦，	司徒司空和司马，	He chooses men we despise,
亶侯多藏。	家财万贯数不清。	Corrupt and greedy all.
不憖⑧遗一老，	老臣一个也不用，	No men of worthy deeds
俾守我王。	这样的人守王廷。	Are left to guard the crown;
择有车马⑨，	选择富贵有车者，	Those who have cars and steeds
以居⑩徂向。	同去向地自为政。	Are removed to his town.

黾⑪勉从事，	我们努力来工作，	I work hard all day long;
不敢告劳；	不敢叫苦有怨言。	Of my toil I'm not proud.
无罪无辜，	本来无罪又无辜，	I have done nothing wrong;

---

① 艳妻：指褒姒(sì)。② 抑：噫。③ 彻：通"撤"。④ 汙(wū)：同"污"，水池阻塞。莱(lái)，田地荒芜。⑤ 戕(qiāng)：残。⑥ 向：地名，在今河南尉氏县。⑦ 有事：有司，官名。⑧ 憖(yìn)：愿。⑨ 有车马：指富家。⑩ 居：语气词。⑪ 黾(mǐn)勉：努力，勉力。

谗口嚣嚣①。	众多小人进谗言。	Against me slander's loud.
下民之孽,	世间人们遭祸灾,	Distress of any kind
匪降自天。	不怪上天降灾祸。	Does not come from on high.
噂沓②背憎,	表面相合背后憎,	Good words or bad behind
职竞由人。	都是人为惹得祸。	Would raise a hue and cry.

悠悠我里③,	我的身体病悠悠,	My homeland's far away;
亦孔之痗④。	忧愁又加重病恙。	I feel so sad and drear.
四方有羡⑤,	四方民众都如愿,	Other people are gay;
我独居忧。	唯独有我心怀忧。	Alone I am grieved here.
民莫不逸,	民众无不很安逸,	When all people are free,
我独不敢休。	唯独有我不敢休。	Why can't I take my ease?
天命不彻⑥,	老天糊涂不行道,	I dread Heaven's decree;
我不敢效我友自逸。	不敢学人自安乐。	I can't as my friends do what I please.

雨无正　　　　　　　　Untimely Rain*

浩浩昊天,	广大无边的苍天,	The heaven high,
不骏⑦其德。	有德也是不久长。	Not kind for long,
降丧饥馑,	降临死亡与饥荒,	Spreads far and nigh
斩伐四国。	天下民众都遭殃。	Famine on throng.
旻天⑧疾威,	苍天暴虐太无当,	Heaven unfair,

---

① 嚣嚣:众多的样子。② 噂(zǔn)沓:喻两面派。③ 里:痛。④ 痗(mèi):病。⑤ 羡:宽裕。⑥ 彻:规律。⑦ 骏:经常。⑧ 旻(mín)天:泛指天。

* The speaker was a groom of the chambers.

弗虑弗图。	从不为民来着想。	You have no care
舍彼有罪，	有罪之人且放过，	Nor have you thought.
既伏①其辜。	隐藏真凶瞒真相。	Sinners are freed;
若无此罪，	清白无辜实冤枉，	Those who sin not,
沦胥②以铺③。	全都受迫遭祸殃。	Why should, they bleed?

周宗④既灭，	镐京已经被灭亡，	Where can I go after the fall
靡所止戾⑤。	没有居所能住长。	Of Zhou's capital?
正大夫离居，	长官大臣已离职，	Ministers gone,
莫知我勚⑥。	我的辛劳有谁知。	None knows my toil
三事大夫，	三公大夫都失职，	Nor serves the throne
莫肯夙夜。	不肯早晚辅君忙。	But all recoil.
邦君诸侯，	各国君王与诸侯，	Of the lords none
莫肯朝夕。	不再早晚参君王。	At court appear.
庶⑦曰式臧，	希望他们能改过，	No good is done
覆出为恶。	谁知反而更猖狂。	But evil here.

如何昊天！	怎奈昊昊的苍天，	Why isn't just word
辟⑧言不信。	乖张邪僻不守言。	Believed when heard?
如彼行迈，	就像行人向前走，	Travelers know
则靡所臻⑨。	没有方向如何到。	Nowhere to go.
凡百君子，	所有在朝的君子，	O lords, he good
各敬尔身。	各自慎重先保身。	And show manhood!

---

①伏：藏，隐。②胥：相继。③铺：通"痛"(pū)，痛苦。④周宗：镐京。⑤戾(lì)：定。⑥勚(yì)：疲惫。⑦庶：庶几，表示希望之词。⑧辟：邪僻。⑨臻(zhēn)：至。

胡不相畏，	为何彼此不相敬，	Don't you revere
不畏于天？	竟连苍天也不畏。	Heaven you fear?

戎①成不退，	战祸至今未消除，	After the war
饥成不遂，	饥荒也还没结束。	Famine's not o'er.
曾我暬御②，	只因我是侍御臣，	I, a mere groom,
憯憯日瘁。	终日惨惨熬苦心。	Am full of gloom.
凡百君子，	若有好话就禀报，	Among lords who
莫肯用讯③。	如是恶言赶紧逃。	Will speak the true?
听言④则答，	君王喜听顺耳言，	They like good word;
譖⑤言则退。	敢进忠言遭斥退。	Bad one's not heard.

哀哉不能言，	不能说话真可悲，	Alas! What's true
匪舌⑥是出，	不是舌头有毛病，	Cannot be said,
维躬是瘁。	只怕患病身遭殃。	Or woe on you,
		Your tongue and head.
哿⑦矣能言，	小人嘴巧招喜欢，	If you speak well
巧言如流，	好话说得流水长，	Like stream ne'er dry,
俾躬处休⑧。	身居要职心安康。	You will excel
		And soon rise high.

维曰于仕，	就说入仕来做官，	It's hard to be
孔棘且殆。	情势危险又紧急。	An officer.
云不可使，	如果说个"使不得"，	The wrongs you see
得罪于天子。	必将得罪于天子。	Make you incur
		Displeasure great

---

①戎：兵。②暬(xiè)御：侍御。③讯：进谏。④听言：顺从的话。⑤譖(zèn)言：谗言。⑥匪舌：惟躬，病。⑦哿(gě)：嘉。⑧休：福禄。

亦云可使,	如果说了"可以办",	Of Heaven's Son,
怨及朋友。	朋友一定会埋怨。	Or in the state
		Friends you have none.

谓尔迁于王都,	让你迁回到王都,	Go back to capital!
曰予未有室家。	说我没有房屋住。	You say your home's not there.
鼠思①泣血,	忧思啼泣呕心血,	My bitter tears would fall
无言不疾。	各种表现皆激烈。	To say what you can't bear:
昔尔出居,	那日你离王都去,	"When you left, who
谁从作尔室?	有谁帮你建家室?	Built house for you?"

小 旻

Counselors*

旻天疾威,	苍天幽远真残暴,	The Heaven's ire
敷②于下土。	降下灾荒遍国土。	On earth descends.
谋犹③回遹④,	谋算计划真邪僻,	The counsels dire
何日斯沮⑤?	哪天才能终停止?	Go without ends.
谋臧不从,	好的计谋他不用,	They follow one
不臧覆用。	反而恶计受恩宠。	Not good but bad.
我视谋犹,	那些谋划由我看,	The good not done,
亦孔之邛⑥!	纰漏太多不可用。	I feel so sad.

| 潝潝⑦訿訿⑧, | 小人党同又伐异, | Controversy |

---

① 鼠思:忧思。② 敷:布满。③ 犹:谋。④ 遹(yù):邪僻。⑤ 沮(jǔ):止。⑥ 邛(qióng):病。⑦ 潝潝(xìxì):相互附和的样子。⑧ 訿訿(zǐzǐ):互相抵触的样子。

* This was a lamentation over the recklessness and incapacity of the king's plans and of his counsellors.

亦孔之哀。	此举真是太悲哀。	Is to be rued.
谋之其臧,	那些良好的谋划,	They disagree
则具是违。	没有一个照着做。	On what is good.
谋之不臧,	那些不好的规则,	On what is bad
则具是依。	全都照行无违背。	They will depend.
我视谋犹,	这些谋划由我看,	I feel not glad;
伊于胡厎①!	不知何时才终止。	How will this end?

我龟既厌,	卜筮灵龟已厌倦,	The tortoise bored,
不我告犹。	不再告知我凶吉。	Nothing's foretold.
谋夫孔多,	出主意的人太多,	Men on the board
是用不集②。	没有哪个能做成。	No right uphold.
发言盈庭,	议论纷纷满朝堂,	The more they say;
谁敢执其咎?	责任有谁敢担当?	The less they do.
如匪行迈谋,	行路不知有所问,	They won't start on their way.
是用不得于道。	方向不明难成行。	How can we ask them to?

哀哉为犹,	国政混乱真可哀,	Alas! formers of plan
匪先民是程③,	不知取法效先祖,	Won't follow those of yore.
匪大犹④是经;	也不遵循天地经。	No principles they can
维迩言是听,	浅薄话儿偏爱听,	Formulate as before.
维迩言是争。	也会由此起纷争。	They follow counselors
如彼筑室于道谋,	就像建屋问路人,	Who can nothing good yield. They ask the wayfarers

---

① 厎(zhǐ):至。② 集:成功。③ 程:效法。④ 大犹:大道。

| | | About houses to build. |

是用不溃①于 　人多嘴杂说不清！
　成。

国虽靡止②，　国家虽然范围小，　Though bounded is our state,
或圣或否。　　也有圣贤和愚氓。　Our men may be wise or not.
民虽靡膴③，　民众虽然数量少，　Our numbers are not great;
或哲或谋，　　也有贤哲也有谋，　Some know to plan and plot;
或肃或艾④。　还有严肃治国者。　Others are able to think
如彼泉流，　　就像那些泉水流，　Like stream from spring will flow.
无沦胥⑤以败。不要玷染受污浊。　Together they will sink
　　　　　　　　　　　　　　　In common weal and woe.

不敢暴虎，　　不敢徒手打猛虎，　Don't fight a tiger with bare hand,
不敢冯⑥河。　不敢徒步过江河。　Nor cross without a boat the stream.
人知其一，　　个人只知一方面，　You may know one thing in your land,
莫知其他。　　不能详细知其他。　But not another as you deem.
战战兢兢，　　心惊胆战意恐恐，　Be careful as if you did stand
如临深渊，　　就像身在深水边，　On the brink of the gulf of vice
如履薄冰。　　就像走在薄冰上。　Or tread upon thin ice!

小　宛　　　　　　　　　　　Reflections*

宛⑦彼鸣鸠，　鸣叫的斑鸠真小巧，Small is the cooing dove,
翰⑧飞戾⑨天。高高飞起至青天。　But it can fly above.

---

① 溃：遂。② 止：地基。③ 膴(wǔ)：法则。④ 艾(yì)：干练。⑤ 沦胥：牵连受苦。⑥ 冯(píng)：徒步过河。⑦ 宛(wǎn)：小。⑧ 翰：高。⑨ 戾(lì)：至。

* Some officer, in a time of disorder and misgovernment, urges on his brothers the duty of maintaining their own virtue and of observing the greatest caution.

我心忧伤，	我的心里多忧伤，	My heart feels sad and drear,
念昔先人。	思念逝去的故人。	Missing my parents dear.
明发不寐，	通宵达旦难入睡，	Till daybreak I can't sleep,
有怀二人①。	感怀我的父母亲。	Lost so long in thoughts deep.
人之齐圣②，	人们真的很睿智，	Those who are grave and wise,
饮酒温③克。	喝到微醉能自持。	In drinking won't get drunk;
彼昏不知，	那些昏庸糊涂者，	But those who have dull eyes
壹醉日富。	一醉方休更自满。	In drinking will be sunk.
各敬尔仪，	个人行为要自重，	From drinking be restrained.
天命不又。	天命一去不再有。	What's lost can't be regained.
中原有菽④，	园中有片绿豆苗，	There are beans in the plain;
庶民采之。	百姓争相去摘采。	People gather their grain.
螟蛉⑤有子，	桑虫若是产幼子，	The insect has young ones;
蜾蠃⑥负之。	土蜂赶忙来背负。	The sphex bears them away.
教诲尔子，	教育你的下一代，	So teach and train your sons
式穀⑦似⑧之。	好好行善继祖德。	Lest they should go astray.
题⑨彼脊令，	看那鸟儿名脊令，	The wagtails wing their ways
载飞载鸣。	时而飞来时而鸣。	And twittering they're gone.
我日斯迈，	每天都在向前行，	Advancing are my days;
而月斯征。	你也每月都远征。	Your months are going on.
夙兴夜寐，	早起晚睡要努力，	Early to rise and late to bed!

① 二人：指父母。② 齐圣：聪明睿智。③ 温：蕴藉自持。④ 菽：大豆。⑤ 螟蛉：桑上小青虫。⑥ 蜾蠃(guǒluǒ)：土蜂。⑦ 穀：善。⑧ 似：嗣，继承。⑨ 题：视，看。

| 无忝①尔所生。 | 不要辱没你所生。 | Don't disgrace those by whom you're bred! |

交交②桑扈③,	桑扈飞来又飞去,	The greenbeaks on their tour
率场啄粟。	沿着场院啄粟米。	Peck grain in the stack-yard.
哀我填④寡,	可怜我家本穷苦,	I am lonely and poor,
宜岸宜狱。	先人没落受陷垢。	Unfit for working hard.
握粟出卜,	手握粟米来占卜,	I go out to divine
自何能穀?	可否运好得吉祥?	How can I not decline.

温温恭人,	那人谨慎又恭良,	Precarious, ill at ease,
如集于木。	好比停在高树上。	As if perched on trees;
惴惴⑤小心,	惴惴不安时谨慎,	Careful lest I should ail
如临于谷。	就像面临大深谷。	On the brink of a vale;
战战兢兢,	战战兢兢意恐恐,	I tremble twice or thrice
如履薄冰。	就像行走薄冰上。	As treading on thin ice.

小 弁　　　　　The Banished Prince*

| 弁⑥彼鸒⑦斯, | 那些雅鸟真快乐, | With flapping wings the crows |

---

① 忝(tiǎn):辱没。② 交交:往来的样子。③ 桑扈:窃脂,俗呼青觜(zuǐ),肉食不食粟。④ 填(tiǎn):穷苦。⑤ 惴惴(zhuìzhuì):形容又发愁又害怕的样子。⑥ 弁(pán):"昪(biàn)"字的假借,快乐。⑦ 鸒(yù):鸟名,形似鸟,大如鸽,腹下白色。往往千百成群,鸣声雅雅,又名雅鸟。

* The eldest son and heir-apparent of King You of Zhou bewailed his banishment because the king, enamoured of Lady Shi of Bao and led away by slanderers, announced that a child by Lady Shi should be his successor. When King You was killed in 770 B. C., the banished prince was recalled and became King Ping who removed the capital to the east.

归飞提提①。	飞回巢窝一群群。	Come back, flying in rows.
民莫不穀②，	没有百姓不安居，	All people gay appear;
我独于罹③。	唯我独自心忧伤。	Alone I'm sad and drear.
何辜于天？	我于苍天有何罪，	O what crime have I even
我罪伊何？	我的过错在哪里？	Committed against Heaven?
心之忧矣，	我的心中很忧伤，	With pain my heart's pierced through.
云如之何！	我能把它怎么样？	Alas! what can I do?

踧踧④周道，	各国大道真平坦，	The highway should be plain,
鞫⑤为茂草。	路边满满生茂草。	But it's o'ergrown with grass.
我心忧伤，	我的心中实烦恼，	My heart is wound'd with pain
惄⑥焉如捣，	就像舂米把心捣。	As if I'm pound'd, alas!
假寐⑦永叹，	姑且和衣长叹息，	Sighing, I lie still dressed;
维⑧忧用⑨老。	我因忧愁而衰老。	My grief makes me grow old.
心之忧矣，	我的心里多忧愁，	I feel deeply distressed,
疢⑩如疾首。	头痛欲烈似火烧。	Gnawed by headache untold.

维桑与梓，	看到桑树和梓树，	The mulberry and other
必恭敬止。	毕恭毕敬站那里。	Trees planted by our mother
靡瞻⑪匪父，	我只遵从父教诲，	And father are protected
靡依匪母。	我只依照母叮咛。	As our parents are respected.
不属⑫于毛，	没有毛发可依着，	Without the fur outside
不离⑬于里？	没有皮里可黏附。	And the lining inside,

---

① 提提(shí)：群飞安闲之貌。② 穀：善。③ 罹(lí)：忧。④ 踧踧(dí)：平易。⑤ 鞫(jū)：同"鞠"，穷，阻塞。一说"鞫"读为"茭(jiāo)，荒。⑥ 惄(nì)：忧思。⑦ 假寐：不脱衣而寐。这句是说虽在梦中还是长叹。⑧ 维：以。⑨ 用：而。⑩ 疢(chèn)：热病。⑪ 瞻：依照。依，遵从。⑫ 属(zhǔ)：连。⑬ 离：附着。

天之生我，	上天把我生下来，	Can we live at a time
我辰①安在？	我的好运哪里找？	Without reason or rhyme?

菀彼柳斯，	那些柳树真茂盛，	Lush grow the willow trees;
鸣蜩②嘒嘒③。	上有蝉儿嘒嘒鸣。	Cicadas trill at ease.
有漼④者渊，	有个深渊潭水深，	In water deep and clear
萑苇淠淠⑤。	长着密密的芦苇。	Rushes and reeds appear.
譬彼舟流⑥，	就像小船随水流，	Adrift I'm like a boat;
不知所届。	不知漂流到哪里。	I know not where I float.
心之忧矣，	我的心里多忧伤，	My heart deeply distressed,
不遑假寐。	没有心思去装睡。	In haste I lie down dressed.

鹿斯之奔，	有只小鹿跑过来，	The stag off goes
维足伎伎⑦，	四蹄飞奔快如飞。	At a fast gait;
雉之朝雊⑧，	山鸡清晨来鸣叫，	The pheasant crows,
尚求其雌。	将它雌伴来呼唤。	Seeking his mate.
譬彼坏⑨木，	好像那些衰枯树，	The ruined tree
疾用无枝。	病得叶落枝条秃。	Stript of its leaves
心之忧矣，	我的心中多忧伤，	Has saddened me.
宁莫之知。	难道有谁能知道？	Who knows what grieves?

相⑩彼投兔，	看那落网的兔子，	The captured hare
尚或先之。	或许还能被放回。	May be released;

---

① 辰：时运。② 蜩(tiáo)：蝉。③ 嘒嘒(huì huì)：蝉声。④ 漼(cuǐ)：深貌。⑤ 淠淠(pèi pèi)：草木众盛貌。⑥ 舟流：言无人操纵随舟自流。⑦ 伎伎(qíqí)：奔驰的样子。⑧ 雊(gòu)：雉鸣。⑨ 坏(huì)：树木瘿(yǐng)肿。⑩ 相：视。

行有死人，	路边倒卧的死人，	The dead o'er there
尚或墐①之。	或许还有人葬他。	Buried at least.
君子秉心，	奈何君子的居心，	The king can't bear
维②其忍之。	就会如此的残忍。	The sight of me;
心之忧矣，	我的心里多忧伤，	Laden with care,
涕既陨之。	泪珠缓缓地滑落。	My tears flow free.

君子信谗，	君子相信了谗言，	Slanders believed
如或酬之。	好像接受人敬酒。	As a toast drunk,
君子不惠，	君子没有仁慈心，	The king's deceived,
不舒究之。	不愿细细来追究。	In thoughts not sunk.
伐木掎③矣，	砍伐树时要牵引，	The branch cut down,
析薪④杝⑤矣，	劈柴薪要沿纹理。	They leave the tree.
舍彼有罪，	有罪之人被放过，	The guilty let alone,
予之佗⑥矣。	却把罪责加给我。	They impute guilt to me.

莫高匪山，	高不过那么颠，	Though higher than a mountain
莫浚匪泉。	深不过那流泉。	And deeper than a fountain,
君子无易由⑦言，	君子请莫轻开言，	The king ne'er speaks linght word or jeers,
耳属于垣。	耳朵自贴向墙边。	For even walls have ears.
无逝我梁，	不要前去我的鱼梁，	"Do not remove my dam

---

① 墐(jìn)：埋。② 维：何。③ 掎(jǐ)：牵引。④ 析薪：劈柴。⑤ 杝(chǐ)：就是顺木柴的丝理来劈破。⑥ 佗(tuó)：加。⑦ 由：于。

无发我笱，	不要翻动我的渔篓，	And my basket for fish!"
我躬不阅①，	我自身难以安存，	I can't preserve what I am.
遑恤我后。	又如何顾及身后事忧。	What care I for my wish?

巧　言

Disorder and Slander*

悠悠昊天！	遥远广阔的苍天，	O great Heaven on high,
曰父母且②！	说是下民的父母。	You're called our parent dear.
无罪无辜，	人民无罪又无过，	Why make the guiltless cry
乱如此怃③。	为何降下大灾祸。	And spread turmoil far and near?
昊天已④威，	苍天实在太暴怒，	You cause our terror great;
予慎无罪。	我们实在无过错。	We're worried for the guiltless.
昊天泰怃，	苍天实在太傲慢，	You rule our hapless fate;
予慎无辜。	我们实在很无辜。	We're worried in distress.
乱之初生，	祸乱刚刚开始时，	Sad disorder comes then
僭⑤始既涵。	流言已开始流行。	When untruth is received.
乱之又生，	祸乱再次兴起时，	Disorder comes again
君子信谗。	君王又把谗言听。	When slanders are believed.
君子如怒，	君王如能斥谗言，	If we but blame falsehood,
乱庶遄⑥沮⑦。	祸乱立即就停止。	Disorder will decrease.
君子如祉⑧，	君王处理能得当，	If we but praise the good,

① 阅：收容。② 且(jū)：语气词。③ 怃(hū)：大。④ 已：大，甚，很。⑤ 僭(zèn)：谗言。⑥ 遄(chuán)：迅速。⑦ 沮：终止。⑧ 祉：福。

* The speaker, suffering from the king through slander, appealed to Heaven, dwelled on the nature and evil of slander and expressed his detestation of and contempt for the slanderers.

乱庶遄已。	祸乱铲除国兴隆。	Disorder soon will cease.
君子屡盟，	君王屡盟无信用，	If we make frequent vows,
乱是用长。	所以祸乱在增长。	Disorder will still grow.
君子信盗，	君王偏信欺骗者，	If we to thieves make bows,
乱是用暴。	所以祸乱更猖獗。	They will bring greater woe.
盗言孔甘，	骗人谎言很动听，	What they say may be sweet;
乱是用餤①，	祸乱由此更增深。	The woe grows none the less.
匪其止共②，	小人做事不守礼，	The disorder complete
维王之邛③。	只能给王添烦愁。	Will cause the king's distress.
奕奕④寝庙，	宗庙雄伟真宽敞，	The temple's grand,
君子作之。	先王亲自来督造。	Erected for ages.
秩秩大猷，	各种政策俱完善，	Great work is planned
圣人莫⑤之。	全由圣人来谋划。	By kings and sages.
他人有心，	如果他人有异心，	Judge others' mind
予忖度之。	一眼我就能测度。	But by your own.
跃跃⑥毚⑦兔，	狡猾兔子疾奔逃，	The hound can find
遇犬获之。	猎犬能将它捉到。	Hares running down.
荏染⑧柔木，	幼小树苗多柔软，	The supple tree
君子树之。	君王把它来栽种。	Plant'd by the good,
往来行言，	流言四起纷纷传，	From slander free,
		You can tell truth from falsehood.

---

① 餤(tán)：增多。② 共：恭敬。③ 邛(qióng)：病。④ 奕奕(yìyì)：大。⑤ 莫：谋。⑥ 跃跃(tìtì)：快速跳跃的样子。⑦ 毚(chán)：兔，狡兔。⑧ 荏染(rěnrǎn)：柔弱的样子。

心焉数①之。　　真相如何心中明。　　Grandiose word
蛇蛇②硕言，　　美言夸夸说不停，　　Should not be heard.
出自口矣!　　　汩汩流淌谗人口。　　Sweet sounding one
巧言如簧，　　　巧言美妙如吹簧，　　Like organ-tongue.
颜之厚矣!　　　颜面真是厚如墙。　　Can deceive none
　　　　　　　　　　　　　　　　　　Except the young.

彼何人斯，　　　那是一个什么人，　　Who is that knave
居河之麋③。　　住在河边水草旁。　　On river's border,
无拳④无勇，　　也无力气也无勇，　　Nor strong nor brave,
职为乱阶。　　　祸乱都由他源起。　　Root of disorder?
既微⑤且尰⑥，　 小腿溃烂脚又肿，　　You look uncanny.
尔勇伊何?　　　如何显示你神勇?　　How bold are you?
为犹将⑦多，　　你的计谋真是多，　　Your plans seem many;
尔居徒几何?　　你的价值有几何?　　Your followers are few.

何人斯

Friend or Foe? *

彼何人斯?　　　那是一个什么人?　　Who's the man coming here
其心孔艰⑧。　　他的心思难揣测。　　So deep and full of hate?
胡逝我梁，　　　为啥经过我鱼梁，　　My dame he's coming near.
不入我门?　　　又不进入我家门?　　But enters not my gate.
伊谁云从?　　　要问他听谁的话，　　Is he a follower

---

① 数(shǔ)：辨。② 蛇蛇(yíyí)：轻薄的样子。③ 麋(méi)：湄，水边。④ 拳：力。
⑤ 微：足疡。⑥ 尰(zhǒng)：肿。⑦ 将：大。⑧ 艰：阴险。

* The speaker, suffering from slander and suspecting that the slanderer was an old friend, intimated the grounds of his suspicion and lamented his case, while he would welcome the restoration of their former relations.

维暴之云。	暴公说啥他听啥。	Of the tyrant? Yes, sir.

二人从行，	两个人儿一同行，	Two friends we did appear;
谁为此祸？	这祸是由谁闯下？	Alone I am in woes.
胡逝我梁？	为何经过我鱼梁，	My dam he's coming near,
不入唁我。	却不进门来慰问？	But past my gate he goes.
始者不如今，	当初不是这般冷，	He is different now;
云不我可。	如今待我太无情。	He has broken his vow.

彼何人斯，	那是一个什么人？	Who's the man coming here,
胡逝我陈[①]？	为何经过我堂前。	Passing before my door?
我闻其声，	我只听他脚步声，	His voice I only hear,
不见其身。	却不看见他身影。	But see no man of yore.
不愧于人？	面对世人不惭愧，	How can he not fear then
不畏于天？	难道也不怕苍天。	Neither heaven nor men?

彼何人斯？	那是一个什么人？	Who's the man coming forth
其为飘风。	好比风儿飘不定。	Like a whirlwind which roars?
胡不自北，	为何不从北边来，	Why does he not go north
胡不自南？	为何不从南边来。	Nor to the southern shores?
胡逝我梁，	为何经过我鱼梁，	Why comes he near my dam
祇搅我心。	恰好扰乱我内心。	And disturbs what I am?

尔之安行，	你要缓缓向前行，	Even when you walk slow,
亦不遑舍。	却也不及暂停歇。	You won't stop where you are.

[①] 陈：堂前的路。

尔之亟行，	你在路上走得急，	And then when fast you go,
遑脂①尔车。	甭想停住你的车。	How can you grease your car?
壹②者之来，	每次经过我门前，	You will not come to see,
云何其盱③！	我的心中多企盼。	Let alone comfort me.

尔还而入，	你回来时入家门，	If you should but come in,
我心易④也。	我的心情多欢快。	Then I would feel at ease.
还而不入，	你回来时不进家，	But you do not come in,
否⑤难知也。	是何心思实难猜。	I know you're hard to please.
壹者之来，	每次你到我家来，	You won't come to see me,
俾我祇⑥也。	都能够使我心安。	Nor will set my heart free.

伯氏吹埙⑦，	大哥来吹陶埙，	Earthern whistle you blew;
仲氏吹篪⑧。	二哥来吹横笛。	I played bamboo flute long.
及尔如贯，	与你如同一线牵，	When I was friend with you,
谅不我知。	竟然于我无情义。	We had sung the same song.
出此三物⑨，	列出祭物猪狗鸡，	Before offerings now,
以诅尔斯。	一起盟誓表心迹。	Can you forget your vow?

为鬼为蜮⑩，	你是厉鬼和短狐，	I curse you as a ghost,
则不可得。	飘来飘去无踪影。	For you have left no trace.
有靦⑪面目，	只是有个人面目，	I will not be your host
视人罔极⑫。	待人却没有准则。	I see your ugly face.

---

①脂：止住车。②壹：每次。③盱：希望。盱(xù)：忧。④易：高兴。⑤否：语助词，无意义。⑥祇(qí)：病。⑦埙(xūn)：古代吹奏乐器。⑧篪(chí)：横笛(竹制)。⑨三物：指猪、犬、鸡。⑩蜮(yù)：短狐。⑪靦(tiǎn)：露脸见人。⑫极：准则。

作此好歌，	苦心作好此歌谣，	But I sing in distress
以极仅侧。	追究你的不公允。	For you are pitiless.

巷 伯

A Eunuch's Complaint

萋兮斐兮，	彩丝亮啊花线明啊，	A few lines made to be
成是贝锦。	织成贝纹锦。	Fair shell embroidery,
彼谮人者，	那个造谣的害人精，	You slanderers in dress
亦已大甚。	实在太狠心！	Have gone to great excess.
哆兮侈兮，	张开嘴啊咧开唇啊，	The Sieve stars in the south
成是南箕。	成了簸箕星。	Opening wide their mouth,
彼谮人者，	那个造谣的害人精，	You vile slanderers, who
谁适与谋？	谁是他的智多星？	Devise the schemes for you?
缉缉翩翩，	喊喊喳喳鬼话灵，	You talk so much, o well;
谋欲谮人。	一心要挖陷人阱。	In slander you excel.
慎尔言也，	劝你说话加小心，	Take care of what you say.
谓尔不信。	有一天没人再相信。	Will it be believed? Nay.
捷捷幡幡，	花言巧语舌头长，	You may think you are clever,
谋欲谮言。	千方百计将人陷。	Slandering people ever.
岂不尔受？	并非没人来上当，	But deceived, they will learn
既其女迁。	终将自己要遭殃。	You'll be punished in turn.

骄人①好好②，	进谗的人乐忘形，	The proud are in delight,
劳人③草草④。	劳心的人真苦恼。	The crowd in sorry plight.
苍天苍天！	苍天啊苍天，	Heaven bright, heaven bright!
视彼骄人，	你看那人多骄傲，	Look on the proud;
矜⑤此劳人。	这位劳人多可怜。	Pity the crowd!

彼谮人者，	那个散布流言者，	O you vile slanderers,
谁适与谋？	是谁为他出策谋？	Who are your counselors?
取彼谮人，	要把那个造谣者，	I would throw you to feed
投畀⑥豺虎。	扔到荒野喂豺虎。	The wolf's or tiger's greed.
豺虎不食，	豺虎嫌臭不肯食，	If they refuse to eat,
投畀有北⑦。	把它扔到北方去。	I'd tread you down my feet
有北不受，	严寒地方也不收，	Or cast you to north land
投彼有昊⑧。	它投到天上去发落！	Or throw to Heave's hand.

杨园之道，	杨园有一条小路，	The eunuch Mengzi, I
猗⑨于亩丘⑩。	逶迤附着在亩丘。	Go to the Garden High
寺人⑪孟子，	我是宦臣名孟子，	By a willowy road long
作为此诗。	亲自作了这首诗。	And make this plaintive song.
凡百君子，	恳请朝廷各大臣，	Officials on your way,
敬而听之。	态度端正认真听。	Hearken to it, I pray.

---

① 骄人：指谗者。② 好好：喜悦。③ 劳人：忧人，指被谗者。④ 草草：慅慅(sāosāo)：忧伤的样子。⑤ 矜(jīn)：哀怜。⑥ 畀(bì)：与。⑦ 有北：北方极寒无人之境。⑧ 有昊：昊天。⑨ 猗(yǐ)：加。⑩ 亩丘：有垄界像田亩的丘。一说是丘名。⑪ 寺人：阉官。

谷风之什

Fifth Decade of Odes

谷 风

Weal and Woe*

习习①谷风，	和煦东风微微吹，
维风及雨。	阴雨潇潇绵绵落。
将恐将惧，	当初遇难恐慌时，
维予与女。	你我相依在一起。
将安将乐，	如今生活很安乐，
女转弃予！	你却变心把我弃。

Strong winds hard blow,
Followed by rain.
In times of woe
Firm we'd remain;
Cast off in weal,
Lonely I feel.

习习谷风，	和煦东风微微吹，
维风及颓②。	大风回旋真厉害。
将恐将惧，	当初遇难恐慌时，
寘予③于怀。	将我拥在你怀里。
将安将乐，	如今生活很安乐，
弃予如遗！	你将我遗弃忘记。

Strong winds hard blow
From morn till night.
In times of woe
You held me tight;
Cast off in weal,
How sad I feel!

习习谷风，	和煦东风微微吹，
维山崔嵬。	看那高山真雄伟。
无草不死，	没有小草不干枯，

Strong winds blow high,
But mountains stand.
No grass but die,

---

① 习习：和调的样子。② 颓(tuí)：暴风由上而下。③ 予：我。

* A woman complained of the alienation produced by the change for the better in the circumstances

无木不萎。	没有树木不凋零。	Nor trees in land.
忘我大德，	忘记我的大恩德，	Much good's forgot;
思我小怨！	细小恩怨记心中。	Small faults ale not.

蓼 莪

The Parents' Death*

蓼蓼①者莪，	莪蒿长得真茂盛，	Long and large grows sweet grass,
匪莪伊②蒿。	不是莪蒿是青蒿。	Not wild weed of no worth.
哀哀父母，	我的父母真可怜，	My parents died, alas!
生我劬③劳。	生我养我真辛劳。	With toil they gave me birth.

蓼蓼者莪，	莪蒿长得真茂盛，	Long and large grows sweet grass,
匪莪伊蔚④。	不是莪蒿是蔚蒿。	Not shorter weed on earth.
哀哀父母，	我的父母真可怜，	My parents died, alas!
生我劳瘁。	生我养我真辛劳。	With pain they gave me birth.

瓶之罄⑤矣，	酒瓶之中酒尽了，	When the pitcher is void,
维罍⑥之耻。	这是酒坛的羞耻。	Empty will be the jar.
鲜民之生，	孤苦伶仃在世上，	Our parents' life destroyed,
不如死之久矣！	不如早死无忧伤。	How sad we orphans are!
无父何怙⑦？	没有父亲怎么办？	On whom can I rely,

---

① 蓼(lù)：长大貌。莪(é)：莪蒿，野草名。② 伊：是。③ 劬(qú)：劳苦。④ 蔚(wèi)：牡蒿。⑤ 罄(qìng)：尽。⑥ 罍(léi)：酒器。⑦ 怙(hù)：依靠。

* A son deplored his hard fate in being prevented from rendering the last services to his parents and enlarged on the parental claim.

无母何恃？	没有母亲依靠谁？	Now fatherless and motherless?
出则衔恤①，	远行心怀忧郁情，	Outdoors, with grief I sigh;
入则靡至！	返家无处觅双亲。	Indoors, I seem homeless.

父兮生我，	父亲把我生下来，	My father gave me birth;
母兮鞠②我，	母亲把我来养大。	By mother I was fed.
拊③我畜我，	抚育我呀养活我，	They cherished me with mirth,
长我育我，	护佑我呀教育我，	And by them I was bred.
顾我复④我，	照顾我呀牵挂我，	They looked after me
出入腹⑤我。	出门进门抱着我。	And bore me out and in.
欲报之德，	想要报答此恩德，	Boundless as sky should be
昊天罔极！	不料老天降灾祸。	The kindness of our kin.

南山烈烈⑥，	南山雄伟且高大，	The southern mountain's high;
飘风发发⑦。	暴风呼呼把沙扬。	The wind soughs without cheer.
民莫不穀⑧，	人人都能养爹娘，	Happy are those near by;
我独何害⑨！	唯独有我受灾殃。	Alone I'm sad and drear.

南山律律⑩，	南山雄伟且高大，	The southern mountain's cold;
飘风弗弗⑪。	暴风呼呼把沙扬。	The wind blows a strong blast.
民莫不穀，	人人都能养爹娘，	Happy are young and old;
我独不卒⑫！	唯独我不能送葬。	My grief fore'er will last.

---

① 恤(xù)：忧。② 鞠(jū)：养育。③ 拊(fǔ)：抚摸。④ 复：往来。⑤ 腹：怀抱。⑥ 烈烈：高大的样子。⑦ 发发(bōbō)：疾速的样子。⑧ 穀：养。⑨ 害：忧虑。⑩ 律律：同"烈烈"。⑪ 弗弗：同"发发"。⑫ 卒：为父母养老送终。

大　东

East and West*

有饛①簋②飧③，	食盒里边装满饭，	The tripod's full of food;
有捄④棘匕。	枣木勺柄弯又长。	They eat with spoons of wood.
周道⑤如砥⑥，	大路光滑又平坦，	The road's smooth like whetstone
其直如矢。	方向笔直如箭矢。	For lords to go alone.
君子⑦所履，	王公贵族走上边，	Like arrow it is straight,
小人所视。	百姓只能远远看。	On which no people circulate.
睠⑧言顾之，	回过头来看一眼，	Recalling bygone years,
潸⑨焉出涕。	不禁眼泪落胸前。	In streams run down my tears.
小东大东⑩，	东方大国和小国，	In East states, large and small,
杼柚⑪其空。	织布来回搜刮光。	The looms are empty all.
纠纠葛屦，	葛布鞋子带纠缠，	In summer shoes we go
可以履霜。	可以用来御冰霜。	On winter frost or snow.
佻佻⑫公子，	君子安闲又轻盈，	Even the noble sons
行彼周行。	来来往往大道上。	Walk on foot like poor ones.

---

① 饛(méng)：食物满器之貌。② 簋(guǐ)：古读如"九"，盛食品的器具，圆筒形。③ 飧(sūn)：食。④ 捄(qiú)：通作"觩"，角上曲而长之貌，形容匕柄的形状。⑤ 周道：大道或官路。⑥ 砥(dǐ)：磨刀石，磨物使平也叫砥。⑦ 君子：小人，指贵族与平民。⑧ 睠(juàn)："眷"的异体字。回顾之貌。⑨ 潸(shān)：涕下貌。⑩ 小东大东："东"指东方之国，远为大，近为小。⑪ 杼柚(zhùzhú)：是织机上的两个部分。杼持纬线，柚受经线。⑫ 佻佻(tiáotiáo)：美好。

* The descendents of Shang in the East complained of the inequality between the East and the West ruled by the government of Zhou, and vented their indignation by showing the deceit in Heaven where stars did not live up to their fine names: the Winnowing Fan could not winnow and the Dipper could not hold wine.

| 既往既来， | 折回往返好几趟， | Seeing them come and go, |
| 使我心疚①。 | 使我心中多忧伤。 | My heart is full of woe. |

有冽②氿③泉。	旁流的泉水真清凉，	Cold water passing by,
无浸获薪。	别湿了砍下的柴薪。	Do not soak our firewood!
契契④寤叹，	忧苦失眠又叹息，	Woeful we wake and sigh
哀我惮⑤人。	可怜我们辛苦人。	For scanty livelihood.
薪是获薪，	这些柴火是新柴，	If our firewood is dry,
尚可载也。	还可用车来装载。	We may carry it west.
哀我惮人，	可怜我这劳苦人，	If wet, we can but sigh.
亦可息也。	也该好好休息了。	O when may we have rest?

东人之子，	东方国家的百姓，	We toilers of the east
职劳不来⑥。	承受劳苦无人问。	Are not paid as those of the West;
西人⑦之子，	西周国家的人民，	The western nobles at least
粲粲衣服。	穿着华丽光照人。	Are all splendidly drest.
舟人之子，	船户之家的子弟，	The rich and noble sons
熊罴是裘。	熊罴大衣穿上身。	Don't care about their furs,
私人⑧之子，	即使家奴的后代，	But as slaves the poor ones
百僚⑨是试⑩。	将来也能当官吏。	Serve all the officers.

| 或以其酒， | 有人喝酒喝好酒， | If we present them wine, |
| 不以其浆， | 有人竟无饮酒浆。 | They do not think it fine. |

---

① 疚：病痛。② 冽(liè)：寒。③ 氿(guǐ)：从旁出，流道狭长的泉叫做"氿泉"。④ 契契：忧苦。⑤ 惮(dàn)：亦作"瘅(dàn)"，疲劳。⑥ 来：慰勉。⑦ 西人：指周人。⑧ 私人：私家仆隶之类。⑨ 僚：又作"寮"，官。⑩ 试：用。

鞙鞙①佩璲②，	有人带玉真风光，	If we present them jade,
不以其长。	有人杂佩也没有。	They don't think it well-made.
维天有汉③，	天上银河星灿烂，	The Silver River bright
监④亦有光。	以之为镜亦有光。	Looks down on us in light.
跂⑤彼织女，	织女星座两脚分，	The Weaving Stars are three;
终日七襄⑥。	每天七次把位移。	All day long they are free.

虽则七襄，	虽然每天移七次，	Though all day long they move,
不成报⑦章，	织布难以成纹样。	They weave nothing above.
睆⑧彼牵牛，	牵牛星儿耀眼亮，	Bright is the Cowherd Star,
不以服箱。	也不能够负车厢。	But it won't draw our car.
东有启明⑨，	东方有颗启明星，	Morning Star in the east,
西有长庚。	西方有颗长庚星。	Eight Net Stars catch no beast,
有捄⑩天毕⑪，	天毕星座柄儿长，	Evening Star in the west,
载施之行。	把它倒张在路上。	What use though they don't rest?

维南有箕，	南边有个箕星座，	In south the Winnowing Fan
不可以簸扬。	不能用来筛米糠。	Cannot sift grain for man.
维北有斗⑫，	北方有个斗星座，	In north the Dipper fine
不可以挹⑬酒浆。	不能用来舀酒浆。	Cannot ladle good wine.
维南有箕，	南边那个箕星座，	The Sieve shines in the south,

---

① 鞙鞙(juānjuān)：玉圆的样子。② 璲(suì)：通"瑞"，宝玉。③ 汉：云汉，就是天河。④ 监：鉴，镜子。⑤ 跂(qí)：歧。⑥ 襄：驾。⑦ 报：复，就是往来的意思。⑧ 睆(huǎn)：明貌。⑨ 启明、长庚：同是金星的异名，朝在东方，叫做"启明"，晚在西方，叫做"长庚"。⑩ 捄：形容毕星的柄。⑪ 毕：星名。共八星，形状像田猎时所用的毕网。⑫ 斗：南斗星。⑬ 挹(yì)：用勺酌水。

载翕①其舌。	他的舌头不算长。	Idly showing its mouth.
维北有斗，	北边那个斗星座，	In the north shines the Plough
西柄之揭②。	柄儿一直向西方。	With handle like a bow.

四 月　　　　　　　　Banishment to the South*

四月维夏，	夏历四月已夏天，	From fourth to sixth moon when
六月徂③暑。	六月酷暑正当前。	The summer heat remains,
先祖匪人，	先祖又不是他人，	Our fathers are kind men;
胡宁忍予？	怎能忍心我受苦！	Can they leave me in pains?

秋日凄凄，	秋天来了风凄凄，	The autumn days are chill;
百卉俱腓④。	百种花卉都枯萎。	All plants and grass decay.
乱离瘼⑤矣，	慌乱不断亲戚散，	In distress I am ill.
爰其适归？	何时才能得归还？	Where can I go? Which way?

冬日烈烈，	冬天到来风烈烈，	In winter days severe
飘风发发。	大风呼啸耳边刮。	The vehement wind blows.
民莫不穀，	人们生活都很好，	No one feels sad and drear.
我独何害！	为何只有我受害！	Why am I alone in woes?

---

① 翕(xī)：缩。② 揭：高举。③ 徂(cú)：始。④ 腓(féi)：通"痱"，枯萎。⑤ 瘼(mò)：病。

* An officer banished to the south deplored the misery he had suffered in summer, autumn and winter, compared himself to destroyed tree and muddy water and complained that he was not so free as hawk and fish and that he could not grow like ferns and medlars.

山有嘉卉，　　山上长有好草木，　　Trees on the hill were good
侯栗侯梅。　　既有栗树也有梅。　　And mume trees far and nigh.
废①为残贼②，　人们习惯被残害，　　Who has destroyed the wood?
莫知其尤③。　　没人觉得有过错。　　Who knows the reason why?

相彼泉水，　　看那山间的泉水，　　Water from fountain flows
载清载浊。　　有的清来有的浊。　　Now muddy and now clear.
我日构④祸，　　每天都要遭灾祸，　　But I'm each day in woes.
曷云能穀？　　何时能过好生活？　　How can I not be drear?

滔滔江汉，　　江河滔滔向东流，　　The rivers east and west
南国之纪⑤。　　统揽南方小支流。　　Crisscross in southern land.
尽瘁以仕，　　鞠躬尽瘁为国家，　　In work I did my best.
宁莫我有。　　为何君王看不到。　　Who'd give me helping hand?

匪鹑⑥匪鸢⑦，　做人不是鹰和雕，　　Like hawk or eagle why
翰飞戾天。　　振翅一飞冲云霄。　　Cannot I skyward go?
匪鱣⑧匪鲔，　　做人也不是鱣鲔，　　Like fish why cannot I
潜逃于渊。　　游在深渊真逍遥。　　Go to hide down below?

山有蕨薇，　　山上一片蕨薇草，　　Above grow ferns in throng,
隰有杞桋。　　低处女桑和枸杞。　　And medlars spread below.
君子作歌，　　君子写了这首诗，　　Alas! I've made this song
维以告哀。　　以慰心头的哀伤。　　To ease my heart of woe.

---

①废：习惯。②残贼：害虫。③尤：过。④构：遘，遭遇。⑤纪：纲，约束之意。⑥鹑(tuán)：雕。⑦鸢(yuān)：鹰。⑧鱣(zhān)、鲔(wěi)：鱼名。

北　山		Injustice*
陟彼北山，	爬上北边那座山，	To gather medlars long,
言采其杞。	上山去把枸杞采。	I go up northern height.
偕偕①士子，	武士个个皆强壮，	Being an officer strong,
朝夕从事②。	从早到晚公事忙。	I'm busy day and night
王事靡盬③，	公家的事没个完，	For the royal affairs.
忧我父母④。	想到父母心忧伤。	Who for my parents cares?
溥⑤天之下，	天下如此的广大，	The land under the sky
莫非王土。	哪片土地非王土。	Is all the king's domain;
率⑥土之滨⑦，	凡是天涯范围内，	The people far and nigh
莫非王臣。	哪个不是他臣民。	Are under royal reign.
大夫⑧不均，	大臣分工不公平，	But ministers unfair
我从事独贤⑨。	唯独我们差事苦。	Load me with heavy care.
四牡彭彭⑩，	四匹母马奔走忙，	Four steeds run without rest
王事傍傍⑪。	操办公事也心急。	For state affairs all day long.
嘉我未老，	夸奖我还没衰老，	They say I'm at my best
鲜⑫我方将⑬。	赞美我的体力壮。	And few like me are strong.

---

① 偕偕：强壮貌。② 从事：言办理王事。③ 盬(gǔ)：止息。④ 忧我父母：使父母担忧。
⑤ 溥(pǔ)：犹"普"。⑥ 率：自。⑦ 滨：水边。⑧ 大夫：执政大臣。⑨ 贤：多，劳。⑩ 彭彭：不得休息的样子。⑪ 傍傍：纷至沓来、无穷尽的样子。⑫ 鲜：嘉，善。⑬ 将：壮。

* A petty officer complained of the arduous and continual duties unequally imposed upon him and keeping him away from his duty to his parents, while others were left to enjoy their ease.

| 旅力方刚， | 趁着我还有力量， | I have a robust chest |
| 经营四方。 | 奔走忙碌管四方。 | And may go east and west. |

或燕燕①居息，	有人在家多安逸，	Some enjoy rest and ease;
或尽瘁事国。	有人为了国事忙。	Others worn out for the state.
或息偃②在床，	有的卧倒在床榻，	Some march on without cease;
或不已于行。	有的不停赶路上。	Others lie in bed early and late.

或不知叫号，	有人不知世间苦，	Some know not people's pain;
或惨惨③劬劳。	有人操劳伴终生。	Others toil for state affairs.
或栖迟偃仰，	有人生活很悠闲，	Some long in bed remain;
或王事鞅掌④。	有人公事忙不断。	Others laden with great cares.

或湛⑤乐饮酒，	有人饮酒又行乐，	Some drink all the day long;
或惨惨畏咎。	有人谨慎怕过错。	Others worry for woe.
或出入风议⑥，	有人只会讲空话，	Some only say all's wrong;
或靡事不为。	有人事事都繁忙。	To hard work others go.

无将大车　　　　　　　　Don't Trouble*

无将⑦大车，	牛拉大车不要扶，	Don't push an ox-drawn cart
祇自尘兮。	只会沾惹一身土。	Or you'll raise dust about.
无思百忧，	不要去想烦心事，	Do not trouble your heart

---

① 燕燕：安息。② 偃：卧。③ 惨："懆(cǎo)"，不安。④ 鞅掌：忙乱烦扰的意思。⑤ 湛 (dān)：乐。⑥ 风议：就是放言。⑦ 将(jiàng)：推。

* This ode read like the song of a driver who advised people not to do anything be- yond human power lest it should get them into trouble.

祇①自疻兮。	弄得自己徒忧伤。	Or you'll be ill, no doubt.

无将大车，　　牛拉大车不要扶，　　Don't push an ox-drawn cart
维尘冥冥②。　　尘土滚滚遮人眼。　　Or dust will dim your sight.
无思百忧，　　不要去想烦心事，　　Do not trouble your heart
不出于颎③。　　心中忧愁无前途。　　Or you can't see the light.

无将大车，　　牛拉大车不要扶，　　Don't push an ox-drawn cart
维尘雝④兮。　　扬起尘土路模糊。　　Or dust will darken the way.
无思百忧，　　不要去想烦心事，　　Do not trouble your heart
祇自重⑤兮。　　只给自己添重负。　　Or you will pine away.

小　明　　　　　A Nostalgic Official*

明明上天，　　至明至清的上天，　　O Heaven high and bright,
照临下土。　　光芒普照洒大地。　　On lower world shed light!
我征徂西，　　我今出征到西边，　　Westward I came by order
至于艽⑥野。　　一直走到那荒野。　　As far as this wild border
二月⑦初吉，　　那时正是腊月初，　　Of second month then on the first day;
载离寒暑。　　如今寒去暑也往。　　Now cold and heat have passed away.
心之忧矣，　　我的心中很忧伤，　　Alas! my heart is sad

---

① 祇(qí)：忧病。② 冥冥：尘飞的样子。③ 颎(jiǒng)：光明。④ 雝：蔽。⑤ 重(zhòng)：沉重，劳累。⑥ 艽(qiú)野：远郊荒野。⑦ 二月：夏历十二月。

* An official kept long abroad on distant service deplored the hardships of his lot and tendered good advice to those officials in power at court.

其毒大苦。	就像吃药那般苦。	As poison drives me mad.
念彼共①人，	想到那些服役人，	I think of those in power;
涕零如雨。	涕泗滂沱泪如雨。	My tears fall down in shower.
岂不怀归？	怎能不想回家去？	Will I not homeward go?
畏此罪罟②。	害怕罪责担不起。	I fear traps high and low.

昔我往矣，	想我当初离家时，	When I left home for here
日月③方除。	天地万物萌新芽。	Sun and moon ushered in new year.
曷④云其还，	何时能够把家还，	Now when may I go home?
岁聿⑤云莫。	万物凋零已岁暮。	Another year will come.
念我独兮，	想到孤苦一个人，	I sigh for I am lonely.
我事孔庶⑥。	公事不断正繁忙。	Why am I busy only?
心之忧矣，	我的心中很忧伤，	O how can I feel pleasure?
惮⑦我不暇。	辛苦工作不得闲。	I toil without leisure.
念彼共人，	想到那些服役人，	Thinking of those in power,
睠睠⑧怀顾。	心中眷眷实挂念。	Can I have happy hour?'
岂不怀归？	怎能不想回家去，？	Don't I long for parental roof?
畏此谴怒。	只怕官府要震怒。	I'm afraid of reproof.

昔我往矣，	想我当初离家时，	When I left for the west,
日月方奥⑨。	阳光灿烂天正暖。	With warmth the sun and moon were blest.

---

① 共(gōng)人：指军中征集服役的士兵。② 罟(gǔ)：网。③ 日月：时光。④ 曷(hé)：怎么，何时。⑤ 聿(yù)：古汉语助词，用在句首或句中。⑥ 庶：众。⑦ 惮：劳。⑧ 睠睠(juàn)：怀念。⑨ 奥(yù)：暖。

曷云其还，	何时能够把家还？	When can I go home without cares,
政事愈蹙①。	国家政事更急促。	Busy on state affairs?
岁聿云莫，	一年已经将结束，	It is late in the year;
采萧获菽②。	各种作物都已收。	They reap beans there and here.
心之忧矣，	我的心中很忧伤，	I feel sad and cast down;
自诒伊戚③。	许是自己寻烦恼。	I eat the fruit I've sown.
念彼共人，	想到那些服役人，	Thinking of those in power,
兴④言出宿。	起身夜下独徘徊。	I rise at early hour.
岂不怀归？	怎能不想把家还，	Will I not homeward go?
畏此反复。	害怕君王怒无常。	I fear returning blow.
嗟尔君子，	哎呀诸位服役者，	Ah! officials in power,
无恒安处。	不要贪图求安乐。	There's no e'er-blooming flower.
靖⑤共⑥尔位，	恭敬对待你工作，	When you're on duty long,
正直是与。	秉公办事要正直。	You should know right from wrong.
神之听之，	神灵得知你如此，	If Heaven should have ear,
式穀⑦以女。	定把福禄赐给你。	Justice would then appear.
嗟尔君子，	哎呀诸位服役者，	Ah! officials in power,
无恒安息。	不要贪图求安乐。	There's no e'er-resting hour.
靖共尔位，	恭敬对待你工作，	Should you do duty well,
好是正直。	忠于职守遵规则。	You'd know heaven from hell.

---

① 蹙(cù)：急。② 萧：即艾蒿；菽：即大豆，九谷中最后收获的那一种。③ 戚：忧。④ 兴：起。⑤ 靖：审慎。⑥ 共：通"供"。⑦ 穀：禄。

神之听之，　　神灵得知你如此，　　If Heaven should know you,
介①尔景福。　　赐你齐天的洪福。　　Blessings would come to view.

鼓　钟　　　　　　　　　　　　Bells and Drums*

鼓钟将将，　　敲起钟鼓将将响，　　The bells ring deep and low;
淮水汤汤，　　淮河之水浩汤汤，　　The vast river waves flow.
忧心且伤。　　我的心中很忧伤。　　My heart is full of woe.
淑人君子，　　古代圣贤和君子，　　How can I forget then
怀允②不忘。　　实在想念不能忘。　　Those music-making men?

鼓钟喈喈③，　　敲起钟鼓喈喈响，　　The bells sound shrill and high;
淮水湝湝④，　　淮河之水急急流，　　The river waves flow by.
忧心且悲。　　我的心中很悲伤。　　My heart heaves long, long sigh.
淑人君子，　　古代圣贤和君子，　　How can I forget then
其德不回⑤。　　行为端正德高尚。　　Those music-loving men?

鼓钟伐鼛⑥，　　敲起大鼓咚咚响，　　The bells and drums resound;
淮有三洲，　　淮河之滨有三洲，　　Three isles emerged, once drowned.
忧心且妯⑦。　　忧心忡忡实悲伤。　　My heart feels grief profound.

---

① 介：给予。② 允：信。③ 喈喈(jiējiē)：钟声。④ 湝湝(jiējiē)：水疾流的样子。⑤ 回：邪僻。⑥ 鼛(gāo)：大鼓。⑦ 妯(chōu)：激动。

* This ode was supposed to refer to the expedition of King You to the country of the Huai, where he abandoned himself to the delights of music in 771 B.C., one year before he was killed by the western tribes.

淑人君子，	古代圣贤和君子，	How can I forget then
其德不犹①。	品德高尚行优良。	Those music-playing men?
鼓钟钦钦，	敲起钟鼓钦钦响，	They beat drum and ring bell,
鼓瑟鼓琴，	又弹瑟来又弹琴，	Play lute and zither well,
笙磬同音。	还有笙磬也和唱，	In flute or pipe excel,
以雅以南，	雅乐南乐声悠扬，	Sing odes and southern song
以籥②不僭③。	排箫齐整同登场。	And dance with nothing wrong.

楚 茨

Winter Sacrifice*

楚楚④者茨⑤，	蒺藜茂密丛丛生，	O let us clear away
言抽⑥其棘。	拔去杂草除荆棘。	All the overgrown thorns!
自昔何为？	为何自古都如此，	Just as in olden days
我艺⑦黍稷。	我种高粱和黄米。	We plant millet and corns.
我黍与与⑧，	我的高粱长得旺，	Our millet overgrows
我稷翼翼。	我的黄米也茁壮。	And our barns stand in rows;
我仓既盈，	我的仓库已装满，	Our sorghum overgrows
我庾⑨维亿。	我的谷场也满装。	And our stacks stand in rows.
以为酒食，	备下美酒和佳肴，	We prepare wine and meat
以享以祀。	祭祀祖先和神灵。	For temple sacrifice;
以妥⑩以侑⑪，	请尸安座来劝酒，	We urge spirits to eat

---

① 犹：缺点，过失。② 籥(yuè)：排箫。③ 僭(jiàn)：乱。④ 楚楚：荆棘丛生的样子。
⑤ 茨：蒺藜。⑥ 抽：拔除。⑦ 艺(yì)：通"艺"，种植。⑧ 与与：繁盛貌。翼翼：同"与与"。⑨ 庾(yǔ)：露天谷仓。⑩ 妥：安坐。⑪ 侑(yòu)：劝饮劝食。

* The "spirit" was a representative or personator of the worthy dead or great fathers who were sacrificed to; the "grondson" was the name given to the sacrificer or the king of the Zhou dynasty.

以介景福。	来年赐我好福气。	And invoke blessings thrice.

济济①跄跄，	步伐郑重有威严，	We clean the oxen nice
絜②尔牛羊，	牛羊洗得真干净，	And offer them in heap
以往烝尝③。	秋祭冬祭都举行。	For winter sacrifice.
或剥或亨，	剥去皮毛入锅烹，	We flay and broil the sheep
或肆或将。	陈列上来献神仙。	And cut and carve the meat.
祝④祭于祊⑤，	祝官先来行祊礼，	The priest's at the temple gate
祀事孔明⑥。	祭祀仪式很盛大，	Till service is complete.
先祖是皇，	先祖都请来参加。	Then come our fathers great.
神保⑦是飨。	神灵宗祖来享用，	They enjoy food and wine
"孝孙⑧有庆⑨，	"主祭孝孙好运气。	And to their grandson say,
报以介福，	企盼神灵降大福，	"Receive blessings divine,
万寿无疆！"	万寿无疆福永驻！"	Live long and be e'er gay!"

执爨⑩踖踖⑪，	厨师敏捷又恭敬，	The cooks work with great skill
为俎⑫孔硕，	选用最大的用具。	And prepare all the trays.
或燔⑬或炙。	又烧肉来又烤肝，	They roast or broil at will;
君妇莫莫⑭，	主妇动作很庄严。	Women help them always.
为豆孔庶，	碗中菜肴很丰盛，	Smaller dishes abound
为宾为客⑮。	助祭之人请享用，	For the guests left and right.
献酬交错，	主人敬酒酬客宾，	They raise cups and drink round

---

① 济济：恭敬端庄。② 絜：使之洁。③ 烝(zhēng)尝：冬祭曰烝，秋祭曰尝。④ 祝：祭祀中向神祷告的神职人员。⑤ 祊(bēng)：祭祀的一种，正式祭祀前搜找祖先和神灵的仪式。⑥ 明：备，洁。⑦ 神保：神明。⑧ 孝孙：主祭之人。⑨ 庆：福。⑩ 爨(cuàn)：灶。⑪ 踖踖(jí)：恭敬勤敏。⑫ 俎(zǔ)：盛肉的礼器。⑬ 燔(fán)：燔肉。⑭ 莫莫：敬谨。⑮ 宾客：祭祀中的助祭者。

礼仪卒度，	礼仪周全合规范，	According to the rite.
笑语卒获。	言谈笑语不闹喧。	They laugh and talk at will
神保是格①，	神灵祖先请到来，	When witches come and say,
"报以介福，	"赐予洪福齐天高，	"Receive more blessings still;
万寿攸酢②！"	万寿无疆永不老！"	Live long with glee for aye!"

我孔熯③矣，	我们态度很恭敬，	With respect we fulfil
式礼莫愆④。	取法规矩不犯错。	The due rites one by one.
工祝致告：	祝官传达神旨意，	The priests announce the will
"徂赉⑤孝孙。	"快把福禄赐孝孙。	of spirits to grandson:
苾⑥芬孝祀，	祭祀酒菜真是香，	"Fragrant's the sacrifice;
神嗜饮食，	神灵用罢很喜欢。	They enjoy meat and wine.
卜尔百福。	赐你百种好福气，	They confer blessings thrice
如几⑦如式，	祭祀按时合规矩。	On you for rites divine.
既齐既稷⑧，	办事整齐又迅速，	You have done what is due
既匡既敕。	态度恭敬又严整。	Correctly with good care.
永锡尔极⑨，	永远赐你无限福，	Favors conferred on you
时万时亿。"	成千成亿数不清"。	Will be found everywhere."

礼仪既备，	仪式已经准备好，	The ceremonies done,
钟鼓既戒⑩。	钟鼓乐器也齐备。	Drums beaten and bells rung,
孝孙徂位，	孝孙回到主祭位，	In his place the grandson,
工祝致告；	祝官报告祭礼成。	The priest then gives his tongue:
"神具醉止。"	"神灵畅饮已喝醉，"	"The spirits drunken well,

---

① 格：来。② 酢(zuò)：报。③ 熯(nǎn)：敬惧。④ 愆(qiān)：过失。⑤ 赉(lài)：予。⑥ 苾(bì)：馨香。⑦ 几：期。⑧ 稷：疾。⑨ 极：至。⑩ 戒：齐备。

皇尸①载起,	扮神灵者立起身。	The dead ready to go."
鼓钟送尸,	敲钟打鼓送尸神,	Let's beat drum and ring bell
神保聿归。	奏曲送神归天庭。	For them to go below!
诸宰君妇,	诸位厨师和主妇,	Cooks and women, come here.
废②彻不迟。	即刻撤退此宴席。	Remove trays without delay.
诸父兄弟,	叔伯兄弟都聚齐,	Uncles and cousins dear,
备言燕私。	享用酒宴叙亲情。	At private feast let's stay.
乐具入奏,	乐器移入室内奏,	Music played in the hall,
以绥后禄。	一同享用祭后食。	We eat when spirits go.
尔肴既将,	你的菜肴真是美,	Enjoying dishes, all
莫怨具庆。	全无怨言都喜庆。	Forget their former woe.
既醉既饱,	已经喝足也吃饱,	They drink their fill and eat,
小大稽首。	长幼参拜齐致辞,	Bowing the head, old and young.
"神嗜饮食,	"圣灵享受这饭菜,	"The spirits love your meat
使君寿考。	使你长寿永不老。	And will make you live long.
孔惠③孔时,	祭祀做得很顺利,	Your rites are duly done;
维其尽之。	该做之事都做好。	You are pious and nice.
子子孙孙,	告诫子孙和后代,	Let nor son nor grandson
勿替④引⑤之。"	延续下去礼永葆。"	Forget the sacrifice!"

信南山　　　　Spring sacrifice at the Foot of the Southern Mountain*

信⑥彼南山,	南山绵延真雄伟,	The Southern Mountain stands,

---

①尸:祭祀中假扮神灵的人。②废:拿走。③惠:顺。④替:废。⑤引:续。
⑥信:长远之意。

* This sacrificial ode traced husbandry to its first author, King Yu of Xia (2205-Z197 B. C.).

维禹甸①之。	大禹曾在此治水。	Exploited by Yu's hands.
昀昀②原隰，	高原低洼都平整，	The plains spread high and low
曾孙③田之。	曾孙在此耕种田。	Tilled by grandsons, crops grow.
我疆我理④，	划定疆域细分理，	Of southeast fields we find
南东其亩。	向东向西分垄亩。	The boundaries defined.

上天同⑤云，	阴云密密天上布，	Clouds cover winter sky;
雨雪雰雰⑥。	雪花纷纷空中飘，	Snowflakes fall from on high.
益之以霢霂⑦，	再加小雨滴滴落，	In spring comes drizzling rain;
既优既渥⑧，	田亩润泽水充分，	It moists and wets the plain.
既沾既足，	土地潮湿水充足，	Fertile grow all the fields;
生我百谷。	供我百谷来生长。	Abundant are their yields.

疆埸⑨翼翼，	田亩边界真整齐，	Their acres lie in row;
黍稷彧彧⑩。	黍稷长得也茂盛。	Millet and sorgham grow.
曾孙之穑，	曾孙收获的粮食，	Grandsons reap harvest fine
以为酒食。	储存起来酿美酒。	And make spirits and wine.
畀⑪我尸宾⑫，	献给神主与宾客，	They feast their guests with food
寿考万年。	祈求寿命一万年。	That they may live for good.

| 中田有庐⑬， | 田中有间小棚舍， | Gourds grow amid the field |
| 疆埸有瓜。 | 芦边田畔植瓜菜。 | And melons have gross yield. |

---

① 甸(diàn)：治田。② 昀昀(yúnyún)：平坦整齐的样子。③ 曾孙：主祭者。④ 理：定其小的脉络。⑤ 同：重。⑥ 雰雰(fēnfēn)：纷纷。⑦ 霢霂(màimù)：小雨。⑧ 渥(wò)：雨水丰足。⑨ 埸(yì)：畔，田界。⑩ 彧彧(yùyù)：茂盛。⑪ 畀(bì)：给予。⑫ 尸宾：代表先祖受祭的活人。⑬ 庐：通"芦"，萝卜。

是剥是菹①，	剥去皮叶来腌制，	They are, pickled in slices,
献之皇祖。	献给神灵和祖宗。	Offered in sacrifices,
曾孙寿考，	曾孙寿命长百岁，	That we may receive love
受天之祜②。	这是皇天赐他福。	And long life from Heaven above.
祭以清酒，	清香之酒来祭祀，	We offer purest wine
从以骍③牡，	还有红色大公牛。	To ancesters divine;
享于祖考。	献给祖先来享用，	Kill a bull with red hair
执其鸾刀，	拿起金鸾锋刃刀。	By a knife in hand bare;
以启其毛。	用来割开它的毛，	We rid it of hair red
取其血膋④。	取出它的血和膏。	And take fat from the bled.
是烝⑤是享，	进献佳肴请享用，	During the sacrifice
苾苾芬芬，	手艺不错喷喷香。	The fat burned gives smell nice.
祀事孔明。	祭祀做得很完备，	Our ancesters delight
先祖是皇⑥，	先祖表示很赞赏。	In the service and rite.
报以介福，	赐予洪福作回报，	We grandsons will be blest
万寿无疆！	让你万寿永无疆。	With longest life and best.

---

① 菹(zū)：盐渍。② 祜(hù)：福。③ 骍(xīn)：毛皮红色的马或牛。④ 膋(liáo)：脂膏。
⑤ 烝：进献。⑥ 皇：赞美，嘉许。

甫田之什

Sixth Decade of Odes

甫　田

Harvest*

倬①彼甫田②，	那片田地真开阔，	"Endless extend my boundless fields;
岁取十千。	每年收获万斤粮。	A tenth is levied of their yields.
我取其陈，	我从仓中取陈谷，	I take grain from old store
食我农人。	供养种田的农人，	To feed the peasants' mouth.
自古有年。	自古都有丰收年。	We've good years as of yore;
今适南亩，	今到南田来查看，	I go to acres south.
或耘或耔③，	又除草来又播种，	They gather roots and weed;
黍稷薿薿④。	黍稷长得真茂盛。	Lush grow millets I see.
攸介攸止，	待到五谷成熟时，	Collected by those who lead,
烝⑤我髦⑥士。	田官进献多殷勤。	They are presented to me.
以我齐明⑦，	祭祀供品装满盆，	"I offer millets nice
与我牺羊，	献上硕大的牛羊，	And rams in sacrifice
以社以方。	祭祀土地和四方，	To spirits of the land
我田既臧，	我的农田收成好，	That lush my fields become.
农夫之庆。	耕田农夫多欢畅，	Joyful my peasants stand;

---

① 倬(zhuō)：大。② 甫田：大田。③ 耔(zǐ)：培土。④ 薿薿(nǐnǐ)：茂繁。⑤ 烝(zhēng)：召。⑥ 髦(mào)士：田官。⑦ 齐明：祭器所盛的谷物。

* This ode described husbandry and sacrifices connected with it, and happy under standing between the peasants and their lord, who was the speaker in the first two stanzas.

琴瑟击鼓，	弹奏琴瑟击起鼓，	They play lute and beat drum.
以御^①田祖，	欢天喜地迎农神，	We pray to God of Fields
以祈甘雨，	诚心诚意求雨降。	That rain and sunshine thrives
以介^②我稷黍，	助我稷黍长得好，	To increase our millet yields
以毂我士女。	养活男女和老少。	And bless my men and their wives."

曾孙来止，	曾孙来到田地里，	Our lord's grandson comes near.
以其妇子，	农人带来妻与子。	Our wives and children dear
馌^③彼南亩。	乡亲送饭到田间，	Bring food to acres south.
田畯至喜，	田官见了心欢喜。	The o'erseer opens mouth,
攘^④其左右，	曾孙左右皆回避，	From left to right takes food
尝其旨否。	亲尝食物香甜否。	And tastes whether it's good.
禾易长亩，	禾苗茂盛长满田，	Abundant millets grow
终善且有。	又好又多不可数。	Over acres high and low.
曾孙不怒，	曾孙不怒很满意，	Our lord's grandson is glad;
农夫克敏。	农夫辛苦很勤勉。	His peasants are not bad.

曾孙之稼，	曾孙的庄稼长得好，	The grandson's crops in piles
如茨^⑤如梁。	又像房盖又像桥。	Stand high as the roof tiles.
曾孙之庾，	曾孙的粮屯真丰腴，	His stacks upon the ground
如坻^⑥如京。	就像高大的土丘。	Look like hillock and mound.
乃求千斯仓，	需要粮仓千百间，	He seeks stores in all parts
乃求万斯箱。	需要千万大车厢。	And conveys crops in carts.
黍稷稻粱，	满装黍稷装稻粱，	We peasants sing in praise

① 御(yù)：迎接。② 介：毂，介，助。毂，养。③ 馌(yè)：送饭。④ 攘(rǎng)：推开。⑤ 茨(cí)：草屋顶。⑥ 坻(chí)：水中的高地。

农夫之庆①。　农夫齐聚喜洋洋。　Of millet, paddy, maize.
报以介福，　　天降大福为回报，　He'll be blessed night and day
万寿无疆！　　延年益寿永无疆。　And live happy for aye.

大　田　　　　　　　　　　　Farm Work*

大田多稼，　　宽阔田里庄稼多，　Busy with peasants' cares,
既种②既戒③，　选了种子修农具，　Seed selected, tools repaired,
既备乃事。　　所有事情我动手。　We take our sharp plough-shares
以我覃④耜⑤，　我的犁头很锋利，　When all is well prepared.
俶⑥载⑦南亩。　修整南面的土地，　We begin from south field
播厥百谷，　　百种谷物都播种。　And sow grain far and wide.
既庭⑧且硕，　　庄家长得大又直，　Gross and high grows our yield;
曾孙是若⑨。　　周王看了心欢喜。　Our lord's grandson's satisfied.

既方⑩既皁⑪，　谷粒长出了谷壳，　The grain's soft in the ear
既坚既好，　　挺阔坚硬长势好，　And then grows hard and good.
不稂⑫不莠⑬。　没有稂草和莠草。　Let nor grass nor weed appear;
去其螟⑭螣⑮，　去掉青虫和丝虫，　Let no insects eat it as food.

---

① 庆：赐。② 种：选种子。③ 戒(古音jì)：修农具。④ 覃：通"剡"，锐利。⑤ 耜(sì)：似犁的农具。⑥ 俶(chù)：始。⑦ 载：从事。⑧ 庭：读为"挺"，生出。⑨ 若：顺。⑩ 方：房。⑪ 皁(zào)：谷实才结成的状态。⑫ 稂(láng)：禾粟之生穗而不充实的，又叫"童梁"。⑬ 莠(yǒu)：草名，叶穗像禾。⑭ 螟(míng)：吃苗心的小青虫，长约半寸。⑮ 螣(tè)：虫名，长一寸左右，食苗叶，吐丝。

* The first stanza described the farm work in spring, the second that in summer, the third harvest in autumn and the last sacrifice in winter.

及其螟①贼②，	还有吃根的小毛虫，	All vermins must expire
无害我田稚。	不要残害我稻苗。	Lest they should do much harm.
田祖有神，	土地之神有灵光，	Pray gods to put them in fire
秉畀③炎火。	把它投进烈火中。	To preserve our good farm.

有渰④萋萋，	阴云凄凄天上飘，	Clouds gather in the sky;
兴雨祁祁⑤。	阵雨徐徐降下来。	Rain on public fields come down,
雨我公田，	浇灌公家的田亩，	It drizzles from on high
遂及我私。	再来滋润我私田。	On private fields of our own.
彼有不获稚⑥，	那里有没熟的稻苗，	There are unreaped young grain
此有不敛穧⑦；	这里有遗落的禾束；	And some ungathered sheaves,
彼有遗秉⑧，	那里有成把的谷物，	Handfuls left on the plain
此有滞穗⑨。	这里有漏掉的麦穗，	And ears a widow perceives
伊⑩寡妇之利。	留给孤苦的寡妇。	And gleans and makes a gain.

曾孙来止，	曾孙来到田地里，	Our lord's grandson comes here.
以其妇子。	农人带来妻与子。	Our wives bring food to acres south
馌彼南亩，	乡亲送饭到田间，	Together with their children dear;
田畯至喜。	田官见了心欢喜。	The overseer opens mouth.
来方⑪禋⑫祀，	大王前来祭天地，	We offer sacrifice
以其骍⑬黑，	赤墨两色的牛羊，	With victims black and red,
与其黍稷。	还有收获的黍稷。	With millet and with rice.
以享以祀，	请求神仙来享用，	We pray to fathers dead

---

① 螟(míng)：吃苗根的虫。② 贼：也是虫名，专食苗节，善钻禾秆。③ 畀(bì)：付。 ④ 渰(yǎn)：云起的样子。⑤ 祁祁：徐徐。⑥ 不获稚：因未成熟而不割的禾。⑦ 穧(jì)：收割。⑧ 遗秉：遗漏了的成把的禾。⑨ 滞穗：抛撒在田里的穗子。⑩ 伊：是。⑪ 方：祭四方之神。⑫ 禋(yīn)：精洁致祭。⑬ 骍(xīn)：赤色牲畜。

以介①景福。	降下洪福不可量。	That we may be blessed thrice.

瞻彼洛矣　　　　　　　Grand Review*

瞻彼洛矣，	看那洛河，	See River Luo in spring
维水泱泱②。	大水汤汤。	With water deep and wide.
君子③至止，	天子到这里，	Thither has come the king,
福禄如茨④。	福禄多无量。	Happy and dignified,
韎韐⑤有奭⑥，	红色蔽膝戴身上，	In red knee-covers new,
以作六师。	率领部队练武忙。	Six armies in review.
瞻彼洛矣，	看那洛河，	See River Luo in spring;
维水泱泱。	大水泱泱。	Deep and wide flows its stream.
君子至止，	天子到这里，	Thither has come the king;
鞞琫⑦有珌⑧。	佩刀真漂亮。	Gems on his scabbard gleam.
君子万年，	天子福寿万年长，	May he live long and gay,
保其家室。	保其家室永安康。	His house preserved for aye!
瞻彼洛矣，	看那洛河，	See River Luo in spring;
维水泱泱。	大水泱泱。	Its stream flows deep and wide.
君子至止，	天子到这里，	Thither has come the king;

---

① 介：求。② 泱泱：水深广的样子。③ 君子：指天子。④ 茨(cí)：草屋顶，喻多。⑤ 韎韐(mèigé)：红色皮制蔽膝。⑥ 奭(shì)：赤色。⑦ 鞞琫(bǐběng)：有玉饰的刀鞘。⑧ 珌(bì)：刀鞘玉饰。

* This ode read like a hymn sung by feudal princes met at some gathering in praise of the king as he appeared among them.

福禄既同①。	福禄同此江。	He's blessed and dignified.
君子万年，	天子福寿万年长，	May he live long and great
保其家邦。	保其家国永安康。	And long preserve his state!

裳裳者华

A Noble Lord*

裳裳②者华，	花朵开得真饱满，	Flowers give splendid sight
其叶湑③兮。	叶子青青也旺盛。	With lush leaves by the side.
我觏④之子，	已经见到那个人，	I see the lord so bright;
我心写兮。	非常称心合我意。	My heart is satisfied.
我心写兮，	我心满意自欢喜，	My heart is satisfied;
是以有誉处⑤兮。	从此安乐过生活。	I praise him with delight.
裳裳者华，	花儿开得真饱满，	Flowers give splendid sight;
芸⑥其黄矣。	花瓣纷纷色鲜黄。	They're deep yellow and red.
我觏之子，	已经见到那个人，	I see the lord so bright,
维其有章⑦矣。	美丽花纹附着装。	Elegant and well-bred.
维其有章矣，	服饰华美有文章，	Elegant and well-bred,
是以有庆矣。	从此欢庆喜洋洋。	I bless him with delight.
裳裳者华，	花儿开得真饱满，	Flowers give splendid sight;
或黄或白。	有的白啊有的黄。	They are yellow and white.

---

① 同:会集。② 裳裳:花丰盛的样子。③ 湑(xǔ):茂盛的样子。④ 觏(gòu):遇见。
⑤ 誉处:安乐。⑥ 芸:花叶发黄的样子。⑦ 有章:有才华。

* This ode was said to be responsive to the former; the king celebrated the praises of the chief among the feudal princes.

我觏之子，	已经见到那个人，	I see the lord so bright
乘其四骆①。	驾着四匹黑鬃马，	With four steeds left and right.
乘其四骆，	驾着四匹黑鬃马，	With four steeds left and right,
六辔沃若②。	六条缰绳真灵活。	He holds six reins with delight.

左之左之，	向左转呀向左转，	He goes left if he will,
君子宜之。	君子驾车技术高。	Driving the steeds with skill.
右之右之，	向右转呀向右转，	If he will he goes right,
君子有之。	君子操纵很灵活。	Driving with main and might.
维其有之，	君子才高可任用，	As he has true manhood,
是以似③之。	继嗣祖业有才能。	At what he does he's good.

桑扈　　　　　　　　The Royal Toast*

交交桑扈④，	布谷鸟儿交错飞，	Hear the green-beaks' sweet voice
有莺⑤其羽。	羽毛彩色有花纹。	And see their variegated wings fly.
君子乐胥⑥，	君子生活真快乐，	Let all my lords rejoice
受天之祜⑦。	老天保佑运气好。	And be blessed from on high.

交交桑扈，	布谷鸟儿交错飞，	Hear the green-beaks' sweet voice
有莺其领。	脖颈羽毛有花纹。	And see their feather delicate.
君子乐胥，	君子生活真快乐，	Let all my lords rejoice

---

① 骆(luò)：黑鬃的白马。② 沃若：调试活络的样子。③ 似：嗣。④ 桑扈：窃脂，即布谷鸟。⑤ 莺：鸟羽有文采。⑥ 胥：《集传》，"胥，语词。"⑦ 祜(hù)：福。

* The king, celebrating his feudal princes, expressed his admiration of them and good wishes for them.

万邦之屏。	他是天下的屏障。	And be buttress to the state.

之屏之翰，	他是根基是屏障，	Be a buttress or screen,
百辟①为宪②。	百国以他为榜样。	Set an example fine,
不戢③不难④，	性情温和受尊敬，	Be self-restrained and keen,
受福不⑤那⑥。	享受万福也不多。	Receive blessings divine.

兕觥其觩⑦，	牛角杯子角弯曲，	The cup of rhino horn
旨酒思柔。	甘甜美酒绕舌柔。	Is filled with spirits soft.
彼交⑧匪敖⑨，	不急不躁不傲慢，	Do not feel pride nor scorn,
万福来求⑩。	万福齐聚实难得。	And blessings will come oft.

鸳 鸯　　　　　　　　　The Love-Birds*

鸳鸯于飞，	鸳鸯鸟儿双双飞，	Flying love-birds need rest
毕⑪之罗之。	有人用网来补捉。	When large and small nets spread.
君子万年，	君子长寿有万年，	May you live long and blest,
福禄宜之。	福禄齐聚心安康。	Wealthy and happily wed!

鸳鸯在梁，	鸳鸯鸟儿梁上飞，	On the dam love-birds stay,
戢⑫其左翼。	收起左翼敛起头。	In left wing hid the head.
君子万年，	君子长寿有万年，	May you live safe for aye,

---

① 辟(bì)：国君。② 宪：表率。③ 戢(jí)：收藏。④ 难(nuó)：恐惧。⑤ 不：语气助词。⑥ 那(nuó)：多。⑦ 觩(qiú)：角弯的样子。⑧ 交：侥幸。⑨ 敖：骄。⑩ 求：聚。⑪ 毕：罗网。⑫ 戢(jí)：收敛。

* The love-birds flying in pairs alluded to the newly-wed and the four horses were used to draw the carriage of the bride.

宜其遐①福。	安享洪福以永年。	Duly and happily wed!

乘马在厩②,　　四匹马儿在马房,　　Four horses in the stable
摧③之秣④之。　切碎鲜草将它喂。　With grain and forage fed.
君子万年,　　　君子长寿有万年,　　May you live long and stable,
福禄艾⑤之。　　福禄相宜永不忘。　For you're happily wed.

乘马在厩,　　　四匹马儿在马房,　　Four horses in the stable
秣之摧之。　　　喂它鲜草再切碎。　With forage and grain fed.
君子万年,　　　君子长寿有万年,　　May you live comfortable,
福禄绥⑥之。　　安享福禄家安绥。　For you're happily wed.

頍 弁　　　　　　　　　　　　The Royal Banquet*

有頍⑦者弁⑧,　有人高高戴皮帽,　　Who are those lords so fine
实维伊何?　　　戴上皮帽要做啥?　　In leather cap or hood,
尔酒既旨⑨!　　你的美酒甘且甜,　　Coming to drink your wine
尔殽既嘉。　　　你的佳肴味道好。　　And eat your viands good?
岂伊异人?　　　宴上难道有他人?　　Can they be others?
兄弟非他。　　　都是手足亲弟兄。　　They are your brothers.
茑⑩与女萝,　　茑丝花儿与女萝,　　They are like mistletoe
施⑪于松柏。　　绕于松树柏树间。　　That o'er cypress does grow.

---

① 遐(xiá):长久。② 厩(jiù):马棚,泛指牲口棚。③ 摧(cuò):铡碎的草。④ 秣(mò):用来喂马的杂谷。⑤ 艾:养育。⑥ 绥(suī):安定。⑦ 頍(kuǐ):戴帽子的样子。⑧ 弁(biàn):皮帽。⑨ 旨:嘉,美。⑩ 茑(niǎo):茑丝花。⑪ 施(yì):延及。

* This ode celebrated the king ("you") feasting with his relatives.

未见君子，	没有见到那君子，	When they see you not, how
忧心弈弈①；	心中忧伤不可止。	Can their hearts not be sad?
既见君子，	已经见到那君子，	When they do see you now,
庶几说②怿③。	渐渐就会心欢喜。	They are happy and glad.
有颎者弁，	有人高高戴皮帽，	Who are those lords so fine
实维何期？	戴上皮帽要做啥？	In deer skin cap or hood,
尔酒既旨，	你的美酒甘且甜，	Coming to drink your wine
尔殽既时④。	你的菜肴是时鲜。	And eat your seasonable food?
岂伊异人？	宴上难道有他人？	Can they be others?
兄弟具来。	兄弟捧场都已到。	They are your brothers.
茑与女萝，	菟丝花儿与女萝，	They are like mistletoe
施于松上。	绕于松树柏树间。	That o'er the pine does grow.
未见君子，	没有见到那君子，	When they see you not, how
忧心怲怲⑤；	心中忧伤实难熬。	Can their hearts not feel sad?
既见君子，	已经见到那君子，	When they do see you now,
庶几有臧⑥。	心情慢慢会变好。	They feel all right and glad.
有颎者弁，	有人高高戴皮帽，	Who are those lords so fine
实维在首。	头戴皮帽显精神。	With leather cap on head,
尔酒既旨，	你的美酒甘且甜，	Coming to drink your wine,
尔殽既阜⑦。	你的菜肴真丰盛。	With food the table spread?
岂伊异人？	宴上难道有他人？	O how can they be others?
兄弟甥舅。	都是兄弟和舅甥。	They are our cousins and brothers.

---

① 弈弈(yìyì)：忧愁的样子。② 说：通"悦"。③ 怿(yì)：欢喜、高兴。④ 时：善。⑤ 怲怲(bǐngbǐng)：忧愁的样子。⑥ 臧：善。⑦ 阜(fù)：多。

如彼雨雪，	就像天上降雨雪，	We are like snow or rain;
先集维霰。	雪花冰珠难久长。	Nothing will long remain.
死丧无日，	人生死丧实难料，	Death may come any day;
无几相见。	相见日子也寥寥。	We can enjoy tonight at least.
乐酒今夕，	劝君今晚同一醉，	Drink and rejoice as you may;
君子维宴。	及时宴乐在今宵。	Let us enjoy the feast!

车舝   On the Way to the Bride's House*

间关①车之舝②兮，	车轴转动车轮响，	Having prepared my creaking cart,
思娈③季女逝兮。	美丽女子出嫁了。	I go to fetch my bride.
匪饥匪渴，	不愁吃也不愁喝，	Nor hungry nor thirsty at heart,
德音来括④。	只望女子有品德。	I'll take her as good guide.
虽无好友，	虽无众多好朋友，	Nor good friends come nor priest;
式燕且喜。	且来开宴同庆贺。	We'll rejoice in our feast.

依⑤彼平林，	密密树林真茂盛，	In the plain there's dense wood
有集维鷮⑥。	停着一只美羽鸟。	And pheasants with long tail.
辰⑦彼硕女⑧，	那位女子真是好，	I love my young bride good;
令德来教。	快用美德来相教。	She'll help me without fail.
式燕且誉⑨，	一起宴饮多欢乐，	I'll praise her when we feast,
好尔无射⑩。	永远爱你不厌烦。	Never tired in the least.

---

① 间关：车轮声。② 舝(xiá)：车轴两头的金属键，控制车毂，使之不易脱落。③ 娈(luán)：美好。④ 括：约束。⑤ 依：盛。⑥ 鷮(jiāo)：长尾雉。⑦ 辰：美善貌。⑧ 硕女：德高貌美的女子。⑨ 誉：通"豫"，欢乐。⑩ 射(yì)：厌弃。

* This ode was said to be sung at a wedding and the wood-splitting might allude to love-making in ancient Chinese songs.

虽无旨酒，	虽无甘甜的美酒，	Though we have no good wine,
式饮庶几。	望您能够饮一杯。	We'll drink, avoiding waste.
虽无嘉殽，	虽无上等的佳肴，	Though our viands are not fine,
式食庶几。	望您能够尝一口。	We may give them a taste.
虽无德与女，	虽然我无你德行，	Though no good to you can I bring,
式歌且舞。	也能载舞又载歌。	Still we may dance and sing.
陟彼高冈，	登上那座高山岗，	I climb the mountain green
析其柞薪；	劈下柞树当柴火。	To split oak for firewood.
析其柞薪，	砍下它的小树枝，	Amid leaves lush and green
其叶湑兮。	树上枝叶更繁茂。	I split oak for firewood.
鲜①我觏②尔，	难得能够见到你，	Seeing my matchless bride,
我心写兮。	我实快乐心意足。	I will be satisfied.
高山仰止，	高山需要仰头望，	You're good like mountains high;
景行③行止。	大道穿梭多宽敞。	Like the road you go long.
四牡骓骓，	四匹马儿快快跑，	My four steeds run and hie;
六辔如琴。	六根缰绳似琴丝。	Six reins like lute-strings weave a song.
觏尔新昏，	望着称心新嫁娘，	When I'm wed to my bride,
以慰我心。	以此可以慰我心。	How my heart will be satisfied!

青　蝇　　　　　　　　　Blue Flies*

营营④青蝇，	青头苍蝇嗡嗡飞，	Hear the buzzing blue flies;

---

① 鲜：善。② 觏(gòu)：见。③ 景行(háng)：大道。④ 营营：嘤嘤。

* It was said that this ode was directed against King You who lent a ready ear to slander and blue flies became symbolic of slanderers.

止于樊①。	停落院间篱笆上。	On the fence they alight.
岂弟②君子，	君子平易又通达，	Lord, don't believe their lies;
无信谗言。	切莫听信小人言。	Friend, don't take wrong for right.

营营青蝇，	青头苍蝇嗡嗡飞，	Hear blue flies buzzing, friend;
止于棘。	停息院里枣树上。	They light on jujube trees.
谗人罔极，	小人做事无准则，	The slander without end
交乱四国。	祸害捣蛋乱四国。	Spreads in the state disease.

营营青蝇，	青头苍蝇嗡嗡飞，	Hear blue flies buzzing, friend;
止于榛。	停在那棵榛树上。	They light on hazel tree.
谗人罔极，	小人做事无准则，	The slander without end
构③我二人。	你我之间造事端。	Sets you at odds with me.

宾之初筵　　　　　　　　　Revelry*

宾之初④筵，	宾客入座开宴席，	The guests come with delight
左右秩秩⑤。	宾主肃敬守礼仪。	And take place left and right.
笾豆有楚，	杯盘碗盏列整齐，	In rows arranged the dishes,
殽⑥核维旅。	菜肴果品实在好。	Displayed viands and fishes.
酒既和旨⑦，	美酒味香又甘醇，	The wine is mild and good;
饮酒孔偕。	举杯共饮很热闹。	Guests drink and eat the food.

---

① 樊：竹篱笆。② 岂弟(kǎitì)：平易通达。③ 构：挑拨，离间。④ 初：席。⑤ 秩秩：肃敬的样子。⑥ 殽(yáo)：同"肴"。⑦ 和旨：调美。

* Directed against drunkenness, this ode was a lively picture of the license of the time of King You.

钟鼓既设,　　钟鼓已经摆上来,　　Bells and drums in their place,
举酬逸逸①。　敬酒劝酒杯不绝。　They raise their cups with grace.
大侯②既抗,　　君主箭靶高高挂,　　The target set on foot,
弓矢斯张。　　张弓搭箭向靶心。　　With bows for them to shoot,
射夫既同,　　射者先来选对手,　　The archers stand in row,
献尔发功。　　演练技艺显功夫。　　Ready their skill to show.
发彼有的,　　人人争取中目标,　　If the target is hit,
以祈尔爵③。　好让对手罚饮酒。　You'll drink a cup for it.

籥④舞笙鼓,　　和籥起舞钟鼓鸣,　　They dance to music sweet
乐既和奏。　　一起演奏声和谐。　　Of flute and to drumbeat.
烝⑤衎⑥烈祖,　此番娱乐献列祖,　　Rites are performed to please
以洽百礼。　　百种礼仪要周备。　　Our ancestors with ease.
百礼既至,　　祭礼完备很周到,　　The offerings on hand
有壬⑦有林。　隆重盛大又繁多。　　Are so full and so grand.
锡尔纯嘏⑧,　　神灵赐予你洪福,　　You will be richly blessed,
子孙其湛。　　子孙后代乐陶陶。　　Sons, grandsons and the rest.
其湛曰乐,　　众人高兴又欢乐,　　Happy is every man.
各奏尔能。　　各献射箭真技能。　　Let each do what he can.
宾载手仇⑨,　宾客来把对手找,　　Each guest shoots with his bow;
室人入又。　　主人也来陪一场。　　The host joins in the row.
酌彼康⑩爵,　给你满满斟一杯,　　Let's fill an empty cup.
以奏尔时。　　等你胜利来畅饮。　　When one hits, all cheer up.

① 逸逸:往来不断。② 侯:箭靶。③ 爵:射爵,射箭的礼数,不胜者被罚饮酒。④ 籥(yuè):一种乐器。⑤ 烝(zhēng):进。⑥ 衎(kàn):娱乐。⑦ 壬:大。⑧ 纯嘏(gǔ):大福。⑨ 仇:对手。⑩ 康:大。

宾之初筵，	宾客入座开宴席，	When guests begin to feast,
温温其恭。	个个温顺又恭敬。	They are gentle at least.
其未醉止，	酒过一巡未喝醉，	When they've not drunk too much,
威仪反反。	言行举止守礼仪。	They would observe the rite;
曰既醉止，	喝过数旬都已醉，	When they have drunk too much,
威仪幡幡①。	礼数仪态皆忘形。	Their deportment is light.
舍其坐迁，	离开各自的座位，	They leave their seats and go
屡舞僊僊。	走起路来飘飘然。	Capering to and fro.
其未醉止，	刚刚还未喝醉时，	When they've not drunk too much,
威仪抑抑。	举止行为都慎重。	They are in a good mood;
曰既醉止，	待到酒醉酩酊时，	When they have drunk too much,
威仪怭怭②。	嬉皮笑脸不端庄。	They're indecent and rude.
是曰既醉，	还说已经喝醉酒，	When they are deeply drunk,
不知其秩。	自然不知守礼仪。	They know not where they're sunk.

宾既醉止，	宾客已经全喝醉，	When they've drunk their cups dry,
载号载呶③。	又是叫啊又是闹。	They shout out, brawl and cry.
乱我笾豆，	果碗菜盘被推乱，	They put plates upside down;
屡舞僛僛④。	跌跌撞撞站不稳。	They dance like funny clown.
是曰既醉，	还说已经喝醉酒，	When they have drunk wine strong,
不知其邮⑤。	稀里糊涂不知错。	They know not right from wrong.
侧弁之俄⑥，	皮帽已经戴歪了，	With their cups on one side,
屡舞傞傞⑦。	疯癫不停跳舞蹈。	They dance and slip and slide.

---

① 幡幡：失威仪。② 怭怭(bìbì)：轻薄粗鄙的样子。③ 呶(náo)：喧哗。④ 僛僛(qīqī)：身体歪斜的样子。⑤ 邮：过错。⑥ 俄：倾倒的样子。⑦ 傞傞(suōsuō)：舞动不止的样子。一说为参差不齐的样子。

既醉而出,	如果醉了就出门,	If drunk they went away,
并受其福。	就是大家的福气。	The host would happy stay.
醉而不出,	如果醉了还不走,	But drunk they will not go;
是谓伐德①。	说明品德不太好。	The host is full of woe.
饮酒孔嘉,	饮酒享乐是好事,	We may drink with delight
维其令仪。	只是礼仪很重要。	If we observe the rite.

凡此饮酒,	凡是举杯饮美酒,	Whenever people drink,
或醉或否。	有人喝醉有清醒。	In drunkenness some sink.
既立之监,	已经设立了酒监,	Appoint an inspector
或佐之史。	更有史官记言行。	And keep a register.
彼醉不臧,	醉酒本来就不好,	But drunkards feel no shame;
不醉反耻。	不醉还说你不行。	On others they'll lay blame.
式勿从谓②,	不要劝他再多饮,	Don't drink any more toast,
无俾大怠。	不要让他犯大错。	Or they will wrong the host.
匪言勿言,	不该说的不要说,	Do not speak if you could;
匪由勿语。	不合法的不要做。	Say only what you should.
由醉之言,	酒醉之后胡言语,	Don't say like drunkard born
俾出童羖③。	公羊可以没有角。	You're a ram without horn.
三爵不识,	他的酒量只三杯,	With three cups you've lost head;
矧④敢多又。	怎敢劝他再多喝。	With more you'd be drunk dead.

---

① 伐德:败德。② 从谓:听从别人再劝酒。③ 童羖(gǔ):无角黑色公羊,世上本不存在。④ 矧(shěn):况且。

鱼藻之什　　Seventh Decade of Odes

鱼　藻　　The Fish among the Weed*

鱼在在藻①，	鱼儿躲在水藻中，	The fish among the weed,
有颁②其首。	头儿大大有斑纹。	Showing large head, swims with speed
王在在镐，	大王住在镐京城，	The king in the capital
岂③乐饮酒。	欢快饮酒乐欢颜。	Drinks happy in the hall.
鱼在在藻，	鱼儿躲在水藻中，	The fish swims thereamong,
有莘④其尾。	尾巴长长水中游。	Showing its tail so long.
王在在镐⑤，	大王住在镐京里，	The king in the capital
饮酒乐岂。	欢快饮酒乐悠游。	Drinks cheerful in the hall.
鱼在在藻，	鱼儿躲在水藻中，	The fish among the weed
依于其蒲。	贴着蒲草慢慢游。	Sheltered by rush and reed,
王在在镐，	大王住在镐京里，	The king in the capital
有那⑥其居。	生活安乐且逍遥。	Dwells carefree in the hall.

---

① 藻：水草。② 颁(fén)：指鱼的头很大。③ 岂(kǎi)：欢乐。④ 莘(shēn)：长。⑤ 镐(hào)：镐京。⑥ 那(nuó)：安闲。

* This ode celebrated the praise of King Wu after his triumph over the last king of the Shang dynasty. The fish was in its proper place, enjoying what happiness it could, and so it served to introduce King Wu enjoying himself in his capital.

采菽　　　　　　　　Royal Favours*

采菽①采菽，	采大豆呀采大豆，	Gather beans long and short
筐②之筥之。	装满方筐装圆筐。	In baskets round and square.
君子③来朝，	诸侯远道来朝见，	The lords come to the court.
何锡④之？	大王给他赏点啥？	What suitable things there
虽无予之，	虽然没啥好东西，	Can be given to meet their needs?
路车⑤乘马。	一辆路车四匹马。	A state cab and horses four.
又何予之？	此外还要给他啥？	What else besides the steeds?
玄衮及黼⑥。	黑色龙纹好衣服。	Dragon robes they adore.
觱⑦沸槛泉，	泉水汩汩涌翻腾，	Gather cress long and short
言采其芹。	采摘芹菜在旁边。	Around the spring near by.
君子来朝，	诸侯远道来朝见，	The lords come to the court;
言观其旂。	车上龙旗已看见。	I see dragon flags fly.
其旂淠淠⑧，	旌旗迎风频翻动，	Flags flutter in the breeze,
鸾声嘒嘒⑨。	銮铃急缓有节律。	Three or four horses run,
载骖载驷，	驾着三匹四匹马，	Bells ringing without cease,
君子所届⑩。	诸侯立刻就来到。	The lords come one by one.

---

① 菽(shū)：大豆。② 筐：方筐。筥(jǔ)：圆筐。③ 君子：这里指诸侯。④ 锡："赐"的假借字。⑤ 路车：《集传》，"路车，金路以赐同姓，象路以赐异姓也。"⑥ 衮(gǔn)：有卷龙图纹的衣服。黼(fǔ)，黑白相间礼服。⑦ 觱(bì)沸：泉水翻腾的样子。⑧ 淠淠(pèipèi)，旌旗翻动的样子。⑨ 嘒嘒(huì huì)：銮铃声急缓有节拍。⑩ 届：来到。

* This ode was responsive to the former, celebrating the appearance of the feudal princes at the court, the splendor of their array, the propriety of their demeanor and the favors conferred on them by the king.

赤芾①在股，	皮质蔽膝垂股间，	Red covers on their knees
邪幅②在下。	裹腿斜绑在下边。	And their buskins below,
彼交③匪纾，	不傲慢也不松懈，	They go with perfect ease
天子所予。	天子赏赐真不少。	In what the king bestows.
乐只君子，	诸侯心情多快乐，	They receive with delight
天子命之。	天子命他来辅佐。	High favours from the king;
乐只君子，	诸侯心情多快乐，	They receive with delight
福禄申④之。	又增福来又增禄。	Good fortune in a string.
维柞之枝，	柞树上头枝儿长，	On branches of oak-tree,
其叶蓬蓬⑤。	叶子长得真茂盛。	What riot lush leaves run!
乐只君子，	诸侯心情真快乐，	The lords guard with high glee
殿⑥天子之邦。	平抚四方安国邦。	The land of Heaven's Son.
乐只君子，	诸侯心情真快乐，	They receive with delight
万福攸⑦同。	万种福气全安享。	Blessings from high and low.
平平⑧左右，	左右臣下都能干，	Attendants left and right
亦是率从。	一切命令都遵从。	Follow them where they go.
汎汎杨舟，	杨木小舟水中游，	The boat of willow wood
绋⑨缡⑩维之。	麻绳竹索系船头。	Fastened by band and rope,
乐只君子，	诸侯心情真快乐，	Of happy lords and good
天之葵⑪之。	福气俸禄真是多。	The king scans the full scope.
乐只君子，	心情舒畅乐悠悠，	They receive with high glee

---

① 芾(fú)：皮质的蔽膝。② 邪幅：绑腿。③ 交：衣领。代指衣服。纾(shū)：屈曲。④ 申：重复。⑤ 蓬蓬：茂盛的样子。⑥ 殿：安抚，镇定。⑦ 万福攸(yōu)同：万福之所聚。⑧ 平平(pián pián)：辩治。⑨ 绋(fú)：系船的麻绳。⑩ 缡(lí)：拉船的竹索。⑪ 葵：估量，度量。

福祿膍①之。　厚赏福禄多嘉奖。　All blessings from the king.
优哉游哉，　　生活安逸无忧愁，　They're happy and carefree;
亦是戾②矣。　　悠游安适清福享。　Fortune comes on the wing.

角　弓　　　　　　　　　　Admonition*

骍骍③角弓，　红色角弓样子美，　Tighten the string of the bow,
翩其反矣。　弓背弯曲向两边。　Its recoil will be swift.
兄弟昏姻，　都是兄弟与亲戚，　If brothers alien go,
无胥④远矣。　相互之间莫疏远。　Their affection will shift.

尔之远矣，　你和兄弟相疏远，　If you alienate
民胥然矣。　百姓都会照着办。　Your relatives and brothers,
尔之教矣，　如果你能做榜样，　People will imitate
民胥傚矣。　百姓也会来仿效。　You when you deal with others.

此令兄弟，　兄弟相处要和睦，　When there is brotherhood,
绰绰有裕⑤；　相互包容度量宽。　Good feeling is displayed.
不令兄弟，　若是搞得关系僵，　When brothers are not good,
交相为瘉⑥。　怨恨自然由此生。　Much trouble will be made.

民之无良，　如果百姓不良善，　The people have no grace,

---

① 膍(pí)：厚赐。② 戾(lì)：止，定。③ 骍骍(xīng xīng)：深红色。④ 胥：疏远。⑤ 有裕：气量宽大。⑥ 瘉(yù)：病，引申为怨恨。

* This ode was directed against the king's cold treatment of his relatives and his encouragement to calumniators.

相怨一方，	相互指责怨对方。	They blame the other side;
受爵不让；	接受功勋不谦让，	They fight to get high place
至于己斯亡。	到头谁都命不长。	And come to fratricide.

老马反为驹，	老马反当马驹使，	Old steeds think themselves good;
不顾其后。	不顾后果何不堪。	Of the young they don't think.
如食宜饇①，	就像吃饭要吃饱，	They want plenty of food
如酌孔取。	好比喝酒斟满量。	And an excess of drink.

毋教猱②升木，	莫让猿猴树上爬，	Don't teach apes to climb trees
如涂涂附。	就像泥巴涂抹墙。	Nor add mud to the wall.
君子有徽猷③，	君子若是有良策，	If you do good with ease,
小人与属。	民众便会来效仿。	They'll follow you one and all.

雨雪瀌瀌④，	大雪纷纷满天飘，	Flake on flake falls the snow;
见晛⑤曰消。	太阳出来不见了。	It dissolves in the sun.
莫肯下遗，	不肯低头来谦让，	Don't despise those below.
式居娄⑥骄。	态度傲慢性情骄。	The proud will be undone.

雨雪浮浮⑦，	大雪纷纷满天飘，	The snow falls flake on flake;
见晛曰流。	太阳一出即溶消。	It will melt in sunlight.
如蛮如髦⑧，	就像南方野蛮人，	Let no barbarians make
我是用忧。	令我实在很忧焦。	You fall into a sad plight.

---

①饇(yù)：饱。②猱(náo)：猿猴。③徽：美好。猷，道，即修养。本领。④瀌瀌：雪下得猛烈的样子。⑤晛(xiàn)：日气。⑥娄(lǚ)：屡次。⑦浮浮：同瀌瀌。⑧髦(máo)：西南部族名。

菀柳　　The Unjust Lord*

有菀①者柳，	路边柳树枝叶盛，	Lush is the willow tree.
不尚息焉。	不可依傍而休息。	Who won't rest under it?
上帝甚蹈②。	上天喜怒太无常。	The lord's to punish free.
无自暱焉。	无故不要亲近他。	Don't fall into the pit.
俾予靖③之，	先前让我治邦国，	You lend him hand and arm,
后予极④焉！	而今又要诛杀我。	But he will do you harm.

有菀者柳，	路边柳树枝叶盛，	Lush is the willow tree.
不尚愒⑤焉。	不可休息作屏障。	Who won't shelter 'neath it?
上帝甚蹈，	上天喜怒太无常。	The lord's to punish free;
无自瘵⑥焉。	无故不要接近他。	His ire bursts in a fit.
俾予靖之，	先前让我治邦国，	You lend him arm and hand;
后予迈⑦焉！	而今又来虐待我。	He'll ban you from the land.

有鸟高飞，	鸟儿振翅蓝天上，	The bird flies as it can
亦傅⑧于天。	在那高高天际旁。	Even up to the sky.
彼人之心，	那人心中的欲望，	The heart of such a man
于何其臻？	要到何时是极限？	Will go up far and high.
曷予靖之，	为何叫我治国邦，	Whate'er for him you do,

---

① 菀(yù)：茂盛。② 蹈：指喜怒变化无常。③ 靖：平定。④ 极：诛杀。⑤ 愒(qì)：休息。⑥ 瘵(zhài)：接。⑦ 迈：虐。⑧ 傅：至，到。

* This ode was directed against King Li (877-841 B. C.), tyrannical and oppressive, punishing where punishment was not due, whose court was not frequented by the princes of the States.

居以凶矜①！ 反陷凶险惹祸殃？ He's free to punish you.

都人士　　　　　　　　Men of the Old Capital*

彼都②人士， 京都人士真漂亮， Men of the old capital
狐裘黄黄。 黄色狐袍披身上。 In yellow fox-fur dress,
其容不改， 容貌仪态皆端庄， With face unmoved at all,
出言有章③。 表达清晰有文章。 Spoke with pleasing address.
行归于周④， 即将回到周王朝， At the old capital
万民所望。 万千民众齐盼望。 They were admired by all.

彼都人士， 京都人士真漂亮， Men of the old capital
台笠缁撮⑤。 草笠布帽戴头上。 Wore their hat up-to-date;
彼君子女， 有教养的好女子， The noble ladies tall
绸⑥直如发。 头发黑亮密密直。 Had hair so thick and straight.
我不见兮， 如果多日不见她， Although I see them not,
我心不说。 心中烦忧不舒畅。 Could their face be forgot?

彼都人士， 京都人士真漂亮， Men of the old capital
充耳琇⑦实。 美石宝玉戴耳上。 Wore pendant from the ear;
彼君子女， 有教养的好女子， The noble ladies tall
谓之尹吉⑧。 尹氏吉氏大名姓。 Were fair without a peer.

---

① 矜：危境。② 都(dū)：美。③ 章：有文采，有条理。④ 周：周朝京城。⑤ 撮(cuō)：带子。⑥ 绸：通"稠"，密。⑦ 琇(xiù)：美石。⑧ 尹、吉：都是周氏婚姻的旧姓。

* This was an ode in praise of the lords and ladies of the old capital, written after King Ping removed the capital to the east in 770 B. C.

我不见兮,	如果多日不见她,	Although I see them not,
我心苑①结。	心中郁闷又愁苦。	Could their dress be forgot?

彼都人士,	京都人士真漂亮,	Men of the old capital
垂带而厉②。	腰间垂下长丝带。	With girdles hanging down;
彼君子女,	有教养的好女子,	And noble ladies tall
卷③发如虿④。	头发卷曲向上扬。	With hair like tail of scorpion,
我不见兮,	如果多日不见她,	Of them could I see one,
言从之迈。	愿意时刻随身旁。	After them I would run.

匪伊垂之,	并非有意要垂下,	His girdle hanging there
带则有余。	丝带本就有所长。	Suited so well his gown;
匪伊卷之,	并非有意要卷曲,	Her natural curled hair
发则有旟⑤。	头发本来就飘扬。	Was wavy up and down.
我不见兮,	如果多日不见她,	I see not their return.
云何盱⑥矣!	直立翘首把她望。	How much for trem I yearn!

采 绿   My Lord Not Back*

终朝采绿⑦,	王刍采了一早上,	I gather all the morn king-grass,
不盈一匊⑧。	还是不够一小捧。	But get not a handful, alas!
予发曲局,	我的头发已卷曲,	In a wisp is my hair,

---

① 苑(yù):积压,蕴结。② 厉:带之垂者。③ 卷(quán):发束翘起。④ 虿(chài):虫名,尾巴上翘。⑤ 旟(yú):扬。⑥ 盱(xū):张目盼望的样子。⑦ 绿:一作"菉(lù)",草名。又名王刍。⑧ 匊(jū):即掬。用双手捧起。

* A wife told her sorrow and incapability of attending to anything in the prolonged absence of her husband to whom she was fondly attached.

| 薄言①归沐。 | 我要回家把它洗。 | I'll go home and wash it with care. |

终朝②采蓝,	采蓝采了一早上,	I gather all the morn plants blue,
不盈一襜③。	还是不满一围裳。	But get not an apronful for you.
五日为期,	五天日子就到了,	You should be back on the fifth day.
六日不詹④。	六天不见他到来。	Now it's the sixth, why the delay?

之子于狩,	如果那人去打猎,	If you should hunting go,
言韔⑤其弓。	我将弓箭放套中。	I would put in its case your bow.
之子于钓,	如果那人去钓鱼,	If you should go to fish,
言纶⑥之绳。	我将结好钓鱼绳。	I'd arrange your line as you wish.

其钓维何?	钓鱼钓得怎么样?	What might we take out of the stream?
维鲂⑦及鱮⑧。	只有鳊鱼和鲢鱼。	O tench and bream.
维鲂及鱮,	只有鳊鱼和鲢鱼,	O tench and bream,
薄言观⑨者。	可他总是钓不厌。	With what wild joy my face would beam!

黍 苗

On Homeward Way after Construction*

| 芃芃⑩黍苗, | 黍苗长得真茂盛, | Young millet grows tall and strong, |

---

① 薄言:二字皆语助词,无义。② 终朝(zhāo):从天明到早饭的一段时间。③ 襜(chān):指衣服遮着前面的部分,蔽膝或前裳。④ 詹:到。⑤ 韔(chàng):藏弓的套子。⑥ 纶(lún):拧结。⑦ 鲂:鳊鱼。⑧ 鱮(xù):鲢鱼。⑨ 观:多。⑩ 芃芃(péngpéng):蓬勃茂盛的样子。

* This ode celebrated the service of Duke Mu of Zhao in building the city of Xie (modern Tang County in Henan Province) for the marquisate of Shen established by King Xuan (826-781 B.C.) as a bulwark against the encroachments of wild tribes.

阴雨膏之。	又有雨水来滋润。	Fattened by genial rain.
悠悠南行，	战士悠悠向南行，	Our southward journey's long;
召伯劳之。	幸有召伯来慰问。	The Lord of Zhao cheers the train.
我任①我辇，	又挑重物又挽辇，	Our carts go one by one;
我车我牛。	又驾车来又赶牛。	Our oxen follow the track.
我行既集②，	我的任务已完成，	Our construction is done,
盖云归哉!	何时才能把家还?	So we are going back.
我徒我御，	又步行来又驾车，	We go on foot or run;
我师我旅。	队伍整编安排多。	Our host goes in a throng.
我行既集，	我的任务已完成，	Our construction is done,
盖云归处!	何时才能把家还?	So we are going along.
肃肃③谢功，	谢城修建真神速，	The town of Xie stands strong,
召伯营之。	召伯到此来统治。	Built by our lord with might and main.
烈烈④征师，	随行队伍真威武，	Our expedition's long
召伯成之。	都由召伯来统领。	And our lord leads the train.
原隰⑤既平，	低洼地方已铺平，	Lowland becomes a plain;
泉流既清。	汩汩泉水也变清。	Streams are cleared east and west.
召伯有成，	召伯任务已完成，	Our lord leads the campaign;
王心则宁。	大王终于心安宁。	The king's heart is at rest.

---

① 任:负荷。辇:挽车。② 集:完成。③ 肃肃:迅疾的样子。④ 烈烈:威武的样子。
⑤ 隰(xí):低湿的地方。

隰　桑　　　　　　　　　　The Mulberry Tree*

隰①桑有阿②，	低洼处的桑树真美，	The lowland mulberry tree's fair;
其叶有难③。	叶子长得也很漂亮。	Its leaves are lush and bright.
既见君子，	已经见到那个人儿，	When I see my love there,
其乐如何！	我的心里真是欢喜！	How great will be my delight!

隰桑有阿。	低洼处的桑树真美，	The lowland mulberry tree's fair;
其叶有沃④。	叶子柔美又有光泽。	Its leaves shed glossy light.
既见君子，	已经见到那个人儿，	When I see my love there,
云何不乐？	我的心里怎不欢乐？	How can I not feel delight?

隰桑有阿。	低洼处的桑树真美，	The lowland mulberry tree's fair;
其叶有幽⑤。	叶子长得也很茂盛。	Its leaves darken each day.
既见君子，	已经见到那个人儿，	When I see my love there,
德音孔胶⑥。	德行仪态十分隆盛。	How much have I to say?

心乎爱矣，	我在心中敬爱他，	I love him in my heart,
遐不⑦谓矣？	为何总不告诉他？	Why won't I tell him so?
中心藏之，	这样藏在心里头，	Better keep it apart
何日忘之？	等到何时才能忘？	That sweeter it will grow.

---

① 隰(xí)：低湿的地方。② 阿(ē)：美貌。③ 难：通"傩(nuó)"，盛多。④ 沃(wò)：柔美有光泽。⑤ 幽：茂盛。⑥ 胶：盛。⑦ 遐不：胡不，何不。

* This ode read like a song in which a woman spoke of her admiration and love for a man fair as the mulberry tree and bright as its leaves.

白 华

The Degraded Queen*

白华菅①兮，	细细菅草绽白花，	White flowered rushes sway
白茅束兮。	白茅紧紧捆住它。	Together with white grass.
之子之远，	那人离我已远去，	My lord sends me away
俾我独兮。	剩我孤独度年华。	And leaves me alone, alas!

英英②白云，	白云飘飘降甘露，	White clouds with dewdrops spray
露③彼菅茅。	滋润那些菅和茅。	Rushes and grass all o'er.
天步④艰难，	命运实在太艰难，	Hard is heavenly way;
之子不犹。	那人无德也无道。	My lord loves me no more.

滮⑤池北流.	滮池之水向北流，	Northward the stream goes by,
浸彼稻田。	浸润稻田绿油油。	Flooding the ricefields there.
啸歌伤怀，	长啸高歌真伤感，	With wounded heart I sigh,

---

① 菅(jiān)：茅的一种，又名芦芒。② 英英：白云貌。③ 露：覆，盖。④ 天步：时运。⑤ 滮(biāo)池：古河流名。

* The queen of King You (reigned 780-770 B. C.) complained of being degraded and forsaken for the sake of his fair mistress Lady Shi of Bao. The first stanza suggested the idea of the close connection between rushes and grass as it should be between king and queen. The idea in Stanza 2 seemed to be that the clouds bestowed their dewy influences on rushes and grass while the king neglected the queen. The flooding in Stanza 3 was the greatest benefit to the ricefields, not so did the king deal with the queen. The idea in Stanza 4 seemed to be that the queen had a smaller stove than the king's mistress. Stanza 5 suggested that the king's angry shout was heard without the palace. In Stanza 6 the crane was a clean bird and the heron an unclean one. The idea in Stanza 7 was that the lovebirds were more faithful than the king. Stanza 8 compared the queen to the stone King You trod underfoot.

念彼硕人。	那个人儿令我忧。	Thinking of his mistress fair.

樵①彼桑薪，	摘采那些桑树枝，	Wood's cut from mulberry tree
卬②烘于煁③。	放进灶中作柴薪。	To make fire in the stove.
维彼硕人，	想起那个人儿呀，	His mistress fair makes me
实劳我心。	确实很让我劳心。	Lose the heart of my love.

鼓钟于宫，	宫中鼓钟震天响，	When rings the palace bell,
声闻于外。	声音传到宫墙外。	Its sound is heard without.
念子懆懆④，	心中想你多烦恼，	When I think of him well,
视我迈迈。	你却对我怒冲冲。	I hear but angry shout.

有鹙⑤在梁，	秃鹙梁上把鱼吞，	The heron may eat fish
有鹤在林。	仙鹤忍饥在树林。	While the crane hungry goes.
维彼硕人。	那个人儿真漂亮，	His mistress has her wish
实劳我心。	确实很让我心焦。	While I am full of woes.

鸳鸯在梁，	一对鸳鸯在鱼梁，	The lovebirds on the dam
戢⑥其左翼，	嘴巴插进左翅膀。	Hide their beaks 'neath left wings.
之子无良，	那个人啊不良善，	The woe in which I am
二三其德。	三心二意变无常。	Is what my unkind lord brings.

有扁斯石，	垫脚石头扁又小，	The stone becomes less thick
履之卑兮。	脚踩上去不嫌高。	On which our feet oft tread.

---

① 樵：采。② 卬(áng)：我，此处为女子自称。③ 煁(shén)：可移动的炉灶。④ 懆懆(cǎocǎo)：不安。迈迈，不悦。⑤ 鹙(qiū)：水鸟名。⑥ 戢(jí)：收敛。

之子之远，	那人弃我远离去，	My heart becomes love-sick
俾我疧①兮。	留我一人空悲伤。	For my lord's left my bed.

緜蛮

Hard Journey*

"緜蛮②黄鸟，	"一只小黄鸟，	O hear the oriole's song!
止于丘阿。	停在半山腰。	It rests on mountain slope.
道之云远，	道路真是太遥远，	The journey's hard and long.
我劳如何！"	奔波辛劳若你何！"	How can a tired man cope?
"饮之食之，	"给水喝来给食吃，	Give me food and be kind,
教之诲之。	又教诲来又鼓励。	Help me, encourage me,
命彼后车③，	命令副车停下来，	Tell the carriage behind
谓④之载之。"	让他坐到车上去。"	To stop and carry me!

"緜蛮黄鸟，	"一只小黄鸟，	O hear the oriole's song!
止于丘隅⑤。	停在山角上。	It rests at mountain yon.
岂敢惮⑥行，	怎能害怕走远路，	Do I fear journey long?
畏不能趋。"	只怕疲劳赶不及。"	I fear I can't go on.
"饮之食之，	"给他水来给他食，	Give me food and be kind,
教之诲之。	又教诲来又鼓励。	Help me, encourage me,
命彼后车，	命令副车停下来，	Tell the carriage behind
谓之载之。"	让他坐到车上去。"	To stop and carry me!

---

① 疧(qí)：病。② 緜蛮：小鸟貌。③ 后车：随行副车。④ 谓：归。⑤ 丘隅：丘角。
⑥ 惮：畏。

* Some inferior complained of his toil in an expedition and the neglect with which he was treated by his superiors.

"绵蛮黄鸟，	"一只小黄鸟，	O hear the oriole's song!
止于丘侧。	停在山坡上。	It rests at mountain's bend.
岂敢惮行，	怎能害怕走远路，	Do I fear journey long?
畏不能极①。"	只怕疲劳赶不上。"	I can't get to its end.
"饮之食之，	"给他水来给他食，	Give me food and be kind,
教之诲之。	又教诲来又鼓励，	Help me, encourage me,
命彼后车，	命令副车停下来，	Tell the carriage behind
谓之载之。"	让他坐到车上去。"	To stop and carry me!

瓠叶　　　　　Frugal Hospitality*

幡幡瓠②叶，	葫芦叶子向上翻，	The gourd's waving leaves are fine,
采之亨之。	采摘下来烹煮它。	Taken and boiled in haste.
君子有酒，	君子家中有美酒，	Our good friend has sweet wine;
酌言尝之。	举起杯来先自尝。	He pours it out for a taste.
有兔斯③首，	几只兔子白又肥，	The rabbit's meat is fine
炮④之燔⑤之。	烧过烤过味道好。	When baked or roasted up.
君子有酒，	君子家中有美酒，	Our good friend has sweet wine;
酌言献之。	主人把盏献宾客。	He presents us a cup.
有兔斯首，	几只兔子白又肥，	The rabbit's meat is fine
燔之炙⑥之。	烤过熏过味道好。	When broiled or roasted up,

---

① 极：至。② 瓠(hù)：葫芦。③ 斯：白。④ 炮(páo)：煨，烧。⑤ 燔(fán)：烤。⑥ 炙：熏烤。

* This ode described the simple manners and decency of an earlier time.

| 君子有酒， | 君子家中有美酒， | Our good friend has sweet wine; |
| 酌言酢①之。 | 客人斟酒敬主人。 | We present him a cup. |

有兔斯首，	几只兔子白又肥，	The rabbit's meat is fine
燔之炮之。	烧过烤过味道好。	When baked or roasted up.
君子有酒，	君子家中有美酒，	Our good friend has sweet wines;
酌言酬之。	宾主同饮乐逍遥。	We fill each other's cup.

渐渐之石　　　　　　　Eastern Expedition*

渐渐②之石，	山石雄伟耸立，	The mountain frowns
维其高矣。	山峰直冲云霄。	With rocky crowns.
山川悠远，	山泉绵绵悠远，	Peaks high, streams long,
维其劳③矣。	行路很是辛劳。	Toilsome the throng.
武人东征，	军队奉命东征，	Warriors east go;
不皇④朝矣。	无暇等到天晓。	No rest they know.

渐渐之石，	山石雄伟耸立，	The mountain frowns
维其卒⑤矣。	山峰高峭险峻。	With craggy crowns.
山川悠远，	山泉绵绵悠远，	Peaks high, streams bend.
曷其没⑥矣？	何时才到尽头？	When is the end?
武人东征，	军队奉命东征，	Warriors go east.

---

① 酢(zuò)：回敬。② 渐渐(chánchán)：通"巉"，山石高峻的样子。③ 劳：劳顿。
④ 皇：闲暇。⑤ 卒：高而险。⑥ 没：尽。

* This ode commemorated the hardships of a long and difficult expedition to the east, undertaken in the time of King Li (877-841 B.C.).

不皇出①矣。	无暇顾及休息。	When be released?

有豕白蹢②,	小猪蹄上白毛多,	White-legged swines wade
烝③涉波矣。	众人争相淌过河。	Through streams and fade.
月离④于毕⑤,	月亮快要近毕星,	In Hyades the moon
俾滂沱矣。	大雨滂沱仍未停。	Foretells hard rain soon.
武人东征,	军队奉命去东征,	Warriors east go;
不皇他矣。	他事无暇来照应。	No plaint they show.

苕之华　　　　　　　　Famine*

苕⑥之华?	凌霄花儿绽放,	The bignonia blooms
芸⑦其黄矣。	花瓣纷纷鲜黄。	Yellow and fade.
心之忧矣,	我的心情忧愁,	My heart is full of gloom;
维⑧其伤矣!	内心郁结感伤。	I feel the wound grief's made.

苕之华,	凌霄花儿正放,	The bignonia blooms
其叶青青。	叶子青青鲜亮。	Have left the green leaves dry.
知我如此,	早知此生如此,	Could I foretell what looms,
不如无生!	不如从未出生。	I would not live but die.

牂⑨羊坟⑩首,	母羊身小脑袋大,	The ewe's lean; large its head.

---

① 出:休息。② 蹢(dí):兽蹄。③ 烝(zhēng):众。④ 离:靠近。⑤ 毕:星名。⑥ 苕(tiáo):植物名,蔓生木本,花黄赤色。⑦ 芸:浓艳的黄色。⑧ 维:犹"何"。⑨ 牂(zāng):母绵羊。⑩ 坟:大。

* The speaker lamented the famine and misery in consequence of the general decay of the kingdom.

三星在罶①。　　鱼笼之中闪星光。　　In fish-trap there's no fish.
人可以食，　　　虽然可以供人食，　　Some people may be fed;
鲜可以饱!　　　可是很少能吃饱。　　Few can get what they wish.

何草不黄　　　　　　　　　　Nowhere but Yellow Grass*

何草不黄，　　　什么草儿不枯黄，　　Nowhere but yellow grass,
何日不行。　　　哪日能不在路上？　　Not a day when we've rest,
何人不将②，　　有谁能够不行走，　　No soldier but should pass
经营四方。　　　往来奔忙在四方。　　Here and there, east or west.

何草不玄③，　　什么草儿不枯黄，　　Nowhere but rotten grass,
何人不矜④。　　什么人儿不孤苦？　　None but has left his wife,
哀我征夫，　　　我们征夫真可怜，　　We poor soldiers, alas!
独为匪民⑤。　　唯独我们不是人！　　Lead an inhuman life.

匪兕⑥匪⑦虎，　不是野牛不是虎，　　We're not tigers nor beast.
率⑧彼旷野。　　却要奔跑在旷野。　　Why in the wilds do we stay?
哀我征夫，　　　我们征夫真可怜，　　Alas! we're men at least.
朝夕不暇。　　　从早到晚不得闲。　　Why toil we night and day?

---

① 罶(liǔ)：一种竹制渔具。② 将：行。③ 玄(xuán)：赤黑色，是百草由枯而腐的颜色。
④ 矜(guān)：苦难。⑤ 匪民：非人。⑥ 兕(sì)：野牛。⑦ 匪：彼。⑧ 率：循。

* This was the last odel which read like a song describing the misery of the soldiers constantly employed on expeditionary service and treated without any consideration in the time of King You (780-770 B. C.).

有芃①者狐，	狐狸尾巴真蓬松，	Unlike the long-tailed foxes
率彼幽草。	深草之中来躲藏。	Deep hidden in the grass,
有栈②之车，	一辆高大有篷车，	In our carts with our boxes
行彼周道。	行在周朝大道上。	We toil our way, alas!

---

① 芃(péng)：众草丛生的样子。② 栈：有篷子的车。

大 雅

BOOK OF EPICS

文王之什

First Decade of Epics

文　王

Heaven's Decree*

文王在上，	文王英灵在天上，	King Wen rests in the sky;
於①昭于天！	光辉照耀最明亮。	His spirit shines on high.
周虽旧邦，	岐周虽然是旧邦，	Though Zhou is an old state,
其命维新。	接受天命新气象。	It's destined to be great.
有周不②显③，	周家前途无限好，	The House of Zhou is bright;
帝命不时。	天命周家长兴旺。	God brings it to the height.
文王陟④降，	文王神灵升又降，	King Wen will e'er abide
在帝左右。	常伴上帝在天庭。	At God's left or right side.
亹亹⑤文王，	勤勤勉勉周文王，	King Wen was good and strong;
令闻不已。	美好声誉永不忘。	His fame lasts wide and long.
陈锡⑥哉周，	上帝赐他兴周邦，	God's gifts to Zhou will run

---

① 於（wū）：赞叹。② 不：语气助词，无实义。下文"不时""不亿""无念"之"不"与此同。③ 显：光明。④ 陟：升。⑤ 亹亹（wěi wěi）：勤勉的样子。⑥ 陈锡：重赐，厚赐。

* This was the first epic ode celebrating King Wen (1184-1134 B.C.), dead and alive, as the founder of the Zhou dynasty. It was attributed to the Duke of Zhou for the benefit of the young King Cheng (1114-1076 B.C.). It showed how King Wen's virtue drew to him the favoring regard of Heaven and made him a bright pattern to his descendants and their ministers. Stanza 5 carried on the subject of the descendants of the previous dynasty, called first Shang and then Yin. When they appeared at the court of Zhou, they assisted at the sacrifices of the king in his ancestral temple, which began with a libation of fragrant spirits to bring down the Spirits of the departed. The libation was poured out by the representative of the dead and the cup with the spirits was handed to him by Yin officers.

侯文王孙子。	后世子孙都为王。	From his son to grandson.
文王孙子，	文王子孙代相传，	Descendants of his line
本支①百世。	嫡亲旁支百世昌。	Will receive gifts divine;
凡周之士，	周家群臣和百官，	So will talents and sage
不显亦世②。	也都世世沾荣光。	Be blessed from age to age.
世之不显，	世代显贵沾荣光，	From age to age they're blest;
厥犹翼翼。	谋事小心又周详。	They work with care and zest.
思皇多士，	群臣众多皆贤能，	Brilliant, they dedicate
生此王国。	有幸生在周国里。	Their lives to royal state.
王国克生，	王国能把贤士生，	Born in this royal land,
维周之桢③；	都是周家好栋梁。	They'll support the house grand.
济济多士，	人才济济满朝廷，	With talents standing by,
文王以宁。	文王在天得安宁。	King Wen may rest on high.
穆穆④文王，	端庄恭敬周文王，	King Wen was dignified,
於缉熙⑤敬止！	光明磊落又善良。	Respected far and wide.
假⑥哉天命，	天命伟大不可违，	At Heaven's holy call
有商孙子。	殷商子孙都来归。	The sons of Shang come all.
商之孙子，	殷商子孙蕃衍多，	Those sons of the noblesse
其丽⑦不亿；	成万成亿数不清。	Of Shang are numberless.
上帝既命，	上帝已经发命令，	As Heaven orders it,
侯于周服⑧。	服从周邦为臣子。	They cannot but submit.

---

① 本支：文王的后世子孙。② 不显亦世：即显世，光显于世。③ 桢：干，栋梁。④ 穆穆：容仪谨敬，美好。⑤ 缉熙：光明。⑥ 假：大。⑦ 丽：数目。⑧ 侯于周服：臣服于周。

侯服于周，	殷商称臣服周王，	Submission's nothing strange;
天命靡常。	天命运行本无常。	Heaven's decree may change.
殷士①肤敏②，	殷商诸士多勤敏，	They were Shang's officers;
祼将于京。	助祭镐京陪周王。	They're now Zhou's servitors.
厥作祼③将，	他们助祭行灌礼，	They serve wine in distress
常服黼④冔⑤。	仍然穿戴殷时装。	In Shang cap and Yin dress.
王之荩⑥臣，	都是周王大忠臣，	You loyal ministers,
无念⑦尔祖！	牢记祖德不可忘。	Don't miss your ancestors!
无念尔祖，	牢记祖先别忘记，	Miss no ancestors dear;
聿修厥德。	继承祖业多努力。	Cultivate virtue here!
永言配命，	天命永远不相违，	Obey Heaven's decree
自求多福。	自己多多求福气。	And you'll live in high glee.
殷之未丧师⑧，	殷商未失民心时，	Ere it lost people's heart,
克配上帝。	行为也能合帝意。	Yin played its ordained part.
宜鉴于殷，	殷商灭亡应借鉴，	From Yin's example we see
骏命⑨不易！	永保天命不容易。	It's hard to keep decree.
命之不易，	永保天命不容易，	O keep Heaven's decree
无遏⑩尔躬。	不要断送你身上。	Or you will cease to be.
宣昭义问⑪，	美好声誉要发扬，	Let virtue radiate;
有虞⑫殷自天。	殷朝之鉴是天命。	Profit from Yin's sad fate.

---

① 殷士：殷商之臣属。② 肤敏：敏勉，美好。③ 祼(guàn)：用酒祭祖。行祼之礼，叫做祼将。④ 黼(fǔ)：白黑相间的殷商时的礼服。⑤ 冔(xǔ)：殷商时的礼帽。⑥ 荩(jìn)臣：忠臣。⑦ 无念：不忘。⑧ 师：众人。⑨ 骏命：大命，天意。⑩ 遏：止。⑪ 义问：好名声。⑫ 虞：借鉴。

上天之载①，	上帝之意不可测，	All grow under the sky
无声无臭。	既无气味也无声。	Silently far and nigh.
仪刑②文王，	效法文王好榜样，	Take pattern from King Wen.
万邦作孚③。	天下信任又敬仰。	All states will obey you then.

大 明

Three Kings of Zhou*

明明在下，	文王明德照人间，	Gods know on high
赫赫在上。	赫赫神灵在上天。	What's done below.
天难忱④斯，	天命茫茫不易信，	We can't rely
不易维王。	治国为王实在难。	On grace they show.
天位殷适⑤，	王位本属殷嫡子，	It's hard to retain
使不挟⑥四方。	教令不能达四方。	The royal crown.
		Yin-Shang did reign;
挚仲氏任，	挚国任氏第二女，	It's overthrown.
自彼殷商，	出生地方是殷商。	Ren, Princess Yin,
来嫁于周，	远行出嫁到周国，	Left Shang's town-wall
曰嫔⑦于京，	又在周京做新娘。	To marry in Zhou's capital.
乃及王季，	她跟王季成夫妇，	She wed King Ji,
维德之行。	专做好事美名扬。	The best of men.
大任有身⑧，	不久太任有身孕，	Then pregnant, she
生此文王。	生下一个周文王。	Gave birth to Wen.

---

① 载：事。② 仪刑：效法。③ 孚：相信。④ 忱(chén)：相信。⑤ 适：嫡，嗣子。⑥ 挟：到达。⑦ 嫔：为妇，做新娘。⑧ 有身：怀孕。

* This epic ode celebrated King Ji who married Princess Ren of Yin; King Wen who married Xin; and King Wu who overthrew the dynasty of Shang in 1121 B. C.

维此文王，	就是这位周文王，	When he was crowned,
小心翼翼。	恭敬谨慎又端庄。	Wen served with care
昭事上帝，	懂得怎样敬上帝，	The gods around,
聿怀①多福。	得来福禄无限量。	Blessed here and there.
厥德不回，	对于德行不违背，	His virtue's great,
以受方国②，	四方归民都敬仰。	Fit head of the state.

天监在下，	上天监察人间事，	Heaven above
有命既集③。	天命已经归文王。	Ruled o'er our fate.
文王初载，	文王即位初年时，	It chose with love
天作之合。	上天为他配新娘。	For Wen a mate.
在洽之阳，	她的家乡在洽阳，	On sunny side
在渭之涘。	就在渭水那一方。	Of River Wei
		Wen found his bride
文王嘉止④，	文王大礼已经详，	In rich array.
大邦有子。	大国有个好姑娘。	

大邦有子，	大国有个好姑娘，	Born in a large state,
俔⑤天之妹。	好比天上仙女样。	The celestial bride
文定⑥厥祥，	纳下聘礼定吉祥，	And auspicious mate
亲迎于渭。	文王迎亲渭水边。	Stood by riverside.
造舟为梁，	聚集船只当桥梁，	On birdge of boats they met,
不显其光。	婚礼显耀真荣光。	Splendor ne'er to forget.

| 有命自天， | 上帝有命降下方， | At Heaven's call |

---

① 怀：招来。② 方国：四方臣服的诸侯国。③ 集：成就。④ 嘉止：定婚礼。⑤ 俔(qiàn)：好比。⑥ 文定：指卜算定婚之礼。

命此文王,	命令降予周文王。	Wen again wed In capital
于周于京。	建国为周都为京,	Xin nobly-bred.
缵①女维莘,	继娶莘国好姑娘。	She bore a son
长子维行②,	她是长女嫁文王,	Who should take down,
笃生武王。	生下一个周武王。	When victory's won,
保右命尔,	上天保佑命令他,	The royal crown.
燮③伐大商。	联合诸侯伐殷商。	

殷商之旅,	殷商派出军队来,	Shang troops did wield
其会④如林。	旗帜招展密如林。	Stones on hard wood.
矢⑤于牧野;	武王誓师在牧野:	Wu vowed afield:
"维予侯兴,	"唯我周朝定兴盛,	"To us kinghood!
上帝临女,	上帝亲自照临你,	Gods are behind.
无贰尔心!"	不要二心怀妄想。	Keep your strongmind!"

牧野洋洋⑥,	牧野地方多宽广,	The field is wide;
檀车煌煌,	檀木兵车亮堂堂,	War chariots strong.
驷騵⑦彭彭。	四匹战马真强壮。	The steeds we ride
维师尚父⑧,	三军统帅为尚父,	Gallop along.
时维鹰扬。	好比雄鹰展翅翔。	Our Master Jiang
凉⑨彼武王,	一心辅佐周武王,	Assists the king
肆⑩伐大商,	大举兴兵伐殷商。	To overthrow the Shang
		Like eagle on the wing.
会朝⑪清明!	一朝开创新气象。	A morning bright
		Displaced the night.

---

① 缵(zuǎn):继娶。② 行:出嫁。③ 燮(xiè):和协,相会。④ 会:通"旆",旌旗。⑤ 矢:陈列。⑥ 洋洋:广大,宽阔。⑦ 騵(yuán):赤毛白腹的马。⑧ 师尚父:太公吕望为太师,号尚父。⑨ 凉:通"亮",辅佐。⑩ 肆:疾。⑪ 会朝:一个早上。

緜　　　　　　The Migration in 1325 B. C.

緜緜瓜瓞①。	大瓜小瓜不断长，	Gourds grow in long, long trains;
民之初生，	周族人民初兴旺。	Our people grew in the plains.
自土②沮漆。	杜水沮水到漆水，	They moved to Qi from Tu,
古公亶父③，	古公亶父功业创。	Led by old Duke Tan Fu,
陶复陶穴④，	挖洞筑窑地上下，	And built kilnlike hut and cave
未有家室。	没有房子没有家。	For house they did not have.

古公亶父，	古公亶父不停歇，	Tan Fu took morning ride;
来朝走马⑤；	早晨赶着他的马。	Along the western side
率⑥西水浒⑦，	顺着渭水西岸走，	Of River Wei came he
至于岐下。	来到岐山山脚下。	To the foot of Mount Qi;
爰及姜女，	和他夫人美太姜，	His wife Jiang came at his right
聿来胥宇⑧。	寻找地方重安家。	To find a housing site.

周原⑨膴膴⑩，	周原土地真肥美，	Zhou plain spread at his feet
堇⑪荼如饴。	苦菜也像糖样甜。	With plants and violets sweet.

---

① 瓜瓞(dié)：大瓜叫瓜，小瓜叫瓞。诗人以瓜的绵延和多实来比周民的兴盛。② 土：通"杜"，杜水。"沮""漆"都是水名。③ 古公亶(dǎn)父：周太王。④ 陶复陶穴：陶指挖洞，在地上挖洞为复，在地下挖洞为穴。⑤ 走马：驰马，驱马疾驰。⑥ 率：循，沿着。⑦ 浒：岸边，水边。⑧ 胥宇：察看居处，即考察地势，选择建筑宫室的地址。⑨ 原：广平的土地。⑩ 膴膴(wǔ wǔ)：肥沃，美好。⑪ 堇(jǐn)：堇葵，野生，可以吃。

* This epic ode narrated the beginning and subsequent growth of the House of Zhou, its removal from Bin to the foot of Mount Qi under Duke Tan Fu in 1325 B. C. and its settlement in the plain of Zhou, down to the time of King Wen.

爰始①爰谋，	于是商量又谋划，	He asked his men their mind,
爰契②我龟；	刻龟占卜问神意。	And by tortoise shell divined.
曰止曰时③，	兆示这里作居处，	He was told there to stay
筑室于兹。	此地建屋最吉祥。	And build homes rightaway.
乃④慰乃止，	于是安心住下来，	They settled at the site
乃左乃右；	或左或右把地分。	And planned to build left and right.
乃疆⑤乃理⑥，	丈量土地划疆界，	They divided the ground
乃宣乃亩⑦。	划好田亩好整治。	And dug ditches around.
自西徂东，	从西到东连成片，	From west to east there was no land
周⑧爰执事。	事情样样有人做。	But Tan Fu took in hand.
乃召司空⑨，	召唤司空来管地，	He named two officers
乃召司徒⑩，	召唤司徒来管人。	In charge of laborers
俾立室家。	吩咐他们造房屋，	To build their houses fine.
其绳则直，	拉紧绳子正又直。	They made walls straight with the line
缩版⑪以载，	树起夹板筑土墙，	And bound the frame-boards tight.
作庙翼翼。	建成宗庙好庄严。	A temple rose in sight.
捄⑫之陾陾⑬，	铲土进筐腾腾腾，	They brought basketfuls of earth
度⑭之薨薨⑮，	倒土版内轰轰轰。	And cast it in frames with mirth.

---

① 始：始谋。② 契：刻。③ 时：此时可以动工。④ 乃：古文为"迺"。慰：安。这句是说决定在此定居。⑤ 疆：划定疆界。⑥ 理：分条理。⑦ 亩：治理田垄。⑧ 周：普遍。⑨ 司空：官名，营建的事属司空职掌。⑩ 司徒：官名，调配人力的事属司徒职掌。⑪ 缩版：用绳捆木板，夹土筑墙，版即是筑墙时夹土的木板。⑫ 捄(jiū)：聚土和盛土的动作。⑬ 陾陾(réngréng)：指铲土入筐的声音。⑭ 度(duó)：向版内填土。⑮ 薨薨(hōnghōng)：填土的声音。

筑①之登登，	夯土筑墙登登响，	Then they beat it with blows
削屡②冯冯。	削平凸墙响乒乓。	And pared the walls in rows.
百堵皆兴，	百堵土墙同动工，	A hundred walls did rise;
鼛③鼓弗胜。	擂响大鼓不闻声。	Drums were drowned in their cries.

乃立皋门④，	立起都城外郭门，	They set up city gate;
皋门有伉⑤。	郭门高大多雄伟。	It stood so high and straight.
乃立应门⑥，	立起王宫大正门，	They set up palace door
应门将将⑦。	正门庄严多壮美。	They'd never seen before.
乃立冢土⑧，	堆起土台做祭坛，	They reared an altar grand
戎丑⑨攸行。	出师祈祷列成行。	To spirits of the land.

肆不殄⑩厥愠，	对敌愤怒不曾消，	The angry foe not tame
亦不陨⑪厥问⑫。	民族声望依然保。	Feared our Duke Tan Fu's name.
柞棫拔矣，	拔去柞树和棫树，	Oaks and thorns cleared away,
行道兑⑬矣。	打通往来必经路。	People might go their way.
混夷駾⑭矣，	昆夷望风已奔逃，	The savage hordes in flight
维其喙⑮矣。	困之喘息够狼狈。	Panted and ran out of sight.

| 虞芮⑯质厥成， | 虞芮两国不相争， | The lords no longer strove; |
| 文王蹶⑰厥生⑱。 | 文王感化改天性。 | King Wen taught them to love. |

---

①筑：把土捣实。②削屡(lóu)：是说将墙土隆高的地方削平。③鼛(gāo)：大鼓。④皋门：王都的郭门。⑤伉(kàng)：高大的样子。⑥应门：王宫正门。⑦将将：尊严正肃的样子。⑧冢土：大社，祭土地神的神坛。⑨戎丑：兵众。⑩殄(tiǎn)：绝断。⑪陨(yǔn)：失去。⑫问：名声。⑬兑：通行。⑭駾(tuì)：奔突，逃窜。⑮喙(huì)：窘困。⑯虞芮(ruì)：相传互相争田的虞芮两国国君。⑰蹶：感动，感化。⑱生：性，天性。

予①曰有疏附，	我有疏国来归附，	E'en strangers became kind;
予曰有先后，	我有贤臣前后辅。	They followed him behind.
予曰有奔奏②，	我有良士走四境，	He let all people speak
予曰有御侮。	我有猛将守疆土。	And defended the weak.

棫 朴　　　　King Wen and Talents*

芃芃③棫朴，	棫朴丛生多繁茂，	Oak trees and shrubs lush grow;
薪之槱④之。	劈它作柴堆起来。	They'll make firewood in row.
济济辟王⑤，	文王仪态多端庄，	King Wen has talents bright
左右趣之。	助祭群臣奉圭璋。	To serve him left and right.

济济辟王，	文王仪态最端庄，	King Wen has talents bright
左右奉璋⑥。	左右群臣捧玉璋。	To hold cups left and right
奉璋峨峨⑦，	手捧玉璋貌堂堂，	To offer sacrifice
髦士攸宜。	俊美贤士宜称强。	And pour libations nice.
淠⑧彼泾舟，	船儿顺着泾水流，	On River Jin afloat
烝⑨徒楫之。	众人划水齐举桨。	Many a ship and boat,
周王于迈⑩，	周王挥师去征伐，	The king orders to fight
六师及之。	六军相随威浩荡。	Six hosts of warriors bright.

| 倬⑪彼云汉， | 天上银河广又亮， | The Milky Way on high |

---

① 予：周人自称。② 奔奏：奔走四方传王命的大臣。③ 芃芃(péng péng)：草木繁盛的样子。④ 槱(yǒu)：堆积木柴。⑤ 辟王：指周文王。⑥ 璋：古代祭祀用的酒器，于发兵前祭祀时用。⑦ 峨峨：壮盛的样子。⑧ 淠(bì)：船行摇晃的样子。⑨ 烝(zhēng)徒：众多的船夫。⑩ 于迈：往行。⑪ 倬(zhuō)：广大。

* This epic ode celebrated King Wen using talents in war and in the pre-war sacrifice and breeding or cultivating them after the war.

为章于天。	灿灿光带贯高天。	Makes figures in the sky.
周王寿考,	周王年寿永无疆,	The king of Zhou lives long
遐不作人。	培育人才安国邦!	And breeds talents in throng.

追①琢其章,	雕琢成章是表象,	Figures by chisels made
金玉其相②。	质如金玉最精良。	Look like metal or jade.
勉勉我王,	我王勤奋又努力,	With them our good king reigns
纲纪四方。	条理分明治四方。	Over his four domains.

旱麓

Sacrifice and Blessing*

瞻彼旱③麓④,	看那旱山山脚下,	At the mountain's foot, lo!
榛楛济济。	榛树楛树最茂密。	How lush the hazels grow!
岂弟⑤君子,	君子快乐又平易,	Our prince is self-possessed
干⑥禄岂弟。	求得福禄心欢喜。	And he prays to be blessed.

瑟⑦彼玉瓒⑧,	鲜洁玉把金勺子,	The cup of jade is flne,
黄流在中。	郁香黄酒盛勺里。	O'erflowed with yellow wine.
岂弟君子,	君子快乐又平易,	Our prince is self-possessed;
福禄攸降。	大福大禄赐给你。	He prays and he is blessed.

鸢飞戾天,	鹞鹰展翅飞天上,	The hawks fly in the sky;
鱼跃于渊。	鱼儿跳跃在深渊。	The fish leap in the deep.

---

① 追(duī):雕刻。② 相:本质。③ 旱:山名。④ 麓:山脚。⑤ 岂弟(kǎitì):快乐,平易。⑥ 干:求。⑦ 瑟:鲜亮的样子。⑧ 玉瓒:圭瓒,以圭为柄,黄金为勺,青金为外。

* The prince referred to King Wen blessed by his ancestors.

岂弟君子，	君子快乐又平易，	Our prince is self-possessed;
遐不作人。	培育人才作贡献。	He prays his men be blessed.

清酒既载①，	清酒已经摆上了，	Jade cups of wine are full;
骍牡既备。	红色公牛已备好。	Ready is the red bull.
以享以祀，	虔诚祭祀祖先神，	He pays the sacred rite
以介景福。	祈求大福快来到。	To increase blessings bright.

瑟彼柞棫，	密密一片棫树林，	Oaks grow in neighborhood,
民所燎②矣，	焚烧棫树祭上天。	And are used for firewood.
岂弟君子，	君子快乐又平易，	Our prince is self-possessed;
神所劳③矣。	神灵抚慰保平安。	By gods he's cheered and blessed.

莫莫④葛藟，	郁郁一片野葡萄，	How the creeper and vine
施⑤于条枚。	爬满枝头缠树干。	Around the branches twine!
岂弟君子，	君子快乐又平易，	Our prince is self-possessed;
求福不回⑥。	求福从不违祖德。	He prays right and is blessed.

思 齐　　　　　King Wen's Reign *

思齐⑦大任，	大任肃敬又谨慎，	Reverent Lady Ren
文王之母，	她是文王的母亲。	Was mother of King Wen.
思媚周姜⑧，	周姜为人最可爱，	She loved grandmother dear,

---

① 载:斟。② 燎:烧柴祭天。③ 劳(lào):保佑。④ 莫莫:繁盛的样子。⑤ 施(yì):蔓延。⑥ 回:违背。⑦ 齐(zhāi):庄严,肃敬。⑧ 周姜:周太王之妃。

* This was an ode sung in praise of the virtue of King Wen and the excellent character of his grandmother Jiang, his mother Ren and his wife Si.

京室之妇。	做了主妇住京城，	A good wife without peer.
大姒①嗣徽②音，	大姒继承她德音，	Si inherited her fame;
则百斯男。	多生儿男家旺兴。	From her a hundred sons came.
惠③于宗公，	文王孝顺敬先公，	Good done to fathers dead,
神罔时怨，	神灵满意无怨恨，	Nowhere complaint was spread,
神罔时恫④。	神灵从不感悲痛。	They reposed as they could.
刑于寡妻，	他用礼法待妻子，	King Wen set example good
至于兄弟，	同样对待他弟兄，	To his dear wife and brothers,
以御⑤于家邦。	以此治理国中人。	His countrymen and others.
雝雝⑥在宫，	文王和气在宫廷，	At home benevolent,
肃肃在庙。	宗庙祭礼更恭敬。	In temple reverent,
不显亦临，	暗里也有神监临，	He had gods e'er in view;
无射亦保。	谨慎修身保安宁。	No wrong would he e'er do.
肆⑦戎疾⑧不殄⑨，	大灾大难驱扫尽，	All evils rectified,
烈假⑩不瑕。	大病瘟疫不害民。	No ill done far and wide.
不闻亦式，	好的意见都采纳，	Untaught, he knew the right;
不谏亦入。	逆耳忠言也兼听。	Advised, he saw the light.
肆成人有德，	如今大人品德好，	The grown-up became good;
小子有造。	小孩也能建功勋。	E'en the young showed manhood.

---

① 大姒(sì)：文王之妃。② 徽：美德。③ 惠：恭顺。④ 恫(tóng)：痛。⑤ 御：治理。
⑥ 雝雝(yōngyōng)：和气。⑦ 肆：故。⑧ 戎疾：灾难。⑨ 殄(tiǎn)：断绝。⑩ 烈假：瘟疫。

古之人无斁①,	圣人教育不知倦,	All talents sang in praise
誉髦斯士。	英才辈出皆贤能。	Of King Wen's olden days.

皇　矣　　　　　　　　　　The Rise of Zhou*

皇矣上帝,	伟大上帝真神灵,	O God is great!
临②下有赫。	洞察人间最分明。	He saw our State,
监观四方,	临视天下四方事,	Surveyed our land,
求民之莫③。	了解百姓疾苦情。	Saw how people did stand.
维此二国,	想起夏商两朝末,	Dissatisfied
其政不获。	国家政教不得行。	With Yin-Shang's side,
维彼四国,	思量四方诸侯国,	Then He would fain
爰究爰度。	天下重任谁能当。	Find out again.
上帝耆④之,	上帝心嫌歧周弱,	Another State
憎其式廓⑤。	有心扩大它封疆。	To rule its fate
乃眷西顾,	于是回头望西方,	His eyes turned west;
此维与宅。	可让周王去经营。	Our State was blessed.
作之屏⑥之。	砍掉杂树把地整,	Tai cut the head
其菑⑦其翳⑧。	枯枝死树除干净。	Off the trunk dead
修之平之,	精心修剪枝和叶,	And hewed with blows
其灌其栵⑨。	灌木繁茂新枝生。	The bushy rows.

①斁(dù):厌倦,败坏。②临:临视。③莫:安定。④耆(qí):憎怒。⑤式廓:规模。
⑥屏(bǐng):除去。⑦菑(zī):直立未倒的枯树。⑧翳(yì):倒地的枯树。⑨栵(liè):被砍倒的树干萌发的枝条。

* This epic ode showed the rise of the House of Zhou to the sovereignty of the kingdom and the achievement of King Tai, his son King Ji and his grandson King Wen who conquered the Mi tribe and the Chong State in 1135 B. C.

启之辟之，	开出道路辟地坪，	The rotten trees
其柽①其椐②。	河柳椐树都砍掉。	And mulberries
攘之剔之，	坏树一定要斫除，	Were cleared away
其檿③其柘。	山桑柘树生四处。	Or put in array.
帝迁明德，	上帝佑护明德人，	God made the road
串夷载路。	犬夷疲惫仓忙逃。	For men's abode.
天立厥配，	帝立周王与天配，	King Tai was made
受命既固。	政权兴旺国稳固。	Heaven's sure aide.
帝省其山，	上帝察看那岐山，	God visited Mount Qi
柞棫斯拔，	柞树棫树都拔光，	And thinned oak tree on tree.
松柏斯兑。	松柏挺拔往上长。	Cypress and pines stood straight;
帝作邦作对④，	上帝兴周与天配，	God founded the Zhou State.
自大伯王季。	大伯王季来开创。	He chose Tai as its head,
维此王季，	这位王季品德好，	And Ji when Tai was dead.
因心则友。	心存友爱是天性。	Ji loved his brothers dear;
则友其兄，	王季爱戴他兄长，	His heart was full of cheer.
则笃其庆，	于是周朝得福庆，	When Ji was head of State,
载锡之光。	上天赐他大荣光。	He made its glory great.
受禄无丧，	永享福禄保安康，	The House of Zhou was blest
奄⑤有四方。	拥有天下疆域广。	North to south, east to west.
维此王季，	这个王季真善良，	God gave King Ji
帝度其心，	上帝度量他的心，	The power to see

---

① 柽(chēng)：柽柳，西河柳。② 椐(jū)：灵寿树。③ 檿(yǎn)、柘(zhè)：木名，山桑，黄桑。④ 对：配对。⑤ 奄：全，无余。

貊①其德音。	他的名声传天下。	Clearly right from wrong
其德克明②，	他能明辨是与非，	That he might rule for long.
克明克类③，	区别好人和坏人，	With intelligence great
克长克君。	能为兄长能为君。	He could lead the whole State;
王此大邦，	为王统领这大国，	He ruled with wisdom high,
克顺克比。	百姓和顺上下亲。	Thus obeyed far and nigh.
比于文王，	一直到了周文王，	In his son King Wen's days
其德靡悔。	美好品德无悔恨。	People still sang his praise.
既受帝祉，	已受上帝大福禄，	For God's blessings would run
施于孙子。	千秋万代传子孙。	To his son and grandson.
帝谓文王，	上帝告诫周文王，	To our King Wen God said,
无然畔援④，	不可跋扈休乱行，	"Don't let the foe invade
无然歆⑤羡，	不可贪婪美他人，	Your holy land with might;
诞先登于岸。	先据高位靠自强。	First occupy the height."
密⑥人不恭，	密人态度不恭敬，	The Mi tribe disobeyed,
敢距大邦，	竟敢抗拒周大邦，	On our land made a raid,
侵阮⑦徂共。	侵阮袭共太嚣张。	Attacked Yuan and Gong State;
王赫斯怒，	文王勃然大震怒，	King Wen's anger was great.
爰整其旅，	整顿军队去抵抗，	He sent his troops in rows
以按徂旅。	阻止敌人更向前。	To stop invading foes
以笃于周祜⑧，	周族福气才固强，	That the Zhou House might stand
以对于天下。	民心安定保四方。	And rule over the land.

---

① 貊(mò)：不声张，安静。② 克明：能察是非。③ 克类：能分善恶。④ 畔援：跋扈。⑤ 歆(xīn)羡：羡慕。⑥ 密：古国名，在今甘肃灵台县。⑦ 阮、共：古国名，都在今甘肃泾川县。⑧ 祜(hù)：福祉。

依其在京，	周京军势真强壮，	The capital gave order
侵自阮疆。	班师凯旋自阮疆。	To attack from Yuan border
陟我高冈，	登上高山四处望，	And occupy the height.
无矢①我陵，	不许陈兵我山冈，	Let no foe come with might
我陵我阿，	我的丘陵我山冈。	Near our hill or our mountain
无饮我泉，	不许饮我泉中水，	Nor to drink from our fountain
我泉我池。	我的泉水我池塘。	Nor our pools filled by rain.
度其鲜原，	肥美平原规划好，	King Wen surveyed the plain,
居岐之阳，	定居岐山南向阳，	Settled and occupied
在渭之将②。	住处靠近渭水旁，	Hillside and riverside.
万邦之方③，	你为万国做榜样，	As great king he would stand
下民之王。	天下归心人所向。	For people and the land.
帝谓文王，	上帝告诫周文王，	To our King Wen God said,
予怀明德，	你好品德我赞赏。	"High virtue you've displayed.
不大声以色，	从不疾言和厉色，	You're ever lenient
不长夏④以革⑤；	不仗夏楚和鞭革。	To deal out punishment.
不识不知，	好像无识又无觉，	Making no effort on your part,
顺帝之则。	顺应上帝旧法则。	You follow me at heart."
帝谓文王，	上帝告诫周文王，	To our King Wen God said,
询尔仇方，	团结邻邦多商量，	"Consult allied brigade,
同尔弟兄；	兄弟国家要联合。	Attack with brethren strong,
以尔钩援，	爬城钩梯准备好，	Use scaling ladders long
与尔临冲，	还有临车和冲车，	And engines of assault

---

① 矢：陈军。② 将：侧旁。③ 方：法则。④ 夏：木棍。⑤ 革：皮鞭。

以伐崇墉①。	崇国城墙定能破。	To punish Chong tribe's fault."

临冲闲闲，	临车冲车声势壮，	The engines of on-fall
崇墉言言②。	崇国城墙高又长。	Attacked the Chong State wall.
执讯连连，	拿问俘虏连成串，	Many captives were ta'en
攸馘③安安。	杀敌割耳也从容。	And left ears of the slain.
是类④是禡⑤，	出师祭祀祈胜利，	Sacrifice made afield,
是致是附⑥，	招抚余敌安民众，	We called the foe to yield.
四方以无侮。	四方不再敢欺凌。	The engines of on-fall
临冲茀茀⑦，	临车冲车威力强，	Destroyed the Chong State wall.
崇墉仡仡⑧。	崇国城墙高高耸。	The foe filled with dismay,
是伐是肆，	冲锋陷阵势不挡，	Their forces swept away.
是绝是忽，	消灭崇军有威望，	None dared insult Zhou State;
四方以无拂⑨。	四方无人敢违抗。	All obeyed our king great.

灵　台　　　　　　　　The Wondrous Park*

经始⑩灵台，	开始设计造灵台，	When the tower began
经之营之。	认真设计巧安排。	To be built, every man
庶民攻⑪之，	百姓一起来动手，	Took part as if up-heated,
不日成之。	不用几天就落成。	The work was soon completed.

---

① 墉(yōng)：城墙。② 言言：高大雄伟。③ 馘(guó)：割左耳计算杀敌数量。④ 类：出征前祀神。⑤ 禡(mà)：到所征地祭神。⑥ 附：抚慰，使之来附。⑦ 茀茀(fú fú)：兵车强盛的样子。⑧ 仡仡(yì yì)：高耸的样子。⑨ 拂：违抗。⑩ 经始：创建。⑪ 攻：修建，制作。

* This ode showed the joy of the people in the growing opulence of King Wen who moved his capital to Feng after the overthrow of the State of Chong in 1135 B. C., only one year before his death.

经始勿亟①，	工程本来不急迫，	"No hurry," said the king,
庶民子来。	百姓踊跃完成它。	But they worked as his offspring.

王在灵囿，	周王游览灵园中，	In Wondrous Park the king
麀②鹿攸伏。	母鹿悠闲伏草丛。	Saw the deer in the ring
麀鹿濯濯③，	母鹿体壮毛色润，	Lie at his left and right;
白鸟翯翯④。	白鹤肥大毛羽鲜。	How sweet sang the birds white.
王在灵沼，	周王来到灵沼上，	The king by Wondrous Pond
於牣⑤鱼跃。	满池鱼儿跃动欢。	Saw fishes leap and bound.

虡⑥业维枞⑦，	木柱横板崇牙耸，	In water-girded hall
贲⑧鼓维镛⑨。	悬挂大鼓和大钟。	Beams were long and posts tall.
於论⑩鼓钟，	鼓钟美妙多和谐，	Drums would beat and bells ring
於乐辟雍⑪。	君王享乐在离宫。	To amuse our great king.

於论鼓钟，	鼓钟美妙多和谐，	Drums would beat and bells ring
於乐辟雍。	君王享乐在离宫。	To amuse our great king.
鼍⑫鼓逢逢，	鼍皮大鼓响咚咚，	The lezard-skin drums beat;
矇瞍⑬奏公。	乐师奏乐祝成功。	Blind musicians sang sweet.

---

① 亟(jí)：急。② 麀(yōu)：母鹿。③ 濯濯(zhuózhuó)：肥大润泽的样子。④ 翯翯(hèhè)：洁白的样子。⑤ 牣(rèn)：满。⑥ 虡(jù)：木架以挂钟鼓。⑦ 枞(cōng)：钟、磬的崇牙。⑧ 贲(bēn)：大鼓。⑨ 镛(yōng)：大钟。⑩ 论：和谐。⑪ 辟雍：离宫。⑫ 鼍(tuó)：鳄鱼名。⑬ 矇瞍(méngsǒu)：盲眼的乐师。

下　武　　　　　　　　King Wu

下武①维周，	周邦后人一代代，	In Zhou successors rise;
世有哲王。	世世都有明君生。	All of them are kings wise.
三后②在天，	三位先王在天上，	To the three kings in heaven
王配于京。	武王配天在周京。	King Wu in Hao is given.
王配于京，	武王配天在周京，	King Wu in Hao is given
世德作求。	追求祖先好德行。	To the orders of Heaven.
永言配命，	配合天命能长保，	He would seek virtue good
成王之孚③。	成为周王可信任。	To attain true kinghood.
成王之孚，	成为周王可信任，	To attain true kinghood,
下土之式。	天下百姓好榜样。	Be filial a man should.
永言孝思，	他能永远行孝道，	He'd be pattern for all;
孝思维则。	效法先王是法则。	"Be filial" is his call.
媚④兹一人，	天下敬慕一个人，	All people love King Wu;
应侯顺德。	能从祖德顺法则。	What they are told, they do.
永言孝思，	他能永远行孝道，	Be filial a man should;
昭哉嗣服。	继承王业多荣光。	The bright successor's good.
昭兹来许，	光明磊落后来人，	All bright successors good

---

① 武：继承。② 三后：大王、王季、文王也。③ 孚：信实。④ 媚：爱。

* This ode was sung in praise of King Wu (reigned 1121-1113 B. C.), walking in the ways of his forefathers and by his filial piety securing the throne to himself and his posterity.

绳①其祖武②。	先人事业要继承。	Follow their fatherhood.
於万斯年，	千秋万载把国享，	For long they will be given
受天之祜③。	永享天赐福与禄。	The blessings of good Heaven.

受天之祜，	永享天赐福与禄，	The blessings of good Heaven
四方来贺。	四方诸侯来朝贺。	And good Earth will be given
於万斯年，	千秋万载把国享，	For long yea's without end
不遐有佐。	应有贤臣来辅佐。	To the people's great friend.

文王有声　　　　　　　　Kings Wen and Wu*

文王有声，	文王有个好名声，	King Wen had a great fame
遹④骏⑤有声，	美名盛传人人称。	And famous he became.
遹求厥宁，	唯求天下得安宁，	He sought peace in the land
遹观厥成。	终于国富功业成。	And saw it peaceful stand.
文王烝哉！	文王真是好国君！	O King Wen was so grand!

文王受命，	文王接受上天命，	King Wen whom gods did bless
有此武功：	建立赫赫武功名。	Achieved martial success.
既伐于崇，	讨伐崇国已完成，	Having overthrown Chong,

---

① 绳：继承。② 武：足迹，功业。③ 祜(hù)：福禄。④ 遹(yù)：遵循，一说文言发语词。⑤ 骏：大。

* This epic ode was sung in praise of King Wen and King Wu. The first four stanzas showed how King Wen displayed his military prowess only to secure the tranquility of the people and how this appeared in the building of Feng as his capital city. In Stanza 5 King Yu (reigned 2205-2197 B. C.) referred to the founder of the Xia dy nasty. The last four stanzas showed how King Wu entered, in his capital of Hao, into the sovereignty of the kingdom with the sincere good will of all the people.

作邑于丰。	又在丰邑建都城。	He fixed his town at Feng.
文王烝①哉！	文王真是好国君！	O may King Wen live long!

筑城伊淢②，	筑城又挖护城河，	King Wen built moat and wall
作丰伊匹。	丰邑规模要匹配。	Around the capital
匪棘③其欲，	不是急于图私欲，	Not for his own desire
遹追来孝。	孝顺祖先追前圣。	But for those of his sire.
王后④烝哉！	文王真是好君王！	O our prince we admire!

王公伊濯⑤，	文王功业大无比，	King Wen at capital
维丰之垣。	如同丰邑百丈墙。	Strong as the city wall,
四方攸同，	天下四方同归附，	The lords from state to state
王后维翰。	周家文王为栋梁。	Paid homage to prince great.
王后烝哉！	文王真是好君王！	Our royal prince was great.

丰水东注，	丰水奔流向东方，	The River Feng east flowed;
维禹之绩。	大禹功绩不可量。	Our thanks to Yu we owed.
四方攸同，	天下四方同归附，	The lords from land to land
皇王维辟。	君临天下好榜样。	Paid homage to king grand.
皇王烝哉！	文王真是好君王！	How great did King Wu stand!

镐京辟雍，	镐京建成一辟雍，	He built water-girt hall
自西自东，	无论东方或西方，	At Hao the capital.
自南自北，	无论南方或北方，	North to south, east to west,

---

① 烝(zhēng)：美，盛。② 淢(xù)：护城渠。③ 棘：急。④ 王后：国君。⑤ 濯：显著，大。

无思不服。	谁敢不服周王邦？	By people he was blest.
皇王烝哉！	文王真是好君王！	King Wu was at his crest.

考卜维王，	武王占卜问上苍，	The king divined the site;
宅是镐京，	营建都城在镐京。	The tortoise-shell foretold it right
维龟正之，	神龟有灵作决定，	To build the palace hall
武王成之。	武王建都最成功。	At Hao the capital.
武王烝哉！	武王真是好君王！	King wu was admired by all.

丰水有芑，	水草长满丰水旁，	By River Feng white millet grew.
武王岂不仕？	武王岂不兴业忙？	How could talents not serve King Wu?
诒厥孙①谋，	传授谋略为子孙，	All that he'd planned and done
以燕翼子。	保佑后代子子孙。	Was for the son and grandson.
武王烝哉！	武王真是好君王！	King Wu was second to none.

---

① 孙：通"逊"，顺应。

生民之什   Second Decade of Epics

生 民   Hou Ji, the Lord of corn*

厥初生民①，	初始生下第一人，	Who gave birth to the Lord of Corn?
时维姜嫄。	姜嫄就是那母亲。	By Lady Jiang Yuan he was born.
生民如何？	周人怎样降生的？	How gave she birth to her son nice?
克禋克祀②，	能祭天来能祭神，	She went afield for sacrifice.
以弗③无子。	拔除不祥免无嗣。	Childless, she prayed for a son, so
履帝武④敏⑤歆，	喜踩上帝脚指印，	She trod on the print of God's toe.
攸介攸止。	就在那里停休息。	She stood there long and took a rest,
载震⑥载夙，	胎儿震动不大意，	And she was magnified and blessed.
载生载育，	后来生养一孩子，	Then she conceived, then she gave birth,
时维后稷。	孩子就是那后稷。	It was the Lord of Corn on earth.
诞弥厥月，	姜嫄怀胎整十月，	When her carrying time was done,
先生如达⑦，	头生顺利如羊胎。	Like a lamb slipped down her first son.
不坼⑧不副⑨，	胎衣不破也不裂，	Of labor she suffered no pain;

---

① 民：人，指周人。② 禋（yīn）祀：一种祭天的典祀，一说是郊外祭神求子。③ 弗：通"祓"，除不祥。被无子就是除去无子的不祥，求有子。④ 武：脚印；帝武即上帝的脚印。⑤ 敏：脚拇指。⑥ 震：娠，就是怀孕。⑦ 达：羊胎。⑧ 坼（chè）：胞衣分裂。⑨ 副（pì）：胎盘分离。

* This epic ode was sung in praise of Hou Ji, the Lord of Corn, legendary founder of the House of Zhou.

无菑①无害，	无灾无害真平安。	She was not hurt, nor did she strain.
以赫②厥灵。	这些事情多奇怪。	How could his birth so wonderful be?
上帝不宁，	莫非上帝不愉快，	Was it against Heaven's decree?
不康禋祀，	我的祭祀他不爱，	Was God displeased with her sacrifice.
居然生子。	教我有儿不敢养。	To give a virgin a son nice?

诞寘之隘巷，	婴儿弃在胡同里，	The son abandoned in a lane
牛羊腓③字之；	牛羊一起来喂乳；	Was milked by the cow or sheep.
诞寘之平林，	把他扔在树林里，	Abandoned in a wooded plain,
会④伐平林；	恰有樵夫将救起；	He's fed by men in forest deep.
诞寘之寒冰，	把他扔在寒冰上，	Abandoned on the coldest ice,
鸟覆翼之。	鸟儿展翅暖着他。	He was warmed by birds with their wings.
鸟乃去矣，	鸟儿远去飞走了，	When flew away those birds so nice,
后稷呱矣。	后稷哇哇大哭了。	The cry was heard of the nursling's.
实覃⑤实訏⑥，	哭声又长又响亮，	He cried and wailed so long and loud
厥声载路。	大路之上能听见。	The road with his voice was o'erflowed.

诞实匍匐，	后稷已经会爬了，	He was able to crawl aground
克岐⑦克嶷⑧，	显得有知又有识，	And then rose to his feet.
以就口食。	能把食物放到嘴。	When he sought food around,
蓺⑨之荏菽⑩，	他去种植那大豆，	He learned to plant large beans and wheat.
荏菽旆旆⑪。	大豆棵棵长茁壮，	The beans he planted grew tall;

---

① 菑(zāi)：同"灾"。② 赫：显耀。③ 腓(féi)：庇护，隐蔽。④ 会：适逢。⑤ 覃(tán)：长。⑥ 訏(xū)：大。⑦ 岐：知意。⑧ 嶷：认识。⑨ 蓺(yì)：种植。⑩ 荏(rěn)菽：大豆。
⑪ 旆旆(pèipèi)：茂盛的样子。

禾役穟穟①。	满田稻谷穗穗美，	His millet grew in rows;
麻麦幪幪②，	麻和麦子盖田野，	His gourds teemed large and small;
瓜瓞唪唪③。	瓜儿累累结成堆。	His hemp grew thick and close.

诞后稷之穑，	后稷种植那庄稼，	The Lord of Corn knew well the way
有相之道，	有他用的好方法，	To help the growing of the grain.
茀④厥丰草，	先把茂盛乱草除，	He cleared the grasses rank away
种之黄茂。	后把佳种来播下。	And sowed with yellow seed the plain.

实方⑤实苞，	苗儿齐整又旺盛，	The new buds began to appear;
实种实褎⑥，	长得粗壮又高大。	They sprang up, grew under the feet.

实发实秀⑦，	慢慢抽出穗子来，	They flowered and came into ear;
实坚实好，	坚挺结实人人夸，	They drooped down, each grain complete.

实颖实栗。	无数谷穗沉甸甸。	They became so good and so strong,
即有邰家室。	后稷到邰成了家。	Our Lord would live at Tai for long.

诞降嘉种：	天降良种真神奇：	Heaven gave them the lucky grains
维秬维秠，	两种黑黍秬与秠，	Of double-kernelled millet black
维穈维芑。	又有赤米和白米。	And red and white ones on the plains,

---

① 穟穟（suìsuì）：美好。② 幪幪（měngměng）：茂盛覆地的样子。③ 唪唪（běngběng）：果实累累的样子。④ 茀（fú）：拔除。⑤ 方：整齐。⑥ 褎（yòu）：禾苗渐长的样子。⑦ 秀：出穗扬花。

恒之秬①秠②，	遍种黑黍和麦子，	Black millet reaped was piled in stack
是获是亩；	收割按亩来算计；	Or carried back on shoulders bare.
恒之穈③芑④，	穈和芑也种满地，	Red and white millet growing nice
是任是负；	抱起背起送家里；	And reaped far and wide, here and there,
以归肇祀。	回家开始把神祭。	Was brought home for the sacrifice.

诞我祀如何？	要问祭神怎么样？	What is our sacrifice?
或舂或揄⑤，	舂米舀米人人忙，	We hull and ladle rice,
或簸或蹂⑥，	再次舂米簸糠皮，	We sift and tread the grain,
释⑦之叟叟，	淘起米来沙沙响，	Swill and scour it again.
烝之浮浮。	蒸起米饭气腾腾。	It's steamed and then distilled;
载谋载惟，	然后商量好主意，	We see the rites fulfilled.
取萧祭脂.	采些香蒿和油脂，	We offer fat with southern wood
取羝⑧以軷⑨，	用公羊来祭路神，	And a skinned ram as food.
载燔载烈，	先烧熟来再去烤，	Flesh roast or broiled with cheer
以兴嗣岁⑩。	祈求明年丰产好。	Brings good harvest next year.

卬⑪盛于豆⑫，	祭品盛在木碗里，	We load the stands with food,
于豆于登⑬。	木碗瓦盆都盛些。	The stands of earthernware or wood.
其香始升，	香气开始升上天，	God smells its fragrance rise;
上帝居歆⑭，	上帝安然来受享，	He's well pleased in the skies.

---

① 秬(jù)：黑黍。② 秠(pī)：麦子。③ 穈(mén)：赤苗，红米。④ 芑(qǐ)：白苗，白米。
⑤ 揄(yóu)：舀出，取出。⑥ 蹂(róu)：通"揉"，搓米。⑦ 释：淘米。⑧ 羝(dī)：公羊。
⑨ 軷(bá)：祭祀路神。⑩ 嗣岁：来年。⑪ 卬(áng)：我。⑫ 豆：木制盛肉的食具。
⑬ 登：瓦制的食具。⑭ 歆：享。

胡臭①亶时。	香气真正合时宜。	What smell is this, so nice?
后稷肇祀，	自从后稷创祭礼，	It's Lord of Corn's sacrifice.
庶无罪悔，	无灾无难真安定，	This is a winning way;
以迄于今。	从那直到今日里。	It's come down to this day.

行　苇　　　　　　　　　　Banquet*

敦②彼行苇③，	芦苇丛生聚路旁，	Let no cattle and sheep
牛羊勿践履。	牛羊千万别踩踏。	Trample on roadside rush
方苞方体，	苇草发芽初成长，	Which bursts up with root deep
维叶泥泥④。	叶儿柔嫩正盛旺。	And with leaves soft and lush.
戚戚⑤兄弟，	戚戚相关好兄弟，	We're closely related brothers.
莫远具尔。	彼此亲近莫远离。	Let us be seated near.
或肆之筵，	有人负责摆筵席，	Spread mats for some; for others
或授之几。	有人负责设案几。	Stools will be given here.

肆筵设席，	铺设筵席请人坐，	Mats spread one on another,
授几有缉⑥御。	安排几案态恭敬。	Servants come down and up.
或献或酢，	主人敬酒客还礼，	Host and guests pledge each other;
洗爵奠斝⑦。	洗杯置盏轮番递。	They rinse and fill their cup.
醓醢⑧以荐，	肉汁肉酱献上来，	Sauce brought with prickles ripe
或燔或炙，	有的烧来有的烤。	And roast or broiled meat,
嘉殽脾臄⑨，	牛胃牛舌是佳肴，	There are provisions of tripe,

①臭：香气。②敦(tuán)：聚集的样子。③行(xíng)苇：路边的芦苇。④泥泥：柔嫩茂盛的样子。⑤戚戚：亲密友善的样子。⑥缉(qí)：不断轮换。⑦斝(jiǎ)：酒杯。⑧醓醢(tǎn hǎi)：带汤的肉酱。⑨臄(jué)：舌头。

* This ode celebrated some entertainment given by the king to his relatives, with the trial of archery after the banquet; it also celebrated the honor done on such occasions to the aged.

或歌或咢①。	唱歌击鼓相助兴。	All sing to music sweet.
敦②弓既坚，	雕弓已经很坚劲，	The bow prepared is strong
四镞③既钧，	四支利箭也匀停。	And the four arrows long.
舍矢既均，	拉弓射出中靶心，	The guests all try to hit
序宾以贤。	宾位排列靠本领。	And stand in order fit.
敦弓既句④，	雕弓拉开如月满，	They fully draw the bow
既挟四镞。	四支利箭搭上弦。	And four arrows straight go.
四镞如树，	箭箭射出立靶上，	They hit like planting trees;
序宾以不侮。	排列宾位不轻慢。	Those who miss stand at ease.

曾孙维主，	曾孙成王好主人，	The grandson is the host;
酒醴维醽⑤，	米酒香醇味道好。	With sweet or strong wine they toast.
酌以大斗，	斟来美酒用大斗，	They drink the cups they hold
以祈黄耇⑥。	祈求长寿祝客人。	And pray for all the old.
黄耇台背⑦，	黄发龙钟老年人，	The hoary old may lead
以引以翼。	搀扶呵护侍者仁。	And help the young in need.
寿考维祺，	祝他高寿有祥瑞，	May their old age be blessed;
以介景⑧福。	老天赐予大福分。	May they enjoy their best!

既　醉　　　　　　　　　　Sacrificial Ode*

既醉以酒，	甘醇美酒我已醉，	We've drunk wine strong

---

① 咢(è)：只击鼓不唱歌。② 敦：通"雕"，画。③ 镞(hóu)：箭。④ 句(gòu)：拉满弓。⑤ 醽(rú)：酒味醇厚。⑥ 黄耇(gǒu)：高寿的老人。⑦ 台背：长寿的老人。⑧ 景：大。

* It was said that this ode was responsive to the previous one. The king's relatives expressed their sense of his kindness and their wishes for his happiness, mostly in the words in which the personator of the dead had conveyed the satisfaction of his ancestors with the sacrifice offered to them and promised to him their blessing.

既饱以德。	你的恩惠已饱偿。	And thank your grace.
君子万年,	但愿君子万万岁,	May you live long!
介尔景福。	天赐大福享不尽。	Long live your race!

既醉以酒,	甘醇美酒我已醉,	We've drunk wine strong
尔肴既将①。	你的菜肴真是美。	And eaten food.
君子万年,	但愿君子万万岁,	May you live long!
介尔昭明。	神赐前程多光明。	Be wise and good!

昭明有融,	前程远大多光明,	Be good and wise!
高朗令终。	智慧求得好始终。	By God you're led.
令终有俶②,	善终必有好开始,	See Spirit rise
公尸③嘉告。	神主良言仔细听。	And speak for our dead.

其告维何?	神主祝辞说什么?	What does he say?
笾豆静嘉。	祭品精洁又合适。	Your food is fine.
朋友攸摄④,	朋友宾客来助祭,	Constant friends stay
摄以威仪。	助祭庄严有威仪。	At the service divine.

威仪孔时,	礼节威仪无差错,	With constant friends
君子有孝子。	君子又是大孝子。	And filial sons
孝子不匮⑤,	孝子孝心无穷尽,	There won't be end
永锡尔类⑥。	天赐给你好章程。	For pious ones.

---

① 将:美好。② 俶(chù):开始。③ 尸:祭祀中装扮神灵的人。④ 摄:辅佐。⑤ 匮(kuì):竭尽。⑥ 类:章程,法则。

其类维何？	天赐章程是什么？	To you belong
室家之壸①。	家室安宁天下平。	The pious race.
君子万年，	但愿君子万万岁，	May you live long!
永锡祚②胤③。	天赐给你多福庆。	Be blessed with grace!

其胤维何？	天赐福庆怎么样？	Your race appears
天被尔禄。	上天命你当国王。	By Heaven blessed.
君子万年，	但愿君子万万岁，	You'll live long years,
景命有仆。	天赐妻妾和子孙。	Served east and west.

其仆维何？	妻妾子孙怎么样？	Who will serve you?
厘④尔女士。	赐你女子和男丁。	You will have maids and men.
厘尔女士，	赐你女子和男丁，	Their sons will renew
从以孙子。	子子孙孙都兴旺。	Their service again.

凫　鹥　　　　　　　　　The Ancestor's Spirit*

凫⑤鹥⑥在泾，	野鸭鸥鸟聚泾水，	On the stream waterbirds appear;
公尸来燕来宁。	神尸赴宴多安详。	On earth descends the Spirit good.
尔酒既清，	你的美酒清又澄，	Your wine is sweet and clear,
尔肴既馨。	你的菜肴真是香。	And fragrant is your food.
公尸燕饮，	神尸赴宴饮又尝，	The Spirit comes to drink and eat;

---

① 壸(kǔn)：扩充，广大。② 祚(zuò)：福禄。③ 胤(yìn)：后嗣，子孙。④ 厘：通"赉"，赐予，给予。⑤ 凫(fú)：野鸭。⑥ 鹥(yī)：鸥鸟。

* This ode was appropriate to the feast given to the personator of the departed on the day after the sacrifice in the ancestral temple.

福禄来成①。　　天赐福禄为你降。Your blessing will be sweet.

凫鹥在沙，　　野鸭鸥鸟沙滩上，On the sand waterbirds appear;
公尸来燕来宜②。神尸赴宴心欢畅。On earth enjoys the Spirit good.
尔酒既多，　　你的美酒好又多，Abundant is your wine clear;
尔肴既嘉。　　你的菜肴美又香。Delicious is your food.
公尸燕饮，　　神尸赴宴饮又尝，The Spirit comes to drink and eat;
福禄来为③。　　天赐福禄永安康。Your blessing will be complete.

凫鹥在渚，　　野鸭鸥鸟沙洲上，On the isle waterbirds appear;
公尸来燕来处。神尸赴宴情安舒。In his place sits the Spirit good.
尔酒既湑④，　　你的美酒滤得清，Your wine is pure and clear;
尔肴伊脯⑤。　　你的干肉烹得酥。In slices are your meat and food.
公尸燕饮，　　神尸赴宴饮又尝，The Spirit eats and drinks sweet
　　　　　　　　　　　　　　　　　wine;
福禄来下。　　天赐福禄尽受享。You will receive blessing divine.

凫鹥在潨⑥，　　野鸭鸥鸟水边上，Waterbirds swim where waters
　　　　　　　　　　　　　　　　　meet;
公尸来燕来　　神尸赴宴在高位。The Spirit sits in a high place.
　宗⑦，
既燕于宗，　　已在宗庙设宴席，In his high place he drinks wine
　　　　　　　　　　　　　　　　　sweet;
福禄攸降。　　天赐福禄齐降下。You will receive blessing and grace.

---

①成：成就。②宜：安享。③为：助。④湑(xǔ)：清。⑤脯(pú)：干肉。⑥潨(zhōng)：港汊，水边。⑦宗：尊敬，尊崇。

公尸燕饮，	神尸赴宴饮又尝，	The Spirit drinks and eats his food;
福禄来崇。	天赐福禄重重来。	You'll receive blessing doubly good.

凫鹥在亹①，	野鸭鸥鸟在峡门，	In the gorge waterbirds appear;
公尸来止熏熏②。	神尸赴宴醉醺醺。	Drunken on earth the Spirit good.

旨酒欣欣，	美酒芬芳欣欣乐，	Delicious is your wine clear;
燔炙芬芬。	烧肉味道香喷喷。	Broiled or roast your meat and food.
公尸燕饮，	神尸赴宴饮又尝，	The Spirit comes to drink and feast;
无有后艰。	从此太平无祸殃。	You'll have no trouble in the least.

假 乐　　　　　　　　　　King Cheng*

假乐③君子④，	周王美好多快乐，	Happy and good our king,
显显令德。	品德显著又善良。	Of his virtue all sing.
宜民宜人，	能安百姓用贤良，	He's good to people all;
受禄于天。	所受福禄皆天降。	On him all blessings fall
保右⑤命之，	上天下令保佑他，	And favor from on high
自天申之。	多赐福禄国兴旺。	Is renewed far and nigh.

干⑥禄百福，	求得福禄上百样，	They are blessed, everyone
子孙千亿。	子孙多得千亿强。	Of his sons and grandsons.
穆穆皇皇，	相貌堂堂德行美，	He's majestic and great,

---

① 亹(mén)：峡中两岸对峙如门的地方。② 熏熏：和悦的样子。③ 假乐：嘉乐，喜爱。
④ 君子：指周成王。⑤ 右：通"佑"，佑助。⑥ 干：求。

* This ode was probably sung in praise of King Cheng (1114-1076 B. C.), who succeeded King Wu at the age of thirteen with the Duke of Zhou as regent.

宜君宜王。	宜做国君又为王。	Fit ruler of the State.
不愆①不忘，	没有过错不遗忘，	Blameless and dutiful,
率由旧章。	遵循祖先旧典章。	He follows father's rule.
威仪抑抑②，	仪容美好又端庄，	His bearing dignified,
德音秩秩。	政教法令都守常。	His virtue spreads far and wide.
无怨无恶，	没有怨恨没有恶，	From prejudice he's free,
率由群匹③。	常与群臣共商量。	Revered by all with glee.
受禄无疆，	接受天赐福禄多，	He receives blessings great,
四方之纲。	统治四方作纪纲。	Modeled on from state to state.
之纲之纪，	作为四方好纪纲，	He's modeled on without end;
燕及朋友。	朋友群臣得安康。	Each state becomes his friend.
百辟卿士，	诸侯卿士都说好，	Ministers all and one
媚④于天子。	衷心爱戴我君王。	Admire the Heaven's Son.
不解⑤于位，	勤于职守不懈息，	Dutiful, he is blessed;
民之攸塈⑥。	万民归附国运长。	In him people find rest.

公 刘 Duke Liu *

笃⑦公刘，	诚实厚道的公刘，	Duke Liu was blessed;
匪居匪康。	不图安居把福享。	He took nor ease nor rest.
迺场⑧迺疆，	划分田界划地界，	He divided the fields

---

① 愆(qiān)：过失。② 抑抑：美好的样子。③ 群匹：群臣。④ 媚：爱。⑤ 解(xiè)：通"懈"，懈息。⑥ 塈(jì)：休息。⑦ 笃：诚实忠厚。⑧ 场(yì)：田界。

* This epic ode told the story of Duke Liu, the second legendary hero of the House of Zhou, who moved from Tai to Bin in 1796 B. C.

迺积①迺仓。	堆垛粮食装进仓。	And stored in barns the yields.
迺裹餱②粮,	揉面蒸饼备干粮,	In bags and sacks he tied
于橐③于囊。	放进小袋和大囊。	Up grain and meat when dried.
思辑④用光。	团结人民争荣光。	He led people in rows,
弓矢斯张,	张弓带箭齐武装,	With arrows and drawn bows.
干戈戚扬⑤,	盾牌长矛都扛上,	With axes, shields and spears,
爰方启行。	迈开脚步向前方。	They marched on new frontiers.
笃公刘,	诚实厚道的公刘,	Duke Liu would fain
于胥⑥斯原。	察看这块田原忙。	Survey a fertile plain
既庶既繁,	百姓众多相追随,	For his people to stay.
既顺迺宣,	顺应民情多舒畅,	On that victorious day
而无永叹。	无人怨愤长叹气。	No one would sigh nor rest.
陟则在巘⑦,	一会儿登上山冈,	He came up mountain-crest
复降在原。	一会儿下到平地。	And descended again.
何以舟⑧之?	身上佩带啥东西?	We saw his girdle then
维玉及瑶,	美玉宝石样样装,	Adorned with gems and jade,
鞞琫⑨容刀⑩。	佩刀玉鞘闪闪亮。	His precious sword displayed.
笃公刘,	诚实厚道的公刘,	Duke Liu crossed the mountains
逝彼百泉,	来到泉水岸边上,	And saw a hundred fountains.
瞻彼溥⑪原:	眺望平原多宽广。	He surveyed the plain wide
迺陟南冈,	登上南边高山冈,	By the southern hillside.
乃觏⑫于京。	发现京师好地方。	He found a new capital

---

① 积:在露天堆积粮谷。② 餱(hóu):干粮。③ 橐(tuó):盛干粮的口袋。④ 辑:和睦。⑤ 戚扬:斧子一类的武器。⑥ 胥:察看。⑦ 巘(yǎn):不与大山相连的小山。⑧ 舟:通"周",环绕,带。⑨ 鞞琫(bǐngběng):刀鞘上的装饰品。⑩ 容刀:佩刀。⑪ 溥(pǔ):大。⑫ 觏(gòu):遇见。

京师之野，	就在京邑的旷野，	Wide for his people all.
于时处处，	于是定居建新邦，	Some thought it good for the throng;
于时庐旅，	于是规划建新房。	Others would not dwell there for long.
于时言言，	到处谈笑喜洋洋，	There was discussion free;
于时语语。	到处欢声熙熙攘。	They talked in high glee.

笃公刘，	诚实厚道的公刘，	Duke Liu was blessed;
于京斯依。	定居京师新气象。	At capital he took rest,
跄跄①济济②，	赴宴臣僚多威仪，	Put stools on mats he spread
俾筵③俾几④。	设好坐席与凭几。	For officers he led.
既登乃依，	主宾坐席靠几上，	They leant on stools and sat
乃造其曹。	先祭猪神求吉祥。	On the ornamented mat.
执豕于牢⑤，	捉住神猪在猪圈，	A penned pig was killed;
酌之用匏⑥。	舀酒都用葫芦瓢。	Their gourds with wine were filled.
食之饮之，	酒醉饭饱多欢喜，	They were well drunk and fed;
君之宗之。	推行公刘做君长。	All hailed him as State head.

笃公刘，	诚实厚道的公刘，	Duke Liu would fain
既溥既长，	开辟土地多宽广，	Measure the hill and plain
既景⑦迺冈，	观测日影在高冈，	Broad and long; he surveyed
相其阴阳，	勘察南北与阴阳，	Streams and springs, light and shade;
观其流泉。	察看水源和流向。	His three armies were placed
其军三单，	组织军队分三班，	By the hillside terraced;
度⑧其隰原，	洼地平地都测量，	He measured plains anew

---

① 跄跄(qiāngqiāng)：行动安适的样子。② 济济：庄严的样子。③ 筵：竹席。④ 几：坐时凭倚的矮桌。⑤ 牢：猪圈。⑥ 匏(páo)：匏爵，用葫芦做的酒器。⑦ 景：日影。⑧ 度(duó)：测量。

彻①田为粮。	开垦荒地来种粮,	And fixed the revenue.
度其夕阳,	一直丈量到山西,	Fields were tilled in the west;
豳居允荒②。	豳地居住多宽广。	The land of Bin was blessed.

笃公刘,	诚实厚道的公刘,	Duke Liu who wore the crown
于豳斯馆。	豳地建宫境幽舒。	At Bin had settled down.
涉渭为乱③,	横渡渭水开石料,	He crossed the River Wei
取厉取锻。	采磨石来搬锻石。	To gather stones by day.
止基迺理,	定立基址治田地,	All boundaries defined,
爰众④爰有⑤。	人口众多物富有。	People worked with one mind
夹其皇⑥涧,	住在皇涧两岸边,	On the Huang Riverside
溯其过涧。	顺着过涧住处宽。	Towards Guo River wide.
止旅迺密,	定居大众人口密,	The people dense would stay
芮鞫⑦之即。	河岸两边都住满。	On the shore of the Ney.

泂 酌　　　　　Take Water from Far Away*

泂⑧酌彼行潦⑨,	到那远处取积水,	Take water from pools far away,
挹⑩彼注兹,	舀水倒在这里边,	Pour it in vessels that it may
可以餴⑪饎⑫。	可以蒸饭做酒浆。	Be used to steam millet and rice.
岂弟君子,	君子和乐又平易,	A prince should give fraternal advice

---

① 彻:治理。② 荒:大。③ 乱:水中横渡。④ 众:指人口多。⑤ 有:指物产丰。⑥ 皇:涧名。下文"过",亦涧名。⑦ 芮鞫(ruìjū):水流曲处岸边凹进去的地方叫芮,凸出来的地方叫鞫,统指水边。⑧ 泂(jiǒng):远。⑨ 行潦(lǎo):路边的积水。⑩ 挹(yì):舀。⑪ 餴(fēn):蒸饭。⑫ 饎(xī):酒食。

* This ode was attributed to Duke Kang of Zhao for the admonition to King Cheng to fulfill his duties like a parent to his people so that his people may cling to him.

民之父母。　　为民父母顺民意。　Like parent to his people nice.

泂酌彼行潦，　　到那远处取积水，　Take water from pools far away,
挹彼注兹，　　　舀水倒在这里边，　Pour it in vessels that it may
可以濯罍①。　　可以用它洗祭器。　Be used to wash the spirit-vase.
岂弟君子，　　　君子和乐又平易，　A prince should give fraternal praise
民之攸归。　　　人民归附心向往。　To his people for better days.

泂酌彼行潦，　　到那远处取积水，　Take water from pools far away,
挹彼注兹，　　　舀水倒在这里边，　Pour it in vessels that it may
可以濯②溉③。　　可以用它洗漆尊。　Be used to cleanse everything.
岂弟君子，　　　君子和乐又平易，　To our fraternal prince or king
民之攸塈④。　　人民休息得安宁。　Like water his people will cling.

卷　阿　　　　　　　　　　King Cheng's Progress*

有卷⑤者阿⑥，　　曲折丘陵好风光，　The mountain undulates;
飘风⑦自南。　　旋风吹来自南方。　The southern breeze vibrates.
岂弟君子，　　　君子和乐又平易，　Here our fraternal king
来游来歌，　　　前来游玩把歌唱，　Comes crooning and wandering;
以矢⑧其音。　　献诗献歌兴致昂。　In praise of him I sing.

---

① 罍(léi)：古代的酒器。② 濯(zhuó)：洗涤。③ 溉：漆尊，一种酒器。④ 塈(xì)：休息。
⑤ 卷(quán)：曲。⑥ 阿(ē)：大山丘。⑦ 飘风：旋风。⑧ 矢：陈述。

* This was another ode addressed by Duke Kang of Zhao to King Cheng, desiring for him long prosperity and congratulating him in order to admonish him on the happiness of his people.

伴①奂尔游矣，优游潇洒任游历，　You're wandering with pleasure
优游尔休矣。悠闲自得任休息。　Or taking rest at leisure.
岂弟君子，　　君子和乐又平易，　O fraternal king, hear!
俾尔弥②尔性，终生辛劳何所求，　May you pursue the career
似先公酋矣。承继祖业功千秋。　Of your ancestors dear!

尔土宇昄③章，你的土地和封疆，　Your territory's great
亦孔之厚矣。一望无际最宽广。　And secure is your state.
岂弟君子，　　君子和乐又平易，　O fraternal king, hear!
俾尔弥尔性，终生辛劳有作为，　May you pursue your career
百神尔主矣。天下百神最相配。　As host of gods whom you revere!

尔受命长矣，你受天命久又长，　For long you're Heaven-blessed；
茀④禄尔康矣。赐你福禄又安康。　You enjoy peace and rest.
岂弟君子，　　君子和乐又平易，　O fraternal king, hear!
俾尔弥尔性，终生辛劳百事昌，　May you pursue your career
纯嘏⑤尔常矣。天赐福禄你长享。　And be blessed far and near!

有冯⑥有翼，　依靠良士与贤相，　You've supporters and aides
有孝有德，　　孝敬祖先有德望，　Virtuous of all grades
以引以翼。　　导引辅助左右帮。　To lead or act as wing.
岂弟君子，　　君子快乐又平易，　O our fraternal king,
四方为则。　　四方以你为榜样。　Of your pattern all sing.

---

① 伴(pàn)奂：闲游。② 弥：尽。③ 昄(bǎn)：大。④ 茀：小福。⑤ 嘏(gǔ)：大福。
⑥ 冯(píng)：凭依。

颙颙①卬卬②, 态度温和志气昂, Majestic you appear,
如圭如璋, 德行周正如圭璋, Like jade-mace without peer;
令闻令望。 美名声望传四方。 You're praised from side to side.
岂弟君子, 君子快乐又平易, O fraternal king, hear!
四方为纲。 四方以你为榜样。 Of the State you're the guide.

凤皇于飞, 凤凰青天翩翩飞, Phoenixes fly
翙翙③其羽, 百鸟展翅紧相随, With rustling wings
亦集爰止。 凤停树上百鸟陪。 And settle high.
蔼蔼王多吉士, 周王身边多贤士, Officers of the king's
维君子使, 听从君王献智慧, Employed each one
媚④于天子。 爱戴天子不曾违。 To please the Heaven's Son.

凤皇于飞, 凤凰青天翩翩飞, Phoenixes fly
翙翙其羽, 百鸟展翅紧相随, With rustling wings
亦傅于天。 一起飞到天上去。 To azure sky.
蔼蔼王多吉人, 周王身边多贤士, Officers of the king's
维君子命, 听从君王献智慧, At your command
媚于庶人。 爱护百姓心无愧。 Please people of the land.

凤皇鸣矣, 凤凰鸣叫真吉祥, Phoenixes sing
于彼高冈。 在那高高山冈上。 On lofty height;
梧桐生矣, 梧桐树儿高冈生, Planes grow in spring
于彼朝阳。 东山坡上迎朝阳。 On morning bright.

① 颙颙(yóngyóng):温和恭敬的样子。② 卬卬(ángáng):气宇轩昂的样子。③ 翙翙(huìhuì),众多的样子。④ 媚:顺爱。

菶菶①萋萋，	枝叶苍苍多茂盛，	Lush are plane-trees;
雝雝喈喈。	凤鸣喈喈声悠扬。	Phoenixes sing at ease.
君子之车，	君子有车可以坐，	O many are
既庶且多。	车子既多又华美。	Your cars and steed;
君子之马，	君子有马可以驾，	Your steed and car
既闲且驰。	技艺娴熟能奔驰。	Run at high speed.
矢诗不②多，	献诗奉赋真不少，	I sing but to prolong
维以遂歌。	为谢君王唱成歌。	Your holy song.

民 劳

The People Are Hard Pressed*

民亦劳止，	人民已经够辛劳，	The people are hard pressed;
汔③可小康。	求得可以稍安康。	They need a little rest.
惠此中国，	惠爱京城老百姓，	Do the Central Plain good,
以绥四方。	安抚诸侯定四方。	You'll reign o'er neighborhood.
无纵诡随④，	不要放纵诡诈人，	Of the wily beware;
以谨无良。	谨防小人不善良。	Against the vice take care!
式遏寇虐，	制止暴虐与掠抢，	Put the oppressors down
憯⑤不畏明。	不怕坏人手段强。	Lest they fear not the crown.
柔远能迩，	远近百姓都爱护，	Show kindness far and near;
以定我王。	安定国家保我王。	Consolidate your sphere.

---

① 菶菶(pěngpěng)：草木茂盛的样貌。② 不：语助词，无实义。③ 汔(qì)：乞求。
④ 诡随：不怀好意的人。⑤ 憯(cǎn)：曾。

* This ode was made by Duke Mu of Zhao to reprehend King Li (877-841 B.C.), notorious for his tyranny.

诗经　Book of Poetry

民亦劳止，	人民已经够辛劳，	The people are hard pressed;
汔可小休。	求得可以稍休息。	They need repose and rest.
惠此中国，	惠爱京城老百姓，	Do the Central Plain good,
以为民逑①。	使得人民能安聚。	People will come from neighborhood.
无纵诡随，	不要放纵诡诈人，	Of the wily beware;
以谨惛怓②。	谨防喧闹争名利。	Against bad men take care!
式遏寇虐，	制止暴虐与抢掠，	Repress those who oppress;
无俾民忧。	莫使人民添悲凄。	Relive those in distress.
无弃尔劳③，	不要放弃前功劳，	Through loyal service done
以为王休。	成为国王好名誉。	The royal quiet is won.

民亦劳止，	人民已经够辛劳，	The people are hard pressed;
汔可小息。	求得可以松口气。	They need relief and rest.
惠此京师，	惠爱京师老百姓，	Do good in the capital,
以绥四国。	安抚天下四方地。	You'll please your people all.
无纵诡随，	不要放纵诡诈人，	Of the wily beware;
以谨罔极。	谨防没有准则事。	Against wicked men take care!
式遏寇虐，	制止暴虐与抢掠，	Repress those who oppress
无俾作慝④。	莫让作恶把人害。	Lest they go to excess.
敬慎威仪，	仪容举止要谨慎，	In manner dignified
以近有德。	亲近贤德正自身。	You'll have good men at your side.

民亦劳止，	人民已经够辛劳，	The people are hard pressed;
汔可小愒⑤。	求得可以歇一歇。	They need some ease and rest.

---

① 逑(qiú)：合聚。② 惛怓(hūnnáo)：喧哗纷乱。③ 劳：功劳。④ 慝(tè)：邪恶。
⑤ 愒(qì)：通"憩"，休息。

惠此中国，	惠爱京师老百姓，	Do good in Central Plain
俾民忧泄。	人民忧愁要发泄。	To relieve people's pain.
无纵诡随，	不要放纵诡诈人，	Of the wily beware；
以谨丑厉①。	谨防丑恶奸诈事。	Against evil take care!
式遏寇虐，	制止暴虐与抢掠，	Put the oppressors down
无俾正败。	莫失正道得败坏。	Lest your rule be o'erthrown.
戎②虽小子，	你虽是个年轻人，	Though still young in the State,
而式弘大。	作用巨大当估量。	What you can do is great,

民亦劳止，	人民已经够辛劳，	The people are hard pressed；
汔可小安。	求得可以稍安逸。	They need quiet and rest.
惠此中国，	惠爱京师老百姓，	Do good in Central Plain
国无有残。	国家安定无残患。	Lest people suffer pain.
无纵诡随，	不要放纵诡诈人，	Of the wily beware；
以谨缱绻③，	谨防巴结和奉迎。	Of flattery take care!
式遏寇虐，	制止暴虐与抢掠，	Put the oppressors down
无俾正反。	莫使政权遭反复。	Lest the State be o'erthrown.
王欲玉④女，	衷心成就我君王，	O king, as jade you're nice.
是用大⑤谏。	尽力讽谏深规劝。	Please take my frhnk frank advice!

板　　　　　　　　　　　　Censure*

| 上帝板板⑥， | 上帝行为太荒唐， | God won't our kingdom bless； |

---

① 厉：恶。② 戎：汝，你。③ 缱绻(qiǎnquǎn)：小人纠结不解，比喻朝政纷乱不顺。
④ 玉：好，爱。⑤ 大：郑重。⑥ 板板：反反，无常。

* This was a censure made by Count of Fan (modern Hui County, Henan Province) on the prevailing misery in the times of King Li.

下民卒瘅①！	天下人民都遭殃。	People are in distress.
出话②不然，	光说好话不去做，	Your words incorrect are;
为犹不远。	制定谋略无眼光。	Your plans cannot reach far.
靡圣管管③，	目无圣人自称贤，	You care not what sages do;
不实于亶④。	没有诚意胡乱言。	What you say is not true.
犹之未远，	制定策略无远见，	Your plans are far from nice;
是用大谏。	所以我来大规劝。	So I give you advice.
天之方难，	上天正要降灾难，	Heaven sends troubles down.
无然宪宪⑤。	不要高兴空喜欢。	O how can you not frown?
天之方蹶⑥，	上天正要降动乱，	It makes turmoil prevail;
无然泄泄⑦。	不要喋喋多论断。	You talk to no avail.
辞之辑⑧矣，	如果政令能和缓，	If what you say is right,
民之洽矣。	人民就会抱成团。	'Twill be heard with delight.
辞之怿矣，	如果政令已败坏，	If what you say is not,
民之莫矣。	百姓受苦不得安。	It will soon be forgot.
我虽异事，	我们职事虽不同，	Our duties different,
及尔同寮。	毕竟和你同为官。	We serve the government.
我即尔谋，	我来和你共商量，	I give you advice good;
听我嚣嚣⑨。	听我说话你骄傲。	Your attitude is rude.
我言维服⑩，	我说话语是事实，	My advice is sought after;
勿以为笑。	不要以为话儿戏。	It's no matter for laughter.

---

① 瘅(dàn)：病。② 话：善言。③ 管管：放任自恣，无所依傍。④ 亶(dǎn)：诚信。⑤ 宪宪：欣欣。⑥ 蹶(guì)：动。⑦ 泄泄(yì yì)：多言多语的样子。⑧ 辑(jí)：和。⑨ 嚣嚣(áo áo)：不肯听从别人规劝的样子。⑩ 服：事。

先民有言：	古人有话说得好：	Ancient saying is good:
"询于刍荛①。"	"请教樵夫亦有益。"	"Consult cutters of wood!"

天之方虐，	上天正在发残暴，	Heaven is doing wrong.
无然谑谑。	不要嬉戏瞎胡闹。	How can you get along?
老夫灌灌②，	老夫态度很诚恳，	I'm an old lord sincere.
小子蹻蹻③。	小子轻狂气骄傲。	How can you proud appear?
匪我言耄，	不是我老话糊涂，	I'm not proud of my age.
尔用忧谑。	是你忧患当玩笑。	How can you tease a sage?
多将熇熇④，	多做坏事难收拾，	Trouble will grow like fire,
不可救药。	烈火焚烧无救药。	Beyond remedy when higher.

天之方懠⑤，	上天正在发脾气，	Heaven's anger displayed,
无为夸毗⑥。	不要卑躬又屈膝。	Don't cajole nor upbraid!
威仪卒迷，	君臣威仪都丧乱，	The good and dignified
善人载尸。	贤人闭口如尸般。	Are mute as men who died.
民之方殿屎⑦，	人民痛苦正呻吟，	The people groan and sigh,
则莫我敢葵⑧。	不敢对我乱怀疑。	But none dare to ask why.
丧乱蔑⑨资，	祸丧多端生无计，	Wild disorder renewed,
曾莫惠我师。	无人施惠去救济。	Who'd help our multitude?

天之牖⑩民，	上天诱导老百姓，	Heaven helps people mute
如埙⑪如篪⑫，	好像吹埙和吹篪，	By whistle as by flute,

---

① 刍荛(chúráo)：打草砍柴的人。② 灌灌：诚恳的样子。③ 蹻蹻(juéjué)：骄傲的样子。④ 熇熇(hèhè)：火势炽盛的样子。⑤ 懠(qí)：愤怒。⑥ 夸毗(kuāpí)：柔顺的样子。⑦ 殿屎(xī)：呻吟。⑧ 葵：通"揆"，揣测。⑨ 蔑：无。⑩ 牖(yǒu)：通"诱"。⑪ 埙(xūn)：土制的乐器。⑫ 篪(chí)：竹制的乐器。

如璋如圭， 好像玉璋和玉圭， As two maces form one,
如取如携。 好像取物提东西。 As something brought when done.
携无曰益， 培育扶植不设访， Bring anything you please,
牖民孔易。 教导百姓很容易。 You'll help people with ease.
民之多辟①， 如今人民多邪辟， They've troubles to deplore.
无自立辟②。 不可自把邪辟立。 Don't give them any more!

价③人维蕃， 好人好比是篱笆， Good men a fence install;
大师④维垣， 大众好比是围墙。 The people form a wall.
大邦维屏， 大国好比是屏障， Screens are formed by each State
大宗⑤维翰。 同族好比是栋梁。 And each family great.
怀德维宁， 为政有德国家安， Virtue secures repose,
宗子维城。 宗子就像是城墙。 Walled up by kinsmen close.
无俾城坏， 莫使城墙遭破坏， Do not destroy the wall;
无独斯畏。 不要孤立自遭殃。 Be not lonely after all!

敬天之怒， 上天发怒要敬仰， Revere great Heaven's ire
无敢戏豫。 不敢嬉戏太放荡。 And do not play with fire!
敬天之渝⑥， 老天灾变要敬畏， Revere great Heaven gay
无敢驰驱⑦。 不敢放纵太狂妄。 And don't drive your own way.
昊天曰明， 上天眼睛最明亮， There's nought but Heaven knows;
及尔出王⑧。 随你出入共来往。 It's with you where you go,
昊天曰旦， 上天眼睛最明朗， Great Heaven sees all clear;
及尔游衍⑨。 随你一道共游逛。 It's with you where you appear.

① 多辟：多邪辟行为。② 立辟：立法。③ 价(jiè)：善。④ 师：大众。⑤ 大宗：君子宗族。⑥ 渝(yù)：变。⑦ 驰驱：自恣放纵。⑧ 王：往。⑨ 游衍：游荡。

荡之什

Third Decade of Epics

荡

Warnings*

荡荡①上帝，	败坏法度的上帝，	God's influence spreads vast
下民之辟②。	却是百姓的暴君。	Over people below.
疾威③上帝，	上帝行为太暴虐，	God's terror strikes so fast;
其命多辟。	政令邪僻多无常。	He deals them blow on blow.
天生烝民，	上天生下众百姓，	Heaven gives people birth,
其命匪谌④。	政令无信不真诚。	On whom he'd not depend.
靡不有初，	凡事都有个开头，	At first they're good on earth,
鲜克有终。	很少能够有结果。	But few last to the end.
文王曰咨⑤，	文王开口长声叹：	"Alas!"said King Wen of the west,
咨女殷商！	叹你殷商殷纣王！	"You king of Yin-Shang, lo!
曾是强御，	为何如此施暴强，	How could you have oppressed
曾是掊⑥克，	如此聚敛把民伤，	And exploited people so?

---

① 荡荡：法度废坏的样子。② 辟：君王。③ 疾威：暴虐。④ 谌(chén)：诚信，真诚。⑤ 咨(zī)：嗟叹。⑥ 掊(póu)克：聚敛，搜刮。

* This was a warning addressed to King Li who brought the Zhou dynasty into imminent peril by his violent oppressions, his neglect of good men, his employment of mean creatures, his disannulling the old statutes and laws, his drunkenness and the fierceness of his will, but it was put in the mouth of King Wen delivering his warn ings to the last king of the Shang dynasty, in the hope that King Li would transfer the figure to himself and alter his course so as to avoid a similar ruin.

曾是在位，	如此小人窃高位，	Why put those in high place
曾是在服①。	恶人权势太猖狂。	Who did everything wrong?
天降滔德，	天生这个傲慢人，	Why are those who love grace
女兴是力。	你反助他兴风浪。	Oppressed e'er by the strong?
文王曰咨，	文王开口长声叹：	"Alas!"said King Wen of the west,
咨女殷商！	叹你殷商殷纣王！	"You king of Yin-Shang, lo!
而秉义类，	任用忠贞善良人，	Why not help the oppressed
强御多怼②。	强暴之徒生怨望。	And give the strong a blow?
流言以对，	流言蜚语传得快，	Why let rumors wide spread
寇攘式内。	寇盗抢夺更猖狂。	And robbers be your friend?
侯作侯祝，	诬咒忠臣害贤良，	Let curse fall on your head
靡届靡究。	无穷无尽遭灾殃。	And troubles without end!
文王曰咨，	文王开口长声叹：	"Alas!"said King Wen of the west,
咨女殷商！	叹你殷商殷纣王！	"You king of Yin-Shang, lo!
女炰烋③于中国，	咆哮国中太张狂，	You do wrong without rest.
敛怨以为德。	招来怨恶以为良。	Can good out of wrong grow?
不明尔德，	你的品德不自明，	You know not what is good;
时无背无侧。	前后左右无贤良。	You've no good men behind.
尔德不明，	你的品德不自明，	Good men not understood,
以无陪无卿。	没有辅佐无卿相。	To you none will be kind.

---

① 服：服政事，在位。② 怼(duì)：怨恨。③ 炰烋(páoxiāo)：即"咆哮"。

文王曰咨，	文王开口长声叹：	"Alas!" said King Wen of the west,
咨女殷商！	叹你殷商殷纣王！	"You king of Yin-Shang, lo!
天不湎①尔以酒，	上天没叫你酗酒，	You drink wine without rest;
不义②从式。	不该放纵自恣狂。	On a wrong way you go.
既愆③尔止，	仪容举止失常态，	You know not what's about,
靡明靡晦。	不论日夜酗酒汤。	Nor tell darkness from light.
式号式呼，	又是狂喊又大叫，	Amid clamour and shout
俾昼作夜。	昼夜颠倒太荒唐。	You turn day into night.

文王曰咨，	文王开口长声叹：	"Alas!" said King Wen of the west,
咨女殷商！	叹你殷商殷纣王！	"You king of Yin-Shang, lo!
如蜩如螗④，	怨声载道如蝉噪，	Cicadas cry without rest
如沸如羹。	实似落入沸水汤。	As bubbling waters flow.
小大近丧，	大事小事快灭亡，	Things great and small go wrong
人尚乎由行。	仍然一副旧模样。	But heedless still you stand.
内奰⑤于中国，	国内人人都愤怒，	Indignation grows strong
覃⑥及鬼方⑦。	怒火延伸到远方。	In and out of the land.

文王曰咨，	文王开口长声叹：	"Alas!" said King Wen of the west,
咨女殷商！	叹你殷商殷纣王！	"You king of Yin-Shang's days!
匪上帝不时，	不是上帝不善良，	Not that you're not God-blessed,
殷不用旧。	殷商不守旧典章。	Why don't you use old ways?
虽无老成人，	虽然没有老成人，	You've no experienced men,

---

① 湎(miǎn)：沉迷。② 义：宜，应该。③ 愆(qiān)：过错。④ 蜩(tiáo)、螗(táng)：蝉。
⑤ 奰(bì)：发怒。⑥ 覃(tán)：延伸。⑦ 鬼方：远夷之国，远方。

尚有典刑。	尚有典章可模仿。	But the laws have come down.
曾是莫听,	这些你都不肯听,	Why won't you listen then?
大命以倾。	国家将灭命将亡。	Your State will be o'erthrown.

文王曰咨,	文王开口长声叹:	"Alas!"said King Wen of the west,
咨女殷商!	叹你殷商殷纣王!	"You who wear Yin-Shang's crown!
人亦有言:	古人有话这样讲:	Know what say people blessed:
"颠沛之揭①,	"树木倒下根出土,	When a tree's fallen down,
枝叶未有害,	枝叶还没受损伤,	Its leaves may still be green
本实先拨②。"	树根却已先遭殃。"	But roots exposed to view.
殷鉴不远,	以殷为鉴不太远,	Let Xia's downfall be seen
在夏后之世。	就在夏王朝廷上。	As a warning to you!"

抑　　　　　Admonition by Duke Wu of Wei*

抑抑③威仪,	仪容美好礼彬彬,	What appears dignified
维德之隅。	为人品德端庄正。	Reveals a good inside.
人亦有言:	古人有话说得好:	You know as people say:
"靡哲不愚。"	大智看来似愚笨。	There're no sages but stray.
庶人之愚,	常人众人显得笨,	When people have done wrong,
亦职维疾。	也许天生有毛病。	It shows their sight not long.
哲人之愚,	智者看似不聪明,	When sages make mistakes,
亦维斯戾④。	那是装傻避罪名。	It shows their wisdom breaks.

---

① 揭:树根从土中露出。② 拨:断绝,败坏。③ 抑抑:静密。④ 戾:罪也。

* This ode was made by Duke Wu of Wei at ninety to admonish himself and King Ping who was still young. It was the earliest proverbial ode in Chinese poetry.

无竞①维人，	为政最要是贤人，	If a leader is good,
四方其训之。	四方诸侯有教训。	He'll tame the neighborhood.
有觉②德行，	国君德行端正直，	If his virtue is great,
四国顺之。	天下人民遂归顺。	He'll rule o'er every State.
訏谟③定命，	雄才大略定方针，	When he gives orders,
远犹辰告。	长远国策告人民。	They'll reach the borders.
敬慎威仪，	行为举止须谨慎，	As he is dignified,
维民之则。	人民以此为标准。	He's obeyed far and wide.
其在于今，	形势发展到如今，	Look at the present state:
兴迷乱于政。	国政混乱不堪论。	Political chaos' great.
颠覆厥德，	君臣德行都败坏，	Subverted the virtue fine,
荒湛④于酒。	沉湎酒色醉醺醺。	You are besotted by wine.
女虽湛乐从，	只知纵情贪享乐，	You wish your pleasure last
弗念厥绍。	祖宗帝业不关心。	And think not of the past.
罔敷求先王，	先王治道不讲求，	Enforce the laws laid down
克共⑤明刑。	国家法度怎执行？	By kings who wore a crown!
肆皇天弗尚，	如今皇天不护佑，	Or Heaven won't bless you
如彼泉流，	好像泉水向下流，	Like water lost to view,
无沦胥以亡。	相与沉沦都灭亡。	Till you're ruined and dead.
夙兴夜寐，	早早起身深夜眠，	Rise early, late to bed!
洒扫廷内，	洒扫堂屋除灰尘，	Try to sweep the floor clean;
维民之章。	为民表率好榜样。	Let your pattern be seen.

① 竞：强，最重要的。② 觉：正直。③ 訏谟(xūmó)：大计划,谋略。④ 荒湛(dān)：荒耽。⑤ 共(gōng)：执行。

修尔车马，	车辆马匹准备好，	Keep cars and steeds in rows
弓矢戎兵，	弓箭兵器认真修。	And your arrows and bows.
用戒戎①作，	预防一旦战祸生，	If on alert you stand,
用逷②蛮方。	驱逐蛮夷千秋功。	None dare invade your land.

质尔人民，	安定万众老百姓，	Do people real good;
谨尔侯度，	遵守法度要认真。	Make laws against falsehood.
用戒不虞③。	警惕祸事突然生，	Beware of what's unforeseen;
慎尔出话，	开口说话要谨慎。	Say rightly what you mean.
敬尔威仪，	行为举止要端敬，	Try to be dignified;
无不柔嘉。	处处温和得安宁。	Be kind and mild outside.
白圭之玷④，	白玉之上存污点，	A flaw in white jade found,
尚可磨也；	尚可琢磨除干净。	Away it may be ground;
斯言之玷，	言论如果有差错，	A flaw in what you say
不可为也！	再想挽回不可能。	Will leave its influence to stay.

无易由言，	不要轻率乱发言，	Don't lightly say a word
无曰"苟矣，	莫言"说话可随便。	Nor think it won't be heard.
莫扪朕舌"，	没人把我舌头拴"，	Your tongue is held by none;
言不可逝矣。	一言既出弥补难。	Your uttered words will run.
无言不雠⑤，	言语不会无馈反，	Each word will answered be;
无德不报。	施德总有福禄添。	No deed is done for free.
惠于朋友，	朋友群臣要爱护，	If you do good to friend
庶民小子。	平民百姓须安抚。	And people without end,

①戒戎:戒备兵事。②逷(yì):通"逖",远。③虞:料想。④玷(diàn):缺点。⑤雠(chóu):反应,应验。

子孙绳绳①，	子孙谨慎不怠慢，	You'll have sons in a string
万民靡不承。	万民没有不顺服。	And people will obey you as king.

视尔友君子，	见你招待君子人，	Treat your friends with good grace;
辑柔尔颜，	态度和蔼笑盈盈，	Show them a kindly face.
不遐有愆。	小心过错莫发生。	You should do nothing wrong
相在尔室，	看你一人在室内，	E'en when far from the throng.
尚不愧于屋漏②。	面对神明无惭愧，	Be good when you're alone;
无曰"不显，	莫道"室内光线暗，	No wrong is done but known.
莫予云觏"。	没人能把我看见"。	Think not you are unseen;
神之格思，	神灵来去无踪影，	The sight of God is keen.
不可度思，	何时降临难猜测，	You know not what is in his mind,
矧③可射④思。	哪能厌怠遭罚惩。	Let alone what's behind.

辟尔为德，	修身养性怡情操，	When you do what is good,
俾臧俾嘉。	使它高尚更美好。	Be worthy of manhood.
淑慎尔止，	言谈举止要慎重，	With people get along;
不愆于仪。	端正仪容须礼貌。	In manners do no wrong.
不僭⑤不贼⑥，	不犯过错不害人，	Making no mistakes small,
鲜不为则。	很少不为人效法。	You'll be pattern for all.
投我以桃，	别人送我一只桃，	For a peach thrown on you,
报之以李。	我用李子来回报。	Return a plum as due.
彼童⑦而角，	羊羔无角说有角，	Seeking horns where there's none,
实虹⑧小子。	实是乱你周王朝。	You make a childish fun.

---

① 绳绳：慎戒。② 屋漏：屋子的西北角叫屋漏。指暗处。③ 矧(shěn)：况且。④ 射：厌倦。⑤ 僭(jiàn)：差错。⑥ 贼：伤害。⑦ 童：没有长角的羊。⑧ 虹：溃乱，败坏。

荏①染柔木，	有株树木很柔韧，	The soft, elastic wood
言缗②之丝。	配上丝弦做成琴。	For stringed lute is good.
温温恭人，	态度温和谦恭人，	A mild, respectful man
维德之基。	品德高尚根基深。	Will do good when he can.
其维哲人，	如果你是聪明人，	If you meet a man wise,
告之话言，	善言劝告你能听，	At what you say he tries
顺德之行。	顺应道德去实行。	To do what he thinks good.
其维愚人，	如果你是天性笨，	But a foolish man would
覆谓我僭③，	反说我言不可信，	Think what you say untrue:
民各有心。	大相径庭各有心。	Different is his view.

於乎小子，	可叹小子太年轻，	Alas! young man, how could
未知臧否。	好事坏事分不清。	You tell evil from good?
匪手携之，	非只用手相搀扶，	I'll lead you by the hand
言示之事。	而且教你办事情。	And show you where you stand.
匪面命之，	不但当面教导你，	I'll teach you face to face
言提其耳。	拎住耳朵要你听。	So that you can keep pace.
借曰未知，	假使年幼不懂事，	I'll hold you by the ear,
亦既抱子。	已有儿婴抱怀中。	You too have a son dear.
民之靡盈，	为人虽然存缺点，	If you are not content,
谁夙知而莫成？	谁人早慧却晚成？	In vain your youth is spent.

| 昊天孔昭， | 苍天在上最明白， | Great Heaven fair and bright, |
| 我生靡乐。 | 我的生活多烦忧。 | I live without delight. |

---

① 荏(rén)染：柔软。② 缗(mín)：安上。③ 僭(jiàn)：不相信。

视尔梦梦①，	看你糊涂不懂事，	Seeing you dream all day,
我心惨惨②。	我的心里实在痛。	My heart will pine away.
诲尔谆谆，	谆谆耐心教导你，	I tell you now and again,
听我藐藐③。	你既不听态度傲。	But I advise you in vain.
匪用为教，	不肯把它作教训，	You think me useless one;
覆用为虐。	反而当成大笑话。	Of my words you make fun.
借曰未知，	难道说你没知识，	Can you say you don't know
亦聿既耄④！	真的年龄也不小！	How old today you grow?

於乎小子，	可叹你这年轻人，	Alas! young man, I pray,
告尔旧止，	告你先王旧典章。	Don't you know ancient way?
听用我谋，	你能听用我主张，	Listen to my advice,
庶无大悔。	没有大错大懊丧。	And you'll be free from vice.
天方艰难，	上天正在降灾难，	If Heaven's ire come down,
曰丧厥国。	国势危险要灭亡。	Our State would be o'erthrown.
取譬不远，	让我就近打比方，	Just take example near by,
昊天不忒。	上天赏罚不冤枉。	You'll see justice on high.
回遹⑤其德，	邪僻品行若不改，	If far astray you go,
俾民大棘！	百姓危急遭祸殃。	You'll plunge people in woe.

桑　柔　　　　　　　　Misery and Disorder*

菀彼桑柔，	桑叶柔嫩生长旺，	Lush are mulberry trees;

---

① 梦梦：混乱。② 惨惨：悲伤，不快乐。③ 藐藐：态度傲慢，听不进去的样子。④ 耄(mào)：八九十岁曰耄。⑤ 遹(yù)：邪僻。

* The Earl of Rui mourned over the misery and disorder of the times, with a view to reprehend the misgovernment of King Li, especially his oppressions and listening to bad Counsellors.

其下侯旬①，	树荫宽广遍地凉。	Their shade affords good ease.
捋采其刘②，	桑叶捋尽树枝疏，	When they're stript of their leaves,
瘼③此下民，	树下人民晒难当。	The people deeply grieves.
不殄④心忧，	忧心不断意愁苦，	They're so deeply distressed
仓兄⑤填兮，	丧乱凄凉滋惆怅。	That sorrow fills their breast.
倬⑥彼昊天，	老天在上最高明，	O Heaven great and bright,
宁不我矜！	不肯哀怜我心伤。	Why not pity our plight?

四牡骙骙⑦，	四马奔驰忙不停，	The steeds run far and nigh;
旟旐⑧有翩。	鸟旗龟旗纷乱飘。	The falcon banners fly.
乱生不夷，	祸乱发生不平静，	The disorder is great;
靡国不泯，	四方无不乱纷纷。	There's ruin in the State.
民靡有黎，	百姓困苦丁壮少，	So many killed in clashes,
具祸以烬⑨。	都遭战乱成灰烬。	Houses reduced to ashes.
於乎有哀，	呜呼哀哉真可叹，	Alas! we're full of gloom;
国步斯频！	国家命运急又紧。	The State is near its doom.

国步蔑资⑩，	国贫民困资财光，	Nothing can change our fate;
天不我将⑪。	老天不肯把我帮。	Heaven won't help our State.
靡所止疑⑫，	居无定所无处住，	Where to stop we don't know;
云徂何往？	归宿不知向何方。	We have nowhere to go.
君子实维，	君子认真细思量，	Good men may think and brood;

---

① 旬：树荫遍布，树影均匀。② 刘：树叶剥落稀疏的样子。③ 瘼(mò)：病。④ 殄(tiǎn)：绝断。⑤ 仓兄(chuàngkuàng)：同"怆怳"，凄怆。⑥ 倬(zhuō)：明察。⑦ 骙骙(kuí kuí)：不息。⑧ 旟旐(yúzhào)：鸟隼旗曰旟，龟蛇旗曰旐。⑨ 烬(jìn)：灰烬。⑩ 蔑资：无资财。⑪ 将：养。⑫ 疑：定。

秉心无竞。	心地端正不好强。	They strive not for their good.
谁生厉阶①?	是谁制造此祸根?	Who is the man who sows
至今为梗。	一直作梗害人伤。	The dire distress and woes?

忧心慇慇,	心中隐隐多痛苦,	With heavy heart I stand,
念我土宇。	常常怀念我国土。	Thinking of my homeland.
我生不辰,	我生没有逢佳时,	Born at unlucky hour,
逢天僤②怒。	遭逢老天正盛怒。	I meet God's angry power,
自西徂东,	从那西边到东边,	From the east to the west,
靡所定处。	无处栖身可安宿。	I have nowhere to rest.
多我觏痻③,	我遭祸乱诸多苦,	I see only disorder;
孔棘我圉④。	十分紧急我疆土。	In danger is our border.

为谋为毖⑤,	为国谋划要谨慎,	If you follow advice,
乱况斯削。	祸乱可能得减轻。	You may lessen the vice.
告尔忧恤,	教你如何忧国事,	Let's gain a livelihood;
诲尔序爵。	教你如何封官职。	Put things in order good.
谁能执热,	谁能手持滚烫物,	Who can hold something hot
逝不以濯?	不去用水来洗濯?	If he waters it not?
其何能淑,	国事若真无佳策,	Can remedy be found
载胥及溺。	百姓遭溺命难保。	If the people are drowned?

如彼溯风,	好比人们逆风跑,	Standing against the breeze,
亦孔之僾⑥。	呼吸困难受不了。	How can you breathe at ease?

---

① 厉阶:祸端。② 僤(dàn)怒:重怒。③ 痻(mín):病。④ 圉(yǔ):边疆。⑤ 毖(bì):谨慎。⑥ 僾(ài):窒息,气不畅。

民有肃心，	人民本有进取心，	Could people forward go
荓①云不逮。	苦于有力难用上。	Should an adverse wind blow?
好是稼穑，	重视耕种和收获，	Love cultivated soil;
力民代食。	百姓苦力代耕养。	Let people live on toil.
稼穑维宝，	勤劳种收是个宝，	The grain to them is dear;
代食维好。	代耕之民年年忙！	They toil from year to year.

天降丧乱，	老天降下大灾祸，	Heaven sends turmoil down
灭我立王。	想要毁我所拥王。	To ruin the royal crown.
降此蟊贼，	降下蟊贼等害虫，	Injurious insects reign
稼穑卒痒，	庄稼全部糟踏光。	And devour crop and grain.
哀恫②中国，	哀痛国中的人民，	Alas! in Central State
具赘③卒荒。	遍地灾祸田尽荒。	Devastation is great.
靡有旅力，	人民疲病乏力量，	What can I do but cry
以念穹苍。	无法感动那上苍。	To the boundless great sky?

维此惠君，	只有顺民好君王，	If the king's good and wise,
民人所瞻。	大家拥戴好敬仰。	He's revered in our eyes.
秉心宣犹，	心地光明有智谋，	He'll make his plans with care
考慎其相。	选择贤臣与辅相。	And choose ministers fair and square.
维彼不顺，	只有蛮横强暴君，	If he has no kinghood,
自独俾臧，	以为所用都贤良。	He'll think alone he's good.
自有肺肠，	独有主张坏心肠，	His thoughts are hard to guess,
俾民卒狂。	逼使百姓都发狂。	His people in distress.

---

① 荓(pīng)：使。 ② 恫(tōng)：痛。 ③ 赘(zhuì)：连属。

瞻彼中林，	看那郊外林莽莽，	Behold! among the trees
甡甡①其鹿。	成群麋鹿多欢畅。	The deer may roam at ease.
朋友已谮②，	同僚朋友不信任，	Among friends insincere
不胥以穀③。	没有善意难相容。	You cannot roam with cheer,
人亦有言：	古人曾经说得好：	Nor advance nor retreat
进退维谷。	进退不通是绝路。	As in a strait you meet.
维此圣人，	圣人明哲有智谋，	How wise these sages are!
瞻言百里：	高瞻远瞩过百里。	Their views and words reach far.
维彼愚人，	愚人鼠目寸光浅，	How foolish those men bad!
覆狂以喜。	行为癫狂还自喜。	They rejoice as if mad.
匪言不能，	不是有话不能说，	We can't tell them what we know
胡斯畏忌？	直言畏忌罪加身。	For fear of coming woe.
维此良人，	只有这些善良人，	These good men you avoid,
弗求弗迪④：	不去贪求不钻营。	They are never employed.
维彼忍心，	只有那些忍心者，	Those cruel men in power
是顾是复。	瞻顾求宠多反复。	Are courted from hour to hour.
民之贪乱，	民心思乱有原因，	So disorder is bred
宁为荼毒。	实逢恶政苦难当。	And evil deeds wide spread.
大风有隧⑤。	大风吹时有来路，	The big wind blows a gale
有空大谷。	来自空空大谷中。	From the large, empty vale.

---

① 甡甡(shēn shēn)：众多的样子。② 谮(zèn)：不相信。③ 穀：善。④ 迪(dí)：进取，钻营。⑤ 隧(suì)：风疾速的样子。

维此良人，	只有这位善良人，	What can a good man say?
作为式穀：	举止美好为高尚。	It is of no avail!
维彼不顺，	只有那些悖理者，	In the court bad men stay;
征以中垢。	做事不正行肮脏。	What they say will prevail.

大风有隧，	大风吹时有来路，	The big wind blows its way;
贪人败类。	贪婪小人害宗族。	In the court bad men stay.
听言则对，	好听话语多答对，	When praised, they're overjoyed;
诵言如醉。	听见忠言就装醉。	When blamed, they play the drunk.
匪用其良，	不用忠良贤德人，	Good men are not employed;
覆俾我悖。	反而使我遭悖晦。	In distress they are sunk.

嗟尔朋友，	哎呀我的朋友们，	Alas! alas! my friend,
予岂不知而作。	你的所为我不知。	Can I write to no end?
如彼飞虫，	好比鸟儿高空飞，	Like a bird on the wing,
时亦弋获。	有时被射落网中。	Hit, you may be brought down.
既之阴女，	我来本为庇护你，	Good to you I will bring,
反予来赫。	反而发怒威赫我。	But at me you will frown.

民之罔极，	人民所以行不轨，	Don't do wrong to excess;
职凉善背。	主要相信善欺人。	People fall in distress.
为民不利，	为政暴虐不利民，	If you do people wrong,
如云不克。	就怕害人不能胜。	How can they get along?
民之回遹①，	百姓行为多邪僻，	If they take a wrong course,

---

① 回遹(yù)：邪僻。

职竞用力。	全因暴力来执政。	It's because you use force.

民之未戾①，	人民动荡不安定，	People live in unrest,
职盗为寇。	朝廷执政有盗行。	For robbers spread like pest.
凉曰不可，	诚恳劝说不能从，	I say that will not do；
复背善詈。	背地乱骂不认人。	You say that is not true.
虽曰匪予，	虽说为虐不是我，	Though you think I am wrong,
既作尔歌。	终作此歌盼你听。	I've made for you this song.

云　汉　　　　　　　　　　Great Drought*

倬②彼云汉，	浩瀚银河天上横，	The Silver River shines on high，
昭回于天。	星光灿烂转不停。	Revolving in the sky.
王曰於乎，	国王仰天长叹息：	The king heaves sigh on sigh：
何辜③今之人！	今天人民何罪愆！	"O what wrong have we done?
天降丧乱，	上天降下这丧乱，	What riot has death run!
饥馑荐臻④。	饥荒连年都发生。	Why have famines come one by one?
靡神不举⑤，	没有神灵未祭祀，	What sacrifice have we not made?
靡爱斯牲。	不敢吝惜那牺牲。	We have burned all maces of jade.
圭璧⑥既卒，	祭神圭璧都用到，	Have we not killed victims in herd?

---

① 戾：安定。② 倬(zhuō)：广大的样子。③ 辜(gū)：罪。④ 荐臻：接连着来。⑤ 举：祭祀。⑥ 圭璧：祭祀时用的玉器。

* On occasion of a great drought in 821 B. C. King Xuan expostulated with God and the Spirits who might he expected to succour him and his people, asked them wherefore they were contending with him and detailed the measures he had taken and was still taking for the removal of the calamity. The Silver River in Stanza 1 was the Chinese name for the Milky Way.

| 宁莫我听！ | 为啥祈祷天不听！ | How is it that we are not heard? |

旱既大甚，	旱灾已经很严重，	"The drought has gone to excess;
蕴隆虫虫①。	暑气闷热蒸难当。	The heat has caused distress.
不殄②禋祀，	不停祭祀求降雨，	There's no sacrifice we've not made;
自郊③徂宫④。	郊祭庙祭全举行。	For gods above we've buried jade.
上下奠瘗⑤，	奠酒奉玉祭天地，	There are no souls we don't revere
靡神不宗。	所有神明都祭享。	In temples far and near.
后稷不克⑥，	祖宗后稷不能求，	The Lord of Corn can't stop the drought;
上帝不临。	上帝不来来亲临。	Ruin falls on our land all about.
耗斁⑦下土，	人间田土成灾难，	The Almighty God won't come down.
宁丁我躬！	为啥正当我身上！	Why should the drought fall on my crown!

旱既大甚，	旱灾已经很严重，	"Excessive is the drought;
则不可推。	要想消除不可能。	I am to blame, no doubt.
兢兢业业，	战战兢兢提心胆，	I palpitate with fear
如霆如雷。	如防霹雳和雷声。	As if thunder I hear.
周余黎民，	周地剩余老百姓，	Of people I'm bereft;
靡有孑⑧遗。	几乎全都无所剩。	How many will be left?
昊天上帝，	老天上帝好心狠，	The Almighty on high
则不我遗。	不愿慰问我死生。	Does not care if we die.
胡不相畏，	百姓怎能不惧怕，	O my ancestors dear,
先祖于摧⑨。	祖先祭祀要被毁。	Don't you extinction fear?

① 虫虫：热气熏蒸的样子。② 殄(tiǎn)：断绝也。③ 郊：祭祀天地。④ 宫：祭祀宗庙。⑤ 瘗(yì)：埋。⑥ 克：能，胜。⑦ 斁(dù)：败坏。⑧ 孑(jié)遗：遗留。⑨ 摧：毁灭。

旱既大甚，	旱灾已经很严重，	"Excessive is the drought;
则不可沮。	没有办法可阻挡。	No one can put it out.
赫赫①炎炎，	骄阳似火炎气腾，	The sun burns far and wide;
云我无所。	哪里还有容身地。	I have nowhere to hide.
大命②近止，	死亡大限已临近，	Our end is coming near;
靡瞻靡顾。	瞻前顾后没商量。	I see no help appear.
群公先正，	历代公卿众灵神，	Dukes and ministers dead
则不我助。	不来过问不相帮。	All turn away the head.
父母先祖，	父母先祖显神灵，	O my ancestors dear,
胡宁忍予！	怎能忍我遭灾情。	How can you not appear?

旱既大甚，	旱灾已经很严重，	"The drought spreads far and nigh;
涤涤③山川。	山秃河涸草木尽。	Hills are parched and streams dry.
旱魃④为虐，	旱魃为恶太猖狂，	The demon vents his ire;
如惔如焚。	好比大火遍地燃。	He spreads wide flame and fire.
我心惮暑，	我心畏惧酷热天，	My heart's afraid of heat;
忧心如熏。	心里忧愁如熬煎。	Burned with grief, it can't beat.
群公先正，	历代公卿百官神，	Why don't the souls appear?
则不我闻。	不来过问不相帮。	Won't they my prayer hear?
昊天上帝，	老天上帝降灾情，	Almighty in the sky,
宁俾我遁！	为啥叫我长受困。	Why put on me such pressure high?

旱既大甚，	旱灾已经很严重，	"The drought holds excessive sway,

---

① 赫赫：旱气。② 大命：国命，国运。③ 涤涤(dídí)：除尽。④ 旱魃(bá)：旱神。

黾勉①畏去。	勉力祈祷不辞劳。	But I dare not go away.
胡宁瘨②我以旱？	为啥降旱加害我？	Why has it come from on high?
憯③不知其故。	不知缘由不知故。	I know not the reason why.
祈年孔夙，	祈祷丰年都很早，	Early I prayed for a good year,
方社不莫。	祭祀方社也不迟。	Sacrifice offered there and here.
昊天上帝，	浩渺苍天高上帝，	God in heaven, be kind!
则不我虞④。	也不想想我的苦。	Why won't you bear this in mind?
敬恭明神。	一向恭敬众神灵，	O my reverend Sire,
宜无悔怒。	神明不应有恼怒！	Why vent on me your ire?
旱既大甚，	旱灾已经很严重，	"The drought has spread far and near;
散无友⑤纪。	人人散乱无法纪。	People dispersed there and here.
鞫⑥哉庶正，	公卿百官束无策，	Officials toil in vain;
疚哉冢宰。	宰相痛苦空急切。	The premier brings no rain.
趣马⑦师氏，	趣马师氏来祈雨，	The master of my horses
膳夫左右；	膳夫大臣齐相助。	And leaders of my forces,
靡人不周⑧，	没有一人不出力，	There's none but does his best;
无不能止。	无人停住不去求。	There's none who takes a rest.
瞻卬⑨昊天，	抬头望天无片云，	I look up to the sky.
云如何里！	我的心里多忧苦。	What to do with soil dry?
瞻卬昊天，	仰望苍天万里晴，	"I look up to the sky;
有嘒其星，	闪闪繁星亮晶晶。	The stars shine bright on high.

---

① 黾勉:勉力祈祷。② 瘨(diān):病。③ 憯(cǎn):竟。④ 虞:佑助。⑤ 友:通"有"。
⑥ 鞫(jū):穷困。⑦ 趣马:掌管马的官。⑧ 周:救济。⑨ 卬(yǎng):通"仰"，仰望。

大夫君子，	公卿大夫众君子，	My officers have done their best;
昭假①无赢②。	诚心祭告多真诚。	With rain our land's not blessed.
大命近止，	死亡大限已临近，	Our course of life is run,
无弃尔成！	继续祈祷持不停。	But don't give up what's done.
何求为我，	祈雨不是为自己，	Pray for rain not for me
以戾③庶正。	为安百官与公卿。	But for officials on the knee.
瞻卬昊天，	抬头向上望苍天，	I look up to the sky:
曷惠其宁？	何时惠赐得安宁？	Will rain and rest come from on high?"

崧 高　　　　　　　　Count of Shen *

崧④高维岳，	巍峨四岳高高山，	The four mountains are high;
骏极于天。	高峻耸立入云天。	Their summits touch the sky.
维岳降神，	四岳高山降神灵，	Their spirits come on earth
生甫及申。	申伯甫侯人间生。	To Fu and Shen gave birth.
维申及甫，	就是申伯和甫侯，	The Shen State and Fu State
维周之翰。	周朝栋梁最有名，	Are Zhou House's bulwarks great.
四国于蕃，	保卫四方诸侯国，	They screen it from attack
四方于宣⑤。	天下靠他保安宁。	On the front and the back.
亹亹⑥申伯，	申伯做事最勤敏，	Count Shen was diligent

---

① 昭假：诚心祭告。② 赢：松懈。③ 戾：安定。④ 崧(sōng)：形容山大而高峻。⑤ 宣：垣，城墙。⑥ 亹亹(wěi wěi)：勤勉的样子。

* This epic ode celebrated the appointment by King Xuan of the brother of his mother to be the Count of Shen and defender of the southern border of the kingdom, with the arrangements made for his entering on his charge. The writer was General Ji Fu who appeared in Poem "General Fang" as the commander of an expedition against the tribes of the Huns in the commencement of King Xuan's reign.

王缵①之事。	继承祖业担重任。	In royal government.
于邑于谢，	赐封城邑在谢地，	At Xie he set up capital,
南国是式②。	南国诸侯做榜样。	A pattern for southern States all.
王命召伯，	周王命令召伯虎，	Count Zhao was ordered by the king
定申伯之宅。	去为申伯建新城。	To take charge of the house-building.
登③是南邦，	建成国家在南方，	Of southern States Shen's made the head,
世执其功。	子子孙孙保国土。	Where his great influence will spread.
王命申伯，	周王下令给申伯，	The king ordered Shen's chief
式是南邦。	要在南方树楷模。	To be pattern to southern fief,
因④是谢人，	依靠谢地老百姓，	And employ men of capital
以作尔庸⑤。	建筑新的城与墙。	To build the city wall.
王命召伯，	周王又令召伯虎，	The king gave Count Zhao his command
彻⑥申伯土田。	治理申伯新国疆。	To define Count Shen's land.
王命傅御，	王命太傅和侍御，	The king ordered his steward old
迁其私人⑦。	迁去家臣共生活。	To remove Shen's household.
申伯之功，	申伯迁谢告成功，	The construction of State of Shen
召伯是营。	召伯奉命来经营。	Was done by Count Zhao and his men.
有俶⑧其城，	谢城坚固又厚实，	They built first city walls
寝庙既成。	宗庙寝殿都建成。	And then the temple halls.
既成藐藐，	宫室相连多巍峨，	The great works done by the lord,
王锡申伯。	周王赐赏申伯礼。	The king gave Count Shen as reward

---

①缵(zuǎn)：继承。②式：法则，榜样。③登：建成。④因：依靠。⑤庸：城墙。⑥彻：治理，划定缰界。⑦私人：家臣，家人。⑧俶(hù)：厚实、坚固的样子。

四牡跻跻， 四匹骏马多轩昂， Four noble steeds at left and right
钩膺①濯濯②。 胸前配饰金闪闪。 With breasthooks amid trappings
　　　　　　　　　　　　　　　　　bright.

王遣申伯， 王送申伯去谢城， The king told Count Shen to speed
路车③乘马。 四马大车真漂亮。 To his State in cab and steed.
我图④尔居， 仔细谋划你住处 "I've thought of your town beforehand;
莫如南土。 不如南土好地方。 Nowhere's better than southern land.
锡尔介圭⑤， 赐你大圭作礼物， I confer on you this mace,
以作尔宝。 作为国宝好收藏。 Symbol of dignity and grace.
往迟⑥王舅， 尊贵王舅放心去， Go, my dear uncle, go
南土是保。 确保南方这片疆。 And protect the south from the foe."

申伯信迈， 申伯决定要起程， Count Shen set out for Xie;
王饯于郿。 周王郿地以饯行。 The king feasted him at Mei.
申伯还南， 申伯要到南方去， Count Shen would take command
谢于诚归。 决心离开往谢城。 At Xie in southern land.
王命召伯， 周王命令召伯虎， Count Zhao was ordered to define
彻申伯土疆。 申伯疆土要划清。 Shen's land and border line,
以峙⑦其粻⑧， 路上干粮充备齐， And provide him with food
式遄⑨其行。 日夜兼程不留停。 That he might find his journey good.

申伯番番⑩， 申伯勇武貌堂堂， Count Shen with flags and banners

---

① 钩膺：套在马前胸和颈腹上的带饰。② 濯濯：光泽鲜明的样子。③ 路车：诸侯乘坐的一种大型马车。④ 图：图谋，谋虑。⑤ 圭：古代玉制的礼器，诸侯执此以朝见周王。⑥ 迟(jì)：语助词，犹哉。⑦ 峙：储备。⑧ 粻(zhāng)：粮食。⑨ 遄(chuán)：快速。⑩ 番番(bō bō)：勇武的样子。

既入于谢。	住进谢邑好地方。	Came to Xie, grand in manners.
徒御啴啴①，	随从士卒列成行，	His footmen and charioteers
周邦咸喜。	全城百姓喜洋洋。	Were greeted by the town with cheers.
戎有良翰，	作为国家好栋梁，	The State will be guarded by men
不显申伯。	申伯高贵真荣光。	Under the command of Count Shen,
王之元舅，	周王舅父真威严，	Royal uncle people adore
文武是宪②。	文德武功是榜样。	And pattern in peace as in war.

申伯之德，	申伯仁德有声名，	Count Shen with virtue bright
柔惠③且直。	温良和顺又端庄。	Is mild, kind and upright.
揉此万邦，	安抚诸侯服万国，	He'll keep all States in order,
闻于四国。	天下四方功传扬。	With fame spread to the border.
吉甫作诵④，	吉甫创写这首诗，	I, Ji Fu, make this song
其诗孔硕⑤。	篇幅宏大义深长。	In praise of the count strong.
其风⑥肆好，	曲雅旋律曲调，	I present this beautiful air
以赠申伯。	赠给申伯表衷肠。	To the count bright and fair.

烝　民　　　　　　　　　Premier Shan Fu *

天生烝⑦民，	上天生育众百姓，	Heaven who made mankind

---

① 啴啴(chǎn chǎn)：阵容盛大的样子。② 宪：法式，模范。③ 柔惠：温顺，恭谨。
④ 诵：颂赞之诗。⑤ 孔硕：指篇幅很长。⑥ 风：曲调，旋律。⑦ 烝(zhēng)：众多。

* This epic ode celebrated the virtue of Premier Shan Fu and his despatch to the east to fortify the capital of the State of Qi (modern Shandong Provice). Like the preceding ode, this was also made by General Ji Fu to present to his friend on his departure from the court.

有物有则①。	万事有形有法则。	Endowed him with body and mind.
民之秉彝②，	人人保持生来性，	The people loved manhood.
好是懿德。	全都喜爱好美德。	Could they not love the good?
天监有周，	老天监察我周朝，	Heaven beheld our crown
昭假③于下。	诚心祈祷在下国。	And shed light up and down.
保兹天子，	为了保佑周天子，	To help His son on earth,
生仲山甫。	生下山甫是贤哲。	To Shan Fu He gave birth.

仲山甫之德，	山甫生性好品德，	Cadet Shan Fu is good,
柔嘉维则。	温和善良有原则。	Endowed with mild manhood.
令仪令色，	仪表端庄好气色，	Dignified is his air;
小心翼翼。	谨慎小心不出格。	He behaves with great care,
古训是式，	先王古训能遵循，	He follows lessons old;
威仪是力。	言行尽力与礼合。	He is as strong as bold.
天子是若，	事事顺承天子意，	He follows Heaven's Son
明命使赋④。	传送命令听政策。	That his orders may be done.

王命仲山甫，	天子命令仲山甫，	The king orders him to appear
式是百辟。	要为诸侯作准绳。	As pattern to each peer;
缵戎祖考，	祖先功业来继承，	To serve as his ancestors dear
王躬是保。	辅佐周王保安宁。	And protect the king here;
出纳王命，	王命出入来掌管，	To give orders to old and young
王之喉舌。	作为喉舌责不轻。	And be the king's throat and tongue;
赋政于外，	颁布政令达诸侯，	To spread decrees and orders

---

① 则：法则。② 秉彝(yí)：秉性。③ 昭假：诚心祭告。④ 赋：发布。

四方爰发①。	天下四方都响应。	That they be obeyed on four borders.

肃肃王命，	天命肃肃很严正，	The orders dignified
仲山甫将之。	山甫认真去执行。	Are spread out far and wide.
邦国若否②，	国家事情好与坏，	Premier Shan Fu does know
仲山甫明之。	山甫都能认识清。	The kingdom's weal and woe.
既明且哲，	知识渊博又明理，	He's wise and free from blame,
以保其身。	保持自己好名声。	To guard his life and fame.
夙夜匪解③，	日夜辛劳不松懈，	He's busy night and day
以事一人。	侍奉周王保太平。	To serve the king for aye.

人亦有言：	古人曾经这样说，	As people have said oft,
"柔则茹之，	东西要拣软的吃，	"We choose to eat the soft;
刚则吐之。"	"坚硬东西往外吐。"	The hard will be cast out."
维仲山甫，	只有山甫一个人，	On this Shan Fu cast doubt.
柔亦不茹，	柔软东西不乱吃，	He won't devour the soft;
刚亦不吐；	东西再硬也不吐。	Nor is the hard cast oft.
不侮矜寡，	鳏寡弱者不欺侮，	He'll do the weak no wrong,
不畏强御。	强暴之人也不怕。	Nor will he fear the strong.

人亦有言：	古人经常这样说，	People say everywhere,
"德輶④如毛，	"道德品行轻如毛，	"Virtue is light as air;
民鲜克举之。"	很少有人能举高。"	But few can hold it high."
我仪图⑤之，	暗暗思考细揣度，	I ponder with a sigh:

①发：行动，响应。②否：恶，不好。③解：懈怠。④輶(yóu)：轻。⑤仪图：思考，揣度。

维仲山甫举之，	做到只有仲山甫，	Only Shan Fu can hold it high
爱莫助之。	可惜无力能帮助。	And needs no help from the sky.
衮①职有阙，	龙袍上面有破损，	When the king has defect,
维仲山甫补之。	只有山甫能弥补。	Shan Fu helps him correct.

仲山甫出祖②，	山甫出行祭路神，	Where Shan Fu goes along,
四牡业业③，	四马高大真威风。	Run his four horses strong.
征夫捷捷，	征夫敏捷动作快，	His men alert would find
每怀④靡及。	纵有私情不顾及。	They often lag behind.
四牡彭彭⑤，	四马奔驰走得疾，	His four steeds run east-bound
八鸾锵锵。	八只鸾铃响声齐。	To eight bells' tinkling sound.
王命仲山甫，	周王命令仲山甫，	The king orders him to go down
城彼东方。	建城东方立功勋。	To fortify the eastern town.

四牡骙骙，	四马向前奔跑行，	His four steeds galloping,
八鸾喈喈。	八只鸾铃响不停。	His eight bells gaily ring.
仲山甫徂⑥齐，	山甫动身往齐国，	Shan Fu goes to Qi State;
式遄其归。	盼他早日起回程。	His return won't be late.
吉甫作诵，	吉甫写下这首歌，	I, Ji Fu, make this song
穆如清风。	美如清风爽人心。	To blow like breeze for long.
仲山甫永怀，	临行山甫多牵挂，	O Shan Fu, though we part,
以慰其心。	聊以此歌表心意。	My song will soothe your heart.

---

① 衮(gǔn)：龙袍。② 祖：祭祀道路之神。③ 业业：高大强健的样子。④ 每怀：私情，私事。⑤ 彭彭(bāng bāng)：奔跑的样子。⑥ 徂(cú)：到。

韩奕　　　　The Marquis of Han*

奕奕梁山，	梁山巍峨高又大，	The Liang Mountains are grand;
维禹甸①之，	大禹当年治理它，	Yu of Xia cultivated the land.
有倬②其道。	一条大路通周都。	The Marquis of Han came his way
韩侯受命，	韩侯受命保国家，	To be invested in array.
王亲命之：	周王亲自传旨意：	"Serve as your fathers had done,"
缵③戎祖考，	祖业功业须继承，	In person said the Heaven's Son,
无废朕命。	我的命令不可忘。	"Do not belie our trust;
夙夜匪解，	早晚勤勉别懈怠，	Show active zeal you must.
虔共④尔位。	坚守职位切莫忘。	Let things be well arranged;
朕命不易，	我的命令没变化，	Let no order be changed.
榦⑤不庭方⑥，	讨伐不朝诸侯国，	Assist us to extort
以佐戎辟⑦。"	辅佐君王治天下。	Lords who won't come to court."
四牡奕奕，	四匹公马多强壮，	His cab was drawn by four steeds
孔脩⑧且张。	身体高大气势壮。	Long and large, running high speeds.
韩侯入觐⑨，	韩侯入周来朝见，	The marquis at court did stand,
以其介圭，	手捧大圭上朝堂，	His mace of rank in hand.
入觐于王。	从容拜见周朝王。	He bowed to Heaven's Son,

---

① 甸(diàn)：治理。② 倬(zhuó)：长远。③ 缵(zuǎn)：继承。④ 虔共(gōng)：敬诚恭谨。⑤ 榦(gān)：同"幹"，安定。⑥ 不庭方：不来朝觐的各国诸侯。⑦ 辟：君位。⑧ 孔脩：很长。⑨ 入觐(jìn)：入朝朝见天子。

* This epic ode celebrated the Marquis of Han, his investiture and King Xuan's charge to him; the gifts he received and the parting feast; his marriage; the excellence of his territory and his sway over the region of the north.

王锡韩侯，	周王赏赐韩侯礼，	Who showed him his gifts one by one.
淑旂绥章，	锦绣龙旗有纹饰，	The dragon flags all new
簟茀①错衡，	车上竹篷花车衡，	And screens made of bamboo,
玄衮赤舄，	黑色龙袍大红鞋，	Black robes and slippers red,
钩膺②镂钖③，	马胸马头配饰美，	Carved hooks for horse's head,
鞹鞃④浅幭⑤，	浅色虎皮盖轼上，	A tiger's skin aboard
鞗⑥革金厄。	马辔金环闪亮亮。	And golden rings for the lord.

韩侯出祖，	韩侯临行祭路神，	The marquis went on homeward way
出宿于屠。	出京来到屠地住，	At Tu for the night he did stay.
显父饯之，	显父设宴来饯行，	Xian Fu invited him to dine,
清酒百壶。	席上清酒有百壶。	Drinking a hundred vases of wine.
其肴维何？	宴间菜肴有哪些？	What were the viands in the dishes?
炰鳖鲜鱼。	清蒸团鱼鲜鱼煮。	Roast turtles and fresh fishes.
其蔌⑦维何？	吃的蔬菜有什么？	And what was the ragout?
维笋及蒲，	新鲜竹笋和香蒲。	Tender shoots of bamboo.
其赠维何？	临行送些啥礼物？	What were the gifts furthermore?
乘马路车⑧。	四匹马儿和大车。	A cab of state and horses four.
笾豆⑨有且，	菜肴丰盛色味全，	So many were the dishes fine,
侯氏燕胥。	诸侯赴宴尽欢喜。	The marquis with delight did dine.

| 韩侯取妻， | 韩侯娶一美娇妻， | The marquis was to wed |
| 汾王之甥， | 她是厉王外甥女， | The king's niece in nuptial bed. |

---

① 簟茀(diànfú)：竹制的车篷。② 钩膺：套在马胸前的带饰。③ 镂钖：马额头上的金属饰物。④ 鞹鞃(kuòhóng)：裹着皮革的车前横木。⑤ 幭(miè)：车轼上的皮革。⑥ 鞗(tiáo)革：马辔头。⑦ 蔌(sù)：素菜。⑧ 路车：贵族用的大车。⑨ 笾豆：古代的饮食器皿。

蹶父之子。	蹶父家的小姑娘。	It was the daughter of Gui Fu
韩侯迎止，	韩侯亲自去迎娶，	The marquis came to woo.
于蹶之里。	经过蹶邑大街上。	A hundred cabs came on the way
百两彭彭，	百辆彩车熙攘攘，	To Gui's house in array.
八鸾锵锵，	八只鸾铃响叮当，	Eight bells made tinkling sound，
不显其光。	场面盛大真荣光。	Shedding glory around.
诸娣①从之，	陪嫁姐妹相跟随，	Virgins followed the bride in crowd
祁祁如云。	盛妆打扮如彩云。	As beautiful as cloud.
韩侯顾之，	韩侯举行三顾礼，	The marquis looked round
烂②其盈门。	满庭灿烂真辉煌。	The house in splendor drowned.
蹶父孔武，	蹶父威武有见识，	Gui Fu in war had fame.
靡国不到；	各个地方都去到。	Among the states whence he came，
为韩姞相攸③，	他为韩姞找归处，	He liked Han by the water，
莫如韩乐。	只有韩地最称意。	Where he married his daughter.
孔乐韩土，	位在韩邑安乐多，	In Han there are large streams
川泽訏訏，	河流湖泊多宽阔。	Full of tenches and breams；
鲂鱮甫甫，	鳊鱼鲢鱼肥又大，	The deer and doe are mild
麀鹿噳噳，	母鹿公鹿满山腰。	And tigers and cats wild；
有熊有罴，	林中还有熊和黑，	The bears or black or brown
有猫有虎。	山猫老虎能看到。	Roam the land up and down.
庆既令居，	庆贺找到好地方，	His daughter Ji lived there；
韩姞燕誉④。	韩姞安居乐陶陶。	She found no state more fair.

---

① 娣(dì)：陪嫁的姑娘。② 烂：光彩绚烂。③ 相攸：观察合适的地方。④ 燕誉：安乐。

溥①彼韩城，	城邑宽广是韩国，	The city wall of Han
燕师所完。	燕国工匠修筑成。	Was built by people of Yan.
以先祖受命，	韩国先祖受封礼，	Han ancestors got orders
因时百蛮。	控制北方百蛮族。	To rule o'er tribes on borders.
王锡韩侯，	周王下令赐韩侯，	The marquis has below
其追其貊②，	追貊两国由你领，	Him tribes of Zhai and Mo.
奄③受北国，	北方小国都在内，	He should preside as chief
因以其伯④。	自为方伯担重任。	Of northern states and fief；
实墉⑤实壑，	挖筑壕沟修城墙，	Lay out fields, make walls strong
实亩⑥实籍⑦。	划好田亩再收税。	And dig deep moats along；
献其貔⑧皮，	献上当地白狐皮，	Present skins of bears brown
赤豹黄罴。	豹皮熊皮样样好。	And fox white to the crown.

江　汉　　　　　　　　　　Duke Mu of Zhao*

江汉浮浮⑨。	长江汉水浪滔滔，	Onward the rivers roared；
武夫滔滔。	武夫将士气势高。	Forward our warriors poured.
匪安匪游，	不图安逸不闲游，	There was no rest far and nigh；
淮夷来求⑩。	只将淮夷来征讨。	We marched on River Huai.
既出我车，	我的战车已出动，	Our cars drove on the way

---

① 溥(pǔ)：宽阔，阔大。② 追、貊(mò)：都是部落名。③ 奄：完全。④ 伯：诸侯之长。⑤ 墉：修城墙。⑥ 亩：划分田亩。⑦ 籍：征收赋税。⑧ 貔(pí)：一种猛兽名。⑨ 浮浮：强盛的样子。下句"滔滔"，为广大无边的样子。应当作"江汉滔滔，武夫浮浮"。⑩ 求：诛求，讨伐。

* This epic ode celebrated an expedition in 825 B.C. against the southern tribes of the Huai and the work done for King Xuan by Zhao Hu, Duke Mu of Zhao, with the manner in which the king rewarded him and he responded to the royal favor.

既设我旟。	我的旗帜迎风飘。	Our flags flew on display.
匪安匪舒，	不敢苟安不舒缓，	There was no peace far and nigh;
淮夷来铺①。	要到淮夷去驻扎。	We marched on tribes of Huai.

江汉汤汤，	长江汉水涛浩荡，	Onward the rivers flow;
武夫洸洸②。	武夫威武又雄壮。	Backward our warriors go.
经营四方，	东征西讨营四方，	The State reduced to order,
告成于王。	报告成功向周王。	We come back from the border.
四方既平，	四方叛变已定平，	There is peace east and west;
王国庶定。	国家安定无灾殃。	North and south there is rest.
时靡有争，	从此太平战事息，	An end is put to the strife;
王心载③宁。	周王心里多舒畅。	The king may live a peaceful life.

江汉之浒④，	在那长江汉水边，	On the two rivers' borders
王命召虎：	周王命令召伯虎：	The king gives Zhao Hu orders:
"式辟四方，	"前去开辟四方地，	"Open up countryside
彻⑤我疆土。	精心治理我疆土。	And land and fields divide.
匪疚⑥匪棘⑦，	不扰民来不强迫，	Let people rule their fate
王国来极⑧。	要为王国立楷模。	And conform to our State.
于疆于理，	划定疆界治田地，	Define lands by decree
至于南海。"	直到南海都归附。"	As far as Southern Sea."

王命召虎：	周王命令召伯虎，	The king gives Zhao Hu orders

---

① 铺：列阵，驻扎，指讨伐。② 洸洸（guāngguāng）：威武的样子。③ 载：则。④ 浒（hǔ）：水边。⑤ 彻：开发，治理。⑥ 疚：病，害。⑦ 棘：急。⑧ 极：准则。

来旬①来宣②。	负责巡视和安抚。	To inspect southern borders:
"文武受命，	"文王武王受天命，	"When Wen and Wu were kings,
召公维翰。	召公辅政是支柱。	Your ancestors were their wings.
无曰予小子，	不要归功我小子，	Say not young you appear;
召公是似。	召公事业你继承。	Do as your fathers dear.
肇敏③戎公，	努力建立大功业，	You have well served the State;
用锡尔祉。"	定会赐你大福禄。"	I'll give you favor great."

"釐④尔圭瓒⑤。	"赐你玉柄美玉勺，	"Here is a cup of jade
秬鬯⑥一卣⑦。	芬芳黑黍酒一杯。	And wine of millet made
告于文人⑧，	祭告文德祖先神，	Tell your ancestors grand
锡山土田，	赐你田土和山川。	I'll confer on you more land.
于周受命，	来到周朝受王命，	I'll gratify your desires
自⑨召祖命。"	仍用召祖旧封典。"	As my Sire did your Sire's."
虎拜稽首⑩，	召虎下拜来叩头，	Hu bows aground to say:
"天子万年。"	"天子万寿永无疆。"	"May Heaven's Son live for aye!"

虎拜稽首，	召虎下拜来叩首，	Hu bows aground again
对扬⑪王休。	称颂周王有美德。	In praise of royal reign.
作召公考⑫，	写下召公的颂辞，	He engraves Duke Zhao's song,
"天子万寿。"	"敬颂天子多福寿。"	Wishing the king live long.
明明天子，	仁爱明德周天子，	The Heaven's Son is wise;

---

① 旬：巡视。② 宣：宣抚。③ 肇敏：图谋。④ 釐(lí)：赏赐。⑤ 圭瓒(zàn)：用玉用柄的酒勺。⑥ 秬鬯(jùchàng)：黑黍酒，用于祭祀。⑦ 卣(yǒu)：带柄的一种酒壶。⑧ 文人，先祖中有文德的人。⑨ 自：用。⑩ 稽首：叩头礼，跪下时手、头都要触地。⑪ 对扬：颂扬。⑫ 考：簋(guǐ)的假借字。一种青铜器。

令闻不已。	美好声誉永不息。	His endless fame will rise.
矢①其文德,	施行礼乐与教化,	His virtue is so great
洽②此四国。	和顺天下四方国。	That he'll rule o'er every State.

常　武　　　　　　　Expedition against Xu*

赫赫明明③,	威武英明我周王,	Grand and wise is the sovereign who
王命卿士,	亲命卿士为大将。	Gave charge to Minister
南仲大祖④,	太庙之中命南仲,	And Grand-Master Huang Fu,
大师皇父⑤,	太师皇父讨徐方:	Of whom Nan Zhong was ancestor.
"整我六师,	"整顿六师振士气,	"Put my six armies in order
以脩我戎。	修好弓箭和刀枪。	And ready for warfare.
既敬⑥既戒,	提高警惕严戒备,	Set out for southern border
惠此南国。"	爱护百姓安南国。"	With vigilance and care!"

王谓尹氏,	宣王告诉尹吉甫,	The king told Yin to assign
命程伯休父:	策命程伯任司马。	The task to Count Xiu Fu
左右陈行,	部署队伍左右列,	To march his troops in line
戒我师旅。	告诫我军仔细听。	And in vigilance too;

---

① 矢:施行。② 洽:协合。③ 明明:英明,明智。④ 南仲大祖:在太祖之庙命南仲为卿。⑤ 太师皇父:命令皇父做太师。⑥ 敬:警惕。

* This epic ode celebrated an expedition of King Xuan against the State of Xu, a northern tribe of the Huai. The commander-in-chief was Huang Fu, a descendant of General Nan Zhong who had done good service to the State against the Huns in the times of King Wen (See Poem "General Nan Zhong and His wife"), and not President Huang Fu who was mentioned in Poem "President Huang Fu" as a very bad and dangerous man in the times of King You, King Xuan's son and successor.

率①彼淮浦，	沿着淮河岸边行，	To go along the river shore
省②此徐土。	须对徐国细巡察。	Until they reach the land of Xu;
不留③不处④，	诛其君来吊其民，	And not to stay there any more
三事⑤就绪。	三卿尽职责任明。	When the three tasks get through.

赫赫业业，	威仪堂堂气轩昂，	How dignified and grand
有严天子。	宣王神武又威严。	Did the Son of Heaven show!
王舒保⑥作，	王师从容向前进，	He advanced on the land
匪绍匪游。	不敢闲逛不游行。	Nor too fast nor too slow.
徐方绎⑦骚，	徐军未战内已乱，	The land of Xu was stirred
震惊徐方。	王师威力震徐国。	And greatly terrified
如雷如霆，	声势浩大如雷霆，	As if a thunder heard
徐方震惊。	震惊徐方君与民。	Shook the land far and wide.

王奋厥武，	王师奋发多威武，	The king in brave array
如震如怒。	好比雷霆发震怒，	Struck the foe with dismay.
进厥虎臣，	派出冲锋先头军，	His chariots went before;
阚⑧如虓⑨虎。	威猛如同咆哮虎。	Like tigers did men roar.
铺敦⑩淮濆⑪，	陈兵布阵淮水边，	Along the riverside
仍⑫执丑虏。	捉获徐方众俘虏。	They captured the foes terrified.
截⑬彼淮浦，	截断淮水溃逃路，	They advanced to the rear
王师之所。	王师就把兵驻定。	And occupied their sphere.

---

① 率：循着，沿着。② 省：巡视，察看。③ 留：刘，杀。④ 处：吊，安抚。⑤ 三事：立三个卿大夫。⑥ 舒保：徐缓。⑦ 绎(yì)骚：骚动不安。⑧ 阚(hǎn)：老虎发怒。⑨ 虓(xiāo)：老虎吼叫。⑩ 铺敦：陈列，驻扎。⑪ 濆(fén)：大堤。⑫ 仍：频繁，连续。⑬ 截：截断。

王旅嘽嘽①，	王师气势有威力，	The legions of the king's
如飞如翰②，	好比雄鹰疾飞翔。	Are swift as birds on wings.
如江如汉，	好比江汉浪滔滔，	Like rivers they are long;
如山之苞，	好比群山气势壮，	Like mountains they are strong.
如川之流，	好比大河不可挡，	They roll on like the stream;
绵绵翼翼，	连绵不断声势壮。	Boundless and endless they seem.
不测不克，	不可预测不可胜，	Invincible, unfathomable, great,
濯③征徐国。	大胜徐国定南方。	They've conquered the Xu State.

王犹允塞④，	宣王谋略真可信，	The king has wisely planned
徐方既来⑤，	徐方已经来归降。	How to conquer Xu's land.
徐方既同，	徐方已经来会同，	Xu's chiefs come to submit
天子之功。	天子亲征建功勋。	All through the king's merit.
四方既平，	四方已经定太平，	The country pacified,
徐方来庭。	徐方也来拜朝王。	Xu's chiefs come to the king's side.
徐方不回⑥，	徐方不敢再违抗，	They won't again rebel;
王曰还归。	王命班师回周朝。	The king says, "All is well."

瞻卬　　　　Complaint against King You*

瞻卬⑦昊天，	仰起头来望昊天，	I look up to the sky;
则不我惠。	不肯对我施恩情。	Great Heaven is not kind.

---

① 嘽嘽(dāndān)：盛大的样子。② 翰：高飞的鸟。③ 濯：规模大。④ 允塞：信实。⑤ 来：归服。⑥ 回：违反。⑦ 瞻卬(yǎng)：瞻仰。

* The speaker deplored the misery and oppression that prevailed in the time of King You (780-770B. C.)and intimated that they were caused by the interference of Lady Shi of Bao in the government.

孔填①不宁，	天下许久不安宁，	Restless for long am I;
降此大厉。	降下大祸在人境。	Down fall disasters blind.
邦靡有定，	国家无法能安定，	Unsettled is the State;
士民其瘵②。	害苦平民和百姓。	We're distressed high and low.
蟊贼蟊③疾，	好比害虫吃庄稼，	Insects raise havoc great.
靡有夷届。	没完没了不肯定。	Where's the end to our woe?
罪罟不收④，	罪恶之网不收起，	The net of crime spreads wide.
靡有夷瘳⑤。	人民苦难永止境。	Alas! where can we hide!
人有土田，	别人有了好土地，	People had fields and lands,
女反有之。	你却侵占归己有。	But you take them away.
人有民人，	别人有了老百姓，	People had their farm hands;
女覆夺之。	你又要去强抢夺。	On them your hands you lay.
此宜无罪，	这人本是无辜者，	This man has done no wrong;
女反收之。	你却要把他捕捉。	You say guilty is he.
彼宜有罪，	那人本来有罪过，	That man's guilty for long;
女覆说⑥之。	你却替他去开脱。	You say from guilt he's free.
哲夫成城，	智慧男子能建城，	A wise man builds a city wall;
哲妇倾城。	女人有才使城倾。	A fair woman brings its downfall.
懿厥哲妇，	可恨此妇太聪明，	Alas! such a woman young
为枭⑦为鸱。	如同恶枭猫头鹰。	Is no better than an owl;
妇有长舌，	女人多嘴舌头长，	Such a woman with a long tongue

---

①填(chén)：久。②瘵(zhài)：病。③蟊(máo)疾：病疫。④收：拘收，逮捕。⑤瘳(chōu)：病愈。⑥说(tuō)：通"脱"，脱罪，赦放。⑦枭(xiāo)、鸱(chī)：恶声之鸟，比喻恶之人。

维厉之阶。	祸乱都从她那生。	Will turn everything foul.
乱匪降自天，	祸乱不会从天降，	Disaster comes not from the sky
生自妇人。	大都生于妇人上。	But from a woman fair.
匪教匪诲，	无人教王行暴政，	You can't teach nor rely
时维妇寺①。	女人内侍全都听。	On woman and eunuch for e'er.
鞫②人忮忒③，	专门诬告陷害人，	They slander, cheat and bluff,
谮始竟背。	先去诽谤后背弃。	Tell lies before and behind.
岂曰不极，	难道她还不够凶，	Is it not bad enough?
伊胡为慝④？	为啥继续做恶事？	How can you love a woman unkind?
如贾三倍，	好比商人三倍利，	They are like men of trade
君子是识。	叫他参政岂相宜？	For whom wise men won't care.
妇无公事⑤，	妇人不去做女工，	Wise women are not made
休其蚕织。	她却不肯蚕与织。	For State but household affair.
天何以刺？	上天为何来责罚？	Why does Heaven's blame to you go?
何神不富⑥？	神明为何不赐福？	Why won't gods bless your State?
舍尔介狄⑦，	放纵披甲夷与狄，	You neglect your great foe
维予胥忌；	反而把我来怨恨。	And regard me with hate.
不吊⑧不祥，	天灾人祸不忧虑，	For omens you don't care;
威仪不类。	人君威仪都丧亡。	Good men are not employed.
人之云亡，	忠臣贤士都离去，	You've no dignified air;
邦国殄瘁⑨。	国家危困更遭殃。	The State will be destroyed.

---

① 寺：寺人，阉人。② 鞫(jū)人：奸人。③ 忮忒(zhìtè)：害人。④ 慝(tè)：恶迹。
⑤ 公事：即功事，指女子蚕织之事。⑥ 富：通"福"，施恩德。⑦ 介狄：元凶。指侵犯中国的夷狄。⑧ 吊：闵，体恤。⑨ 殄瘁(tiǎncuì)：困苦不堪。

天之降罔①，	上天降下罪恶网，	Heaven extends its sway
维其优矣。	牢不可破不可防。	Over our weal and woe.
人之云亡，	忠臣贤士都离去，	Good men have gone away;
心之忧矣。	我的心里多忧伤。	My heart feels sorrow grow.
天之降罔，	上天降下无情网，	Heaven extends its sway
维其几②矣。	灾难降临人心慌。	O'er good and evil deeds.
人之云亡，	忠臣贤士都逃亡，	Good men have gone away;
心之悲矣。	我的心里多悲凉。	My heart feels sad and bleeds.
觱沸③槛泉④，	槛泉泉水涌不息，	The bubbling waters show
维其深矣。	泉水源头深无底。	How deep the spring's below.
心之忧矣，	我心忧伤多悲戚，	Alas! the evil sway
宁自今矣？	难道只是从今起？	Begins not from today.
不自我先，	我生之前无灾祸，	Why came it not before
不自我后。	我生之后更没有。	Or after I'm no more?
藐藐昊天，	高远苍茫老天爷，	O boundless Heaven bright,
无不克巩。	约束万物定乾坤。	Nothing is beyond your might.
无忝⑤皇祖，	莫要辱没尊祖先，	Bring to our fathers no disgrace
式救尔后。	更要想到子孙事。	But save our future race!

召 旻　　　　　　　　King You's Times*

旻⑥天疾威，	老天暴虐又疯狂，	Formidable Heaven on high

---

① 罔：通"网"。② 几：危险。③ 觱(bì)沸：泉水喷涌的样子。④ 槛(jiàn)泉：向上涌出的泉水。⑤ 忝(tiǎn)：侮辱。⑥ 旻(mín)天：昊天，天空广大无边。

* The speaker bemoaned the misery and ruin which were going on, showing they were owing to King You's employment of mean and worthless men, and he wished he king would use such ministers as the Duke of Zhao.

天笃降丧。	接连不断降丧亡。	Sends down big famine and disorder.
瘨①我饥馑，	饥馑粮荒遍灾情，	Fugitives wander far and nigh;
民卒流亡。	人民颠沛离家乡。	Disaster spreads as far as the border.
我居圉②卒荒。	疆土荒芜尽苍凉。	

天降罪罟，	老天降下罪恶网，	Heaven sends down its net of crime;
蟊贼内讧。	奸贼内争乱嚷嚷。	Officials fall in civil strife.
昏椓③靡共，	阉宦小人不称职，	Calamitous is the hard time;
溃溃回遹，	昏愦邪僻多放荡，	The State can't lead a peaceful life.
实靖夷我邦。	实在灭亡我家邦。	

皋皋訿訿④，	顽固懒惰又欺骗，	Deceit and slander here and there,
曾不知其玷⑤。	自己不知是污点。	Wrong-doers win the royal grace.
兢兢业业，	言行小心又谨慎，	Restless, cautious and full of care,
孔填不宁，	很久心里不安宁，	We are afraid to lose our place.
我位孔贬。	职位可能还遭贬！	

如彼岁旱，	好比那年有旱象，	As in a year of drought
草不溃茂⑥，	百草不能繁茂畅，	There can be no lush grass,
如彼栖苴⑦。	好比枯草萎又倒。	No withered leaves can sprout.
我相此邦，	我来观察这国家，	This State will perish, alas!
无不溃止。	崩溃混乱要灭亡！	

---

①瘨(diān)：灾害。②居圉(yǔ)：处住。③昏椓(zhuó)：宦官。④訿訿(zǐ zǐ)：诽谤的样子。⑤玷(diàn)：缺点，污点。⑥溃茂：茂盛。⑦苴(chá)：水中浮草。

维昔之富不如时，	昔日富足今日贫，	We had no greater wealth
		In bygone years;
维今之疚①不如兹。	如今时弊更严重。	We're not in better health
		Than our former compeers.
彼疏②斯粺③，	该吃粗粮吃细粮，	They were like paddy fine;
胡不自替？	为啥自己不退让？	We're like coarse rice.
职兄④斯引。	情况严重更发展！	Why not give up your wine
		But indulge in your vice!
池之竭矣，	池塘里面水干竭，	A pool will become dry
不云自频⑤！	岂不起自池塘边。	When no rain falls from the skies;
泉之竭矣，	山里泉流水断绝，	A spring will become dry
不云自中！	岂不起自泉中间。	When no water from below rise.
溥⑥斯害矣，	灾害已经很普遍，	The evil you have done will spread.
职兄⑦斯弘，	情况严重更发展，	Won't it fall on my head?
不烖我躬？	哪能不把我牵连？	
昔先王受命，	从前先王受天命，	In the days of Duke Zhao
有如召公，	贤臣召公掌国政。	Our land ever increased.
日辟国百里，	每天开拓百里地，	Alas! alas! but now
今也日蹙⑧国百里。	如今日损百里地。	Each day our land decreased.
		Men of today, behold!
於乎哀哉！	可悲可叹呜呼哉！	Don't you know anything of old?
维今之人，	如今满朝文武人，	
不尚有旧？	仍有旧日忠良臣？	

---

① 疚(jiù)：贫穷。② 疏：粗米，糙米。③ 粺(bài)：精米，细米。④ 兄(kuàng)：通"况"，更加。⑤ 频：通"濒"，水边。⑥ 溥(pǔ)：遍。⑦ 烖(zāi)：同"灾"。⑧ 蹙(cù)：缩小。

颂

BOOK OF HYMNS

周　颂

Hymns of Zhou

清庙之什

First Decade of Hymns of Zhou

清　庙

King Wen's Temple*

於①穆②清③庙，	啊！深沉清静的宗庙，	Solemn's the temple still;
肃雝显相④。	助祭公侯严肃雍容。	Princes their duties fulfil.
济济⑤多士，	众位执事威仪齐整，	Numerous officers,
秉文之德。	文王德行铭记在心。	Virtuous King Wen's followers,
对越⑥在天，	遥对文王在天之灵，	Worship his soul on high,
骏奔走在庙。	健步如飞奔走在庙庭。	Whom they hurry to glorify.
不⑦显不承，	光大祖德泽被后世，	There are none but revere
无射⑧于人斯！	人民崇敬仰慕无穷。	Tirelessly their ancestor dear.

维天之命

King Wen Deified*

| 维⑨天之命， | 想来天道运行不悖， | Great Heaven goes its way |
| 於穆不已。 | 庄严肃穆永不停歇。 | Without cease and for aye. |

---

① 於(wū)：叹词，相当于"啊"。② 穆：严肃美好的样子。③ 清：清明。清庙，供奉清明有德先祖的宗庙。④ 相：助祭的公侯。⑤ 济济：多而整齐的样子。⑥ 越：于。⑦ 不：同"丕"，发语词。⑧ 射(yì)：无射，无穷无尽。⑨ 维：同"惟"，想的意思。

* This was the first hymn celebrating the reverential manner in which a sacrifice to King Wen (1184-1134 B.C.) was performed.

* This hymn celebrating King Wen's virtue as comparable to that of Heaven was sung when King Cheng performed a sacrifice to his grandfather in 1110 B.C.

於乎不显,	多么显赫啊光明无限,	O King Wen's virtue great
文王之德之纯!	文王的德行真纯正。	Will likewise circulate.
假①以溢②我,	善道仁政令我平静,	His virtue overflows
我其收之。	我们应当好好承继。	And in his descendants grows.
骏惠③我文王,	遵循先祖文王德行,	Whatever King Wen has done
曾孙笃之。	子子孙孙身体力行。	Will profit his grandson.

维 清

King Wen's Statutes*

维清缉熙④,	周朝政治多清明,	The world is clear and bright;
文王之典⑤。	文王真是能征善战。	King Wen's statutes shed light.
肇禋⑥,	祭天征伐由他始,	Begin by sacrificial rite
迄用有成,	直到武王成功业,	And end by victory great.
维周之祯⑦。	真是周朝的吉祥瑞。	God, bless Zhou's State!

烈 文

King Cheng's Inaugural Address*

| 烈文⑧辟公⑨, | 文德双全的众诸侯, | O princes bright and brave |

①假:通"嘉",指仁政。②溢:通"谧",静谧,平静。③骏惠:顺从。④缉熙:光明。⑤典:当指文王用兵打仗之兵法。⑥肇禋(yīn):开始祭天。⑦祯:祥瑞。⑧烈文:有功与德。⑨辟公:指诸侯。

* This was the third hymn appropriate at some sacrifice to King Wen and celebrating his statutes. It was sung to accompany the performance of the dance of King Wen, which consisted in going through a number of bodily movements and evolutions, intending to illustrate the style of fighting introduced by Wen in his various wars.

* This hymn was made on the occasion of King Cheng's accession to the government in 1109 B.C. when he thus addressed the princes who had assisted him in the ancestral temple.

锡①兹祉福。	先王赐与大福祥。	Favored by former kings!
惠②我无③疆，	蒙恩受惠爱无边，	Boundless blessings we have
子孙保之。	子孙永保福无穷。	Will pass to our offsprings.
无封靡④于尔邦，	别让你国有大罪，	Don't sin against your State
维王其崇⑤之。	我王对你才敬重。	And you'll be honored as before.
念兹戎功，	想起先祖的大功劳，	Think of your service great
继序⑥其皇之；	继承发扬更光大。	You may enlarge still more.
无竞⑦维人，	得到贤人最重要，	Try to employ wise men,
四方其训⑧之。	四方悦服竟归顺。	Your influence will spread from land to land.
不显维德，	先王德行昭明，	Try to practise virtue then
百辟其刑之。	诸侯竞相模仿成风。	Your good example will forever stand.
於乎！前王不忘。	啊！先王的功德铭记传颂！	O of all things, Forget not former kings!

天　作　　　　　　　　　Mount Qi*

天作⑨高山⑩，	巍峨岐山浑然天成，	Heaven made lofty hill

---

① 锡：通"赐"，赏赐。② 惠：爱。③ 无：毋。④ 封靡，大罪过。⑤ 崇：尊敬。⑥ 继序：继承。⑦ 无竞：不刚强，意为恭谦有礼。⑧ 训：通"顺"。⑨ 作：生的意思。⑩ 高山：指岐山。

* This hymn was appropriate to a sacrifice to King Tai who labored the land at the foot of Mount Qi (Poem "The Rise of Zhou").

大王荒①之。	大王拓展疆土苦心经营。	For former kings to till.
彼作矣,	大王开创沃野千亩,	King Tai worked the land
文王康②之。	文王安抚百姓安康。	For King Wen to expand.
彼徂③矣,	率领众民聚集岐山,	The former kings are gone;
岐有夷④之行⑤,	岐山的道路平又广。	The mountain path is good to travel on.
子孙保之。	子孙永葆世代盛昌。	O ye son and grandson, Pursue what your forefathers have begun!

昊天有成命　　　　　King Cheng's Hymn*

昊天⑥有成命,	苍天早已有命令,	By great Heaven's decrees
二后⑦受之。	文王武王受命为君主。	Two kings with power were blessed,
成王不敢康,	成王不敢贪图安逸,	King Cheng dare not live at ease
夙夜基⑧命宥⑨密⑩。	日夜勤敬治国安邦。	But day and night does his best
於缉熙,	文武事业更光明,	To rule the State in peace
单⑪厥心,	忠诚之心治国,	And pacify east and west.
肆⑫其靖之!	天下一定能太平。	

---

① 荒:扩大治理的意思。② 康:使安乐,使安康。③ 徂:到,去。④ 夷:平坦。⑤ 行(háng):道路。⑥ 昊天:指苍天;成命,明确的命令。⑦ 后:君王。二后,指文王、武王。⑧ 基:谋。命,政令。⑨ 宥:语助词。⑩ 密:勤勉。⑪ 单:忠诚。⑫ 肆:巩固。

* This hymn was appropriate to a sacrifice to King Cheng (reigned 1109-1076B. G.), son of King Wu and grandson of King Wen.

我 将　　　　　King Wu's Sacrificial Hymn*

我将①我享②，	我把烹好的祭品献上，	I offer sacrifice
维羊维牛，	既有牛来又有羊，	Of ram and bull so nice.
维天其右③。	希望上帝保佑交好运。	May Heaven bless my State!
仪式④刑⑤文王之典，	效法文王的制度典章，	I observe King Wen's statutes great;
日靖⑥四方。	每日谋划安定四方。	I'll pacify the land.
伊嘏⑦文王，	伟大圣明周文王，	O King Wen grand!
既右飨之。	享受祭祀神灵来到。	Come down and eat, I pray.
我其夙夜，	我将日夜勤国政，	Do I not night and day
畏天之威，	崇敬上帝威灵循天道，	Revere Almighty Heaven?
于时⑧保之。	保证国家的太平功告成。	May your favor to me be given!

时 迈　　　　　King Wu's Progress*

| 时⑨迈⑩其邦， | 出发巡视诸侯国， | A progress through the State is done. |

---

① 将：奉献。② 享：祭祀。③ 右：佑。④ 仪式：法度。⑤ 刑：效法。⑥ 靖：安定。⑦ 嘏(jiǎ)：伟大。⑧ 于时：于是。⑨ 时：语气助词。⑩ 迈：行，指巡视，视察。

* This hymn was appropriate to a sacrifice to King Wen in the hall of audience where King Wu assembled all the princes to undertake an expedition against the last king of Shang in 1121 B. C.

* This hymn was appropriate to King Wu's sacrifice to Heaven and to the Spirits of the Mountains and Rivers on a progress through the kingdom after the overthrow of the Shang dynasty in 1121 B. C.

昊天其子之，　上帝视我为子嗣，　　O Heaven, bless your son!
实右①序②有周。保佑周朝国运昌。　　O bless the Zhou House up and
　　　　　　　　　　　　　　　　　　　　　　down!

薄言震之，　　刚刚出兵讨伐纣王，　　Our victory is so great
莫不震叠③。　天下诸侯莫不惊慌。　　That it shakes State on State.
怀柔④百神，　祭祀四方山川神灵，　　We revere gods for ever
及河乔岳⑤。　遍及大河与高山。　　　Of mountain and of river.
允⑥王维后。　武王实昭彰后世的　　　Our king is worthy of the crown.
　　　　　　　好君王！
明昭有周，　　大周德行光明照四方，Zhou's House is bright and full
　　　　　　　　　　　　　　　　　　　of grace：
式⑦序在位。　百官都贤良忠诚。　　　Each lord is in his proper place,
载戢⑧干戈，　收起干戈，　　　　　　With spears and shields stored
　　　　　　　　　　　　　　　　　　　up in rows,
载櫜⑨弓矢。　装好弓箭。　　　　　　And in their cases arrows and
　　　　　　　　　　　　　　　　　　　bows.
我求懿德⑩，　前去访求有德之士，　　The king will do his best
肆⑪于时夏。　遍施善政天下四方，　　To rule the kingdom east and
　　　　　　　　　　　　　　　　　　　west.
允王保之。　　周王定能保土封疆。　　O may our king be blessed!

---

① 右：同"佑"。② 序：助。③ 叠：通"慑"，惊惧。④ 怀柔：安抚、取悦。⑤ 乔岳：高山。
⑥ 允：确实。⑦ 式：发语词。⑧ 戢（jí）：收藏。⑨ 櫜（gāo）：盛弓矢的袋子。⑩ 懿德：
有美德的人。⑪ 肆：实行。

执 竞　　　　　Kings Cheng and Kang*

执①竞武王，	武王制服强暴，	King Wu was full of might;
无竞②维烈③。	功业举世无双。	He built a career bright.
不显成康④，	成康二王赫显，	God gives Cheng and Kang charge
上帝是皇⑤。	上帝赞扬更嘉赏。	This glory to enlarge.
自彼成康，	始自成，康时代，	Kings Cheng and Kang are blessed
奄有四方，	一统天下拥四方，	To rule from east to west.
斤斤⑥其明。	英明洞察锐目光！	How splendid is their reign!
钟鼓喤喤，	鸣钟擂鼓喤喤响，	Hear drums' and bells' refrain.
磬筦⑦将将⑧，	击磬吹管声铿锵，	Hear stones and flutes resound.
降福穰穰⑨。	上天为你多福降。	With blessings we are crowned.
降福简简，	鸿福大无边，	Blessings come to our side;
威仪反反⑩，	祭礼多端庄。	Our lords look dignified.
既醉既饱，	神灵酒足饭饱后，	We are drunk and well fed;
福禄来反。	再降福禄予武王。	Blessings come on our head.

思 文　　　　　Hymn to the Lord of Corn*

思⑪文⑫后稷，	先王后稷有文德，	O Lord of Corn so bright,

---

①执：制服。②竞：强暴，这里指商纣王。③烈：功业。④成康：成就安定的局面。⑤皇：嘉赏。⑥斤斤：精明的样子。⑦筦(guǎn)：同"管"，一种竹制乐器。⑧将将(qiāngqiāng)：同"锵锵"。⑨穰穰(rǎngrǎng)：众多的样子。⑩反反：慎重的样子。⑪思：语气助词。⑫文：文德，指建设国内的功德，与"武功"相对。

* This hymn was appropriate to a sacrifice to Kings Wu, Cheng and Kang.

克①配彼天。 功德堪比天。 You're at God's left or right.
立②我烝民， 养育我们众百姓， You gave people grain-food;
莫匪尔极③。 人人受您的恩惠。 None could do us more good.
贻我来牟④， 留给我们大麦小麦， God makes us live and eat;
帝命率⑤育。 天命养育人民。 You told us to plant wheat,
无此疆尔界， 农政不再分疆界， Not to define our border
陈常⑥于时夏。 全国上下都施行。 But to live in good order.

---

① 克：能。② 立：养育。烝民，百姓。③ 极：最，极大的恩惠。④ 来牟(móu)：小麦和大麦。⑤ 率：用。⑥ 常：农政。

* This hymn was appropriate to the border sacrifice when Hou Ji, the Lord of Corn, was worshipped as the correlate of God (Poem "Hou Ji, the Lord of Corn").

臣工之什

Second Decade of Hymns of Zhou

臣 工

Husbandry*

嗟嗟①臣工②，	群臣百官啊，	Ah! ye ministers dear,
敬尔在公。	公事需努力。	Attend to duties here.
王釐③尔成，	周王赐你耕作法，	The king's set down the rule,
来④咨⑤来茹⑥。	你要细致钻研。	You should know to the full.
嗟嗟保介⑦，	农官田官啊，	Ah! ye officers dear,
维⑧莫⑨之春，	暮春正要抓紧农事。	It is now late spring here.
亦又何求？	你们还有啥要求？	What do you seek to do?
如何新畬⑩？	生田熟田怎么种？	Tend the fields old and new.
於⑪皇⑫来牟，	麦种壮实多肥美，	Wheat grows lush in the field.
将受厥⑬明。	收成一定会很好。	What an enormous yield!
明⑭昭上帝，	光明伟大的上帝，	Ah! Heaven bright and clear
迄⑮用康年。	请赐我们丰收年。	Will give us a good year.
命我众人，	命令我的农夫们，	Men, get ready to wield
庤⑯乃钱⑰镈⑱，	备全锄头和铁锹，	Your sickles, spuds and hoes

---

① 嗟嗟：发语词。② 臣工：大臣、官员。③ 釐：通"赉"，赐予。④ 来：是。⑤ 咨：商量，询问。⑥ 茹：忖度。⑦ 保介：田官。⑧ 维：是。⑨ 莫：同"暮"。⑩ 畬(yú)：开垦了三年的熟田。⑪ 於：赞叹词。⑫ 皇：美好。⑬ 厥：其、它的。⑭ 明：收成。⑮ 迄：至。⑯ 庤(zhì)：准备。⑰ 钱(jiǎn)：铁锹。⑱ 镈(bó)：锄头。

* This was instructions given to the officers of husbandry, probably after the sacrifice in spring for a good year.

奄①观铚②艾。 收割就要开始了。 And reap harvest in rows.

噫 嘻

King Kang's Prayer*

噫嘻③成王！ 周王祈祷唤苍天， O King Cheng in the sky,
既昭④假⑤尔。 一片虔诚达上苍。 Please come down from on high.
率时⑥农夫， 率领农夫们下地， See us lead the campaign
播厥百谷。 安排播种百谷。 To sow all kinds of grain,
骏⑦发⑧尔私⑨， 迅速开发私田， And till our fields with glee
终三十里。 三十里地都种遍。 All over thirty li!
亦服⑩尔耕， 大家一起来耕作， Ten thousand men in pairs
十千维耦⑪。 万人耦耕在田间。 Plough the land with the shares.

振 鹭

The Guest Assisting at Sacrifice*

振⑫鹭于飞， 一群白鹭展翅翔， Rows of egrets in flight
于彼西雝⑬。 正在西边大泽上。 Over the marsh in the west.
我客戾⑭止， 我有贵客光临， Like those birds dressed in white,
亦有斯容⑮。 他也仪容高洁。 Here comes our noble guest.

---

① 奄：同。② 铚(zhì)艾：收割。③ 噫嘻：祈祷天神的呼喊声。④ 昭：表明。⑤ 假：达、至。⑥ 时：是，此。⑦ 骏：迅速。⑧ 发：开发。⑨ 私：私田。⑩ 服：从事。⑪ 耦(ǒu)：二人并耕的耕作方法。⑫ 振：群飞的样子。⑬ 雝(yōng)：水泽。⑭ 戾(lì)：至。⑮ 斯容：好仪容。

* This hymn was said to be King Kang's prayer to King Cheng for a good year.

* This hymn celebrated the representative of the former dynasty who had come to court to assist at sacrifice. It might have been sung when the king was dismissing the guest in the ancestral temple.

在彼无恶，	他在本国无人怨，	He's loved in his own State;
在此无斁①。	来到我邦受敬仰。	He is welcome in ours.
庶几夙夜，	望你日夜勤勉国事，	Be it early or late,
以永终②誉。	美名长存天下颂扬。	His fame for ever towers.

丰 年   Thanksgiving*

丰年多黍多稻③，	丰年黍米稻谷多，	Millet and rice abound this year;
亦有高廪④，	粮仓高大全装满，	High granaries stand far and near.
万亿⑤及秭⑥。	成万成亿真不少。	There are millions of measures fine;
为酒为醴，	酿成醇酒和甜酒，	We make from them spirits and wine
烝畀⑦祖妣。	进献先妣与先考。	And offer them to ancestors dear.
以洽⑧百礼，	配合各种祭品，	Then we perform all kinds of rite
降福孔皆。	普降恩泽福星照。	And call down blessings from Heaven bright.

有 瞽   Temple Music*

| 有瞽⑨有瞽， | 盲乐师啊盲乐师， | Musicians blind, musicians blind, |

① 无斁(yì)：没有人讨厌。② 终：众。③ 稻(tú)：稻谷。④ 廪(lǐn)：粮仓。⑤ 亿：周代十万为亿。⑥ 秭(zǐ)：数量名，一万亿为一秭。⑦ 畀(bì)：给予。⑧ 洽：配合。⑨ 瞽：盲乐官。

* This ode of thanksgiving for a plentiful year was used at the sacrifice in autumn and winter.

* This hymn was made on the occasion of the Duke of Zhou's completing his instruments of music and announcing the fact in a grand performance in the temple of King Wen.

在周之庭。	排列周庙大庭上。	Come to the temple court behind.
设业①设虡②,	钟鼓架子都摆好,	The plume-adorned posts stand
崇牙③树羽④。	架上饰有彩羽毛。	With teeth-like frames used by the band;
应田县鼓⑤,	小鼓大鼓与悬鼓,	From them suspend drums large and small,
鞉⑥磬⑦柷⑧圉⑨。	鞉磬柷圉列成道。	And sounding stones withal.
既备乃奏,	乐器齐备始演奏,	Music is played when all's complete;
箫管备举。	笛箫齐鸣音缭绕。	We hear pan-pipe, flute and drumbeat.
喤喤厥声,	乐音交响又洪亮,	What sacred melody
肃雝和鸣,	徐缓肃穆声美妙,	And solemn harmony!
先祖是听。	先祖神灵同欣赏,	Dear ancestors, give ear;
我客戾止,	诸位贵宾也光临,	Dear visitors, come here!
永观厥成。	欣赏佳音久绕梁。	You will enjoy our song And wish it to last long.

---

① 业:悬挂钟、磬的木架横梁上的锯齿状大板。② 虡(jù):悬挂钟、磬的木架。③ 崇牙:业上用来悬挂乐器的木钉。④ 树羽:崇牙上装饰的五彩羽毛。⑤ 应田县鼓:各种各样的鼓,县,通"悬"。⑥ 鞉(táo):摇鼓。⑦ 磬:玉石制的古代打击乐器。⑧ 柷(zhú):木质漆桶状的打击乐器,击柷表示音乐的开始。⑨ 圉(yǔ):古击乐器,状如伏虎,背上有二十七锯齿,以木尺划之发声,击圉表示音乐的结束。

潜　　　　　　　　　　Sacrifice of Fish*

猗与①漆沮②，	漆水沮水景秀美啊，	In Rivers Ju and Qi
潜③有多鱼；	鱼儿深藏在水里。	Fish in warrens we see.
有鳣④有鲔⑤，	有黄鱼也有鲟鱼，	There're sturgeos large and small,
鲦⑥鲿⑦鰋⑧鲤。	还有鲿鲦、鲇和鲤。	Mudfish, carp we enthral
以享以祀，	用来供奉祖先，	For temple sacrifice
以介景福。	求降鸿福无边。	That we may be blessed twice.

雝　　　　　　　　　King Wu's Prayer to King Wen

有来雍雍⑨，	来时雍容和睦，	We come in harmony；
至止肃肃⑩。	到此恭敬严肃。	We stop in gravity,
相⑪维辟公，	诸侯公卿助祭，	The princes at the side
天子穆穆。	天子仪容端庄。	Of the king dignified.
於荐⑫广牡，	进献肥美牲畜，	"I present this bull nice
相予肆祀⑬。	帮我摆陈祭品。	And set forth sacrifice

---

① 猗与：感叹词。② 漆、沮(jū)：周代的两条河。③ 潜：深藏。④ 鳣(shān)：鲤鱼。
⑤ 鲔(wěi)：鲟鱼。⑥ 鲦(tiáo)：白条鱼。⑦ 鲿(cháng)：黄颊鱼。⑧ 鰋(yǎn)：鲇鱼。
⑨ 雍雍：和睦庄重的样子。⑩ 肃肃：严肃恭敬的样子。⑪ 相：助祭。辟公，诸侯。
⑫ 荐：献祭。广牡，肥壮的公畜。⑬ 肆祀：陈设祭品。

* This hymn was sung in the last month of winter and in spring when the king presented a fish in the ancestral temple as an act of duty and an acknowledgement that it was to his ancestors favor that the king and the people were indebted for the supplies of food which they received from the waters.

* This prayer was said to be appropriate at a sacrifice by King Wu to his father Wen.

| 假①哉皇考②！ | 伟大光荣的先王， | To royal father great. |
| 绥③予孝子。 | 保佑我这个孝子。 | Bless your filial son and his State! |

宣哲④维人，	百官智慧通达，	"You're a sage we adore,
文武维后。	君王文韬武略。	A king in peace and war.
燕⑤及皇天，	上天保佑周朝安宁，	O give prosperity
克昌厥后。	子孙后代繁荣盛昌。	To Heaven and posterity!

绥我眉寿⑥，	赐我平安长寿，	"Bless me with a life long,
介以繁祉⑦。	佑我福禄无疆。	With a State rich and strong!
既右⑧烈考，	既请先父受祭享，	I pray to father I revere
亦右文母⑨。	又请先母来品尝。	And to my mother dear."

载 见

King Cheng's Sacrifice to King Wu*

载⑩见辟王，	诸侯开始来朝周王，	The lords appear before the king
曰求厥章⑪。	考求车服之类典章。	To learn the rules he ordains.
龙旂阳阳，	龙纹旗帜多么明亮，	The dragon flags are bright
和铃央央。	车上的铃儿响叮当。	And the carriage bells ring.
鞗⑫革有鸧⑬，	辔头装饰金碧辉煌，	Glitter the golden reins,
休有烈光。	华丽美好闪耀光芒。	His splendor at its height.

---

① 假：美、嘉。② 皇考：指文王，是武王对去世父亲的美称。③ 绥：安抚。④ 宣哲：聪明智慧。⑤ 燕：安。⑥ 眉寿：长寿。⑦ 繁祉：多福。⑧ 右：通"侑"，劝侑。⑨ 文母：文王的妻子大姒。⑩ 载：初始。⑪ 章：泛指关于车、服装方面的典章制度。⑫ 鞗(tiáo)革：马缰绳。⑬ 有鸧(qiāng)：形容车马缰绳上的金饰非常艳丽。

* This hymn was appropriate to an occasion when the feudal princes were assisting King Cheng at a sacrifice to King Wu in 1113 B. C.

率见昭考①，	率领众人祭奠武王，	The filial king leads the throng
以孝以享。	敬献祭品虔行祭享。	Before his father's shrine.
以介眉寿，	祈求赐予年寿绵长，	He prays to be granted life long
永言保之。	永保子孙得安康。	And to maintain his rights divine.
思皇多祜，	大福大禄又吉祥，	May Heaven bless his State!
烈文辟公。	有功有德众位诸侯。	The princes brave and bright
绥以多福，	神灵多多赐福禄，	Be given favors great
俾缉熙于纯嘏②。	使我前途光明无疆。	That they may serve at left and right.

有　客

Guests at the Sacrifice*

有客有客，	远方有客来我家，	Our guests alight
亦白其马。	驾驭一匹白骏马。	From horses white.
有萋③有且，	随从人员一大群，	Their train is long,
敦琢其旅。	诸位都是品德良好。	A noble throng.

有客宿宿，	客人头夜在此宿，	Stay here one night;
有客信信④。	三天四天一再留。	Fasten their horses tight.
言授之絷，	最好拿条绊马绳，	Stay here three nights or four;
以絷其马。	拴住马脚不让行。	Let no horse leave the door!

---

① 昭考：此处指周武王。② 嘏(gǔ)：福。③ 萋、且(jū)：随从众多的样子。④ 信：住两夜，一宿为宿，再宿为信。

* This ode celebrated the Viscount of Wei on one of his appearances at the capital and assisting at the sacrifice in the ancestral temple of Zhou. Uncle of the last king of the Shang dynasty, he was made Duke of Song to continue the sacrifices of the House of Shang.

薄言追①之，	客人将去我饯行，	Escort guests on their way;
左右绥之。	文武百官同相送。	Say left and right, "Good day!"
既有淫威，	客人既已受款待，	Say "Good day" left and right
降福孔夷。	请神赐予更大福。	Till day turns into night.

武

Hymn to King Wu Great and Bright*

於皇武王，	多么伟大的周武王啊，	O King Wu great and bright,
无竞维烈。	丰功伟业举世无双。	Matchless in main and might.
允文文王，	文德显著周文王，	King Wen beyond compare
克开厥后。	万代的基业他开创。	Opened the way for his heir.
嗣武受之，	武王继成受天命，	King Wu after his Sire
胜殷遏刘②，	制止杀戮胜殷商，	Quelled Yin's tyrannic fire.
耆③定尔功。	巩固政权绩辉煌。	His fame grows higher and higher.

---

① 追：饯行，送别。② 刘：杀，征伐。③ 耆(zhǐ)：致使；达到。
* This hymn was sung in the ancestral temple to the music regulating the dance in honor of the achievements of King Wu.

闵予小子之什

Third Decade of Hymns of Zhou

闵予小子

Elegy on King Wu*

闵①予小子，	可怜我年纪轻轻，
遭家不造②，	竟遭丧父真不幸，
嬛嬛③在疚④。	孤苦无依忧心忡，
於乎皇考，	称赞伟大先父周武王，
永世克孝。	终生能把孝道行。
念兹皇祖，	追念我的祖父周文王，
陟降⑤庭止。	任用臣子无私公正。
维予小子，	想我嗣位年纪轻，
夙夜敬止。	日夜勤政应恭敬。
於乎皇王，	文王武王请放心，
继序⑥思不忘。	继承大业永铭记。

Alas! how sad am I!
Over my deceased father I cry.
Lonely, I'm in distress
To lose my father whom gods bless.
Filial all your life long,
You loved grandfather strong
As if he were ever in courtyard.
Fatherless, I am thinking hard
Of you both night and day.
O kings to be remembered for aye!

访落

King Cheng's Ascension to the Throne*

访⑦予落止，　执政之初认真谋划，

I take counsel on early days:

---

① 闵：通"悯"，怜悯。② 不造：不幸，不详。③ 嬛嬛(qióngqióng)：孤独无依。④ 疚(jiù)：忧伤，痛苦。⑤ 陟降：上下，即提升或降级的意思。⑥ 序：绪,事业。⑦ 访：谋划、商讨。

* This elegy was appropriate to the young King Cheng, declaring his sentiments in the temple of his father.

* This seemed to be a sequel to the former hymn. The young king told of his difficulties and incompetences, asked for counsel to help to follow the example of his father, stated how he meaned to do so and concluded with an appeal to King Wu.

率①时昭考。	要遵循武王行德政。	How to follow my father's ways?
於乎悠哉!	任务重大道路远啊，	Ah! but he is far above me
朕未有艾②。	少有经验无甚才。	And to reach him I am not free.
将予就之③，	帮我实行先王的章法，	Please help me to get to his side,
继犹判涣④。	继续谋求大业成。	To learn on what I should decide.
维予小子，	想我如今年纪轻，	I am a young king not so great
未堪家多难。	家国多难担承不起。	To shoulder hard tasks of the State.
绍⑤庭上下，	先父遵循先人法度，	I will follow him up and down,
陟降厥家。	用人得当国家安宁。	Take counsel to secure the crown.
休⑥矣皇考，	武王神灵真英明，	Rest in peace, royal father dear,
以保明⑦其身。	保佑我身得安宁。	O help me to be bright and clear!

敬 之　　　　　King Cheng's Consultation*

敬⑧之敬之!	为人处世小心谨慎，	Be reverent, be reverent!
天维显思。	天理昭昭最显明。	The Heaven's way is evident.
命不易哉!	保持国运真困难，	Do not let its favor pass by
无曰高高在上。	莫言苍天高在上。	Nor say Heaven's remote on high.

---

① 率：遵循。② 艾：阅历。③ 将予就之：指将遵循先人的法典。④ 判涣：分散，使广大。⑤ 绍：继承。⑥ 休：美。⑦ 明：勉励。⑧ 敬：警戒。

* This dialogue might be a portion of the consultation which took place in the temple between King Cheng and his ministers. The first half was the admonition of the ministers and the second the reply of the king.

陟降厥士①，	任用群臣要顺应天意，	It rules over our rise and fall
日监在兹。	每日监视这下边。	And daily watches over all."
维予小子，	想我年轻人刚刚即位	"I am a young king of our State,
不聪②敬止。	敢不听从不恭敬？	But I will show reverence great.
日就③月将④，	日积月累时常学习，	As sun and moon shine day and night,
学有缉熙于光明。	学问积渐向光明。	I will learn to be fair and bright.
佛⑤时⑥仔肩，	群臣辅我担大任，	Assist me to fulfill my duty
示我显德行。	告诉我治国的美德。	And show me high virtue and beauty!"

小 毖⑦　　　　　　King Cheng's Self-Criticism*

予其惩⑧，	我要惩前毖后，	I blame myself for woes gone by
而毖后患。	却无人给我指引。	And guard against those of future nigh.
莫予荓⑨蜂，	无人扯我去往哪里，	A wasp is a dangerous thing.
自求辛螫⑩。	真是自寻苦辛劳。	Why should I seek its painful sting?
肇允彼桃虫⑪，	开始以为小鷦鷯，	At first only a wren is heard;

---

① 士：通"事"。② 聪：听。③ 就：久。④ 将：长。⑤ 佛(bì)：通"弼"，辅助。⑥ 时：是。仔肩，责任。⑦ 毖(bì)：谨慎。⑧ 惩(chéng)：警戒。成语"惩前毖后"即源于此。⑨ 荓(píng)蜂：牵引扶住的意思。⑩ 螫(shì)：勤劳。⑪ 桃虫：一种极小的鸟。

* King Cheng acknowledged that he had erred and stated his purpose to be careful in the future; he would guard against the slightest beginning of evil and was penetrated with a sense of his own incompetencies. This piece might be considered as the conclusion of the service in the ancestral temple with which it and the previous three were connected.

拚①飞维鸟。　忽成大鸟飞上天。　When it takes wing, it becomes a bird.

未堪家多难，家国多难受不了，　Unequal to hard tasks of the State,

予又集于蓼②。陷入困境更难堪。　I am again in a narrow strait.

载 芟

Cultivation of the Ground*

载芟③载柞④，开始除草又除杂树，　The grass and hushes cleared away,

其耕泽泽⑤。接着用力耕田松土。　The ground is ploughed at break of day.

千耦⑥其耘⑦，成千上万农夫锄草，　A thousand pairs weed, hoe in hand;

徂隰⑧徂畛⑨。走向洼地的小路。　They toil in old or new-tilled land.

侯⑩主⑪侯伯⑫，田主带着长子，　The master comes with all his sons,

侯亚⑬侯旅⑭，跟着许多子孙晚辈，　The older and the younger ones.

侯彊⑮侯以⑯。壮汉雇工一起劳作。　They are all strong and stout;

有嗿⑰其馌⑱，送饭的人说说笑笑，　At noon they take meals out.

---

① 拚(fān)：通"翻"，翻飞。② 蓼(liǎo)：水草名,其味苦辣。③ 芟(shān)：锄草。④ 柞(zé)：砍伐树木。⑤ 泽泽(shìshì)：土松散的样子。⑥ 耦：二人并耕。⑦ 耘：去田间的草。⑧ 隰(xí)：低湿的田地,即指田地所在。⑨ 畛(zhěn)：田边的小路。⑩ 侯：语气助词。⑪ 主：家长。⑫ 伯：长子。⑬ 亚：长子以次的诸子。⑭ 旅：众,指晚辈。⑮ 彊：指强壮有力的人。⑯ 以：用或干。⑰ 嗿(tǎn)：众饮食的声音。⑱ 馌(yè)：送到田间的饭。

* This piece was an accompaniment of some royal sacrifice.

思①媚②其妇，	妇女个个样貌美好。	They love their women fair
有依③其士④。	男子个个干劲旺盛。	Who take of them good care.
有略⑤其耜⑥，	犁锹雪亮锋利。	With the sharp plough they wield,
俶载南亩。	开始耕种南面土地。	They break the southern field.
播厥百谷，	各种禾谷播种下去。	All kinds of grain they sow
实函⑦斯活⑧。	粒粒种子饱含生气，	Burst into life and grow,
驿驿其达，	苗儿不断冒出来。	Young shoots without end rise;
有厌⑨其杰⑩，	杰出的苗儿特美，	The longest strike the eyes.
厌厌其苗，	一般的整整齐齐。	The grain grows lush here and there;
绵绵⑪其麃⑫。	稻穗连绵颗粒饱满，	The toilers weed with care.
载获济济，	开始收获硕果累累，	The reapers come around;
有实⑬其积⑭，	场上粮食堆积如山，	The grain's piled up aground.
万亿及秭⑮。	算来有千亿万亿。	There're millions of stacks fine
为酒为醴⑯，	用来酿造醇和美酒，	To be made food or wine
烝⑰畀祖妣，	将它们进献给先祖，	For our ancestors' shrine
以洽⑱百礼。	供应各种祭礼。	And for the rites divine.
有飶⑲其香，	祭筵酒气芬芳，	The delicious food
邦家之光。	邦国光大家庭昌盛。	Is glory of kinghood.
有椒其馨，	醇和的甜酒真芬芳，	The fragrant wine, behold!
胡考⑳之宁。	老人长寿享安康。	Gives comfort to the old.

---

①思：语助词。②媚：美好。③依：通"殷"，壮盛的样子。④士：指在田中耕作的男子。⑤略：锋利。⑥耜(sì)：农具名，犁头，用来插地起土。⑦函：含藏。⑧活：有生气的样子。⑨厌：美好的样子。⑩杰：先长特出的苗。⑪绵绵：连绵不断的样子。⑫麃(biāo)：禾苗的末梢。⑬实：满。⑭积：在露天堆积粮谷。⑮秭(zǐ)：万亿。⑯醴：甜酒。⑰烝(zhēng)：进。⑱洽：合。百礼，各种祭礼。⑲飶(bì)：本字为"苾"，芬芳。⑳考：寿考。

匪且①有且，	如此繁荣超过期望，	We reap not only here
匪今斯今，	丰收并非破天荒，	But always in good cheer.
振②古如兹。	自古就有这般景象。	We reap not only for today
		But always in our fathers' way.

良 耜

Hymn of Thanksgiving *

畟畟③良耜，	犁头雪亮又锋利，	Sharp are plough-shares we wield;
俶载南亩。	先耕南边田地。	We plough the southern field.
播厥百谷，	播下多种禾谷，	All kinds of grain we sow
实函斯活。	颗颗饱含生气。	Burst into life and grow.
或来瞻女，	有人前来看望，	Our wives come to the ground
载筐及筥④，	拿着方篓圆筐，	With baskets square ahd round
其饟⑤伊黍。	送来米饭热气腾。	Of millet and steamed bread,
其笠伊纠，	头戴编织的斗笠，	With straw-hat on the head.
其镈⑥斯赵，	挥动锄头齐心协力，	We weed with hoe in hand
以薅⑦荼蓼⑧。	薅除杂草田亩清理。	On the dry and wet land.
荼蓼朽止，	杂草烂掉在田地，	When weeds fall in decay,
黍稷茂止。	庄稼长得真茂密。	Luxuriant millets sway.
获之挃挃⑨，	挥动镰刀刷刷响，	When millets rustling fall,

①且(zū)：此，指丰收。②振：起。③畟畟(cècè)：形容器物的锋利。④筥(jǔ)：圆形的竹筐。⑤饟(xiǎng)："饷"的异体字，将食物给人叫做"饷"。⑥镈(bó)：农具名，锄头，用来除草。⑦薅(hāo)：拔除田草为薅。⑧荼、蓼：两种野草。⑨挃挃(zhìzhì)：割取禾穗的声音。

* This hymn was made for the thanksgiving to the spirits of the land and the grain in autumn and it was proper therefore that it should set forth the beginning and the end of the labors of husbandry.

积之栗栗①，	场上粮食高堆积。	We reap and pile them up all
其崇如墉，	堆得城墙一般高，	High and thick as a wall.
其比②如栉③，	堆得梳篦一般密，	Like comb teeth stacks are close;
以开百室④。	成千上百仓开启。	Stores are opened in rows.
百室盈止，	仓屋全部都装满，	Wives and children repose
妇子宁止。	妇女儿童得休息。	When all the stores are full.
杀时犉⑤牡，	宰牛献到祭坛，	We kill a tawny bull,
有捄⑥其角。	牛角向上弯弯。	Whose horns crooked appear.
以似以续，	祭祀社稷之神，	We follow fathers dear
续古之人。	永远继承先人传统。	To perform rites with cheer.

丝 衣   Supplementary Sacrifice*

丝衣其紑⑦，	身着丝衣洁净鲜明，	In silken robes clean and bright,
载弁俅俅。	头戴皮帽美丽端正。	In temple caps for the rite,
自堂徂基⑧，	从庙堂一直到门槛，	The officers come from the hall
自羊徂牛。	有着牛羊等做牺牲。	To inspect tripods large and small,
鼐⑨鼎及鼒⑩。	还有大鼎和小鼎。	To see the sheep and oxen down and up

---

① 栗栗：众多的样子。② 比：排列迫近。③ 栉（zhì）：理发用具，梳篦总名。④ 百室：指储藏谷子的仓屋。⑤ 犉（rún）：牛长七尺为犉。⑥ 捄（qiú）：通作"觩"，角上曲而长之貌，形容匕柄的形状。⑦ 紑（fóu）：洁净新鲜的样子。⑧ 基：畿的假借词，门槛。⑨ 鼐（nǎi）：大鼎。⑩ 鼒（zī）：小鼎。

* This piece belonged to the entertainment of the personator of the dead in connection with the supplementary sacrifice on the day after one of the great sacrifices in the ancestral temple.

兕觥其觩。	兕角杯儿弯弯如月，	And rhino horns used as cup,
旨酒思柔。	斟满美酒温柔清醇。	To see if mild is wine,
不吴①不敖，	不敢喧哗不傲慢，	If there is noise before the shrine
胡考之休！	保佑我们都长寿。	In sacrifice to lords divine.

酌

The Martial King*

於②铄③王师，	武王军队战绩辉煌，	The royal army brave and bright
遵养时晦④。	挥兵攻取昏庸纣王。	Was led by King Wu in dark days
时纯熙⑤矣，	一时间普天都得光明，	To overthrow Shang and bring back light
是用大介。	天降恩泽大吉祥。	And establish the Zhou House's sway.
我龙受之，	顺应天意得天下，	Favored by Heaven, I
蹻蹻⑥王之造。	武王功业四海扬。	Succeed the Martial King.
载用有嗣，	后世子孙要铭记，	I'll follow him as nigh
实维尔公⑦允师。	先人是我们好榜样。	As summer follows spring.

---

① 吴：大声喧哗。② 於(wū)：赞美词。③ 铄(shuò)：辉煌的样子。④ 时晦：不利之时。⑤ 纯熙：明亮。⑥ 蹻蹻(jué)：勇武的样子。⑦ 尔公：你的先人。

* This was King Cheng's hymn in praise of King Wu or the Martial King who reigned 1121-1115 B. C. It was made to announce in the temple of King Wu the completion of the dance intended to represent the achievements of the king in the overthrow of the Shang and the establishment of the Zhou dynasty. Poem "Hymn to King Wu" and the three that followed this were also sung in connection with that dance.

桓　　　　　　　　　　Hymn to King Wu*

绥①万邦，	武王平定天下万邦，	All the States pacified,
娄丰年。	年年喜获好收成。	Heaven favors Zhou far and wide,
天命匪解②。	天命在周要久长。	Rich harvest from year to year.
桓桓③武王，	武王英明又威武，	How mighty did king Wu appear
保有厥士。	拥有辽阔的疆域。	With his warriors and cavaliers
于以四方，	于是镇抚四方国，	Guarding his four frontiers
克定厥家。	齐家治国平天下。	And securing his State!
於昭于天，	武王光辉照天上，	Favored by Heaven great,
皇④以间⑤之！	代替殷商享天下。	Zhou replaced Shang by fate.

赉　　　　　　　　　　King Wu's Hymn to King Wen*

文王既勤止，	文王一生太勤劳，	King Wen's career is done;
我应受之。	我当好好来继承。	I will follow him as son,
敷⑥时绎⑦思，	施行政令要三思，	Thinking of him without cease.
我徂⑧维求定。	天下安定是我求。	We have conquered Shang to seek peace.
时周之命。	周王命令须奉行，	O our royal decree

---

① 绥：安定。② 解(xiè)：懈怠。③ 桓桓：威武的样子。④ 皇：君王。⑤ 间(jiàn)：代。
⑥ 敷：布的意思。⑦ 绎：寻绎、不断的意思。⑧ 徂：往的意思。

* This hymn was considered as a portion of the larger piece sung to the dance celebrating the merit and success of King Wu.

* This hymn celebrating the praise of King Wen was said to be the third of the pieces sung to the dance mentioned in the note on Poem "The Martial King".

於①绎思！	文王政令要谨记。	Should be done in high glee.

般

The King's Progress *

於皇时周，	啊，大周的天下多壮丽。	O great is the Zhou State!
陟其高山。	登至那座高山向下望，	I climb up mountains high
堕②山乔岳③，	丘陵峰峦都在眼前，	To see hills undulate
允犹翕④河。	合祭黄河献上美酒。	And two rivers flow by.
敷天之下，	普天之下的神灵，	Gods are worshipped, I see,
裒⑤时之对，	同聚一起齐享受，	Under the boundless sky,
时周之命。	保佑大周国运永昌！	All by royal decree.

---

① 於(wū)：叹辞。② 堕(duò)：狭长的小山。③ 乔岳：高大的山。④ 翕(xì)：合，指合祭。⑤ 裒(póu)：聚集。

* This hymn was said to be the fourth of the six pieces sung to the dance celebrating the greatness of Zhou and its firm possession of the kingdom, as seen in King Wu's progress.

鲁　颂　　Hymns of Lu

駉　　　　　　　　Horses*

駉駉①牡马，	群马雄健又高大，	How sleek and large the horses are
在坰②之野。	放牧远郊和水边。	Upon the plain of borders far!
薄言駉者：	要问良马有几种，	What color are these horses bright?
有驈③有皇，	白胯黑马浅黄马。	Some black and white, some yellow light,
有骊有黄，	骊马纯黑赤马黄，	Some are pure black, others are bay.
以车彭彭④。	驾起车来强有力，	What splendid chariot steeds are they!
思无疆，	鲁公深谋又远虑，	The Duke of Lu has clear fore-sight:
思马斯臧。	马儿优良再无加。	He has prepared his steeds to fight.

駉駉牡马，	群马高大又强壮，	How sleek and large the horses are
在坰之野。	牧放远郊和水边。	Upon the plain of borders far!
薄言駉者：	要问良马有几种，	What color are these horses bright?
有骓⑤有駓⑥，	杂色白马黄白马，	Some piebald, others green and white;
有骍有骐，	骍马青黑赤黄骐，	Some brownish red, others dapple grey.

---

① 駉駉(jiōngjiōng)：马肥壮的样子。② 坰(jiōng)：远。③ 驈(yù)：黑色的马白色的胯。④ 彭彭(bāngbāng)：马强壮有力的样子。⑤ 骓(zhuī)：苍白杂毛的马。⑥ 駓(pī)：黄白杂毛的马。

* This was an ode celebrating Duke Xi of Lu (658-626 B. C.) for his constant and admirable thoughtfulness, especially as seen in the number and quality of his horses.

以车伾伾①。	驾起车来有力气。	What fiery chariot steeds are they!
思无期，	鲁公深谋又远虑，	The Duke of Lu has good fore-sight：
思马斯才。	马儿成才真堪嘉。	He will employ his steeds in fight.

驷驷牡马，	群马雄壮又高大，	How sleek and large the horses are
在坰之野。	放在远郊近山坡。	Upon the plain of borders far!
薄言驷者：	要问良马有几种，	What color are these steeds well-trained?
有骓②有骆，	骓马青黑骆马白，	Some flecked, some white and black-maned,
有骊有雒，	赤色骊马黑色雒，	Some black and white-maned, others red.
以车绎绎③。	驾起车来快如梭。	They are chariot horses well-bred.
思无斁④，	鲁公深谋又远虑，	The Duke of Lu has fine fore-sight：
思马斯作。	马儿振作撒欢跳。	He has bred and trained his steeds to fight.

驷驷牡马，	群马肥壮强有劲，	How sleek and large the horses are
在坰之野。	放牧郊野近山边。	Upon the plain of borders far!
薄言驷者：	要问良马有几种，	What color are these horses bright?
有𬳿⑤有騢⑥，	红白騢马灰白𬳿，	Some cream-like, others red and white；
有驔⑦有鱼⑧，	黄脊驔马白眶驹，	Some white-legged, others fishlike-eyed.

---

①伾伾(pīpī)：有力的样子。②骓(tuó)：青黑色而有白鳞花纹的马。③绎绎(yìyì)：跑得快的样子。④斁(yīn)：厌倦。⑤𬳿(yīn)：浅黑和白色相杂的马。⑥騢(xiá)：赤白杂毛的马。⑦驔(diàn)：黑色黄脊的马。⑧鱼：两眼眶有白圈的马。

以车祛祛①。	驾起车来脚步轻。	They drive war chariots side by side.
思无邪，	鲁公深谋又远虑，	The Duke of Lu has grand fore-sight;
思马斯徂。	马儿俊美能疾行。	He will drive his brave steeds to fight.

有 駜

The Ducal Feast*

有駜②有駜，	马儿肥壮又高大，	Sleek and strong, sleek and strong,
駜彼乘黄。	驾上四匹黄骠马。	Four brown steeds come along.
夙夜在公，	早晚忙碌为国家，	The officers are wise,
在公明明③。	鞠躬尽瘁无闲暇。	Stay late but early rise.
振振④鹭，	一群白鹭飞上天，	Like egrets white
鹭于下。	忽而上升忽而下。	Dancers alight.
鼓咽咽⑤，	鼓儿咚咚不停响，	The drums resound;
醉言舞。	酒醉起舞影婆娑。	Tipsy, they dance aground
于胥乐兮。	大家欢乐笑开颜。	In happiness they are drowned.

有駜有駜，	马儿高大多肥壮，	Sleek and strong, sleek and strong,
駜彼乘牡。	四匹公马气昂昂。	Four stallions come along.
夙夜在公，	早晚忙碌在公堂，	The officers drink wine;
在公饮酒。	公事之余把酒尝。	Early and late they are fine.
振振鹭，	一群白鹭飞上天，	Like egrets white
鹭于飞。	渐展羽翅高高飞。	Dancers in flight.

---

① 祛祛(qūqū)：强健。② 駜(bì)：马肥壮有力的样子。③ 明明：操劳勤勉。④ 振振：鸟群飞的声音。⑤ 咽咽(yīn)：有节奏的鼓声。

* This piece related how Duke Xi of Lu feasted together with his officers and how the officers expressed their good wishes.

鼓咽咽，	鼓儿敲起咚咚响，	The drums resound;
醉言归。	酒醉饭饱人散场。	Drunk, they go round;
于胥乐兮。	大家心里喜洋洋。	In happiness they are drowned.
有驖有驖，	马儿强壮多有劲，	Sleek and strong, sleek and strong,
驖彼乘骃①。	四匹青马真雄壮。	Four grey steeds come along.
夙夜在公，	早晚办事在公堂，	The officers eat food
在公载燕。	公事之余齐举觞。	Early and late they are good.
自今以始，	打从今年开始，	From now and here,
岁其有。	年年都是丰收年。	Abundant be each year!
君子有穀②，	君子有德做善事，	The duke has well done,
诒孙子。	子孙后代永相传。	So will his son and grandson,
于胥乐兮。	大家欢喜笑开颜。	They will be happy everyone.

泮　水　　　　　　　　The Poolside Hall*

思乐泮③水，	泮水之滨喜气洋，	Pleasant is the pool half-round
薄采其芹④。	人在水中采水芹。	Where plants of cress abound.
鲁侯戾止⑤，	鲁侯大驾将光临，	The Marquis of Lu comes nigh;
言观其旂。	只见大旗龙纹影。	His dragon banners fly,
其旂茷茷⑥，	车上旌旗随风展，	His flags wave on the wing
鸾声哕哕。	铃儿叮当响不停。	And his carriage bells ring.

---

① 骃(xuān)：青黑马。② 穀：善，福禄。③ 泮(pàn)水：水名。④ 芹：水菜。⑤ 戾止：到达。⑥ 茷茷(pèipèi)：旗帜飘扬的样子。

* This was an ode in praise of Marquis or Duke Xi of Lu, celebrating his interest in the State college built by the poolside and his exaggerated triumph over the tribes of the Huai, celebrated in the poolside hall.

无小无大，	百官无论大与小，	Officers old and young
从公于①迈。	跟随鲁侯向前行。	Follow him all along.

思乐泮水，	游乐泮水乐陶陶，	Pleasant is the pool half-round
薄采其藻。	人在水中采水藻。	Where water-weeds abound.
鲁侯戾止，	鲁侯大驾已来到，	The Marquis of Lu comes near;
其马蹻蹻②。	马儿强健四蹄骄。	His horses grand appear.
其马蹻蹻，	马儿强健四蹄骄，	His horses appear strong;
其音昭昭③。	随行人儿多热闹。	His carriage bells ring long.
载色④载笑，	鲁侯和颜又悦色，	With smiles and with looks bland,
匪怒伊教。	从不发怒耐心教。	He will instruct and command.

思乐泮水，	游乐泮水乐悠悠，	Pleasant is the pool half-round
薄采其茆⑤。	采摘莼菜忙不休。	Where mallow plants abound.
鲁侯戾止，	鲁侯大驾已来到，	The Marquis pays a call
在泮饮酒。	泮水岸边摆美酒。	And drinks wine in the hall.
既饮旨酒，	美酒已经举杯饮，	After wine, it is foretold,
永锡难老⑥。	祝君长寿年岁久。	"You will never grow old.
顺彼长道⑦，	顺着大道向前走，	If along the way you go,
屈此群丑。	征服叛贼不用愁。	You will overcome the foe."

穆穆鲁侯，	鲁公端庄又威严，	The Marquis' virtue high
敬明其德。	恭敬勤勉振朝纲。	Is well-known far and nigh.
敬慎威仪，	注意威仪有礼貌，	His manner dignified,

---

① 于：往，迈，行。② 蹻蹻(jiāojiāo)：马强壮的样子。③ 昭昭：响亮。④ 色：和颜悦色。
⑤ 茆(mǎo)：即江南的莼菜。⑥ 老：长寿的意思。⑦ 长道：远路。

维民之则。	真是人民好榜样。	He is ever people's guide.
允文允武,	又能文来又能武,	He is bright as well as brave,
昭假①烈祖。	英明能及诸先王。	Worthy son of ancestors grave.
靡有不孝,	遵循祖训无不孝,	He is full of filial love
自求伊祜,	自求福佑保吉祥。	And seeks blessings from above.
明明鲁侯,	鲁公勤勉又努力,	The Marquis of Lu bright
克明其德。	能修品德讲法度。	Sheds his virtuous light.
既作泮宫,	已把泮宫建设好,	He has built the poolside hall;
淮夷攸服。	淮夷人民都归顺。	Huai tribes pay him homage all.
矫矫②虎臣,	将帅英勇如猛虎,	His tiger-like compeers
在泮献馘③。	献敌左耳泮水旁。	Presents the foe's left ears.
淑问④如皋陶,	审讯得法似皋陶,	His judges wisdom show;
在泮献囚。	泮宫献上阶下囚。	They bring the captive foe.
济济多士,	百官济济人才多,	His officers aligned
克广德心。	鲁侯善心得传扬。	With their forces combined
桓桓⑤于征;	三军威武出征去,	Drove in martial array
狄彼东南。	平定东南去祸殃。	Southeastern tribes away.
烝烝皇皇⑥,	声势盛大军容壮,	They came on backward way
不吴不扬。	肃静无哗列队过。	Without noise or display.
不告于讻⑦,	宽待俘虏不穷究,	At poolside hall they show
在泮献功。	泮宫献功赐玉帛。	What they have done with the foe.

---

① 昭假:诚心祭告。② 矫矫(jiǎojiǎo):勇武的样子。③ 馘(guó):割下敌人的左耳以记功。④ 淑问:善于审讯。⑤ 桓桓:威武的样子。⑥ 烝烝皇皇:形容一种盛况。⑦ 讻(xiōng):争辩。

角弓其觩①，	角弓弯弯硬又强，	They notch their arrows long
束矢其搜。	众箭齐发嗖嗖响。	On bows with bone made strong.
戎车孔博②，	战车坚固千百辆，	Their chariots show no fears,
徒御无斁。	战士英勇斗志昂。	With tireless charioteers.
既克淮夷，	淮夷已经被征服，	The tribes of Huai they quell
孔淑不逆。	俯首听命不违抗。	Dare no longer rebel.
式固尔犹③，	坚决执行好计谋，	As the Marquis would have it,
淮夷卒获。	淮夷终于得扫荡。	The tribes of Huai submit.
翩彼飞鸮④，	翩翩飞翔猫头鹰，	The owls flying at ease
集于泮林。	落在泮水岸边林。	Settle on poolside trees.
食我桑黮⑤，	吃了我的紫桑椹，	They eat our mulberries
怀我好音。	为我歌唱有佳音。	And sing sweet melodies.
憬⑥彼淮夷，	如今淮夷有觉悟，	The chief of Huai tribes brings
来献其琛。	献来珍宝表衷心。	All rare and precious things:
元龟象齿，	既有大龟和象牙，	Ivory tusks, tortoise old,
大赂⑦南金。	还有南方珍贵金。	Southern metals and gold.

闷 宫　　　　　Hymn to Marquis of Lu *

闷⑧宫有侐⑨，	姜嫄之庙多静寂，	Solemn the temples stand,

---

① 觩(qiú)：弓弯曲强硬的样子。② 博：多。③ 犹：通"猷"，计谋。④ 鸮(xiāo)：猫头鹰。⑤ 黮(shèn)：通"椹"，桑椹。⑥ 憬(jǐng)：觉悟的意思。⑦ 赂(lù)：赠送财物。⑧ 闷(bì)：神；闷宫，神庙，指供奉后稷的母亲姜嫄的庙。⑨ 侐(xù)：清静的样子。

* This was the longest epic ode or hymn in praise of Marquis or Duke Xi of Lu, celebrating his magnificent career of success. It was written by Xi Si on an occasion when the Marquis had repaired on a large scale the temple of the State of Lu.

实实①枚枚。	又高又大人迹稀。	Well-built, well-furniahed, grand.
赫赫姜嫄，	姜嫄光明又伟大，	There we find Jiang Yuan's shrine:
其德不回②。	品德端正无邪瑕。	Her virtue was divine.
上帝是依③，	上帝凭依在她身，	On God she did depend
无灾无害。	无灾无害有妊娠。	And safely by the end
弥月不迟，	怀孕十月不延迟，	Of her ten months was born
是生后稷，	生下儿子是后稷。	Hou Ji, our Lord of Grain or Corn.
降之百福，	上天赐予百种福，	Blessed by Heaven, he knew
黍稷重穋，	黍稷成熟有早晚，	When sowing time was due
稙④穉⑤菽麦。	豆麦先后播下土。	For wheat and millet early or late.
奄⑥有下国，	后稷拥有全天下，	Invested with a State,
俾民稼穑。	教会人民种庄稼。	He taught people to sow
有稷有黍，	既有高粱和黍子，	The millet and to grow
有稻有秬⑦。	还有香稻和黑黍。	The sorghum and the rice.
奄有下土，	四海之内都归顺，	All over the country nice
缵⑧禹之绪。	大禹事业得承继。	He followed Yu of Xia's advice.

后稷之孙，	说起后稷子孙旺，	The grandson of Hou Ji
实维大王⑨，	古公亶父谥太王。	King Tai came to install
居岐之阳，	住在岐山向阳地，	Himself south of mount Qi,
实始翦⑩商。	开始准备灭殷商。	Nearer to Shang capital.
至于文武，	传到文王和武王，	Then came Kings Wen and Wu;
缵大王之绪；	太王事业更发扬。	They both followed King Tai.

---

① 实：广大的样子。② 回：邪。③ 依：凭依。④ 稙(zhí)：早种的谷物。⑤ 穉(zhí)：晚种的谷物。⑥ 奄：包括。⑦ 秬(jù)：黑黍。⑧ 缵(zuǎn)：继承。⑨ 大(tài)王：文王的祖父古公亶父。⑩ 翦：消灭。

致天之届，	替天行道伐殷纣，	King Wu beat Shang in Mu,
于牧之野。	牧野一战殷商亡。	Decreed by Heaven high.
"无贰无虞①，	"莫怀二心莫欺诳，	"You should have nor fear nor doubt
上帝临女！"	人人头顶有上苍！"	For great God is with you.
敦②商之旅，	集合殷商之俘获，	You'll wipe Shang forces out,
克咸厥功。	成就大业世无双。	With victory in view."
王曰"叔父③，	成王开口叫"叔父，	King Cheng said to his uncle great,
建尔元子④，	封你长子为侯王，	"I will set up your eldest son
俾侯于鲁。	使他为王在鲁邦。	As Marquis of Lu State
大启尔宇⑤，	大大开拓你土疆。	And enlarge the land you have won
为周室辅。"	辅卫周室作屏障。"	To protect the Zhou State."

乃命鲁公，	成王下令给鲁公，	The Duke of Lu was made
俾侯于东，	建立侯国在东方。	Marquis in the east obeyed,
锡之山川，	赐他山川与土地，	And given land to cultivate,
土田附庸⑥。	还有小国做附庸。	Hills, rivers and attached State.
周公之孙，	周公远孙鲁僖公，	He was Duke of Zhou's grandson
庄公之子⑦，	庄公之子是英雄。	And Duke Zhuang's eldest son.
龙旂⑧承祀，	打着龙旗来祭祀，	With dragon banners at command,
六辔耳耳⑨。	六条缰绳把马控。	He came six reins in hand.
春秋匪解，	四时祭祀不懈怠，	He made his offering
享祀不忒。	玉帛牺牲按时供。	In autumn as in spring
皇皇后帝，	光明伟大的上帝，	To God in Heaven great
皇祖后稷，	还有后稷老祖宗。	And Hou Ji of Zhou State.

①虞：欺骗。②敦：聚集。③叔父：指周公。④元子：长子，指周公的长子伯禽。⑤宇：居，引申为领土。⑥附庸：小国。⑦庄公之子：指鲁僖公。⑧龙旂：画着交龙的旗帜。⑨耳耳：华丽的样子。

| 诗经 Book of Poetry |

享以骍牺，　　献上牺牲金色牛，　He offered victims nice
是飨是宜①，　　神灵享受兴味浓，　For the great sacrifice
降福既多。　　　降下洪福千万种。　And received blessings twice
周公皇祖，　　　伟大先祖周公旦，　From his ancestors dear;
亦其福女。　　　也将赐你福无穷。　Even the Duke of Zhou did appear.

秋而载尝②，　　秋天尝祭庆丰收，　In summer came the rite;
夏而楅衡，　　　夏天设栏先养牛。　In autumn horns were capped of bull.
白牡骍刚。　　　公牛有白也有黄，　There were bulls red and white,
牺尊③将将，　　漂亮酒樽美酒装。　Bull-figured goblets full,
毛炰④胾⑤羹，　　生烤乳猪肉片汤，　Roast pig, soup and minced meat,
笾豆大房⑥。　　大盘小碗都满装。　And dishes of bamboo and wood,
万舞⑦洋洋，　　场面盛大万舞跳，　And dancers all-complete.
孝孙⑧有庆。　　保佑子孙清福享。　Blessed be ye grandsons good!
俾尔炽而昌，　　使你昌盛又兴旺，　May you live in prosperity
俾尔寿而臧，　　使你长寿且吉祥。　And protect the eastern land!
保彼东方，　　　愿你能安定东方，　May you have longevity
鲁邦是常。　　　守卫鲁国国运长。　And may the land of Lu long stand!
不亏不崩，　　　江山永固不崩溃，　Unwaning moon, unsunken sun,
不震不腾；　　　如水长流不震荡。　Nor flood nor earthquake far and nigh.
三寿⑨作朋，　　寿比三老百年长，　In long life you are second to none,
如冈如陵。　　　稳如丘陵和山冈。　And firm as mountain high.

---

① 是飨是宜:指两种祭名。② 尝:秋祭名。③ 牺尊:形状像卧牛的酒杯。④ 毛炰(páo):去毛的小烤猪。⑤ 胾(zì)羹:肉片汤。⑥ 大房:一种盛大块肉的食器,形如高足盘。⑦ 万舞:一种舞蹈的名称。⑧ 孝孙:祭祀的孙子,指僖公。⑨ 三寿:指上寿、中寿、下寿。

公车千乘，	鲁公兵车有千辆，	A thousand war chariots were seen;
朱英绿縢①，	红缨长矛绳缠弓	Each had two spears with tassels red
二矛重弓。	弓矛一时都具备。	And two bows bound by bands green.
公徒三万，	鲁公步卒有三万，	Thirty thousand men the duke led
贝胄②朱绥，	红线缀贝饰盔上，	In shell-adorned helmets were dressed.
烝徒增增③。	大军人多势力强	They marched in numbers great
戎狄是膺④，	痛击北狄和西戎，	To quell the tribes of north and west
荆舒是惩，	荆舒两国受严惩，	And punish southern State.
则莫我敢承⑤。	谁人还敢反抗我。	None of them could stand your attack.

俾尔昌而炽，	使你兴旺又繁荣，	May you enjoy prosperity!
俾尔寿而富，	使你长寿又年丰，	With hoary hair and wrinkled back,
黄发台背⑥，	老人驼背头发黄，	May you enjoy longevity!
寿胥与试。	寿高还把重任扛。	Age will give you advice.
俾尔昌而大，	使你昌盛又强大，	May you live great and prosperous
俾尔耆而艾⑦，	使你年高又寿长，	To a thousand years old or twice!
万有千岁，	千年万岁寿无疆，	May you live long and vigorous
眉寿⑧无有害。	长命百岁无灾殃。	As eyebrows long unharmed by vice!

泰山岩岩⑨，	泰山高峻多险峰，	Lofty is Mountain Tai
鲁邦所詹。	鲁国对它最推崇。	Looked up to from Lu State.
奄有龟蒙，	龟山蒙山都属鲁，	Mounts Gui and Meng stand nigh
遂荒大东，	边境一直伸向东。	And eastward undulate

---

①縢(téng)：缠在弓上的丝绳。②贝胄：贝壳做的头盔。③增增：形容兵士蜂拥前进的样子。④膺：击。⑤承：抵挡。⑥黄发台背：都是老人的象征。⑦耆、艾：都是长寿的意思。⑧眉寿：长寿的特征。⑨岩岩：高峻的样子。

至于海邦,	还有海滨各属国,	As far as eastern sea.
淮夷来同①。	淮夷带头来朝贡。	Huai tribes make no ado
莫不率从,	无人胆敢不服从,	But go down on their knee
鲁侯之功。	功劳应归鲁僖公。	Before the Marquis of Lu.
保有凫②绎,	保有凫山和绎山,	We have Mounts Fu and Yi
遂荒徐宅。	徐国也在控制中。	And till at Xu the ground
至于海邦,	沿海小国都归附,	Which extends to the sea
淮夷蛮貊③。	淮夷蛮貊都俯首。	Where barbarians are found.
及彼南夷,	还有荆楚南夷国,	No southern tribe dare disobey
莫不率从。	没有谁人不服从。	The Marquis of Lu's command;
莫敢不诺④,	无人胆敢不听话,	None but would homage pay
鲁侯是若。	顺从鲁侯态度恭。	To the Marquis of Lu grand.
天赐公纯嘏⑤,	天赐鲁公大吉祥,	Heaven gives Marquis blessings great
眉寿保鲁。	高寿长命保鲁地。	And a long life to rule over Lu.
居常与许⑥,	收回常许两边邑,	He shall restore Duke of Zhou's State
复周公之宇。	恢复周公之疆土。	And dwell at Chang and Xu.
鲁侯燕喜,	鲁侯宴饮多欢喜,	The Marquis feasted his ministers
令妻寿母。	贤妻良母受称颂。	With his fair wife and mother old
宜大夫庶士,	大夫诸臣都和睦,	And other officers
邦国是有⑦。	国家始终能兴旺。	For the State he shall hold.

---

① 来同:来朝。② 凫(fú):凫山,在今山东邹县西南。③ 蛮貊(mò):东南方的异族。④ 诺(nuò):答应,顺从。⑤ 纯嘏(gǔ):大福。⑥ 常、许:地名。⑦ 有:保有。

既多受祉，	既受天赐多福祉，	He shall be blessed with golden hairs
黄发儿①齿。	返老还童生新齿。	And juvenile teeth like his heir's.

徂徕②之松，	徂徕山上长松树，	The hillside cypress and pine
新甫③之柏，	新甫山上柏树生，	Are cut down from the root;
是断是度④，	砍下树木又劈开，	Some as long as eight feet or nine,
是寻是尺。	用寻用尺细丈量。	Others as short as one foot.
松桷⑤有舄⑥，	松木椽子直又大，	They are used to build temples new
路寝⑦孔硕，	建成宫殿气恢弘，	With inner chambers large and long.
新庙奕奕⑧。	新修宗庙真漂亮。	Behold! the temples stand in view.
奚斯⑨所作，	奚斯作成诗一首，	It is Xi Si who makes this song
孔曼且硕，	长篇巨制有文采，	Which reads so pleasant to the ear
万民是若。	人人赞扬好诗才。	That people will greet him with cheer.

---

①儿(ní)："齯"的假借词。②徂徕：山名，在今山东泰安县东南。③新甫：山名，也叫梁山，在泰山旁。④度(duó)："剫"的假借词，劈开。⑤桷(jué)：方木椽。⑥舄(xì)：粗大的样子。⑦路寝：古代帝王处理政事的宫室。⑧奕奕(yìyì)：同"绎绎"，相连的样子。⑨奚斯：鲁大夫公子鱼。

商 颂
Hymns of Shang

那
Hymn to King Tang*

猗①与那与！	多么盛大又富丽，	How splendid! how complete!
置我鞉②鼓。	堂上安放置立鼓。	Let us put drums in place.
奏鼓简简，	鼓儿咚咚响起来，	Listen to their loud beat,
衎③我烈祖。	用此娱乐我先祖。	Ancestor of our race.
汤孙④奏假，	汤孙奏乐告神明，	Your descendants invite
绥我思成。	赐我太平天下安。	Your spirit to alight
鞉鼓渊渊⑤，	立鼓声儿咚咚响，	By resounding drumbeat
嘒嘒⑥管声。	箫管呜呜多清亮。	And by flute's music sweet.
既和且平，	曲调和谐歌太平，	In harmony with them
依我磬声。	玉磬配合更悠扬。	Chimes the sonorous gem.
於赫汤孙，	商汤子孙真显赫，	The descendants with cheer
穆穆⑦厥声。	乐队乐声美肃庄。	Listen to music bright.
庸鼓有斁⑧，	敲钟击鼓响铿锵，	Bells and drums fill the ear
万舞有奕。	洋洋万舞好排场。	And dancers seem in flight.
我有嘉客，	助祭嘉宾已来临，	Our visitors appear

① 猗(ē)、那：形容乐队盛大的样子。② 鞉(táo)鼓：一种鼓乐器，类似今天的拨浪鼓。③ 衎(kàn)：欢乐的意思。④ 汤孙：商汤的子孙。⑤ 渊渊：形容鼓声嘈杂。⑥ 嘒嘒(huìhuì)：吹奏管乐器清亮的声音。⑦ 穆穆：美好的样子。⑧ 斁(yì)：形容乐器声很响亮。

* This hymn was appropriate to a sacrifice to King Tang the successful who overthrew the dynasty of Xia and founded that of Shang in 1765 B.C. It dwelt on the music and the reverence with which the service was performed.

亦不夷①怿！	大家一起喜洋洋。	Also full of delight.
自古在昔，	遥想古代我先王，	Our sires since olden days
先民有作。	早把祭礼安排好。	Showed us the proper ways
温恭朝夕，	态度温和又恭敬，	To be meek and poiite
执事有恪②。	小心谨慎祭祀忙。	And mild from morn to night.
顾予烝尝③，	冬祭秋祭神灵来，	May you accept the rite
汤孙之将。	商汤子孙奉酒浆。	Your filial grandson pays！

烈　祖　　　　　　　　　Hymn to Ancestor*

嗟嗟烈祖，	烈烈先祖多荣光，	Ah! ah! ancestor dear,
有秩斯祜④。	不断降下大福祥。	Shower down blessings here.
申⑤锡无疆，	无穷无尽多赐赏，	Let your blessings descend
及尔斯所。	恩泽遍布我国疆。	On your sons without end.
既载清酤，	先祖神前设清酒，	Our wine is clear and sweet.
赉⑥我思成。	赐我国土享安康。	Make our happiness complete.
亦有和羹⑦，	还有调和美味汤，	Our soup is tempered well,
既戒既平。	五味齐全又适当。	Good in flavor and smell.
鬷⑧假无言，	心中默默向神祷，	We pray but silently:
时靡有争。	次序井然无争嚷。	Bless us with longevity,
绥我眉寿⑨，	神灵赐我百年寿，	White hair and wrinkled brow.

---

① 夷：喜悦的意思。② 恪（kè）：恭敬的样子。③ 烝尝：冬祭名烝，秋祭名尝。④ 祜：福气。⑤ 申：重、又。⑥ 赉（lài）：赏赐。⑦ 和羹：调制好的羹汤。⑧ 鬷（zōng）：同"奏"。⑨ 眉寿、黄耇（gǒu）：都是长寿的意思。

* This was another hymn appropriate to sacrifice to King Tang of Shang, Shang dwelling on the spirits, the soup and the gravity of the service and assisting princes.

黄耇无疆。	长寿无疆永安康。	We have no contention now.
约軝错衡，	车毂裹皮辕雕花，	In cars with wheels leather-bound,
八鸾鸧鸧①。	四马八铃响叮当。	At eight bells' tinkling sound,
以假以享，	祭告神灵献祭品，	The princes come to pray
我受命溥将②。	我受天命封土广。	We might be blessed for aye.
自天降康，	安定幸福从天降，	O give us far and near
丰年穰穰③。	五谷丰登多米粮。	Rich harvest year by year!
来假来飨，	先祖降临受祭飨，	O ancestor, alight!
降福无疆。	赐我福分无限量。	May you accept the rite
顾予烝尝，	冬祭秋祭神赏光，	Your filial grandsons pay
汤孙之将。	汤孙祭祀情意长。	And bless us as we pray!

玄　鸟　　　　　　　　　　The Swallow*

天命玄鸟④，	上天命令神燕降，	Heaven sent Swallow down
降而生商⑤，	生育契后才有商，	To give birth to the Sire
宅殷土芒芒⑥。	住居殷地多宽广。	Of Shang who wore the crown
古帝命武汤，	当时上帝命成汤，	Of land of Yin entire.
正⑦域彼四方⑧。	治理天下管四方。	God ordered Martial Tang,

---

① 鸧鸧(qiāngqiāng)：铃声。② 溥将：广大的样子。③ 穰穰(rángráng)：禾黍众多的样子。④ 玄鸟：黑色的燕子。玄，黑色，燕子为黑色，故称玄鸟。⑤ 商：指商朝的始祖契，传说有娀氏之女简狄吞下燕子卵而怀孕，生下契，契建国于商（今河南省商丘）。⑥ 芒芒：同"茫茫"，广大的样子。⑦ 正：治理的意思。⑧ 方：通"旁"，普遍的意思。

* This hymn was appropriate to a sacrifice in the ancestral temple of Shang. The Sire of Shang was said to be born around 2300 B. C. when his mother bathing in some open place took and swallowed an egg dropped by a swallow. The Martial Tang founded the dynasty and his grandson moved the capital to Yin. This hymn was intended to do honor to King Wu Ding (1328-1263B. C.).

方命厥后，	号令天下众诸侯，	To conquer four frontiers,
奄有九有。	九州全部为商疆。	To appoint lords of Shang
商之先后①，	商之先王受天命，	To rule over nine spheres.
受命不殆，	国运长久无祸殃，	The forefathers of Shang
在武丁孙子。	武丁子孙有福祥。	Reigned by Heaven's decree.
武丁孙子，	后裔武丁多贤良，	King Wu Ding, descendant of Tang.
武王靡不胜②，	成汤事业他承当。	Now rules over land and sea.
龙旂十乘，	十乘大车插龙旗，	Wu Ding is a martial king,
大糦是承。	满载黍稷供享祭。	Victor second to none.
邦畿③千里，	幅员辽阔上千里，	Ten dragon chariots bring
维民所止，	人民安居好地方。	Sacrifice on the run.
肇域彼四海。	四海之内都来投，	His land extends a thousand lis
四海来假，	四方夷狄也来降，	Where people live and rest.
来假祁祁④。	来朝人多纷且忙。	He reigns as far as the four seas;
景⑤员维河？	景山四周绕黄河，	Lords come from east and west.
殷受命咸宜，	殷受天命最合适，	They gather at the capital
百禄是何⑥。	享天祉福永无疆。	To pay homage in numbers great.
		O good Heaven, bless all
		The kings of the Yin State!

长　发　　　　　　　　The Rise of Shang*

濬⑦哲维商，	深谋明智是商王，	The Sire of Shang was wise;

---

① 先后：先王，指商汤。② 胜：胜任的意思。③ 畿(jī)：疆域。④ 祁祁：众多的样子。
⑤ 景：景山，在今河南省商丘县。⑥ 何：同"荷"，担负，蒙受。⑦ 濬(ruì)：睿的假借词，明智的意思。

* This epic ode celebrated Qi the Sire of Shang who helped King Yu of the Xia dynasty to stem the deluge around 2200 B. C.; Xiang Tu his grandson; Tang the Martial King who founded the Shang dynasty; and Yi Yin or A Heng, Tang's chief minister, on occasion of a great sacrifice when all the previous kings of the dynasty and the lords of Shang and their famous ministers were honored in the service, probably in the year 1713 B. C.

长发①其祥。	上天常常现吉祥。	Good omens had appeared for long.
洪水芒芒，	远古洪水白茫茫，	Seeing the deluge rise,
禹敷下土方②。	大禹治理定四方。	He helped Yu stem the current strong,
外大国是疆，	扩张夏朝大国界，	Extend the State's frontier
幅陨③既长。	幅员由此广且长，	And domain far and wide.
有娀④方将，	有娀之国也兴旺，	He was son born from Swallow queer
帝立子生商。	简狄为妃生玄王。	And Princess of Rong, its bride.

玄王⑤桓拨，	玄王商契真英明，	He held successful sway
受小国是达，	受封小国政令行，	Over states large and small.
受大国是达。	受封大国也能成。	He followed his proper way
率履⑥不越，	遵守礼法不越轨，	To inspect all and instruct all.
遂视既发。	遍加视察尽施行。	Xiang Tu, his martial grandson,
相土⑦烈烈，	相土治国真威严，	Ruled over land and sea he had won.
海外有截⑧。	四海诸侯都听命。	Heaven's favor divine
帝命不违，	上帝之命不敢违，	Lasted down to the Martial King.
至于汤齐。	代代相传到成汤。	Toward his lords benign,
汤降不迟，	成汤谦卑不怠慢，	In praise of God he'd often sing.
圣敬日跻⑨。	圣明美德日向上，	His virtue grows day by day;
昭假⑩迟迟，	虔诚祈祷不停息，	It is God he reveres.
上帝是祗⑪。	只把上帝来爱敬。	God orders him to hold sway

---

① 长发：常常发现。② 方：四方。③ 幅陨：幅员，疆域。④ 有娀(sōng)：上古国名，在今山西运城。⑤ 玄王：即契。⑥ 率履：循礼。⑦ 相土：契的孙子。⑧ 有截：即截截，整齐的样子。⑨ 跻(jī)：上升的意思。⑩ 昭假(gé)：虔诚祈祷。⑪ 祗(qí)：尊敬的意思。

| 帝命式于九围①。 | 帝令九州都效仿。 | And be model to the nine spheres. |

受小球大球，	接受上天大小法，	He received ensigns large and small
为下国缀旒②。	表率诸侯做榜样，	From subordinate princes far and nigh.
何③天之休，	承蒙老天赐福祥。	He received blessings from gods all
不竞不絿④，	不竞争来不急躁，	For which he did nor seek nor vie.
不刚不柔，	不示弱也不逞强。	To lords he was nor hard nor soft;
敷政优优，	施行政令很宽和，	His royal rule was gentle oft.
百禄是遒⑤。	百般福禄聚一堂。	He received favors from aloft.

受小共大共，	接受小法和大法，	He received tributes large and small
为下国骏厖⑥。	各国诸侯受庇护。	From princes subordinate.
何天之龙⑦，	承蒙上天多宠爱，	He received favors from gods all;
敷奏其勇。	施展才能显英勇。	He showed his valor great.
不震不动，	既不震惊不摇动，	Unshaken, he was fortified,
不戁⑧不竦，	不胆怯也不惶恐。	Unscared, unterrified.
百禄是总。	百般福禄都聚拢。	All blessings came to his side.

武王载旆⑨，	汤王出征伐夏后，	His banners flying higher,
有虔秉钺，	手拿大斧多刚强。	His battle-ax in his fist,
如火烈烈，	好比烈火熊熊烧，	The Martial King came like fire
则莫我敢曷⑩。	谁敢阻挡迎我锋。	Whom no foe could resist.

---

① 九围：即九城，九州的意思。② 缀旒(zhuìliú)：表率、榜样的意思。③ 何：通"荷"，负荷的意思。④ 絿(qiú)：急躁的意思。⑤ 遒(qiú)：聚会。⑥ 骏厖(máng)：保佑的意思。⑦ 龙：通"宠"，荣誉。⑧ 戁(nǎn)：恐惧。⑨ 旆：通"发"，出发。⑩ 曷：通"遏"，害。

苞有三蘖①，	一棵树干三枝杈，	Xie Jie was like the roots
莫遂莫达。	没有一株枝叶长。	Which could no longer grow
九有有截，	九州一齐归殷商。	When he lost his three shoots,
韦顾②既伐，	韦顾两国都投降，	Wei, Gu, Kun Wu, Tang's former foe.
昆吾夏桀。	昆吾夏桀也灭亡。	The Martial King destroyed the brutes
		And he ruled high and low.

昔在中叶，	从前商代中期时，	In times when ruled King Tang,
有震③且业。	国力强大镇四方。	There was prosperity for Shang.
允也天子，	成汤真是天之子，	Heaven favored his son
降予卿士，	贤卿名士从天降，	With Premier A Heng to run
实维阿衡④，	就是伊尹号阿衡，	The government and state
实左右商王。	实为辅佐商汤王。	At left and right of the prince great.

殷　武　　　　　　　Hymn to King Wu Ding*

挞⑤彼殷武，	殷王大军真迅猛，	How rapid did Yin troops appear!
奋伐荆楚。	奋勇挥师伐荆楚。	They attacked Chu State without fear.
罙⑥入其阻，	长驱直入险阻地，	They penetrated into its rear
裒⑦荆之旅。	大败楚军捉俘虏。	And brought back many a captive's ear.
有截其所⑧，	所到之处捷报传，	Wu Ding conquered Chu land.

---

① 蘖(niè)：树枝。② 韦顾：韦、顾，都是国名。③ 震：威武的样子。④ 阿衡：伊尹的号。⑤ 挞(tà)：迅速的样子。⑥ 罙(shēn)："深"的古字。⑦ 裒(póu)：俘虏。⑧ 有截其所：指楚国土地整齐划一。

* This was an epic ode celebrating the war of King Wu Ding against the southern tribe of Chu, its success and the general happiness and virtue of his reign. This hymn was probably made when a special temple was built for him in 1256 B. C.

汤孙之绪。	商汤子孙赫赫功。	What an achievement grand!

维女荆楚，	荆楚只帮要听真，	The king gave Chu command,
居国南乡。	一直住在宋南方。	"South of our state you stand.
昔有成汤，	我的远祖是成汤，	In the time of King Tang
自彼氐羌。	即使僻远如氐羌。	Even the tribes of Jiang
莫敢不来享①，	谁人敢不来进贡，	Dared not but come to pay
莫敢不来王，	谁人敢不来朝王？	Homage under his sway.
曰商是常②。	都说服从我殷商。	Such was the rule of Shang."

天命多辟③，	上天下令诸侯国，	Heaven gave lords its orders
设都于禹之绩④，	大禹治水建国邦，	To build their capitals within Yu's borders,
岁事来辟，	年年祭祀来朝见，	To pay homage each year,
		To do their duties, not to fear
勿予祸⑤适，	宽大不愿施谴责，	Its punishment severe
稼穑匪懈。	切莫松懈误农桑。	If farmwork is well done far and near.

天命降监，	上天在上察四方，	Heaven ordered the lords to know
下民有严⑥。	下民肃敬又端庄。	The reverent people below.
不僭⑦不滥，	不敢妄为违礼制，	They should do no wrong nor be
不敢怠遑⑧。	不敢怠惰把业荒！	Indolent and carefree.
命于下国，	天子命令我宋国，	To each subordinate State
封建厥福。	努力治国福禄多。	May be brought blessings great!

---

① 享：进献。② 常：服从。③ 辟：诸侯。④ 绩：迹的假借字。⑤ 祸：罪过。适：谴责。⑥ 严：恭敬庄重的样子。⑦ 僭：越礼。⑧ 遑：闲暇。

商邑翼翼①，	商都繁华又整齐，	The capital was full of order,
四方之极②。	它是四方好榜样。	A model for States on the border.
赫赫厥声，	他有赫赫好名声，	The king had great renown
濯濯③厥灵。	他的威灵放光芒。	And brilliance up and down.
寿考且宁，	商王长寿又安康，	He enjoyed longevity.
以保我后生。	保我子孙万代昌。	May he bless his posterity!

陟彼景山，	登上高高景山巅，	We climbed the mountain high
松柏丸丸④。	苍松翠柏上参天。	Where pine and cypress pierced the sky.
是断是迁，	锯断松柏运回家，	
方斫⑤是虔。	斫成柱子削成梁。	We felled them to the ground
		And hewed them square and round.
松桷⑥有梴⑦，	松树椽子长又长，	We built with beams of pine
旅楹有闲，	根根柱子多粗壮，	And pillars large and fine
寝成孔安。	寝庙建成神灵安。	The temple for Wu Ding's shrine.

---

① 翼翼：整齐繁盛的样子。② 极：榜样、标准。③ 濯濯：光明。④ 丸丸：光滑而笔直的样子。⑤ 斫(zhuó)：砍。虔，截断。⑥ 桷(jué)：方的椽子。⑦ 梴(chān)：木材长长的样子。